*Timothy D. Barnes*

Early Christian Hagiography and Roman History

Tria Corda

Jenaer Vorlesungen zu Judentum,
Antike und Christentum

Herausgegeben von

Walter Ameling, Karl-Wilhelm Niebuhr
und Meinolf Vielberg

5

Timothy D. Barnes

# Early Christian Hagiography and Roman History

Second, revised edition

Mohr Siebeck

*Timothy D. Barnes,* born 1942; 1966–70 Junior Research Fellow, The Queen's College, Oxford; 1970 D. Phil; 1970–72 Assistant Professor of Classics, 1972–76 Associate Professor of Classics, University College, Toronto; 1976–2007 Professor, Department of Classics, University of Toronto; since 2008 Honorary Fellow, Schools of Divinity and History, Classics and Archaeology, University of Edinburgh.

ISBN 978-3-16-154497-2
ISSN 1865-5629 (Tria Corda)

Die Deutsche Nationalbibliothek lists this publication in the Deutsche Nationalbibliographie; detailed bibliographic data is available on the Internet at *http://dnb.dnb.de.*

First edition 2010

© 2016 by Mohr Siebeck, Tübingen, Germany. www.mohr.de

The book was typeset by Martin Fischer in Tübingen using Garamond typeface, printed by Gulde-Druck in Tübingen on non-aging paper and bound by Nädele in Nehren.

Printed in Germany.

L'hagiographie critique est une branche
de la science historique
*Hippolyte Delehaye*

It would be hard to think of any field of critical or
historical research that could prove more fruitful
in every kind of problem, or one in which a greater
variety of skills and disciplines could be employed
*David Knowles*

# Preface

All scholarly works are inevitably to some extent the product of their own, often unique intellectual and academic milieu. Thus the second edition of the *Oxford English Dictionary,* published in 1989, had an entry for 'prosopography' (originally published in a supplement in 1982) in which two separate meanings of the word were identified.[1] The first was the sole meaning registered in the first edition ('a description of the person or personal appearance'), which was stated to be obsolete by the time of the publication of the fascicule containing it in September 1909.[2] The second meaning, which was absent from the first edition, required a long definition as 'a study or description of an individual's life and career; hence, historical inquiry, especially in Roman history, concerned with the study of (political) careers and family connections; a presentation of evidence relating to this study.' This new meaning was lavishly illustrated with no fewer than fourteen quotations dating between 1929 and 1976: an archaeological report of excavations at Sparta led the way, closely followed by Ronald Syme in 1934, then Arnaldo Momigliano in 1954 at his silliest ('so-called

---

[1] A Supplement to the Oxford English Dictionary 3, ed. R. W. Burchfield (Oxford, 1982), 845.

[2] The dates at which each separate section and part of the first edition were published are documented by J. McMorris, Lexicography and the OED. Pioneers in the Unknown Forest, ed. C. Mugglestone (Oxford, 2000), 228–231.

prosopography, which, as we all know, claims to have ir-
refutably established the previously unknown phenomenon
of family ties'). Moreover, the adjective 'prosopographical'
and the adverb 'prosopographically' received equally full
treatment. All this reflects the fact that the compiler of
these entries was a classicist with a sense of humour who
had studied Roman history as an undergraduate.[3] In the
Oxford of the later twentieth century, however, few who
studied or taught Roman history had any interest at all in
hagiography. Hence the entry for 'hagiography' in the new
*Oxford English Dictionary* is a sorry disappointment, for it is
identical word for word with the entry originally published
in March 1898. Two meanings are registered for the word.
The first is the obsolete use of the word to refer to the so-
called *Hagiographa,* that is, the third part of the Old Testament, comprising the twelve books other than the Law and
the Prophets. The second meaning, illustrated for 1821 with
a jibe of Robert Southey against 'Romish hagiography,' is
still current: 'the writing of the lives of saints; saints' lives as a
branch of literature or legend.' The present work sometimes
uses the word in that sense, but normally employs a third
meaning which has long been current among scholars, and

---

[3] In fact the term 'prosopography' was introduced into the English
language long before 1929 as I noted in Prosopography: Approaches
and Applications. A Handbook, ed. K. S. B. Keats-Rohan. Prosopo-
graphica et Genealogica 13 (Oxford, 2007), 71–82. Although the
version of the *OED* available online in 2009 has regrettably removed
the revealing quotation from Momigliano, it quotes much earlier attestations of the noun 'prosopography,' the adjective 'prosopographical'
and the adverb 'prosopographically' from three American classical journals published in 1904, 1908 and 1896 respectively. Since the adverb
presupposes the noun, I suspect that an occurrence of 'prosopography'
earlier than 1896 lurks undetected somewhere among the scholarly
literature of the late nineteenth century.

is duly recognised in dictionaries produced outside Oxford, viz., the study of the evidence relating to saints and martyrs.[4] This meaning, well attested in French, can perhaps best be illustrated from the opening sentences of the two most helpful introductions to the subject: 'l'hagiographie critique est une branche de la science historique'; 'l'hagiographie … c'est, d'après l'étymologie du mot, l'étude scientifique des saints, de leur histoire et de leur culte.'[5] It corresponds exactly to the two definitions that Hippolyte Delehaye gave of the obsolete word 'hagiology' in the classic eleventh edition of the *Encyclopedia Britannica:* 'that branch of the historical sciences which is concerned with the lives of the saints, … the critical study of hagiographic remains.'[6]

Soon after I began research in Oxford in 1964, my supervisor Sir Ronald Syme encouraged me to investigate early

---

[4] The two senses are run together in the Random House Dictionary of the English Language[2] (New York, 1987), 858: 'the writing and critical study of the lives of the saints.' The French equivalent is glossed 'branche de l'histoire religieuse qui étudie la vie et les actions des saints' in the Grand Larousse de la langue française 3 (Paris, 1973), 2365. In the interests of clarity, let me state that I use the word 'martyrology' only in the first sense stated in OED 6 (1933), 195 = OED[2] 9 (1989), 415, viz., 'a list or register of martyrs': in the present book it never (except in quotations) has either of the other two main meanings stated there – 'an account of those who have suffered death in a cause' and 'the histories of martyrs collectively, that department of ecclesiastical history or literature which deals with the lives of martyrs.'

[5] Delehaye, Méthode (1934), 7; R. Aigrain, L'Hagiographie. Ses sources, ses méthodes, son histoire (Poitiers & Paris, 1953), 7.

[6] H. De(lehaye), 'Hagiology,' Encyclopedia Britannica[11] 12 (New York, 1911), 816–817. This sense of 'hagiology' is not registered at all in the Oxford English Dictionary: the second edition merely reprints the entry from the first edition, which was first published in March 1898 (OED[2] 6 [1989], 1015 = OED 5 [1901], 21). The very possibility of critical hagiography is held up to ridicule by L. Grig, Making Martyrs in Late Antiquity (London, 2004), 146, 184.

Christian texts and documents in a spirit of extreme scepticism. Syme saw nothing intrinsically wrong with the atti-
tude which Momigliano had derided when he complained
that Otto Seeck 'never believed anything to be authentic
if he could help it.'[7] Syme suggested that I investigate the
letters of Ignatius of Antioch and the *acta martyrum* of the
second and third centuries on the assumption that every
text needed to establish its claims to veracity and ought to
be treated as inauthentic until it was proved otherwise. This
was perhaps the most salutary and productive single item of
advice that Syme ever gave me. For, while my investigation
of the letters of Ignatius led nowhere at the time,[8] it revealed
to me the superb scholarship of Bishop Joseph Barber
Lightfoot, who held the see of Durham from 1879 to 1889,
and it convinced me that understanding of Ignatius had not
progressed significantly in the three quarters of a century
after Lightfoot. In my first year of research, therefore, I
learned two fundamental truths about scholarship that are
too often neglected: first, the most useful study of any subject or problem need not be either the most recent or indeed
at all recent in date; second, that sound scholarship remains
sound scholarship despite the passage of time and changes
in intellectual fashion. Moreover, investigation of the early
*acta martyrum* conventionally accepted as authentic very
quickly made me aware that a prosopographical approach
could produce new and sometimes startling results. On one
level, therefore, the present book is a logical sequel to the
study of pre-Decian *acta martyrum* which I wrote more than
forty years ago.[9] Its primary aim is to describe how Christian

---

[7] A. Momigliano, Studies in Historiography (London, 1966), 150.

[8] Though see now Expository Times 120 (2008), 119–130.

[9] JTS, N.S. 19 (1968), 509–533.

hagiography began in the second century as the commemoration of martyrs, but became a vehicle for deliberate fiction in the fourth century and then a normal mode of literary composition.

Although the present book has its ultimate origins in research that I undertook at the very beginning of my academic career, the stimulus to begin its composition was an invitation from the President and Fellows of Wolfson College, Oxford to deliver the Ronald Syme Memorial Lecture on 19 October 1995, for which I chose the title 'Hagiography and Roman History.' It was while preparing this lecture that the idea came to me of expanding its main themes into a book. I was also encouraged to do so by Michael Redies, who came from Berlin to study in Toronto for a year : it was he who first drew my attention to the historical importance of the funerary speech for John Chrysostom (mentioned in Chapter VI). Much of the book was then drafted between 1997 and 2001 while I was the recipient of a generous research grant from the Social Sciences and Humanities Research Council of Canada, which enabled me to spend three months at the American Academy in Rome and subsequently to employ Daniel Thornton as a research assistant for trawling through the not yet digitised *Acta Sanctorum* for usable material. Before, during and after that period my work was materially assisted by the University of Toronto, which granted me a year's research leave in 1997/98, and which for nearly four decades provided me with constant access to its excellent libraries, above all to the library of the Pontifical Institute of Mediaeval Studies.

In their present form, the first five chapters are revised versions of lectures delivered in German at the University of Jena on 10–14 November 2008. Hence the finished book owes a great deal to Walter Ameling and Meinolf Vielberg whose kind invitation to deliver a series of lectures in the series Tria Corda revived my flagging interest in hagiography and whose warm and generous hospitality during the unforgettable week which my wife and I spent in Jena stoked my enthusiasm for the subject even further. The audiences who heard the lectures made many helpful suggestions of substance which I have incorporated in my final text. I am particularly grateful to Meinolf Vielberg and Hugo Brandenburg for their gracious reactions to criticism of ideas that they held dear: they will see how their friendly ripostes have reshaped my opinions on some important issues. My greatest debt, however, is to Walter Ameling, who most kindly corrected numerous mistakes of grammar and idiom in the rough German draft of my lectures before they were delivered, spared no effort to make my week in Jena a thoroughly enjoyable one, saved me from many errors of fact and interpretation in both the lectures and the final version of the book, and has performed a work of supererogation in taking charge of preparing the final version of the book for the printer according to German typographical conventions. It need hardly be added that I alone accept responsibility for the mistakes and misjudgements that doubtless remain, for (as my doctoral supervisor memorably said) 'none is immune from error.'

The English translations of Greek and Latin sources are entirely my own except where I acknowledge the use of published translations, which I have often modernised or modified quite freely.

Edinburgh, 17 September 2009        Timothy D. Barnes

# Table of Contents

Tables

Appendices . . . . . . . . . . . . . . . . . . . . . . . . . . . . . . 329

Indexes . . . . . . . . . . . . . . . . . . . . . . . . . . . . . . . . 415

# Frequently used Abbreviations

The names of ancient authors are normally given in full, while conventional abbreviations are often used for their individual works. Hagiographical writings are normally identified either by their number in the lists enumerated in Appendix 2 or by their number(s) in the Bollandist *Bibliotheca Hagiographia Graeca, Bibliotheca Hagiographia Latina* and *Bibliotheca Hagiographia Orientalis*. The easy availability of electronic search-engines has removed the necessity of providing a formal bibliography, but an index is provided of modern scholars whose views are discussed (though not for bare citiations of their work). The titles of journals and of the series in which books or monographs have been published are either given in an abbreviated form based on the abbreviations used in *L'année philologique* or stated in full. Books and series which are cited with abbreviated titles are noted in the following list.

| | |
|---|---|
| AASS | Acta Sanctorum quotquot toto orbe coluntur, vel a catholicis scriptoribus celebrantur, ed. J. Bolland and others Brussels, Tongerloo, Paris and Rome (1643–1925: incomplete)[1] |
| Athanasius (1993) | T. D. Barnes, Athanasius and Constantius. Theology and Politics in the Constantinian Empire (Cambridge, MA, 1993) |
| Atti (1987) | A. A. R. Bastiaensen and others, Atti e passioni dei martiri (Milan, 1987) |

---

[1] All references to AASS are given by (i) month in the conventional Latin abbreviation, (ii) volume in Roman numerals and (iii) page(s) in the Palmé reprint of 1863–1870 for volumes as far as Oct. XIII (also sometimes, where it is relevant, to the original publication): a concordance of the original edition and reprints of each volume is given by Delehaye, L'œuvre (1959), 172–173.

| | |
|---|---|
| Barnes I etc. | See Appendix 2 |
| BHG | Bibliotheca hagiographica graeca, 3rd edition. Subsidia Hagiographica 8a (Brussels, 1967), with Auctarium. Subsidia Hagiographica 47 (Brussels, 1969) |
| BHL | Bibliotheca hagiographica latina antiquae et mediae aetatis. Subsidia Hagiographica 6 (Brussels, 1898–1901), with Supplementi editio altera auctior. Subsidia Hagiographica 12 (Brussels, 1911) and Novum Supplementum. Subsidia Hagiographica 70 (Brussels, 1986) |
| BHO | P. Peeters, Bibliotheca hagiographica orientalis. Subsidia Hagiograhica 10 (Brussels, 1910) |
| Comm. Mart. Rom. (1940) | H. Delehaye and others, Propylaeum ad Acta Sanctorum Decembris. Martyrologium Romanum ad formam editionis typicae scholiis historicis instructum (Brussels, 1940) |
| Constantine (1981) | T. D. Barnes, Constantine and Eusebius (Cambridge, MA, 1981) |
| CPG | M. Geerard, Clavis Patrum Graecorum, 5 vols. (Turnhout, 1974–1987); M. Geerard & J. Noret, Supplementum (Turnhout, 1998); J. Noret, Clavis Patrum Graecorum 3A: Addenda volumini III (Turnhout, 2003) |
| CPL | E. Dekkers & E. Gaar, Clavis Patrum Latinorum, 3rd edition (Steenbrugge, 1995) |
| Delehaye, Culte (1933) | H. Delehaye, Les origines du culte des martyrs, 2nd edition. Subsidia Hagiographica 20 (Brussels, 1933) |
| Delehaye, Légendes (1927) | H. Delehaye, Les légendes hagiographiques, 3rd edition. Subsidia Hagiographica 18 (Brussels, 1927)[2] |

---

[2] The first edition was published in 1905; the second (1906) was translated into English by V. M. Crawford as The Legends of the Saints: An Introduction to Hagiography (London & Norwood, PA, 1907; reprinted South Bend, 1961). The fourth edition (1955) is a reprint of the third with the addition of a memoir of Delehaye by P. Peeters and

| | |
|---|---|
| Delehaye, Mélanges (1966) | H. Delehaye, Mélanges d'hagiographie grecque et latine. Subsidia Hagiographica 42 (Brussels, 1966) |
| Delehaye, Méthode (1934) | H. Delehaye, Cinq leçons sur la méthode hagiographqiue. Subsidia Hagiographica 21 (Brussels, 1934) |
| Delehaye, L'œuvre (1959) | H. Delehaye, L'œuvre des Bollandistes à travers trois siècles 1615–1915, 2nd edition. Subsidia Hagiographica 13A (Brussels, 1959)[3] |
| Delehaye, Passions (1966) | H. Delehaye, Les passions des martyrs et les genres littéraires, 2nd revised edition. Subsidia Hagiographica 13B (Brussels, 1966) |
| Gebhardt I etc. | See Appendix 2 |
| Halkin, Études (1973) | F. Halkin, Études d'épigraphie grecque et d'hagiographie byzantine. Variorum Series: Collected Studies 20 (London, 1973) |
| Jones, LRE (1964) | A. H. M. Jones, The Roman Empire. A Social, Economic and Administrative Survey (Oxford, 1964) |
| K-K-R | See Appendix 2 |
| Lazzati, Sviluppi (1956) | G. Lazzati, Gli sviluppi della letterature sui martiri nei primi quattro secoli. Con appendice di testi (Turin, 1956) |
| Musurillo | See Appendix 2 |
| New Empire (1982) | T. D. Barnes, The New Empire of Diocletian and Constantine (Cambridge, MA, 1982) |
| PLRE 1 (1971) | A. H. M. Jones, J. Martindale & J. Morris, The Prosopography of the Later Roman Empire 1: A. D. 260–395 (Cambridge, 1971) |
| PLRE 2 (1980) | J. Martindale, The Prosopography of the Later Roman Empire 2: A. D. 395–527 (Cambridge, 1980) |

---

a bibliography of his scholarly writings: it was translated anew by D. Attwater as The Legends of the Saints (London, 1962; reprinted 1998).

 [3] There is an English version of the first edition by an unnamed translator: The Work of the Bollandists through Three Centuries 1615–1915 (Princeton & London, 1922).

| | |
|---|---|
| Quentin, Marty-rologes (1908) | H. Quentin, Les martyrologes historiques du moyen âge. Étude sur la formation du Martyrologe romain (Paris, 1908) |
| Ruinart, Acta Martyrum (1689), (1713) | T. Ruinart, Acta primorum martyrum sincera et selecta (Paris, 1689; 2nd expanded ed., Antwerp, 1713) |
| SC | Sources chrétiennes (Lyon & Paris, 1943–1944; Paris, 1945–) |
| SH | Subsidia Hagiographica (Brussels, 1886–) |
| SP | Studia Patristica (volumes 1–16 published in the series Texte und Untersuchungen [Berlin, 1963–1985]; volume 17 by the Pergamon Press [Oxford, 1982]; volume 18 by Cistercian Publications [Kalamazoo, 1989–1990]; and volumes 19 onward by Peeters [Leuven, 1989–]) |
| ST | Studi e Testi (Rome, then Vatican City, 1900–) |
| Syn. eccl. Cpl. | Synaxarium Ecclesiae Constantinopolitanae, ed. H. Delehaye. Acta Sanctorum, Propylaeum ad Novembrem (Brussels, 1902) |
| Tertullian (1971) | T. D. Barnes, Tertullian. A Historical and Literary Study (Oxford, 1971: 2nd edition with unchanged pagination and postscript, 1985) |
| TTH | Translated Texts for Historians (Liverpool, 1985–) |
| TU | Texte und Untersuchungen zur Geschichte der altchristlichen Literatur (Leipzig, 1883–1942; Berlin, 1952–) |

# Postscript

This second edition confines itself to the correction of typographical and other minor errors (except at p. 239 n. 15).

T. D. Barnes, 20 November 2015

# Apostles and Martyrs:
# Hagiography and the Cult of the Saints

The Crucifixion stands at the centre of the Christian faith. Jesus was sentenced to die on the cross by Pontius Pilatus, the *praefectus* of Judaea, which was at that time part of the Roman province of Syria.[1] Pilate executed Jesus as a rebel, for that is the only interpretation that can be put upon the words of the placard that he had placed on the cross above the head of Jesus in Latin, Greek and Aramaic – 'Jesus of Nazareth, King of the Jews' (John 19.19–20, cf. Matthew 27.37; Mark 15.26; Luke 23.38).[2] Two other condemned criminals were crucified with Jesus, whom two of the gospels describe as robbers, bandits or brigands using the Greek word that corresponds to the Latin *latro* (Matthew 27.38: δύο λησταί; Mark 15.27: δύο ληστάς).[3] Jesus was executed at a Jewish Passover, on 14 Nisan (John 18.28, 19.14)[4] in a year

---

[1] W. Eck, Rom und Judaea (Tübingen 2007), 23–51.

[2] For recent discussion, see J. Geiger, SCI 15 (1996), 202–208; P. L. Maier, Hermes 124 (1996), 58–75; Eck (n. 1), 160–161.

[3] Luke 23.32, cf. 39 has the vaguer κακοῦργοι δύο; John 19.18 the completely imprecise ἄλλους δύο.

[4] Although all four gospels agree that Jesus was crucified on the day before the Jewish sabbath, that is, on a Friday (Matthew 28.1; Mark 15.42, 16.2; Luke 23.56, 24.1; John 19.31, 20.1), they notoriously disagree over the day of the month: the synoptic gospels put the Crucifixion on 15 Nisan, since they make Jesus eat the Passover meal with his disciples, after which he was arrested during the night (Matthew 26.17–20; Mark 14.12–17; Luke 22.7–16). John's date of 14 Nisan

which ancient authors usually stated as the consular year of Rubellius Geminus and Fufius Geminus (often *duobus Geminis consulibus*),[5] that is, A. D. 29,[5] but for which recent estimates have ranged between 27 and 36, though with a strong preference for either 7 April 30 or 3 April 33.[6]

For fully three decades after the crucifixion of Jesus, beyond the period covered by the *Acts of the Apostles,* his followers, who first called themselves Christians in Antioch (Acts 11.26: ἐγένετο δὲ ... χρηματίσαι τε πρώτως ἐν Ἀντιοχείᾳ τοὺς μαθητὰς Χριστιανούς),[7] were treated by the Roman authorities, such as Gallio the proconsul of Achaea in 51 or 52 (Acts 18.12–17),[8] as members of local Jewish communi-

---

has almost always been preferred to that of the other gospels on the convincing grounds that an execution on 15 Nisan would have been a profanation of a holy day (Exodus 12.16; Leviticus 23.5–8).

[5] So Tertullian, *Adversus Iudaeos* 8.18; Lactantius, *Mort. Pers.* 2.1. Similarly, a calendaric work transmitted among the writings of Cyprian puts the crucifixion in the sixteenth year of Tiberius, 215 years before consular year 243 (De pascha computus 20–22 [PL 4.965–968 = CSEL 3.3.267–268]).

[6] J. Finegan, Handbook of Biblical Chronology[2] (Peabody, MA, 1998), 353–369; L. Holford-Strevens, Oxford Companion to the Year, ed. B. Blackburn & L. Holford-Strevens (Oxford, 1999), 772–778, adducing B. E. Schaefer, Quarterly Journal of the Royal Astronomical Society 31 (1990), 53–67. The date of 36 proposed by N. Kokkinos, Chronos, Kairos, Christos, ed. J. Vardaman & E. M. Yamaguchi (Winona Lake, 1989), 133–157, cf. id.,The Herodian Dynasty (Sheffield, 1998), 264–271, was enthusiastically accepted by R. Lane Fox, The Unauthorized Version (London, 1991), 33–36, 120, 304, 423 n. 27.

[7] E. J. Bickermann, Studies in Jewish and Christian History III (Leiden, 1986), 139–151.

[8] Gallio, the brother of Seneca, is attested as proconsul of Achaea in the first half of 52 (Sylloge[3] 801 D = Fouilles de Delphes 3.4.286: his proconsular year was therefore 51–52: PIR[2] J 757; B. E. Thomasson, Laterculi Praesidum I (Gothenburg, 1984), 191.

ties. This situation suddenly and unexpectedly changed when a large part of the city of Rome was destroyed by fire in July 64: according to Tacitus, of the fourteen districts (*regiones*) into which Augustus had divided the city, only four were completely untouched; three were levelled to the ground and 'in the other seven there survived a few traces of housing, mauled and charred' (*Ann.*15.40.2, trans. A. J. Woodman).[9] There were persistent rumours that Nero himself had ordered the fire to be started in order to build a vast new palace in the centre of the city; when normal measures failed to staunch the rumours, the emperor sought a scapegoat and fixed upon the Christians. He accused the tiny community of Christians in Rome of starting the fire and unleashed a pogrom against them. At this time it seems highly probable that the Christians of Rome were concentrated in the modern Trastevere, a quarter occupied largely by dockers and labourers which had remained unscathed by the conflagration because it lay across the River Tiber from the main part of the city.[10] All who could be identified as Christians were arrested and their admission that they were Christians was treated as tantamount to a confession of arson. The local authorities then handed them over to the emperor so that he could exercise his talents as a provider of spectacles for the people while diverting suspicion from himself.

Nero wished to make the punishment fit the crime. Hence he devised novel methods of execution to emphasise and advertise the guilt of his victims, who were presented as both arsonists and inveterate enemies of the whole human

---

[9] On the fire and its consequences, see now E. J. Champlin, Nero (Cambridge, MA & London, 2003), 48–49, 121–126, 178–200.

[10] P. Lampe, From Paul to Valentinus. Christians at Rome in the First Two Centuries, (London, 2003), 19–24, 47–58.

race. Tacitus provides the only detailed account of this episode to survive (*Ann.* 15.44), and its historicity has withstood ferocious critical attacks.[11] In accordance with his normal stylistic habits, however, Tacitus is brief and allusive. Moreover, the text of the relevant passage is corrupt in the only independent manuscript, so that many modern discussions have proceeded on the basis of a false reading.[12] The best two recent editions of the *Annals,* by Franz Römer and Heinz Heubner, accept the diagnosis of the textual problem offered by Georg Andresen nearly a century ago and print the passage as follows:

*et pereuntibus addita ludibria, ut ferarum tergis contecti laniatu canum interirent aut crucibus adfixi [aut flammandi atque] ubi defecisset dies in usum nocturni luminis urerentur.*[13]

And, as they perished, mockeries were added, so that, covered in the hides of wild beasts, they expired from mutilation by dogs, or were burned fixed to crosses for use as nocturnal illumination on the dwindling of daylight.[14]

Tacitus here describes mockeries added to the normal modes of execution (*pereuntibus addita ludibria*). Ted Champlin's recent study of Nero identifies the innovations of Nero's

---

[11] Tertullian names Tacitus as his authority and his account is completely dependent on him (*Apol.* 5.3), while Eusebius derived his knowledge of the episode from a Greek translation of Tertullian's Apologeticum (*HE* 2.25.4, cf. 2.2.4–6).

[12] For example, H.-W. Kuhn, ANRW 2.25.1 (1982), 698–701, registers not only the apostle Peter, but also the victims of Nero as among the very few attested crucifixions in Rome itself.

[13] F. Römer, P. Corneli Taciti Annalium libri XV–XVI. (Vienna, Cologne & Graz, 1976), 67; H. Heubner, P. Corneli Taciti libri quae supersunt 1² (Stuttgart and Leipzig, 1994), 369.

[14] A. J. Woodman, Tacitus: The Annals (Indianapolis & Cambridge, 2004), 326 (with modifications).

devising.[15] The first group of Christians were not exposed to wild beasts in the normal fashion: instead they were dressed in animal skins as themselves being wild beasts and then exposed to attack by hunting dogs. The second group of Christians were set alight as torches, presumably after being clothed in inflammable tunics, in symbolic revenge for their alleged burning of the Temple of Luna Noctiluca (that is, 'Luna Light of the night') on the Palatine, which was probably illuminated at night. The punishment meted out to these Christians of Rome in 64 was thus not (as has normally been assumed) a modified form of crucifixion, but a modified form of burning alive. Indeed, there is no reliable evidence that Christians were ever crucified for being Christians, except in the last paroxysm of pagan violence and sadism at the very end of the 'Great Persecution.'[16]

One of Nero's victims in 64 was the apostle Peter. The legend that Peter was crucified, and crucified head downwards, is not attested in Christian authors before the end of the second century, when Tertullian (*Praescr. Haer.* 36.3) and Origen in his lost commentaries on Genesis referred to his presumed crucifixion (quoted by Eusebius, *HE* 3.1.2).[17] But the story that Peter was crucified head downwards at his own request occurs in the apocryphal *Martyrdom of Peter* (37–39[8–10] = 8.3–4.1 Zwierlein), which implies that it was already current some time earlier.[18] There is, however,

---

[15] Champlin, Nero (n. 9), 122–123, 302 n. 29.

[16] App. 1.

[17] The known fragments of this lost work of Origen are listed at CPG 1410. For an analysis of Tertullian's argument, see M. Monaca, Pietro e Paolo. Il loro rapporto con Roma nelle testimonianze antiche (Rome, 2001), 431–444.

[18] R. A. Lipsius, Acta Apostolorum Apocrypha 1 (Leipzig, 1891), 92–97, translated into English by J. K. Elliott, The Apocryphal New

much earlier evidence of impeccable authority that points
to a very different mode of execution. In the gospel of John,
the risen Jesus says to Peter:

ἀμὴν ἀμὴν λέγω σοι, ὅτε ἦς νεώτερος, ἐζώννυες σεαυτὸν καὶ περιεπάτεις
ὅπου ἤθελες· ἦταν δὲ γηράσῃς, ἐκτενεῖς τὰς χεῖράς σου, καὶ ἄλλος σε ζώσει
καὶ οἴσει ὅπου οὐ θέλεις. τοῦτο δὲ εἶπεν σημαίνων ποίῳ θανάτῳ δοξάσει τὸν
θεόν (John 21.18–19)

The crucial verb (ζώννυμι), which occurs both in the second
person singular of the imperfect tense and in the third
person singular of the future, has been translated rather differently in modern English versions of the New Testament:

Verily, verily, I say unto thee, When thou wast young, thou girdest
thyself, and walkedst whither thou wouldest; but when thou shalt be
old, thou shalt stretch forth thy hands, and another shall gird thee,
and carry thee whither thou wouldest not. This spake he, signifying
by what death he should glorify God. (Authorized Version)

'Very truly, I tell you, when you were younger, you used to fasten
your own belt and go wherever you wished. But when you grow old,
you will stretch out your hands, and someone else will fasten a belt
around you and take you where you do not wish to go.' (He said this
to indicate the kind of death by which he would glorify God.) (New
Revised Standard Version)

'I tell you most solemnly, / when you were young
you put on your own belt / and walked where you liked;
but when you grow old / you will stretch out your hands,
and somebody else will put a belt around you

Testament. A Collection of Apocryphal Christian Literature in an
English Translation (Oxford, 1993), 424–426; O. Zwierlein, Petrus
in Rom. Die literarischen Zeugnisse (Berlin & New York, 2009), 414.
According to this text, Peter was executed by 'the prefect Agrippa:' H.
Waldmann, Das Christentum in Indien und der Königsweg der Apostel
in Edessa, Indien und Rom (Tübingen, 1996), 87–96, identified this
invented character with D. Haterius Agrippa, consul in 22, and argued
that he was *praefectus urbi* from 62/63 to 65.

and take you where you would rather not go.'
In these words he indicated the kind of death by which Peter would give glory to God.
(Jerusalem Bible, printing Jesus' words as Hebrew-style verse)

Both the New Revised Standard Version and the Jerusalem Bible take the Greek verb ζώννυμι in a narrower sense than the Authorized Version. Although another gospel uses the corresponding noun (ζωνή) for a belt in which a man might carry money (Matthew 10.9), the original and primary meaning of the verb ζώννυμι was 'to surround with a belt or girdle, gird' and it was used especially of preparing for a pugilistic conflict, an athletic contest or battle.[19] The King James translators correctly referred to an earlier verse of the same chapter where they render τὸν ἐπενδύτην διεζώσατο, ἦν γὰρ γυμνός as 'he girt his fisher's coat unto him (for he was naked),' where the New Revised Standard Version has 'he put on some clothes, for he was naked' and the Jerusalem Bible, even more colloquially, 'Simon Peter, who had practically nothing on, wrapped his clothes around him' (John 21.7). Whatever the precise nuances of ἐζώννυες σεαυτόν and ἄλλος σε ζώσει, therefore, the risen Jesus is saying that, whereas Peter used to clothe himself, another will clothe him when he is put to death.

All Christians, all New Testament scholars, all historians of the early church know this passage, but they have virtually without exception misunderstood it because they have so far always interpreted it in the light of the later legend that Peter was crucified. But in that case what does ἄλλος σε

---

[19] H. G. Liddell & R. Scott, revised by H. S. Jones, *A Greek-English Lexicon*[9] (Oxford, 1940), 759; H. G. Liddell & R. Scott, revised by H. S. Jones, *A Greek-English Lexicon*[9] (Oxford, 1940), 759; Supplement (1968), 68. The Supplement (Oxford, 1968), 68, adds the sense 'for walking,' adducing John 21.18, Acts 12.8.

ζώσει mean? When criminals were crucified, the executioners stripped them completely naked and took their clothes for themselves, as the Roman soldiers did who cast dice for the robe of Jesus (Matthew 27.35; Mark 15.24; Luke 23.34; John 19.23–24).[20] The crucified Messiah did not hang upon the cross with his genitals decently hidden from view by a loincloth, as he has almost invariably been depicted in Christian art from the fourth century to paintings by great artists from the Renaissance to the twentieth century (for example Fra Angelico, van Dyck, El Greco, Rembrandt, Velázquez and Salvador Dali).[21] Christ was crucified naked, as Peter too would have been. Had Peter been crucified, his executioners would not have put clothes or a belt on him; they would have taken his clothes off and stripped him naked. In that case, however, the prediction of the risen Christ would have been false: another would not have girt, girded or clothed Peter, but stripped him. If another put clothes on Peter before his execution, as John makes Christ explicitly say, then he cannot have been crucified.

The allusion to the death of Peter that the fourth evangelist puts into the mouth of the risen Christ should not be interpreted in the light of later legend, but in the light of

---

[20] Artemidorus, Oneirocritica 2.53: γυμνοὶ γὰρ σταυροῦνται καὶ τὰς σάρκας ἀπολλύουσιν οἱ σταυρωθέντες, cf. T. Mommsen, Römisches Strafrecht (Leipzig, 1899), 918–921.

[21] On depictions of the Crucifixion in art, see esp. A. Kartsonis, Byzance et les images. Cycle de conférences organisé au Musée du Louvre par le Service culturel du 5 octobre au 7 décembre 1992, ed. A. Guillou & J. Durand (Paris 1994), 151–188; M. Lisner, Holzkruzifixe in Florenz und in der Toskana von der Zeit um 1300 bis zum frühen Cinquecento (München 1970), figs. 111–113, 142–143, 146–148; L. Steinberg, The Sexuality of Christ in Renaissance Art and Modern Oblivion[2] (Chicago & London, 1996), 91–94; 135–139, 199–203, 261–266.

Tacitus' account of the first known persecution of Christians.[22] Nero's Christian victims in 64 were all clothed by another, since they were either dressed as wild animals or clad in something that caught fire easily, presumably the combustible tunic described by Seneca in a contemporary letter (*Ep.* 14.5: *cogita hoc loco … illam tunicam alimentis et inlitam et textam*). But it was only the latter category of Christians who perished with hands outstretched in a parody of the crucifixion of Jesus. It follows that Peter was burnt alive in 64 – a fact which is very relevant to the question of whether his body was ever recovered for burial.

A little more than forty years after Nero's death (probably in 110), in a city on the south coast of the Black Sea, which must be either Amisus or Amastris,[23] Christians were denounced before the ex-consul Pliny, who had been sent as a legate of the emperor Trajan to the province of Bithynia (which included Pontus).[24] Pliny tells Trajan that he had

---

[22] The recent discussion by Zwierlein, Petrus in Rom (n. 18), 119–124, voices justified doubts about the traditional interpretation, but he strangely fails to discuss Tacitus, *Ann.* 15.44 anywhere in more than 300 pages, contenting himself with bare references to the passage and a few brief and sundry remarks in another context (311–312).

[23] The place is deduced from the fact that Pliny wrote *Ep.* 10.92 from Amisus, *Ep.* 10.98 from Amastris: the date lies between 18 September and 3 January in Pliny's second year in Bithynia-Pontus, that is, in the autumn of either 110 or 111: A. N. Sherwin White, The Letters of Pliny (Oxford, 1966), 80–82, 529–533, 691.

[24] Pliny was a *legatus pro praetore* of the emperor sent with proconsular rank by senatorial decree to a province normally governed by proconsuls: CIL 5.5262 = ILS 2927 (originally from Comum); CIL 6.1552 = 11.5272 (Hispellum), cf. Thomasson, Laterculi Praesidum I (n. 8), 247. The trials took place between 18 September and 3 January during Pliny's second year in Bithynia, that is, in the autumn of 110, 111 or 112: Sherwin-White, Letters of Pliny (n. 23), 80–82, 529–533, convincingly dates Pliny's arrival in Bithynia to 109.

never been present at the trial of Christians before, but, since he knew that Christians were *eo ipso* criminals, he had no hesitation at all in sentencing those who admitted to being Christians to condign punishment: those who were not Roman citizens he executed on the spot, while those who possessed Roman citizenship he sent to Rome in accordance with normal administrative procedures (Pliny, *Ep.* 10.96.1–4).[25] Pliny was equally certain how he should treat those who denied that they were Christians or ever had been: he made them invoke the gods, make a symbolic sacrifice to an image of the emperor and curse Christ, then set them free (5: *cum praeeunte me deos adpellarent et imagini tuae … ture ac vino supplicarent, praeterea male dicerent Christo, … dimittendos putavi*). What of those who admitted that they had been Christians in the past, but asserted that they were Christians no longer? Pliny was uncertain whether to convict or acquit them. After compelling them to venerate the gods and the emperor's image and to curse Christ (6), he then adjourned the trial, keeping this category of accused in prison while he consulted Trajan (9). Pliny's question to the emperor was simple, practical and pressing: should he execute or release the large number still in custody (9: *visa est enim mihi res digna consultatione, maxime propter periclitantium numerum*)? In reply, Trajan commended Pliny for his condemnation and execution of those Christians who had been formally accused and found guilty (Pliny, *Ep.* 10.97.1) But he also rebuked him explicitly for acting on the basis of anonymous accusations, and implicitly both for listening to an informer and for making the accused sacrifice to an image of himself (2). But Trajan's rescript to Pliny had a

---

[25] F. Millar, JRS 56 (1966), 159, 165; P. Garnsey, *Social Status and Legal Privilege in the Roman Empire* (Oxford, 1970), 72–79.

general application in that it laid down the legal principle that was to define the legal status of Christianity until 250:

They are not to be sought out; if they are formally accused and found guilty, they are to be punished, with the reservation that anyone who denies that he is a Christian and makes that clear in reality, that is, by making an offering to our gods, gains pardon by his change of mind, though suspect for his past actions. But accusations posted up anonymously ought to have no standing in any charge. That sets a most evil precedent and is unworthy of our <enlightened> age.

It is unfortunate that Pliny's elegant and decorous language combined with his eloquent plea for Trajan to show clemency, which emphasises that his investigations have uncovered no criminality beyond a 'depraved and immoderate superstition' (*Ep.* 10.96.7–8) and urges that mild treatment of the apostates will help to foster traditional religious practices (9–10), have blinded many modern exegetes to the precise nature of the legal question on which he sought the emperor's clarification.[26]

Of the Christians killed in Rome in 64, condemned to death between 64 and 110, executed by Pliny or put to death by the Roman authorities before 150, the name is transmitted of precisely one individual besides Peter, Paul and other apostles. He is Symeon the son of Clopas, the bishop of Jerusalem: he was a relative of Jesus who claimed descent from King David and was crucified in the reign of Trajan as a potential rebel leader (Eusebius, *HE* 3.32.1–6, quoting Hegesippus). Moreover, when Eusebius composed

---

[26] JRS 58 (1968), 36, cf. JTS, N. S. 20 (1969), 300, complaining that R. Freudenberger, Das Verhalten der römischen Behörden gegen die Christen im 2. Jahrhundert dargestellt am Brief des Plinius an Trajan und den Reskripten Trajans und Hadrians (Munich, 1968), failed to state clearly anywhere that Pliny's letter 'is a request for guidance on an urgent problem: are those still in prison to be punished or set free?'

the first history of the early church close to the year 300, he could find no evidence for the Bithynian Christians executed by Pliny except Tertullian, whose *Apologeticum* he quoted in Greek translation (*HE* 3.33.3, cf. Tertullian, *Apol.* 2.6–7).[27] This absence of documentation reflects the fact that no Christian who died for his faith before the reign of the emperor Antoninus Pius (138–161) was or could be commemorated as a martyr because the concept of martyrdom did not yet exist. The concept, which was 'solidly anchored in the civic life of the Graeco-Roman world of the Roman Empire' and 'inextricably rooted in a society and culture peculiar to that world,' was invented in the second quarter of the second century.[28]

The Greek nouns μάρτυς, μαρτύριον and μαρτυρία and their cognate verb μαρτυρεῖν had long been used in their original sense of 'witness', 'testimony,' 'evidence' and 'to bear witness' or 'to testify' respectively: indeed μάρτυρος is used as a metrically more convenient form of μάρτυς eight times in the epics attributed to Homer (*Iliad* 1.338, 2.302, 3.280, 14.274, 22.255; *Odyssey* 1.273, 14.394, 16.423). This traditional usage carried no hint either that the witness validated his testimony by dying for it or that the testimony was validated by the death of the witness. The Greek words only acquired their familiar meanings of 'martyr,' 'martyrdom' and 'to suffer martyrdom' in the second century of the common era. A careful lexicographical study by Norbert

---

[27] A. Harnack, TU 8.4 (Leipzig, 1892), 3–36.

[28] G. W. Bowersock, Martyrdom and Rome (Cambridge, 1995), xi, 41–57, cf. T. Baumeister, Die Anfänge der Theologie des Martyriums (Münster, 1980), 260: 'der Martystitel ist in den Jahrzehnten zwischen Ignatius und dem Polykarpmartyrium in Kleinasien aufgekommen.' An enormous modern bibliography is duly catalogued by M. Slusser, TRE (1992), 210–212.

Brox in 1961 showed, against the consensus of previous scholarship, that both the noun μάρτυς and the verb μαρτυρεῖν were invariably used in their traditional sense not only in the New Testament and in Jewish texts of the first and second centuries, but also in Christian writings of the post-apostolic age, such as the letter of the church of Rome to the church of Corinth (commonly styled I Clement) and the Shepherd of Hermas.[29] The new meaning and the ideology of martyrdom are foreshadowed in the Fourth Book of

---

[29] N. Brox, Zeuge und Märtyrer. Untersuchungen zur frühchristlichen Zeugnis-Terminologie (Munich, 1961), cf. J. W. van Henten, Internationales Josephus-Kolloquium IV, Brussels 1998, ed. J. U. Kalms & F. Siegert (Münster, 1999), 124–141, on the absence of the concept from Josephus. Scholars before Brox had come close to seeing this important truth: see esp. J. B. Lightfoot, Apostolic Fathers[2] 1. S. Clement of Rome 2 (London, 1890), 26–27, in his comment on 1 Clement 5; Delehaye, Sanctus (1927), 76–80; H. von Campenhausen, Die Idee des Martyriums in der alten Kirche (Göttingen, 1936), 27–29, 51–55. All three correctly noted that the later meaning of μάρτυς and its cognates is absent from the Shepherd of Hermas, which was probably written between 100 and 150, while Lightfoot and Delehaye also conceded its absence from the New Testament; all three, however, made the crucial mistake of allowing that the participle μαρτυρήσας in 1 Clement 5.3, 7, could mean 'by suffering martyrdom,' while Campenhausen both derived the concept of martyr from Johannine theology and claimed to find it in Revelation (Idee 1, 43–45, 53–55). In disproof, see Brox, Zeuge und Märtyrer, 196–201. In the preface to the second edition of his book, Campenhausen confessed that his explanation of the origin of the title of martyr had been completely disproved by Brox (Die Idee des Martyriums in der alten Kirche[2] [Göttingen, 1964], vii). The concept of martyrdom is nevertheless read into the New Testament in several essays in the volume Suffering and Martyrdom in the New Testament. Studies presented to G. M. Styler by the Cambridge New Testament Seminar, ed. W. Horbury and B. McNeil (Cambridge, 1981). Contrast Baumeister, Die Anfänge (n. 28), 2–4, 258–260: although he assumes '[die] Verwurzelung der christlichen Märtyreridee in der jüdischen Martyriumsdeutung' (1), he correctly explains the undeniable simi-

Maccabees, which may have been composed as late as the reign of Hadrian,[30] and both are certainly implicit in several passages in the letters of Ignatius, for both Ignatius and IV Maccabees speak of heroic death for one's religious beliefs.[31]

Several passages in the *Martyrdom of Polycarp*, which was written in 157, provide the earliest clear and indubitable attestation of the new meaning, as has long been recognised (1.1, 2.1, 13.2, 17.1, 18.3, 19.1).[32] But there may be an isolated attestation of the word μαρτύριον with the new

---

larities between Ignatius and IV Maccabees as the product of the same cultural milieu, not direct derivation in either direction (277–289).

[30] On the vexed problem of the date of IV Maccabees, which was probably written in south-eastern Asia Minor and which is conventionally dated c. 100 A.D., see esp. J. W. van Henten, Tradition and Reinterpretation in Jewish and Early Christian Literature, ed. J. W. van Henten and others (Leiden, 1986), 136–149; Märtyrer und Märtyrerakten, ed. W. Ameling (Stuttgart, 2002), 62–69.

[31] D. Boyarin, Dying for God. Martyrdom and the Making of Christianity and Judaism (Stanford, 1999), 93–105, asserts that 'it is obvious that the pre-Christian *2 Maccabees* already contains a martyr text' on the basis of the minimalist definition of 'martyr text' offered by J. W. van Henten, The Maccabean Martyrs as Saviours of the Jewish People: A Study of 2 and 4 Maccabees (Leiden, 1997), 7, and proposes that 'we think of martyrdom as a "discourse".' That does not do justice to Bowersock's demonstration that the *Martyrdom of Polycarp* is the earliest text in which the concept of martyrdom is undubitably attested. On the vocabulary of Ignatius, see Brox, Zeuge und Märtyrer (n. 29), 203–225; K. Bommes, Weizen Gottes. Untersuchungen zur Theologie des Martyriums bei Ignatius von Antiochien. (Cologne & Bonn, 1976), 29–50, 147–164, 221–227; C. Munier, ANRW 2.27.1 (1993), 455–463; on similarities of thought and expression that Ignatius shares with *IV Maccabees,* O. Perler, Riv. arch. crist. 25 (1949), 47–72; Bowersock, Martyrdom and Rome (n. 28), 10–12, 15–17, 77–81. Bowersock correctly rejects the thesis that Ignatius is dependent on IV Maccabees, which has been widely accepted, e. g., by W. H. C. Frend, Martyrdom and Persecution in the Early Church (Oxford, 1965), 197–201.

[32] Delehaye, Sanctus (1927), 76–80 ('sans contestation possible').

meaning more than a decade earlier – in one of the seven surviving letters that Ignatius, the bishop of Antioch wrote during his journey from Antioch to execution in Rome. Although Eusebius of Caesarea dated the death of Ignatius to the reign of Trajan, who died in 117,[33] that date must be too early, since one passage in the letters rebuts a striking Christological formulation of Ptolemaeus, the disciple of Valentinus, preserved by Irenaeus (*Letter to Polycarp* 3.2, cf. Irenaeus, *Adversus Haereses* 1.1.11 Harvey = 1.6.1 Rousseau / Doutreleau), while another contradicts Valentinus' assertion that Christ was born of Silence / Sige (*Letter to the Magnesians* 8.2), from which it follows that Ignatius was writing no earlier than c. 140.[34]

In a famous passage Ignatius looks forward to fighting with wild beasts in Rome, presumably in the Amphitheatrum Flavianum (or Colosseum) and the opportunity of showing himself to be a true disciple of Christ (*Letter to the Ephesians* 1.2). Modern texts of the authentic version of the letters of Ignatius (the so-called Middle Recension) follow Theodor Zahn in printing the passage as follows:

ἀκούσαντες γὰρ δεδεμένον ἀπὸ Συρίας ὑπὲρ τοῦ κοινοῦ ὀνόματος καὶ ἐλπίδος, ἐλπίζοντα τῇ προσευχῇ ὑμῶν ἐπιτυχεῖν ἐν Ῥώμῃ θηριομαχῆσαι, **ἵνα διὰ τοῦ ἐπιτυχεῖν** δυνηθῶ μαθητὴς εἶναι, <ἰδεῖν ἐσπουδάσατε>.[35]

---

[33] *Chronicle* pp. 218–219 Karst; *HE* 3.21–22; 3.36.2–12; 4.1; Jerome, *Chronicle* 194ᶠ–195ᵃ Helm.

[34] T. D. Barnes, Expository Times 120 (2008), 119–130, esp. 123–126.

[35] T. Zahn, Patrum Apostolicorum Opera 2. Ignatii et Polycarpi Epistulae Martyria Fragmenta (Leipzig, 1876), 4. Zahn's text is reproduced (with or without a critical apparatus and with or without noting the manuscript reading) by F. X. Funk, Die apostolischen Väter. Sammlung ausgewählter kirchen- und dogmengeschichtlicher Quellenschriften II.1 (Tübingen and Leipzig, 1901), 81; A. Hilgenfeld, Ignatii Antiocheni et Polycarpi Smyrnaei epistulae et martyria (Berlin,

For <you hastened to see me>, hearing that I was being brought in chains from Syria because of our shared name and hope, and that I was hoping by your prayer to obtain <the privilege of> fighting with wild beasts in Rome, so that by attaining martyrdom I might be able to be a <true> disciple.

Lightfoot concurred with Zahn in his classic edition of the Apostolic Fathers except for supplying the infinitive ἱστορῆσαι instead of ἰδεῖν.[36] But the sole manuscript of the Middle Recension not only contains the word μαρτύριον in the sense of 'martyrdom,' but also the additional clause, suppressed in modern editions, 'of him who delivered himself to God for our sake as an offering and sacrifice,' which contains a quotation from the *Letter to the Ephesians* traditionally ascribed to the apostle Paul.[37] It transmits the passage as follows:

---

1902), 213.7; K. Lake, The Apostolic Fathers 1 (Cambridge, Mass. and London, 1912), 174; O. von Gebhardt, A. Harnack and T. Zahn, Patrum Apostolicorum Opera[6] (Leipzig, 1920), 87; K. Bihlmeyer, Die apostolischen Väter: Neubearbeitung der Funkschen Ausgabe[3], ed. W. Schneemelcher (Tübingen, 1956; reprinted 1970), app. to 82.15, reproduced photographically by A. Lindemann and H. Paulsen, Die apostolischen Väter: Griechisch-deutsche Parallelausgabe (Tübingen, 1992), 178; P.-T. Camelot, Ignace d'Antioche (SC 10bis[4], 1969), 58; J. B. Lightfoot & J. R. Harmer, The Apostolic Fathers. Greek Texts and English Translations of their Writings[2], edited and revised by M. W. Holmes (Grand Rapids, 1992), 136 n. 6; J. A. Fischer, Schriften des Urchristentums 1. Die apostolischen Väter[10] (Darmstadt, 1993), 142.12 (first edition 1959); B. D. Ehrman, The Apostolic Fathers 1 (Cambridge, Mass., 2003), 220.

[36] J. B. Lightfoot, Apostolic Fathers[2] 2. S. Ignatius. S. Polycarp 2 (London, 1889), 31.

[37] The full sentence in Ephesians 5.2 reads as follows: ὁ Χριστὸς ἠγάπησεν ἡμᾶς καὶ παρέδωκεν ἑαυτὸν ὑπὲρ ἡμῶν προσφορὰν καὶ θυσίαν τῷ θεῷ εἰς ὀσμὴν εὐωδίας.

ἀκούσαντες γὰρ δεδεμένον ἀπὸ Συρίας ὑπὲρ τοῦ κοινοῦ ὀνόματος καὶ ἐλπίδος, ἐλπίζοντα τῇ προσευχῇ ὑμῶν ἐπιτυχεῖν ἐν ʿΡώμῃ θηριομαχῆσαι, **ἵνα διὰ τοῦ μαρτυρίου ἐπιτυχεῖν** δυνηθῶ μαθητὴς εἶναι τοῦ ὑπὲρ ἡμῶν ἑαυτὸν ἀνενεγκόντος θεῷ προσφορὰν καὶ θυσίαν.

Something is clearly amiss here, since the sentence lacks both a main verb and a verbal form governing the participles in the accusative case, and also perhaps a first person pronoun to provide a referent for these participles. The Anglo-Latin translation supplies the first and second missing elements. It reads

*audientes enim ligatum a Syria pro communi nomine et spe, sperantem oratione vestra potiri in Roma cum bestiis pugnare, ut per potiri possim dicipulus esse, videre festinastis.*[38]

For, hearing that I was being brought in chains from Syria because of our shared name and hope, and that I was hoping by your prayer to obtain <the privilege of> fighting with wild beasts in Rome, so that by attaining martyrdom I might be able to be a <true> disciple, you hastened to see me.

But the word order of the Anglo-Latin translation does not necessarily imply that the missing words ἰδεῖν ἐσπουδάσατε should be added after εἶναι rather than earlier in the sentence. And a first person pronoun is easily supplied. Hence, in accordance with Hefele's placing of the necessary supplement and Cureton's proposal to add an enclitic με,[39] it may be conjectured that what Ignatius originally wrote was

ἀκούσαντες γὰρ δεδεμένον ἀπὸ Συρίας ὑπὲρ τοῦ κοινοῦ ὀνόματος καὶ ἐλπίδος <ἰδεῖν με ἐσπουδάσατε>, ἐλπίζοντα κτλ.

---

[38] Lightfoot, Apostolic Fathers[2] 2.3 (1890), 22.11–13; F. Diekamp, Patres apostolici 2[3] (Tübingen, 1913), 278.

[39] C. J. Hefele, Patrum Apostolicorum Opera[4] (Tübingen, 1855), 152; W. Cureton, Corpus Ignatianum. A Complete Collection of the Ignatian Epistles (London, 1849), 17.

But what of the rest of the sentence? The Syriac version agrees with the Anglo-Latin translation in omitting the Pauline quotation, but the manuscripts of the Long Recension here paradoxically offer a briefer text than the transmitted version of the Middle Recension, which they replicate exactly except for the omission of the second ἐπιτυχεῖν. A finely balanced choice must be made. If Ignatius wrote διὰ τοῦ μαρτυρίου ἐπιτυχεῖν, then he was expressing the hope that he might become a true disciple through attaining martyrdom; if he did not write these words, then he never used the vocabulary of martyrdom, even though all the components of the concept are already there in many passages of his letters. Robert Joly has argued against Zahn and Lightfoot that the author of the Long Recension possessed a text of the Middle Recension of Ignatius which read διὰ τοῦ μαρτυρίου ἐπιτυχεῖν, found the repetition of the infinitive ἐπιτυχεῖν inelegant and therefore deleted the whole phrase.[40] Is this explanation of the paradosis correct? The question can perhaps only be decided definitively when a proper critical edition of the Middle Recension is produced. Until then it may be wisest to leave open the question whether or not Ignatius used the phrase διὰ τοῦ μαρτυρίου in the new sense of 'by martyrdom' or even invented the concept. What is historically important is that, whether or not Ignatius invented it, the concept of martyrdom is first indubitably attested in the *Martyrdom of Polycarp,* where the noun μαρτυρία and the verb μαρτυρεῖν occur with this meaning six times in all (1.1, 2.1, 13.2, 17.1, 18.3, 19.1). Like the martyrdom of Polycarp, the martyrdom of

---

[40]  R. Joly, *Le dossier d'Ignace d'Antioche* (Brussels, 1979), 70–71.

Ignatius probably falls within the reign of Antoninus Pius (138–161).[41]

Polycarp, in the account of whose martyrdom the new terminology is used as if already current, was not only the recipient of one of Ignatius' letters, but may also be identified as the editor who put together the corpus of seven letters known to Eusebius which survives as the Middle Recension.[42] The available evidence therefore suggests that the concept of martyrdom was invented, probably in an urban context and certainly in Christian circles, in the reign of Antoninus Pius, and it might conceivably have been Ignatius of Antioch who invented it. More important, it was only when the new concept of martyrdom had been invented that two linked and parallel phenomena could come into existence – Christian hagiography and the cult of the saints.

Both the new vocabulary of martyrdom and the cult of the saints are indubitably attested for the first time in the letter of the church of Smyrna, commonly known as the *Martyrdom of Polycarp,* which was almost certainly written in 157.[43] From Rome at almost exactly the same period come accounts of the trials of Christians and material evidence of the cult of Saint Peter. Justin, originally a native of Neapolis in Palestine, was the first to attempt a synthesis between Christianity and Greek philosophy.[44] He settled in Rome during the reign of Antoninus Pius and during the later 150s composed a defence of the Christians which he addressed to Pius, the princes Verissimus and Lucius, and

---

[41] Barnes (n. 34) 130. Zwierlein, Petrus in Rom (n. 18). 31–33, 183–237, proposes to date the letters of Ignatius between 170 and 190.

[42] Lightfoot, Apostolic Fathers[2] 2.1 (1889), 125–126, 423–430.

[43] App. 4.

[44] H. Chadwick, Early Christian Thought and the Classical Tradition. Studies in Justin, Clement, and Origen (Oxford, 1966), 9–30.

the Senate and people of Rome (*Apol.* 1.1, cf. 68.3).[45] Justin's so-called *Second Apology*, a piece without either a formal beginning or formal end, which he may have composed as an integral part of a single apology,[46] starts with a story of martyrdom, although, significantly, the word itself is not used. A wanton woman married to a wanton husband was converted to Christianity, reformed herself and tried to convert her husband. When he persisted in his old ways, she refused to sleep with him, and, when he went to Alexandria, she divorced him. He then denounced her as a Christian, but she petitioned the emperor and obtained protection. The husband then persuaded a centurion whom he knew to arrest his wife's Christian instructor Ptolemaeus and to ask him whether he was a Christian. When Ptolemaeus naively admitted it, the centurion imprisoned him and at length brought him before the *praefectus urbi* Urbicus, who asked Ptolemaeus whether he was a Christian and, when he admitted it, ordered his execution. Thereupon one Lucius, who was present in court, protested that this was unjust. When Lucius admitted that he was also a Christian, Urbicus sentenced him too to death, together with another who also protested.

---

[45] Justin was clearly writing before the death of Antoninus Pius on 7 March 161, and he refers (1) to a petition requesting permission to be castrated submitted to the prefect of Egypt Felix, (*Apol.* 1.29.2–3) and (2) to events in Rome while Urbicus was praefectus urbi (2.1.1, 3; 2.12, 15–16): L. Munatius Felix was prefect of Egypt from 150 to 154 (PIR² M 723), while Q. Lollius Urbicus appears to have been *praefectus urbi* from 146 to 160 (PIR² L 327).

[46] On the problems posed by the so-called *Second Apology*, see recently C. Munier, Justin: Apologie pour les Chrétiens (SC 507, 2006), 29–38; P. Parvis & D. Minns, Justin: Philosopher and Martyr: *Apologies* (Oxford, 2009), 21–31, 54–56.

Justin goes on immediately to state that he expects soon to be fixed to a stake after an accusation from the husband or the centurion, if not from his enemy, the Cynic philosopher Crescens (3.1). An account of the predicted trial, which has the form of a documentary record, survives in a variety of recensions.[47] The presiding magistrate was the *praefectus urbi* Q. Junius Rusticus, consul for the second time in 162.[48] Justin was questioned first, then his associates Chariton and Charito, Euelpistus, Hierax and Liberianus. After all had admitted to being Christians, Rusticus sentenced them to be scourged and executed.

For the first generations of Christians the most important authority figures had been the apostles, that is, eleven of Jesus' original twelve disciples, with the addition of Matthias who, according to the evangelist Luke, was elected to replace Judas Iscariot immediately after the Resurrection (Acts 1.13–14),[49] and the convert Saul of Tarsus, a Roman citizen by birth who subsequently took the Roman *cognomen* Paulus to celebrate his conversion of L. Sergius Paullus the procon-

---

[47] K-K-R pp. 125–126 = Musurillo IV, Recension A (Barnes II) is the most primitive version, K-K-R IV = Musurillo IV, Recension B a reworked version, K-K-R pp. 127–129 = Musurillo IV, Recension C a still more elaborate version.

[48] PIR² J 814. Rusticus' prefecture is usually assumed to run from 162 to 168, but analogy suggests that it began before he became consul for the second time on 1 January 162: accordingly, he may be presumed the immediate successor of the *praefectus urbi* whose death is registered during 160 by the Fasti Ostienses, and who is normally identified as Lollius Urbicus (L.Vidman, Fasti Ostienses² (Prague, 1982), 52, frag. R: *[— Q. Lollius Urbicus praef(ectus) u]rb(is) excessi[t]) …*

[49] Lists are given in Matthew 10.2–4; Mark 3.14–19; Luke 6.14–16: they disagree over the tenth name, who is Lebbaeus in Matthew, Thaddaeus in Mark and Judas the son of James in Luke.

sul of Cyprus (Acts 13.4–12).[50] The prestige of the apostles
led later generations of Christians to identify the authors of
the first and fourth Gospels as the Matthew and John who
were two of the original twelve – without evidence and in
defiance of probability (Eusebius, *HE* 3.24.3–13).[51] And it
was still a matter of importance to Eusebius as the first historian of the Christian church around 300 to track the fate
of each of Jesus' disciples individually wherever he could.[52]
But all the apostles died before the world ended as they
had once confidently expected. In the middle of the second
century, when the concept of martyrdom was invented, the
status of the apostles as authority figures came to depend
in large part on whether they had suffered martyrdom. The
earliest shrines for Christian heroes were constructed almost
as soon as the apostles who had until then been revered as
disciples of Jesus came to be venerated as martyrs as well as
apostles. It can hardly be an accident that the cult of the
saints is first attested in the earliest known document of
Christian hagiography: the *Martyrdom of Polycarp* records
that the Christians of Smyrna collected the bones of their
dead bishop which they deemed 'more precious than jewels
and more valuable than gold' (18.2).

---

[50] H. Dessau, Hermes 41 (1906), 347–365. Unfortunately, Paul's
gentilicium is unknown.

[51] Eusebius could not deny that Luke's gospel lacked apostolic
authority (*HE* 3.24.14–15, quoting Luke 1.1–4), but he believed, with
appeal to Papias of Hierapolis and Clement of Alexandria, that Mark
was a follower of Peter, who authorised his gospel to be read during
church services (*HE* 2.15, cf. 3.39.15; 6.14.5–7).

[52] Eusebius, *HE* 2.1.1 (Matthias); 2.1.4 (James the son of Al-
phaeus); 2.1.6, cf. 1.13 (Thaddaeus); 2.25.5–8 (Peter); 3.1.1 (Andrew
and Thomas); 3.18.1–3, 3.23 (John); 3.30–31 (Philip); 3.39.4–5
(Thomas); 3.39.10 (Matthias); 5.10.3 (Bartholomew).

Within a very few years of the death of Polycarp there began a cult of Peter as a martyr in Rome, which can be documented from literary, liturgical, epigraphical and archaeological evidence. Despite occasional scholarly denials, the obvious implication of a letter in the New Testament attributed to Peter is that he came to Rome – and the inference is valid whether or not the letter with its salutation from 'the chosen church in Babylon' was in fact written by Peter (1 Peter 5.13: ἀσπάζεται ὑμᾶς ἡ ἐν Βαβυλῶνι συνεκλεκτὴ καὶ Μᾶρκος ὁ υἱός μου).[53] Hans Lietzmann long ago set out a range of evidence that shows that the apostles Peter and Paul were venerated separately in the late second century, on the Vatican and beside the Via Ostiensis respectively, and venerated jointly at the third milestone on the Via Appia from 258 to some date in first half of the fourth century, when large basilicas were constructed on the Vatican and on the Via Ostiensis.[54] After Lietzmann wrote, excavations conducted under the basilica of St Peter's between 1940 and 1949 showed that a shrine was built for Peter c. 160.[55] Since the publication of the results of the Vatican excavations in

---

[53] In favour, E. G. Selwyn, *The First Epistle of Peter*[2] (London, 1947), 7–63, 243–245, 303–305 (arguing for a date before July 64); O. Cullmann, *Petrus. Jünger-Apostel-Märtyrer* (Zurich, 1952), 87–92; *Peter: Disciple-Apostle-Martyr*[2], trans. F. V. Filson (London & Philadelphia, 1962), 83–88; F. W. Beare, *The First Epistle of Peter*[3] (Oxford, 1970), 28–50 (accepting a much later date); against, Zwierlein, *Petrus in Rom* (n. 18), 7–12.

[54] H. Lietzmann, *Petrus und Paulus in Rom. Liturgische und archäologische Studien*[2] (Berlin & Leipzig, 1927), esp. 109–126, 145–169, with a long and important 'Beilage' by A. von Gerkan, 'Die christlichen Anlagen unter San Sebastiano neu aufgenommen und beschrieben' (248–301).

[55] B. M. Apollonj Ghetti, A. Ferrua, E. Josi and E. Kirschbaum, *Esplorazioni sotto la Confessione di San Pietro in Vaticano eseguite negli anni 1940–1949* (Vatican City, 1951).

1951, they have attracted a vast and contentious bibliography.[56] In the present context, however, it will suffice to summarise briefly what is known about the shrine constructed on the Vatican in the second century and the relation of the fourth century basilica to it, and about the joint cult of Peter and Paul on the Via Appia.

Eusebius of Caesarea quoted two writers of the late second century as evidence that the apostles Peter and Paul were martyred in Rome (*HE* 2.25.7–8). The earlier is Dionysius, the bishop of Corinth, writing to the church of Rome c. 170:

ταῦτα καὶ ὑμεῖς διὰ τῆς τοσαύτης νουθεσίας τὴν ἀπὸ Πέτρου καὶ Παύλου φυτείαν γενηθεῖσαν Ῥωμαίων τε καὶ Κορινθίων συνεκεράσατε. καὶ γὰρ ἄμφω καὶ εἰς τὴν ἡμετέραν Κόρινθον φυτεύσαντες ἡμᾶς ὁμοίως ἐδίδαξαν, ὁμοίως δὲ καὶ εἰς τὴν Ἰταλίαν ὁμόσε διδάξαντες ἐμαρτύρησαν κατὰ τὸν αὐτὸν καιρόν.

In this way by your impressive admonition you have bound together all that has grown from the seed which Peter and Paul sowed in Romans and Corinthians alike. For both of them sowed in our Corinth (1 Corinthians 1.12) and taught us jointly; in Italy too they taught jointly in the same city and were martyred at the same time (trans. G. A. Williamson, rev. A. Louth)

The other authority quoted by Eusebius for the deaths of Peter and Paul in Rome is an otherwise unknown Gaius who was writing when Zephyrinus was bishop of Rome (199–217). The manuscripts of the *Ecclesiastical History* present Eusebius' brief quotation from Gaius' lost work against the Montanist Proclus as follows:

---

[56] The modern bibliography is enormous: more than forty years ago A. A. de Marco, The Tomb of Saint Peter. A Representative and Annotated Bibliography of the Excavations (Leiden, 1964), listed 870 numbered items.

ἐγὼ δὲ τὰ τρόπαια τῶν ἀποστόλων ἔχω δεῖξαι. ἐὰν γὰρ θελήσῃς ἀπελθεῖν ἐπὶ τὸν Βασικανὸν ἢ ἐπὶ τὴν ὁδὸν τὴν Ὠστίαν, εὑρήσεις τὰ τρόπαια τῶν ταύτην ἱδρυσαμένων τὴν ἐκκλησίαν.

I can point out the monuments of the victorious apostles. If you[57] will go as far as the Vatican or the Ostian Way, you will find the monuments of those who founded this church (trans. G.A. Williamson, rev. A. Louth)

In his classic edition Eduard Schwartz printed the text as transmitted, diagnosing Βασικανόν as a pre-Eusebian corruption.[58] Rufinus, however, has a fuller version of the conditional clause:

*Ego, inquit, habeo tropaea apostolorum, quae ostendam. Si enim procedas via regali, quae ad Vaticanum ducit, aut via Ostiensi, invenies tropaea defixa, quibus ex utraque parte statutis Romana communitur ecclesia.*

Frédéric Tailliez accordingly argued that a line of about 20–22 letters has dropped out of the manuscripts of Eusebius in the course of transmission through haplography, and he emended the transmitted text on the basis of Rufinus' version to read[59]

ἐγὼ δὲ τὰ τρόπαια τῶν ἀποστόλων ἔχω δεῖξαι. ἐὰν γὰρ θελήσῃς ἀπελθεῖν ἐπὶ τὴν βασιλ<ικὴν ὁδὸν τὴν εἰς τὸν Βατι>κανὸν ἢ ἐπὶ τὴν ὁδὸν τὴν Ὠστίαν, εὑρήσεις τὰ τρόπαια τῶν ταύτην ἱδρυσαμένων τὴν ἐκκλησίαν.

I myself can point out the trophies of the apostles. For, if you wish to leave the city by the imperial road which leads to the Vatican hill or

---

[57] Either the indefinite 'you' or the Montanist Proclus against whom Gaius directed his lost work.

[58] E. Schwartz, Eusebius Werke 2.1 (GCS 9.1, Berlin & Leipzig, 1903), 178.4, with the comment 'voreusebianischer Fehler.'

[59] F. Tailliez, Orientalia Christiana Periodica 9 (1943), 431–436. In order to illustrate the haplography, Tailliez printed the relevant passage with the missing line inserted as follows: ... ἀπελθεῖν ἐπὶ τὴν βασι / λικὴν ὁδὸν ἐπὶ τὸν Βατι / κανόν, ἢ ἐπὶ τὴν ὁδὸν τὴν Ὠστίαν ...

by the Ostian way, you will find the trophies of those who founded
this church.

Eusebius' two quotations are of very unequal value. Dionysius offers nothing more than empty rhetoric: when he says
that Peter and Paul were martyred 'at the same time,' he is
merely reflecting the contemporary belief that both apostles
died under Nero. Gaius, however, had seen the trophies
of the two apostles and hence counts as an eye-witness for
the existence of cults of Peter and Paul at the time when he
visited Rome.

The 'explorations under the Confessio Petri on the Vatican' conducted between 1940 and 1949' found a shrine (or
*aedicula*) constructed around the year 160 as an integral
part of the so-called Red Wall as a memorial to Peter in a
mid-second century cemetery which must be the 'trophy' of
Peter to which Gaius referred a generation later; and they
established that when a large and magnificent basilica was
built on the site in the second quarter of the fourth century,
no expense or effort was spared, despite the sharp slope of
the terrain, to ensure that its focal point was centred exactly
above the aedicula, which had itself deliberately been constructed exactly above an empty space.[60] This area, which
lies immediately beneath the high altar of St Peter's, had
in the first century been used for the unpretentious burials
of humble folk; about the middle of the second century, a

---

[60] For critical assessments of the archaeological evidence, see esp.
J. Toynbee and J. Ward Perkins, The Shrine of St. Peter and the Vatican
Excavations (London, 1956), 135–167; Lampe, From Paul to Valenti-
nus (n. 10), 104–116; H. G. Thümmel, Die Memorien für Petrus und
Paulus in Rom. Die archäologischen Denkmäler und die literarische
Tradition. Arbeiten zur Kirchengeschichte 76 (Berlin & New York,
1999), 15–72, 96–102. On the bones claimed to be those of Peter and
the Vatical graffiti, see Apps. 8, 9.

number of contiguous burial chambers were constructed, all with several niches to receive individual bodies, all decorated, some luxuriously decorated, with stucco, paintings or mosaics reflecting very varied tastes and interests; and in this complex of pagan tombs, after the foundations of the Red Wall had been laid, but before the wall itself was built, there was constructed an *aedicula* or shrine corresponding to the 'trophy' of Peter on the Vatican to which Gaius referred. The archaeological evidence, therefore, establishes that about or shortly after the middle of the second century the Christians of Rome built a memorial shrine at the place where they believed that the apostle Peter was buried.[61]

The Vatican hill was not the only location in Rome where the cult of Peter was celebrated in later times, when festivals of Peter and Paul were held on three roads (PL 17.1215: *trinis celebratur viis / festum sacrorum martyrum*), that is, of Peter on the Vatican, Paul on the Via Ostienis, and Peter and Paul together on the Appian Way. There is literary, hagiographical and liturgical evidence that a joint cult of Peter and Paul was celebrated in the late third century from 258 onwards *ad catacumbas,* under the later church of San Sebastiano.[62] The force of this evidence was recognised in the nineteenth century by two excellent scholars who knew their Rome well,[63] and it was confirmed by archaeological and epigraphical evidence unearthed in excavations beneath San Sebastiano in the early twentieth century.[64] Graffiti

---

[61] Lietzmann, Petrus und Paulus² (n. 54), 109–126, 145–169; Thümmel, Die Memorien für Petrus and Paulus (n. 60), 15–72.

[62] Thümmel, Die Memorien für Petrus and Paulus (n. 60), 8–10.

[63] viz., M. Armellini, Le catacombe romane (Rome, 1880), 388–420 ('La platonia ove furono deposti i corpi dei ss apostoli Pietro e Paolo'); L. Duchesne, Le Liber Pontificalis 1 (Paris, 1883), civ–cvii.

[64] P. Styger, RQ 29 (1915), 73–110, 149–205; cf. A. von Gerkan,

inscribed on the walls of a late third century construction
invoke the prayers of the two apostles in formulae such
as '*Paule ed Petre petite pro Victore,*' '*Paule Petre pro Erate
rogate,*' '*Petre et Paule subvenite Prim[itivo] peccatori,*' and
'*[Petre et] Paul[e] in [mente nos h]abete in ora[tion]ibus
vestris,*'[65] while other graffiti record the celebration of *refri-
geria,* 'refreshment meals' eaten in commemoration of and
shared with the dead (for example, '*Petro et Paulo Tomius
Coelius refrigerium feci*' and '*at [=ad] Paulu[m] et Pet[rum]
refri[geravi]*).[66] Moreover, after the basilicas of Peter on the
Vatican and Paul on the Via Ostiensis had been built in
the first half of the fourth century, the Christians of Rome
continued to believe that the relics of Peter and Paul had
rested *ad catacumbas* for a period: the first two lines of a
metrical inscription composed by Damasus as bishop of
Rome between 366 and 384 and erected at the site record
the fact that Peter and Paul 'formerly dwelt here' (ILCV 951
= Damasus, *Epigrammata* 26 Ihm = 20 Ferrua: *hic habitasse*

---

in Lietzmann, Petrus und Paulus (n. 54), 248–301; F. Tolotti, Memorie
degli apostoli in Catacumbas. Rilievo critico della Memoria e della
Basilica Apostolorum al III miglio della Via Appia. Collezione "Amici
delle Catacombe" 19 (Vatican City, 1953); Thümmel, Die Memorien
für Petrus and Paulus (n. 60), 73–95. It seems clear, on purely archaeological grounds, that the *memoria* of Peter and Paul on the Appian Way
was constructed between 238 and 260: Toynbee & Ward Perkins,
Shrine (n. 60), 167–182, 268, citing R. Marichal, CRAI 1953. 60–68.
[65] P. Styger, Dissertazioni della Pontificia Accademia Romana di
Archeologia, Serie II. 13 (1918), 58, 59, 64 n. 9, 70 n. 55. For
photographs, see Tolotti, Memorie degli apostoli (n. 64), 17, fig. 1;
Guarducci, Pietro (1983), Tavola XLVII). For the formula, compare
a graffito from the crypt of the Diocletianic martyrs Marcellinus
and Peter, which reads '*Marcelline / Petre petite / [p]ro Gallicanu / [C]
hristiano*' (ICUR, N. S. 6.15963 = ILCV 2334).
[66] Styger, Dissertazioni, (n. 65), 59, 61; Toynbee & Ward Perkins,
Shrine (n. 60), 171–172, 189–190 n. 56.

*prius sanctos cognoscere debes / nomina quisq(ue) Petri pariter Pauliq(ue) requiris*[67] and the *Acta Sebastiani* assume that the 'traces' of both apostles were to be found 'at the beginning of the crypt' during the Diocletianic persecution (PL 17.1150).[68]

The cult of Peter and Paul *ad catacumbas* began on 29 June 258. The date is attested in an almanac compiled in Rome for New Year's Day 354, which has been the subject of several modern studies,[69] even though there is no complete critical edition which prints together all its varied texts and illustrations.[70] The almanac incorporates an earlier docu-

---

[67] The words *hic habitasse prius* were taken to mean that Peter and Paul lodged together on the site before 64 by J. Wilpert, RQ 26 (1912), 117–122, citing a graffito reading '*domus Petri*'; Delehaye, Sanctus (n. 28), 265. But the area was being used for quarrying pozzolana in the first century: Toynbee & Ward Perkins, Shrine (n. 60), 172–173. For the correct interpretation of *habitasse,* see Armellini, Le catacombe (n. 63), 392: 'hanno abitato, vale a dire hanno santificato coi loro corpi il luogo.' Damasus used similar vocabulary in the epigram that he wrote for the tomb of the martryr Gorgonius on the Via Labicana: '*Martyris hic tumulus … hic quicumq(ue) venit sanctorum limina quaerat / inveniet vicina in sede habitare beatos*' (31 Ihm = 32 Ferrua, lines 1, 3–4). It seems most unlikely that *hic* means merely 'here in Rome' and alludes to the martyrdoms of Peter and Paul, which was proposed as a possible interpretation by V. Saxer, Saecularia Damasiana. Atti del convegno internazionale per il XVI centenario della morte di Papa Damaso I (11-12-384 – 10/12-12-1984) (Vatican City, 1986), 67.

[68] App. 7.

[69] Esp. H. Stern, Le calendrier de 354. Étude sur son texte et ses illustrations (Paris, 1953); M. R. Salzman, On Roman Time. The Codex-Calendar of 354 and the Rhythms of Urban Life in Late Antiquity (Berkeley, Los Angeles & Oxford, 1990).

[70] Separate editions of different parts are available, none of them very recent: T. Mommsen, Chr. Min. 1 (1892), 39–148; J. Strzygowski, Die Calenderbilder des Chronographen vom Jahre 354. JDAI, Ergänzungsheft 1 (Berlin, 1888); A. Riese, Anthologia Latina 1.2 (Leipzig, 1906), 135–136 n. 665 (*Monosticha de mensibus*); CIL 1²,

ment entitled *depositio martyrum,* that is, a list of martyrs celebrated in Rome (Chr. min. 1.71–72). Unfortunately, the entry relating to Peter and Paul is transmitted in an incomplete form in the sole manuscript of the almanac. Its full text can, however, be recovered from the corresponding entry in the *Martyrologium Hieronymianum,* which drew on the *depositio martyrum* as one of its sources.[71] The original text may be restored as follows:

*III kal(endas) Iul(ias) Petri in <Vaticano et Petri et Pauli ad> catacumbas Tusco et Basso cons(ulibu)s et Pauli Ost<i>ense.*[72]

No rational explanation of the consular date of 258 has ever been advanced other than that it marks the inauguration of a joint celebration of Peter and Paul *ad catacumbas* in that year, whether or not the transfer of cult included the transfer of the relics or mortal remains of Peter and Paul

---

pp. 254–279 (the *natales Caesarum*), cf. J. Divjak, Textsorten und Textkritik. Tagungsbeiträge, ed. A. Primmer, K. Smolak & D. Weber (Vienna, 2002), 19–38; W. Wischmeyer ib. 45–57.

[71] Delehaye, Mélanges (1966), 353.

[72] Lietzmann, Petrus und Paulus [2] (n. 54), 113–114, cf. Armellini, Le catacombe (n. 65), 394–397; T. Mommsen, Liber Pontificalis, Pars Prior. MGH, Gesta Pontificum Romanorum 1 (Berlin, 1898), 4.10n, 28.1n. In their classic editions of the Liber Pontificalis and the Chronographer of 354, both Duchesne, Liber pontificalis 1 (n. 63), 11–12, and Mommsen, Chr. min. 1.71, printed the text as transmitted ('*III kal(endas) Iul(ias) Petri in Catacumbas et Pauli Ost(i)ense Tusco et Basso cons(ulibu)s*') In 1898 Mommsen argued that the original compiler of the Liber Pontificalis read '*Petri <in Vaticano et Petri et Pauli> in Catacumbas*' in his text of this list of Roman festivals, and Lietzmann accepted this supplement as correct. I have preferred a supplement that retains the correct designation of the place as *ad catacumbas*; indeed I believe that the transmitted *in catacumbas* indicates that words have fallen out between the preposition *in* and the following noun. The original lineation was presumably: '*Petri in <Vaticano et / Petri et Pauli ad> catacumbas / Tusco et Basso cons(ulibu)s / et Pauli Ost<i>ense.*'

from the Vatican and the Via Ostiensis.[73] But there is no archaeological trace, at least no archaeological trace that survives critical scrutiny, for the presence of the mortal remains of Peter underneath the *aedicula* constructed on the Vatican hill c. 160 or of either Peter or Paul in the third century shrine on the Via Appia.[74] Moreover, if Peter was one of the Christians whom Nero burned alive as part of a public entertainment by the banks of the River Tiber, it seems doubtful whether the Christians of Rome in 64 would have been able to recover his body for burial, or perhaps even to recognise it.

What real knowledge did the Christians of the late second century possess about the lives of Jesus' original disciples or the apostle Paul beyond what they could read in the gospels and in the *Acts of the Apostles,* which records the death of only one of them, namely, James the bother of John, who was killed on the orders of King Herod Agrippa (12.2)? The cases of the apostle Paul and the author of the fourth gospel provide a suggestive indication.

The *Acts of the Apostles* notoriously ends without closure.[75] Paul remained in custody in Rome for two years, receiving visitors, proclaiming the kingdom of God and teach-

---

[73] Lietzmann, Petrus und Paulus (n. 54), 109–126; A. von Gerkan, BJb 158 (1958), 103–104; W. H. C. Frend, The Archaeology of Early Christianity. A History (Minneapolis, 1996), 211. For a survey of modern opinions on each side of the question, see Saxer, Saecularia Damasiana (n. 67), 65–66 n. 8.

[74] See esp. Toynbee & Ward Perkins, Shrine (n. 60), 167–182; Thümmel, Die Memorien für Petrus and Paulus (n. 60), 93–95; H. Brandenburg, Ancient Churches of Rome from the Fourth to the Seventh Century, trans. A. Kropp (Turnhout, 2005), 66–69.

[75] H. Omerzu, Das Ende des Paulus, ed. F. W. Horn 106 (Berlin & New York, 2001), 127–156, cf. M. Tilly, ib. 107–125 on Syriac versions of the passage.

ing about Jesus Christ freely and without hindrance (*Acts* 28.30–31). Although *Acts* gives the impression that Paul was under house-arrest, the letter of Paul to the Philippians says that he was in chains in the *praetorium* (1.13), which seems to imply that he was imprisoned in the camp of the praetorian guard. What happened after the two years were over? Later Christian tradition is completely unanimous in reporting that Paul was beheaded in the reign of Nero.[76] It is not clear, however, that any of this derives from authentic memory of Paul's death rather being an inference from the fact that he was a Roman citizen by birth (*Acts* 22.28). For the tradition that Paul died in Rome cannot be traced further back in time than the very late second century and is contradicted by earlier evidence.

Some time before Paul came to Rome, he had written a letter to the Christians of the city in which he declared his intention of proceeding from Rome to Spain (Romans 15.28). The two earliest items of surviving evidence that refer to Paul's death indicate that he did in fact go to Spain.[77] The letter of the church of Rome to the church of Corinth, which is traditionally attributed to Clement,

---

[76] Dionysius of Corinth and Gaius, quoted by Eusebius, *HE* 2.25. 8, 7 (above, p. 24–6); Tertullian, *Praescr. haer.* 36.3; *Scorp.* 15.3; Clement of Alexandria, *Strom.* 7.106.3; Origen in the lost third tome of his commentary on Genesis, quoted by Eusebius, *HE* 2.1.3; Lactantius, *Div. Inst.* 4.21.5; *Mort. Pers.* 2.5–6; Eusebius, *HE* 2.22; *Dem. Ev.* 3.5.65.

[77] 2 Timothy 4.16–22 is not evidence that its author believed that Paul returned to the East after acquittal, since the dramatic date of the letter, which makes Paul say 'I have left Trophimus in Miletus suffering from illness' (20), is before his final journey to Jerusalem, during which he was arrested (cf. *Acts* 20.16–17, 21.1–8). Some scholars have allowed themselves to be misled by Eusebius' dating of 2 Timothy to the period immediately preceding Paul's execution (*HE* 2.22.2–8).

canonically regarded as the third bishop of Rome, can hardly be dated later than c. 100.[78] A complicated passage describes the sufferings and deaths of the apostles Peter and Paul:[79]

Διὰ ζῆλον καὶ φθόνον οἱ μέγιστοι καὶ δικαιότατοι στῦλοι ἐδιώχθησαν καὶ ἕως θανάτου ἤθλησαν. λάβωμεν πρὸ ὀφθαλμῶν ἡμῶν τοὺς ἀγαθοὺς ἀποστόλους· Πέτρον, ὃς διὰ ζῆλον ἄδικον οὐχ ἕνα οὐδὲ δύο, ἀλλὰ πλείονας ὑπήνεγκεν πόνους καὶ οὕτω μαρτυρήσας ἐπορεύθη εἰς τὸν ὀφειλόμενον τόπον τῆς δόξης. διὰ ζῆλον καὶ ἔριν Παῦλος ὑπομονῆς βραβεῖον ἔδειξεν· ἑπτάκις δεσμὰ φορέσας, φυγαδευθείς, λιθασθείς, κῆρυξ γενόμενος ἔν τε τῇ ἀνατολῇ καὶ ἐν τῇ δύσει τὸ γενναῖον τῆς πίστεως αὐτοῦ κλέος ἔλαβεν· δικαιοσύνην διδάξας ὅλον τὸν κόσμον καὶ ἐπὶ τὸ τέρμα τῆς δύσεως ἐλθὼν καὶ μαρτυρήσας ἐπὶ τῶν ἡγουμένων, οὕτως ἀπηλλάγη τοῦ κόσμου καὶ εἰς τὸν ἅγιον τόπον ἀνηλήμφθη, ὑπομονῆς γενόμενος μέγιστος ὑπογραμμός.

Because of jealousy and envy the greatest and most upright pillars were persecuted and contended even unto death. Let us set before our eyes the good apostles. There is Peter, who because of unjust jealousy endured not one or two hardships, but many, and having thus borne witness he travelled to the place of glory that he deserved. Because of jealousy and strife Paul showed a prize for endurance. Seven times he bore chains, he was sent into exile and stoned, he became a herald both in the East and in the West, and he received a noble reputation for his faith. He taught righteousness to the whole world, he went to the limits of the West, he bore witness before the authorities,[80] and thus he was released from this world and taken up

---

[78] Lightfoot, Apostolic Fathers² 1.1 (1890), 346–361.

[79] For elucidation of the writer's train of thought, see esp. H. Löhr, Das Ende des Paulus, ed. F. W. Horn 106 (Berlin & New York, 2001), 197–213.

[80] The traditional translation of ἐπὶ τῶν ἡγουμένων as 'before the rulers' is seriously misleading. The phrase designates provincial governors: see the passages collected by H. J. Mason, Greek Terms for Roman Institutions. A Lexicon and Analysis (Toronto, 1974), 52, to which add Dio 72(71).22.2 (3.264.3 Boissevain), Eusebius, *HE* 3.33.3; 4.2.2, 8.6, 15.19; 6.3.3, 19.15, 41.21; 7.11.25; 9.1.2.

to the holy place, having become the greatest example of endurance.
(1 Clement 5)[81]

Despite its obscurities, this passage could hardly state more
clearly and unambiguously that Paul went to Spain. For,
when a letter from Rome informs its addressees in Corinth
in Greece that Paul went as far as 'the boundary of the West,'
this boundary must lie to the west of Italy. The letter also
says that Paul bore witness before the Roman authorities
in Spain. On the other hand, the passage does not state
that Paul was executed in Rome; on the contrary, it implies
rather that he was executed in Spain. Paul's journey to Spain
is explicitly attested in the so-called Muratorian Canon,
which was compiled in Rome before the end of the second
century.[82] This catalogue of the books of the New Testament
with a series of comments on them has the following entry
for Luke:

*Lucas obtime theofile conprindit quia sub praesentia eius singula gere-*
*bantur sicute et semote passionē petri evidenter declarat. Sed profectionē*

---

[81] My translation differs significantly from that offered by Ehrman,
Apostolic Fathers 1 (n. 35), 43–45. In particular, Ehrman not only
repeats the traditional and misleading 'before the rulers' for ἐπὶ τῶν
ἡγουμένων, but also translates ἐπὶ τὸ τέρμα τῆς δύσεως ἐλθὼν tenden-
tiously as 'came to the limits of the West,' thus tacitly assuming or
making the text seem to say that Paul died in Rome. Since the participle
ἐλθὼν can refer to either coming or going, in this context it surely means
that Paul 'went to the limits of the West,' that is, to Spain.

[82] CPL 83a = CPG 1862, critically edited by H. Lietzmann, Das
Muratorische Fragment und die monarchischen Prologe zu den Evan-
gelien (Berlin, 1902), 5–11; for a careful discussion of the date, see E.
Ferguson, JTS, N. S. 44 (1993), 691–697, reviewing G. M. Hahne-
man, The Muratorian Fragment and the Development of the Canon
(Oxford, 1992).

*pauli au*[83] *urbes ad spaniā proficescentis* (Milan, Ambrosianus I 101 sup. fol. 10 verso, lines 4–8)[84]

For the most excellent Theophilus Luke summarises the individual events which were done in his own presence, as he makes manifestly clear by omitting the passion of Peter and also the departure of Paul as he set out from the city to Spain.[85]

Some of the apocryphal *Acts of the Apostles* also preserve memories of Paul's journey to Spain.[86] If normal criteria of historical criticism are applied – which does not always happen in the study of early Christianity -, then it may be deduced that Paul was tried and executed by a provincial governor in Spain. If that was the case, then the transfer of the place of his martyrdom to Rome is easily explicable as part of the attempt by those who called themselves 'catholic Christians' to use the concept of apostolic succession as a defence against heterodox Christians in the later second century.

---

[83] Corrected to *ab* by a later hand.

[84] I quote the diplomatic transcript by E.S. Buchanan, JTS 8 (1907), 540–541.

[85] My translation smooths the awkwardness of the Latin on the grounds that it is an overly literal translation from a Greek original: the English translation by G. Ogg in E. Hennecke & W. Schneemelcher, New Testament Apocrypha, ed. R. McL. Wilson 1 (London, 1963), 43, renders the German of E. Hennecke & W. Schneemelcher, Neutestamentliche Apokryphen in deutscher Übersetzung 1³ (Tübingen, 1959), 19, not the Latin of the *Muratorian Fragment* itself. Somewhat surprisingly, this passage seems to receive no discussion whatever in Zwierlein, Petrus in Rom (n. 18).

[86] *Actus Petri cum Simone* (BHL 6656) 1, 6; *Martyrium sanctorum apostolorum Petri et Pauli* (BHG 1491) 1, ed. R.A. Lipsius, Acta Apostolorum Apocrypha 1 (Leipzig, 1891), 45.8–15, 51.25–28; 118.2–3. The first two passages are translated into English by G.C. Stead, New Testament Apocrypha, ed. Wilson 2 (London, 1965), 279, 286; Elliott, The Apocryphal New Testament (n. 18), 499, 503.

The ignorance of Christians in the later second century about life of the apostle John is even more blatant, since it can be demonstrated from the text of one of the works attributed to him. The apostle John appears together with Peter in the first few chapters of the *Acts of the Apostles* (1.13, 3.1–4.22, 8.14), but disappears from sight even before the conversion of Saul on the road to Damascus (9.1–19). From Irenaeus onwards, however, Christian writers are completely unanimous in asserting not only that John was the disciple 'whom Jesus loved' (John 13.23; 21.7, 20) and that he lived on into the reign of Trajan, but that he wrote both the fourth gospel and the book of Revelation in that order and that he saw the visions on the island of Patmos recorded in Revelation (1.9) while he was in exile after being banished by the emperor Domitian.[87] No sane modern New Testament scholar, however conservative or radical his or her views, any longer accepts that the author of the fourth gospel, which is normally dated to the 80s of the Christian era, can possibly be identical with the young John, the son of Zebedee and brother of James, who took up the call to follow Jesus in Galilee more than fifty years earlier (Matthew 4.21; Mark 1.19; Luke 5.10).[88] Tradition could be correct in holding that a man called John wrote both Revelation and the fourth gospel, though it is certainly mistaken in dating Revelation with its deliberately Hebraic Greek later than the gospel. For, alone of all the texts that

---

[87] Irenaeus, *Adv. Haer.* 5.30.3; Clement of Alexandria, *Quis dives salvetur?* 42; Eusebius, *HE* 3.18.1–3 (adducing Irenaeus); 3.23 (quoting Irenaeus and Clement); 3.24.3–5.

[88] The tradition that the author of the gospel is indeed the beloved disciple, the son of Zebedee, has been argued in the recent age by J. A. T. Robinson, *The Priority of John*, ed. J. F. Coakley (London, 1985), 1–122.

make up the New Testament, the book of Revelation can be dated precisely – because it alludes to the political situation in which the author was writing.

The dating of Revelation must proceed from the fact that it contains no detectable allusion to any historical event later than the supersession of Nero by another emperor in 68 and the hopes and fears of his imminent return which began to circulate within weeks of his death. For the 'persecution of Domitian,' though widely accepted as historical by later writers both ancient and modern, is not attested by any reliable evidence at all.[89] It is rather a polemical invention by Melito of Sardis (quoted in Eusebius, *HE* 4. 26.7–11), designed as a stratagem to sustain the cherished, though completely false, contention of Christian apologists that it was only under 'bad' emperors that Christians were persecuted: on this a priori thesis, Domitian must have been a persecutor and an imitator of Nero simply because he was a 'bad' emperor.[90] For determining the precise date of Revelation two passages are decisive in combination:

---

[89] A. A. Bell, NTS 25 (1979), 94–97; J. C. Wilson, NTS 39 (1993), 587–605. In particular, the reference to 'Danaids and Dircae' in 1 Clement 6.2 shows that the persecution to which the letter refers must be Nero's fatal entertainments in 64. For elucidation of the mythical allusions, see Champlin, Nero (n. 9), 123–125, which is apparently not known to Zwierlein, Petrus in Rom (n. 18), 27–30, who proposes to delete the words Δαναΐδες καὶ Δίρκαι, following L. Abramowski in her postscript to H. C. Brennecke, ZKG 88 (1977), 302–308. The words were obelised by Lightfoot, Apostolic Fathers[2] 1.2 (1890), 32–33, even though he (unlike Zwierlein) noted the relevance of Nero's 'combination of theatrical representations with judicial punishments.'

[90] The theme was developed by Tertullian, *Apol.* 5.4: *temptavit et Domitianus, portio Neronis de crudelitate.* Lactantius, *Mort. Pers.* 3.1–4.1, went so far as to claim that before 250 Christians were not persecuted under any Roman emperors except Nero and Domitian, asking '*quis enim iustitiam nisi malus persequatur?*' (4.1).

No one can buy or sell who does not have the mark, that is, the name of the beast or the number of its name. This calls for wisdom: let anyone with understanding calculate the number of the beast, for it is the number of a person. Its number is six hundred and sixty-six.

This calls for a mind that has insight: the seven heads are seven mountains on which the woman is seated; also, they are seven kings, of whom five have fallen, one is living, and the other has not yet come; and when he comes, he must remain for only a little while. As for the beast that was and is not, it is an eighth but it belongs to the seven, and it goes to destruction. (13.17–18; 17.9–11: New Revised Standard Version)

This pair of passages was written after the death of Nero on 9 June 68 and before the final victory of Vespasian over Vitellius in the autumn of 69.[91] For there can be no doubt that the beast represents Nero. The letters of Nero's name and title when transcribed from the Greek Νέρων Καῖσαρ to the Aramaic נרון קסר and interpreted as numbers add up to 666, and the identification is confirmed by the fact that some textual witnesses state the number of the beast as 616, which corresponds to an Aramaic transcription of the Latin Nero Caesar without the nu or nin (נרו קסר).[92] The seven kings are clearly Roman emperors. The five who have fallen, that is to say, who are dead, are the first five emperors Augustus, Tiberius, Caligula, Claudius and Nero.

---

[91] A. A. Bell, NTS 25 (1979), 93, 97–102; C. Rowland, The Open Heaven: A Study of Apocalyptic in Judaism and Early Christianity (London, 1982), 403–413; Revelation. Epworth Commentaries (London, 1993), 16–17; J. W. Marshall, Parables of War. Reading John's Jewish Apocalypse (Waterloo, Ont., 2001), esp. 1–2, 88–97. Marshall's excellent and convincing book receives no mention whatever from T. Witulski, Die Johannesoffenbarung und Kaiser Hadrian. Studien zur Datierung der neutestamentlichen Apokalypse (Göttingen, 2007), who dates Revelation to the period of the Bar Kochba rebellion in 132–135.

[92] R. H. Charles, Studies in the Apocalypse (Edinburgh, 1913), 47–49, cf. 57.

The sixth, who now reigns, is therefore Galba, who supplanted Nero, which implies that the passage was written before news reached John of the assassination of Galba in Rome on 15 January 69 and his immediate replacement by Otho. The identity of the eighth king, 'the beast who was and is not,' is equally clear. He is Nero, one of the seven, whose return was widely expected in the East in 68 and 69; indeed, the first of a series of false Neros appeared on the island of Cythnus early in 69 and gained adherents until the governor of Galatia-Pamphylia had him killed (Tacitus, *Hist.* 2.8–9). Who then is the seventh king? Logic suggests that he is probably intended to be Vespasian, the governor of Judaea. For, when Vespasian received news of the death of Nero in the summer of 68, he practically ceased military operations against the Jewish rebellion, even though he had already surrounded Jerusalem, and he sent his son Titus to Rome in the hope that Galba would adopt him as his successor (Tacitus, *Hist.* 2.1–2). Revelation fits perfectly into the political circumstances of the late autumn of 68, when the regime of Galba was tottering, Vespasian the governor of Judaea and Licinius Mucianus the governor of Syria (who was childless) had put aside their long-standing enmity for their joint political interests, and the son of the former was travelling along the south coast of Asia Minor on his way from Syria to Rome, where he hoped for (and many others presumably expected) designation as the next emperor after the aged and childless Galba. In the event, Titus turned back after reaching Corinth as soon as he heard of Galba's death, but his journey must have caused great excitement in the Greek cities along the south coast of Asia Minor.

The author of Revelation was writing in the Roman province of Asia while Jerusalem was surrounded by Roman armies but the Jewish Temple still stood (11.2, 11.8, 11.19,

21.2, 21.10–27). It has recently and convincingly been demonstrated that he was a Jewish Christian or Christian Jew writing for an audience like himself at a time when the Christian churches in Asia still regarded themselves as part of the worldwide Jewish community (2.9, 3.9, 7.4–9, 12.17, 14.1–6, 14.12 .[93] Contemplating the world late in the year 68 as both a Jew and a Christian, he awaited the imminent end of the world in a convulsion that would destroy Rome and create a new heaven and a new earth. Such hopes were dead long before the traditional date of Revelation.

To sum up. This introductory chapter has argued a series of controversial theses, which it may be helpful to recapitulate in chronological order:

1. The apostle Peter was burned to death as part of Nero's entertainments after the fire of Rome in 64; he died by the banks of the River Tiber in 64 and his body was probably not recovered for burial;
2. The apostle Paul was executed in Spain;
3. The book of Revelation was written in Asia Minor in the winter of 68–69 and there is no valid obstacle to identifying its author as the man who later wrote the fourth gospel;
4. The concept and ideology of martyrdom, which are both first clearly attested by the *Martyrdom of Polycarp* in 157, were formulated in Asia Minor or Roman Syria between c. 130 and c. 140, and Ignatius of Antioch may have used them c. 140;

---

[93] Marshall, Parables of War (n. 90), esp. 10–24. At the outset Marshall states that 'putting it bluntly, I argue that the Apocalypse is a Jewish and not a Christian document' (2). That is probably a false antithesis for a work written in Asia Minor in 68–69, and Marshall's arguments surely prove that Revelation is both.

5. The construction of a shrine of Peter on the Vatican hill c. 160 presupposes his veneration as a martyr as well as an apostle;

6. On 29 June 258 the Christian community of Rome transferred the cults of Peter on the Vatican and Paul on the Ostian Way to the site *ad catacumbas* on the Appian Way in a public ceremony.

# II

## Documents from the Period
## of Persecution (to 260)

Eusebius of Caesarea was not only the first to write a history of the Christian church, but also the first hagiographer whose name is known. But Eusebius was not the first to collect hagiographical texts. In his *Ecclesiastical History*, whose first edition he may have largely have composed and perhaps even completed before the onset of the 'Great Persecution' in 303,[1] he refers four times to a 'collection of ancient martyrdoms.' Eusebius had himself compiled and published this collection before he wrote the *Ecclesiastical History*, in which he refers his readers to 'the early martyrdoms which I have collected' (*HE* 4.15.47).[2] In his *Ecclesiastical History* Eusebius prefaces his lengthy quotation of one of these early martyrdoms with a clear statement of his intent in including it in his *History*:

---

[1] As argued in GRBS 21 (1980), 191–201; Constantine (1981), 128–129, 148. For strong arguments against such an early date, see R. W. Burgess, JTS, N. S. 48 (1997), 474–501; Studies in Eusebian and Post-Eusebian Chronology 1 2 (Stuttgart, 1999), 21–98. But placing the conception and the whole of the composition of the Ecclesiastical History during the Diocletianic persecution fails to explain why Eusebius' history of the Christian church in Books I–VII concludes c. 280.

[2] The known fragments are collected in PG 20.1519–1534: BHG, Auct. 1182. The list of martyrs attributed to Eusebius' collection by V. Saxer, AB 102 (1984), 85–95, is absurdly optimistic – a total of no fewer than twenty three including Perpetua and Felicitas.

ἄλλοι μὲν οὖν ἱστορικὰς ποιούμενοι διηγήσεις, πάντως ἂν παρέδωκαν τῇ
γραφῇ πολέμων νίκας καὶ τρόπαια κατ᾽ ἐχθρῶν στρατηγῶν τε ἀριστείας
καὶ ὁπλιτῶν ἀνδραγαθίας, αἵματι καὶ μυρίοις φόνοις παίδων καὶ πατρίδος
καὶ τῆς ἄλλης ἕνεκεν περιουσίας μιανθέντων· ὁ δέ γε τοῦ κατὰ θεὸν πο-
λιτεύματος διηγηματικὸς ἡμῖν λόγος τοὺς ὑπὲρ αὐτῆς τῆς κατὰ ψυχὴν
εἰρήνης εἰρηνικωτάτους πολέμους καὶ τοὺς ἐν τούτοις ὑπὲρ ἀληθείας μᾶλλον
ἢ πατρίδος καὶ μᾶλλον ὑπὲρ εὐσεβείας ἢ τῶν φιλτάτων ἀνδρισαμένους
αἰωνίαις ἀναγράψεται στήλαις, τῶν εὐσεβείας ἀθλητῶν τὰς ἐνστάσεις καὶ
τὰς πολυτλήτους ἀνδρείας τρόπαιά τε τὰ κατὰ δαιμόνων καὶ νίκας τὰς κατὰ
τῶν ἀοράτων ἀντιπάλων καὶ τοὺς ἐπὶ πᾶσι τούτοις στεφάνους εἰς αἰώνιον
μνήμην ἀνακηρύττων.

Other composers of historical narratives would certainly have committed to writing victories in war, triumphs over enemies, the prowess
of generals and the brave deeds of soldiers defiled with the blood of
many thousands whom they slaughtered for the sake of their children, fatherland and also material possessions. But our exposition
of God's commonwealth will inscribe on everlasting monuments
the record of most peaceful wars on behalf of the very peace of the
soul and of those who in them showed bravery on behalf of truth
rather than fatherland, of piety rather than their nearest and dearest,
proclaiming for everlasting memory the constancy and the courage
amid much suffering of the champions of piety, their triumphs over
demons and victories over invisible adversaries, and their crowns <of
martyrdom> when all was done (*HE* 5.pr. 4: translation of Lawlor
and Oulton freely modified).

But Eusebius also reveals that his collection of early martyrdoms incorporated an earlier, already existing collection:

In the same document concerning him (sc. Polycarp) are attached
other martyrdoms too which took place in the same city of Smyrna
about the same period of time as Polycarp's martyrdom. Among
them Metrodorus, who seems to have been a priest of the Marcionite
heresy, who was put to death by being committed to the fire. Of those
of that day there was also a certain celebrated martyr Pionius … And
following this, there are preserved memoirs of others too who suffered martyrdom in Pergamum, a city of Asia – Carpus, Papylas and
a woman Agathonice, who were gloriously perfected after very many
splendid confessions. (*HE* 4.15.46, 48)

Eusebius had therefore found together in a single document
(1) the *Martyrdom of Polycarp* (Barnes I), which was written
in the year 157,[3] (2) the *acta* of Carpus, Papylas and Agathonice in a more primitive version than either of versions
that survive in Greek and Latin (K-K-R II = Musurillo II),[4]
and (3) the *Passion of Pionius* (Barnes V), which includes an
account of the martyrdom of the Marcionite priest Metrodorus (21–22), and he assigned all three to the joint reign
of Marcus Aurelius and Lucius Verus, that is, to the period
between 161 and 169 (cf. *HE* 4.14.10; 19/20). This earlier
collection also contained the letter of the churches of Vienna
and Lugdunum describing the pogrom at Lugdunum /
Lyon conventionally dated to 177 (quoted by Eusebius, *HE*
5.1.3–3.4, whence K-K-R V = Musurillo V, cf. Eusebius,

---

[3] App. 4.

[4] On these *acta*, see esp. H. Lietzmann, Festgabe für Karl Müller
(Tübingen, 1922), 46–57, reprinted in his Kleine Schriften 1 (TU
67, 19580, 239–250; M. Simonetti, Studi agiografici (Rome, 1955,
97–107; F. Halkin, Mullus. Festschrift für Theodor Klauser, JbAC,
Ergänzungsband 1 (Münster, 1964), 150–154; T.D. Barnes, JTS,
N.S. 19 (1968), 514–515; S.G. Hall, Studies in Church History 30
(1993), 9–10; F. Scorza Barcellona, Hagiographies, ed. G. Philippart
3 (Turnhout, 2001), 72–74. The date of the martyrdoms is unclear.
Neither of the two extant recensions can be completely authentic and
neither contains an explicit date: the proconsul's question *prinicipalis
es?* (3 Latin) where the Greek has βουλευτὴς εἶ; (24 Greek) has been
argued to point to the third century rather than the second (Barnes,
JTS, N.S. 19 [1968], 514–515), but J. den Boeft & J. Bremmer,
Vig. Chr. 36 (1982), 383–387, note that the mandata of Severus and
Caracalla used the phrase *de decurionibus et principalibus civitatium*
(*Digest* 48.19. 27 = Callistratus, frag. 35 Lenel) and argue that the fact
that Papylus came from Thyatira (27 Greek) implies that the Acts were
written before Thyatira became an assize centre when Caracalla visited
the city in 215 (OGIS 517), since before that date the inhabitants of
Thyatira were obliged to come to Pergamum to have their cases heard
(Pliny, *NH* 5.126).

*HE* 5 pr. 2; 4.3). To these Eusebius added an account of the trial of Apollonius in Rome during the reign of Commodus (*HE* 5.21.5), and perhaps other similar documents that he used in his *History*, but did not explicitly cite. Eusebius did not find the *Acts of Apollonius* in the earlier collection, and he implausibly reports that Apollonius was tried by the Roman Senate with the praetorian prefect Perennis presiding.[5] Moreover, the versions that survive, in this case in Greek and Armenian (Gebhardt VI; Greek only in K-K-R VII = Musurillo VII), cannot be authentic and are not the *Acts of Apollonius* known to Eusebius.[6]

A significant conclusion follows from these facts. Eusebius' collection of ancient martyrdoms incorporated a preexisting earlier collection of martyrdoms compiled in the province of Asia. For it follows from what Eusebius says that someone had already combined together in a single document accounts of martyrs of Smyrna and Pergamum together with the letter of the Gallic churches, which was addressed to Christians in Asia and Phrygia (*HE* 5.1.2–3, 3.4). This unknown hagiographer compiled this earlier

---

[5] Sex. Tigidius Perennis was praetorian prefect from c. 179 to 185: see M. Absil, Les préfets du prétoire d'Auguste à Commode. 2 avant Jésus-Christ – 192 après Jésus-Christ (Paris, 1997), 184–185; O. Hekster, Commodus. An Emperor at the Crossroads (Amsterdam, 2002), 60–64. As an equestrian, who was not a member of the Senate, Perennis could not have presided over a trial in the Senate: R. J. A. Talbert, The Senate of Imperial Rome (Princeton, 1984), 460–480, 519.

[6] See Barnes, JRS 58 (1968), 46–48; R. Freudenberger, ZNW 60 (1969), 111–130; V. Saxer, Rendiconti della Pontificia Accademia di Archeologia 55–56 (1982–84), 265–298. There are serious divergences between Eusebius' report and the extant *Acts of Apollonius*, which transport the trial to Asia, make Perennis proconsul of Asia, and transform Apollonius into 'the holy and greatly renowned apostle Apollo, also called Sakkeas.'

collection of martyrdoms after 250, which is the year in which Pionius was put to death. It may be suggested that he did so shortly after 260 because he thought that the age of persecution was over.

Both lost collections of early martyrdoms, the earlier collection which Eusebius expanded no less than the collection which he himself compiled, were heterogeneous. They contained texts that described the trials of Christians in protocol form, letters written immediately after an outbreak of persecution by one church to other churches, and texts which, though classified as martyrdoms in the manuscripts and modern collections, are better styled passions because of their literary form and striving for literary elegance. Modern collections with the words 'acts of the early Christian martyrs' or *acta martyrum* in English, German or Italian in their titles are even more heterogeneous. At the extreme, Oscar Gebhardt's *Acta Martyrum Selecta* of 1902 includes two *libelli* of the Decian persecution, a rescript of the emperor Maximinus, the proceedings of two official enquiries into the conduct of African and Numidian bishops during the Diocletianic persecution and even the unhistorical *Acts of Paul and Thecla* as its final item (Gebhardt XVIII–XXII).

The more recent collection by Herbert Musurillo, published in 1972, reprints sixteen texts that date or are claimed to date from the period of the persecutions down to 260. Among these texts *acta martyrum* proper, that is, texts largely in the form of a record of judicial proceedings, are in the minority (Musurillo II, IV, VI, VII, XI). The majority of texts are either passions, that is, literary accounts of the deaths of martyrs composed by Christians for other Christians (Musurillo VIII, X, XII, XIII, XIV, XV), letters in which the Christians of one area describe for the Christians of another area a persecution and martyrdoms which they have witnessed (Musurillo I, V) or extracts from literary works (Musurillo III = Justin, *Apol.* 2.2; Musurillo IX = Eusebius, *HE* 6.5; Musurillo XVI = Eusebius, *HE* 7. 15). Excluded from all modern collections, however, are two highly significant texts. One is a letter of Dionysius, who was bishop of Alexandria from 247 to 264, which Eusebius quotes *in extenso*: in it Dionysius not only provides a narrative of the Valerianic persecution in his city, but also quotes at length from the official record of his appearance in court before the acting governor of Egypt (Eusebius, *HE* 7.11.6–11).[7] The other is a literary work which carries a seriously misleading title. It is the so-called *Life of Cyprian* by the deacon Pontius, which is not a biography at all, but a speech probably delivered in Carthage on the first anniversary of the bishop's martyrdom (Barnes X). Both its function and its content stamp it as a work of hagiography.

All but two of the authentic hagiographical documents of the period down to 260 which have survived (Barnes I–X) come from Roman Africa and the Roman province of Asia, the exceptions being the *Acts of Justin* from Rome (Barnes II) and the *Martyrdom of Fructuosus*, the bishop of Tarragona in Spain (Barnes VII). This geographical distribution, however, does not necessarily imply that there was either a larger number of Christian martyrs or a higher incidence of persecution in Africa and Asia than elsewhere. The Asian documents survive as a result of the editorial activity of the unknown hagiographer whom Eusebius used, the African documents because accounts of prominent martyrs were

---

[7] On the importance of Eusebius' quotation from Dionysius for evaluating independently preserved acta martyrum, see Delehaye, Passions (1966), 304–308. It gives the lie direct to the proposition that early Christian hagiographical texts never incorporate authentic court records.

preserved in Carthage. On the other hand, the chronological distribution of the authentic documents over the whole period from 150 to 313 does to a great extent mirror the actual course of persecution. Christian hagiography presupposes the idea of martyrdom, which came into existence in Asia not long before Polycarp was martyred in Smyrna.[8] Only ten independently preserved early Christian hagiographical documents from the period down to 260 have fully withstood intense historical scrutiny: the earliest is the *Martyrdom of Polycarp* of 157, the next four in chronological order come from the 160s, 180, 204 (or possibly 203) and 250, and no fewer than five belong to 258 and 259.[9]

At least since the reign of Trajan, Christians throughout the Roman Empire had confronted a constant threat of persecution provoked by a riot in reaction to natural disaster, from accusation by a personal enemy or an aggrieved neighbour, or with the arrival of a new governor prepared to entertain, encourage or even invite the denunciation of Christians, and this situation continued until the reign of Caracalla, the son of Septimius Severus (211–217). But the danger of Christians being put to death for their religion began to diminish greatly after the death of Marcus Aurelius. Marcus' son and successor Commodus (180–192) had a favourite concubine who, if not a Christian herself, protected Christians ([Hippolytus], *Ref. omn. haer.* 9.12.10–11). Under Septimius Severus (193–211) and his son Caracalla there begins to be evidence of Christians in the imperial household: according to Tertullian, Severus appropriated the Christian Proculus, the agent of the doctor Euodus who had once cured him, and kept him in

---

[8] Chapter I; App. 4.
[9] App. 2.

his palace until his death (*Scap.* 4.5), and a fine Christian sarcophagus survives of M. Aurelius Prosenes, who served Caracalla as his *a cubiculo* and accompanied him to the East (ILS 1738 = ILCV 3332),[10] Tertullian alleges that a recent governor of Cappadocia treated Christians with cruelty because of his wife's conversion, fell seriously ill and died as 'almost a Christian' himself (*Scap.* 3.4),[11] while Eusebius records that an early third century governor of Arabia asked the prefect of Egypt to send Origen to him to expound Christian teaching (Eusebius, *HE* 6.19.15). Moreover, although it must be conceded that, except at Dura-Europus on the Euphrates, which the Persians sacked in 256, the archaeological evidence for both Christian cemeteries and churches is very sparse before the fourth century,[12] stray allusions reveal that Christian communities owned cemeteries in Carthage in 203/204 (Tertullian, *Scap.* 3.1) and in Rome shortly after the death of Bishop Zephyrinus in 217 ([Hippolytus], *Ref. omn. haer.* 9.12.14),

---

[10] On Prosenes, see esp. H. U. Instinsky, Marcus Aurelius Prosenes – Freigelassener und Christ am Kaiserhof. SB Mainz, Geistes- und Sozialwiss. Kl. 1964, 114–129.

[11] viz., L. Claudius Hieronymianus, on whom see E. Klebs, PIR¹ C 713; E. Groag; PIR² C 888. His name is printed with the impossible order Claudius Lucius Hieronymianus in CCSL 2.1129; CSEL 76.12. He had built at temple of Serapis at York while he was in Britain as *legatus legionis VI Victricis* (CIL 7.240 = ILS 4384 = RIB 658).

[12] R. Krautheimer, Early Christian and Byzantine Architecture (Harmondsworth, 1965), 4–15; G. F. Snyder, Ante Pacem. Archaeological Evidence of Church Life before Constantine (Macon, GA, 1985), 67–117; L. M. White, Building God's House in the Roman World. Architectural Adaptation among Pagans, Jews, and Christians (Baltimore & London, 1990), 6–25, 102–148; id., The Social Origins of Christian Architecture 2. Texts and Monuments for the Christian Domus Ecclesiae and its Environment (Valley Forge, PA, 1997), 121–257

while a commentary on Daniel written in the early third century, apparently in the East, refers to the digging up of 'holy resting-places' and the exhumation and scattering of relics (Hippolytus, *In Dan.* 4.51: κοιμητηρίων ἁγίων ἀνασκαπτομένων, καὶ λειψάνων ἀνορυσσομένων καὶ ἐν πεδίῳ ῥιπτουμένων).[13] Still more significant are the attested contacts between the philosopher and speculative theologian Origen and two empresses. Julia Mammaea, to whom Hippolytus addressed a treatise on the Resurrection, possibly in the form of a letter,[14] summoned Origen to lecture before herself and her son the emperor Severus Alexander in Antioch in 232 or 233 (*HE* 6.21.3–4). Origen not only corresponded with Otacilia Severa, the wife of the emperor Philippus (244–249), but also referred to an occasion when Philip attended a Christian service as a young man (*HE* 6.34, 36.3, 39.1)[15]

During the same period, Christians start to appear in the upper echelons of Roman provincial society. Clement of Alexandria wrote for Christians of some social standing in that city: one of his works has a title ('What rich person may be saved?') which would have been pointless if it had not

---

[13] Quoted more fully in App. 1. On the provenance of the commentary on Daniel, see J. A. Cerrato, Hippolytus between East and West. The Commentaries and the Provenance of the Corpus (Oxford, 2002), 134–137, 152–157, 162–165, 168–171, 230, 238–242. It is not necessary to enter further here into the controverted question of the identity of Hippolytus or the attribution of works transmitted under his name: for the inscribed list of works on the statue at Rome often alleged to be that of Hippolytus, see M. Guarducci, Epigrafia greca 4 (Rome, 1978), 515–545 no. 3.

[14] CPG 1900, cf. M. Richard, SP 12 (Berlin, 1975), 69.

[15] Constantine (1981), 351 n. 95, cf. H. Crouzel, Gregorianum 56 (1975), 545–550.

been addressed to rich Christians.[16] In Africa the Christians of Carthage to whom Tertullian addressed most of his voluminous and usually polemical writings included all strata of society from the humblest to the highest – slaves and freedmen, soldiers, manual workers and tradesmen, merchants and other well-to-do persons, decurions, even members of the senatorial class.[17]

Tertullian himself, the outstanding Latin orator of his age, belonged to the *ordo equester*, as his *De Pallio* makes clear.[18] In this work Tertullian addresses the citizens of Carthage in general, not primarily the Christians among them (*Pall.* 1.1: *principes semper Africae, viri Carthaginienses, vetustate nobiles, novitate felices*), and defends himself for wearing the philosopher's pallium instead of a toga in public. Why did Tertullian need to defend his wearing of the philosopher's cloak? It was perfectly permissible and indeed normal to wear the pallium when doing philosophy: at the age of seventeen, that is, after he had taken the *toga virilis*, the future emperor Marcus Aurelius began to wear the garb of a philosopher, he donned a pallium while studying and slept on the bare floor (*HA, Marcus* 2.6, cf. 1.10). Explanation was necessary because four categories of person were legally obliged to wear the toga in public to denote their status: they were advocates and Roman

---

[16] L. W. Countryman, The Rich Christian in the Church of the Early Empire. Contradictions and Accommodations (New York & Toronto, 1980), 47–68, cf H. Chadwick, Early Christian Thought and the Classical Tradition. Studies in Justin, Clement and Origen (Oxford, 1966), 31–65.

[17] See the detailed arguments of G. Schöllgen, Ecclesia sordida? Zur Frage der sozialen Schichtung frühchristlicher Gemeinden am Beispiel Karthagos zur Zeit Tertullians (Münster, 1984; pub. 1985), 155–267.

[18] Schöllgen, Ecclesia sordida? (n. 17), 176–184.

magistrates, and since Hadrian senators and *equites Romani* (*HA, Hadr.* 22.2) and the concluding section of the *De Pallio* shows that it was to the last of these categories that Tertullian belonged.[19] Despite the extreme preciosity of its language and the rococo bravura of its style, the *De Pallio* has a simple overall argument. Tertullian contends that change, including change of dress is ubiquitous, natural and inevitable. At the end he allows the pallium to speak on its own behalf. The personified garment argues that it is worn not only by philosophers, but by all practitioners of the liberal arts (*Pall.* 6.2). To which Tertullian retorts in his own voice: 'Obviously after Roman knights' (6.3: *plane, post Romanos equites*). When the pallium then replies that the toga, not the pallium, is worn by shameful arsonists and gladiators (presumably an allusion to the emperors Nero and Commodus), Tertullian concludes his work with the comment: 'Rejoice, pallium, and exult! A better philosophy has now considered you worthy since you began to be worn by a Christian' (*Pall.* 6.4).

Christianity became socially respectable during the reign of Septimius Severus,[20] and this new-found acceptance among pagans was reflected on the legal plane. Tertullian reports that out of the twenty three or so proconsuls of Africa between c. 190 and 212 no fewer than four either discouraged or dismissed accusations of Christianity (*Scap.* 4.3–4).[21] Moreover, between the late summer

---

[19] Schöllgen, Ecclesia sordida? (n. 17), 183.

[20] D. E. Groh, SP 14 (1976), 41–47.

[21] Tertullian names in order: Cingius Severus, cos. suff. c. 181, proconsul, c. 195; Vespronius Candidus (Sallustius Sabinianus), cos. suff. c. 176, proconsul c. 190; (C.) Julius Asper, cos. suff. c. 185, cos. II ord. 212, proconsul c. 200; (C.) Valerius Pudens, cos. suff. c. 194, proconsul

or autumn of 212, when Tertullian composed a petition
in the form of an open letter to the proconsul Scapula
protesting against his harassment of Christians (*Scap.* 1.2:
*hunc libellum ... misimus*), and 250, when the emperor
Decius required all his subjects except Jews to sacrifice to
the gods for the common weal, there is scarcely a hint of
the execution of Christians. On the contrary, some years
after Tertullian's plea to Scapula, Minucius Felix composed
a dialogue which celebrates the conversion of a M. Caecilius
from Cirta, who appears to be identical with the M. Caecilius Quirinius who had earlier held the highest magistracy
in Cirta under Caracalla.[22] The dialogue is entitled *Octavius*
after the Christian interlocutor whose arguents convert
Caecilius, and it was almost certainly written in Carthage
(rather than either Rome or Cirta). The persecutions of
Decius and Valerian were both quite short-lived affairs, and
when Valerian was taken prisoner by the Persian king in
260, his son and co-ruler Gallienus granted the Christians
freedom of worship.

## Court Transcripts and Eye-witness Accounts[23]

Few (if any) original official documents survive from the
Greco-Roman world: what survive are copies of official

---

209/211. For the dates of their proconsulates and their earlier careers,
A. R. Birley, Bull. Inst. Arch. 29 (1992), 37–68.

   [22] The identification was first proposed and defended by H. Dessau,
Hermes 15 (1880), 471–474; 40 (1905), 373–386, and finally proved
by M. M. Sage, Cyprian (Cambridge, Mass., 1975). 46, 51–53, 63–73.
On the date and milieu of the *Octavius*, see now NECJ 36 (2009), 8–9.

   [23] On the former category, see G. Lanata, Gli atti dei martiri come
documenti processuali (Milan, 1973).

documents on bronze, stone and papyrus, that is, copies which someone or some group of people decided to preserve on bronze, stone or papyrus.[24] Among such copies preserved on papyrus in the dry climatic conditions of Egypt are numerous copies of reports of court proceedings in all types of legal case from the more than six centuries when Egypt was under Roman administration.[25] The surviving reports are virtually all private copies made by or for interested individuals from official records or archives.[26] Hence it is clear that Christians must have had the opportunity to make copies of official transcripts of the trials of Christians, so there is (and never was) any good reason to deny on a priori grounds that shorthand notes taken in court and later written up for official archives could form the basis of those accounts of the trials of martyrs which observe protocol style.[27] In fact, a letter of Dionysius of Alexandria appeals to court records

---

[24] The distinction drawn here may be illuminated by a modern analogy: my birth certificate, which was written in longhand on an official form on the day that I was born and is for all official purposes treated as the original record of my birth, describes itself as a copy of what stands in the official register of the town where I was born.

[25] What follows is heavily indebted to R. A. Coles, Reports of Proceedings in Papyri. Papyrologica Bruxellensia 4 (Brussels, 1966), esp. 23–27. However, I am unconvinced by Coles' claim that some papyri are 'the official account from the archives' or 'the original report' (23). His prime example is P. Strasbourg grec inv. 1168, published by U. Wilcken, Archiv für Papyrusforschung 4 (1908), 115–117, which Wilcken argued to be the original *Sitzungsprotokoll* of proceedings of the town council of Antinoopolis in 258, not a copy: comparison with the similar documents listed by A. K. Bowman, The Town Councils of Roman Egypt. American Studies in Papyrology 11 (Toronto, 1971), 164–172, seems to me to discountenance Wilcken's inference.

[26] Coles, Reports of Proceedings (n. 25), 16.

[27] As did J. Geffcken, Archiv für Stenographie 57 (1906), 81–89.

of his own hearing before L. Mussius Aemilianus, who was at that time acting prefect of Egypt:[28]

But hear exactly what was said on both sides as it was placed on record:

When Dionysius, Faustus, Maximus, Marcellus and Chaeremon had been brought into court, Aemilianus the acting prefect said: … I also talked off the record about the generosity (φιλανθρωπία) which our lords have displayed concerning you. For they have given you the opportunity of safety if you should be willing to turn towards what is natural and worship the gods who preserve their rule, and to forget unnatural gods. What do you say to this? For I do not expect you to be ungrateful for their generosity, since they urge you towards the better course.

Dionysius replied: Not all men worship all gods, but each community worships those they consider gods. We therefore venerate and worship the one God and Maker of all things, who entrusted rule <over us> to the Augusti, Valerian and Gallienus, who enjoy God's favour, and we pray incessantly to Him that their rule may remain unshaken.

Aemilianus the acting prefect said to them: Who prevents you from worshipping this God too (if indeed he is a god) together with the natural gods? For you have been ordered to venerate the gods, that is, gods whom everyone recognises as gods.

Dionysius replied: We worship no other God.

Aemilianus the acting prefect said to them: I see that you are both ungrateful and unappreciative of the clemency (πρᾳότης) of our Augusti. Accordingly, you shall not be in this city, but depart to the region of Libya and be in a place called Cephro, which I have chosen in accordance with the order of our Augusti. Under no circumstances will it be allowed for either you or any others to hold assemblies or to enter the so-called resting-places (κοιμητήρια). If anyone were to be discovered not having gone to the place that I have ordered or to

---

[28]  Several papyri attest Aemilianus as performing the functions of the prefect without holding the office of prefect from summer 257 to autumn 258, then as prefect from late summer 259 to May 261, at which latter date he was supporting the rebellion of Macrianus and Quietus (PIR² M 757).

be found in any gathering, he will bring danger on himself and the appropriate correction will not be lacking. Depart therefore where you have been ordered. (Eusebius, *HE* 7.11.6–11)

This corresponds closely to the structure and formulae in the protocols of trials in Roman Egypt, which normally have four distinct sections.[29] First comes the introductory formula, which states the name and title of the official who presided over the case, the date and location of the hearing, and the names of the parties in the case. Then comes the body of the trial: each speaker is identified and usually described on his first appearance, and what he says is introduced by the commonest verbs for speaking (where the protocol is in Greek, these are εἶπε(ν) and sometimes ἀπεκρίνατο, as in the proceedings before Aemilianus as quoted by Dionysius); there may also be brief intermediate narrative passages, especially passages recording the reading of documents on the instructions of the presiding officer. The record of the actual proceedings in court ends with the decision rendered by the presiding governor or official. Documents preserved on papyrus, however, usually have a concluding section which is lacking in the reports of the trials of Christians, viz., the official certification of the copy as an accurate record with a subscription from the clerk who has certified it as such. Two contrasting features of Dionysius' report of his interchange with Aemilianus are relevant to the general question of the source and reliability of *acta martyrum*: on the one hand, Dionysius quotes the legal proceedings as they were officially recorded (ὡς ὑπεμνηματίσθη); on the other, he gives a highly coloured

---

[29] Coles, Reports of Proceedings (n. 25), 29–54, G. A. Bisbee, Pre-Decian Acts of Martyrs and Commentarii (Philadelphia, 1988), 33–64.

account which does not fully reflect the extracts from the official record that he quotes.[30]

In and of itself, however, protocol style provides no guarantee of authenticity, historicity or derivation from an official documentary record even at a distant remove. Writers of hagiographical fiction quickly learned how to use the documentary style in order to lend a bogus air of authenticity to accounts of trial which were wholly their own invention, as in the *Acts of Tarachus, Probus and Andronicus* (AASS, Oct. V.566–584: BHG 1574, with the order Probus, Tarachus and Andronicus). Although Ruinart included these *acta* in his collection of authentic documents,[31] they are now rightly assigned to the category of 'epic passions.'[32] The normal introductory formulae of a court record here read as follows:

In the consulate of Diocletian the Augustus <for the third time and Maximian the Augustus> for the first,[33] on the eighth day before the kalends of April (25 March 287), when Flavius Caius Numerianus Maximus[34] was governor of Cilicia, in Tarsus the metropolis, with the same Maximus sitting before the tribunal Demetrius the centurion said: Those brought before your magnificence, my lord, <sent>

---

[30] F. Millar, JTS, N. S. 24 (1973), 242.

[31] Ruinart, Acta martyrum (1689), 458–492 = (1713), 423–448.

[32] Comm. Mart. Rom. (1940), 447; F. Halkin, Inédits byzantins d'Ochrida, Candie et Moscou (SH 38, 1963), 210, publishing a metaphrastic version of the acts (BHG 1574b) from a manuscript in Moscow and another in Jerusalem (211–252).

[33] I have restored the correct formula on the assumption that the author looked up the consular date for 287 in a chronological table or fasti.

[34] The name is mangled in the introductory formula, but stated thus at the start of the second and third examinations of Tarachus and his companions (AASS, Oct. V. 570, 575).

from[35] the city of Pompeiopolis by the *speculatores* Eutolmius and Palladius as being of the most impious religion of the Christians because they do not obey the orders of the emperors, stand before your most holy tribunal.

The trial of Tarachus, Probus and Andronicus is described at inordinate length and always in the same protocol style. The martyrs are then executed at Anazarbus: after a bear and a lion refuse to attack them in the amphitheatre, Maximus orders gladiators to kill them with the sword, after which their bodies are recovered by other Christians. An appendix gives the date of the martyrdom of as 11 October 'in the first year of the persecution.' These *acta* betray themselves as a later confection through anachronistic nomenclature. The protocol states the first element of the governor's name as Flavius, which only came into use as a designator of official status under Constantine, that is, after 324 in the East.[36] Moreover, even in an authentic or contemporary document, protocol style does not necessarily reflect quotation from the official record of a martyr's trial. The *Martyrdom of Polycarp* (Barnes I), which is a letter of the church of Smyrna to other churches, has passages in protocol style which reflect not a document, but what Christians who witnessed Polycarp's trial in the stadium of Smyrna saw and heard.[37] When Polycarp entered the stadium, a voice

---

[35] Reading ἀπό for ἐπί and supplying 'sent' which appears to be needed for the sense.

[36] J. G. Keenan, ZPE 11 (1973), 33–63; 13 (1974), 283–304; 53 (1983), 245–250.

[37] For contrasting (and sometimes complementary) treatments of this much discussed text, see B. Dehandschutter, Martyrium Polycarpi: een literair-kritische Studie (Leuven, 1979); ANRW 2.27.1 (1993), 485–522; G. Buschmann, Martyrium Polycarpi – Eine formkritische Studie. Ein Beitrag zur Frage nach der Entstehung der Gattung Märtyrerakte. Beihefte zur ZNW 70 (Berlin & New York, 1994); Vig. Chr.

was heard saying 'Be strong, Polycarp, and play the man' (9.1, cf. Joshua 1.6). The letter then describes the course of Polycarp's trial in something very close to protocol style: the proconsul speaks briefly and simply, as was normal, the bishop at greater length, while the crowd bays for his blood. The trial begins:

> When he had been brought before him, the proconsul asked him if he was Polycarp. When he admitted it, he urged him to deny, saying 'Have respect for your age.' and other related things, which it is customary for them to say: 'Swear by the Fortune of Caesar, repent, say "Away with the atheists."' But Polycarp looked with a stern face on the whole crowd of lawless pagans in the stadium, shook his hand at them, groaned, looked up to heaven and said: 'Away with the atheists!' When the proconsul persisted and said: 'Swear and I will release you; revile Christ,' Polycarp said: 'For eighty-six years I have served him and he has done me no wrong. How can I blaspheme my king, who has saved me.' (9.2–3)

Some exchanges between the proconsul and the bishop are in strict protocol style:

> The proconsul said: I have wild beasts; I shall set you before them if you do not change your mind. Polycarp said: Summon them! A change of mind from the better to the worse is impossible for us, though it is good to change from wickedness to justice. (11.1)

But much of the trial of Polycarp is presented in a more narrative style and there is no need to imagine that the writer of the letter quotes or reworks a document: since the proconsul interrogated and tried Polycarp in the stadium before a

---

49 (1995), 105–145; J. Lieu, Image and Reality: The Jews in the World of the Christians in the Second Century (Edinburgh, 1996), 57–102; Buschmann, JECS 5 (1997), 181–221. Chapter 4 of the Martyrdom has often been held to be a later interpolation, as by Hall, Studies in Church History 30 (1993), 9–10.

crowd watching the games,[38] there were spectators close at hand who could hear the proceedings, and there is no good reason to exclude the possibility that some Christians were close enough to hear every word that passed between the proconsul and Polycarp. It may be significant that the proconsul did not read out the verdict of the trial himself from a tablet, as was normal, but sent a herald into the middle of the stadium to proclaim that 'Polycarp has three times confessed that he is a Christian' (12.1).[39]

The letter of 'the servants of Christ dwelling in the cities of Vienna and Lugdunum to their brothers in Asia and Phrygia who have the same belief in and hope of redemption,' which Eusebius quotes *in extenso* (*HE* 5.1.3–3.4, whence K-K-R IV = Musurillo IV), is very similar to the letter of the church of Smyrna about the martyrdom of Polycarp.[40] Indeed, it may have been inspired by the earlier letter

---

[38] Bisbee, Pre-Decian Acts of Martyrs (n. 29), 121–122, considers a trial in the stadium as 'most improbable' and hence postulates a preceding trial pro tribunali for which a documentary record existed that the Martyrdom of Polycarp omits. See, however, J. Colin, Les villes libres de l'Orient gréco-romain et l'envoi au supplice par acclamations populaires (Brussels, 1965), 126–130.

[39] For the correct punctuation here (taking τρίς with what follows), see J. den Boeft & J. Bremmer, Vig. Chr. 39 (1985), 111–113.

[40] On the significance of the collocation 'Asia and Phrygia,' see G. W. Bowersock, Martyrdom and Rome (Cambridge, 1995), 85–98, arguing that it reflects authentic administrative details of the 170s. Bowersock had previously claimed that the phrase was anachronistic and pointed to a date c. 300 for the prescript of the letter (Les martyrs de Lyon [Paris, 1978], 249–256). Eusebius, *HE* 5.pr.1, dates the martyrdoms at Lyon to 'the seventeenth year of Marcus Aurelius' after Eleutherus had become bishop of Rome: the actual date must therefore be later than c. 175, but, since there is no reason to believe that Eusebius possessed any evidence for the precise year, it could be after the death of Maecus Aurelius in 180, as argued by T. D. Barnes,

since a textual note in some manuscripts of the *Martyrdom of Polycarp* implies that Irenaeus, who had been a disciple of Polycarp when young before he came first to Rome and then to Lugdunum, where he succeeded the martyred Pothinus as bishop, possessed a copy, which he could have brought with him from Asia to Gaul.[41] This letter is an important document. The judicial trials of the Christians named (Sanctus, Maturus, Blandina, Attalus and Alexander) play a small role in the narrative, and they were all conducted in public before thousands of spectators. But the letter shows how greatly the governor wished to please the assembled crowds, who evinced savage hostility to the Christians, even to the extent of sentencing Attalus to be exposed to wild beasts to please them, although as a Roman citizen he should have been beheaded like the other Roman citizens whom he had condemned to death (Eusebius, *HE* 5.1.44, 51, cf. 47).[42] The letter also provides the only example of the execution of apostates, that is, of those who agreed to deny Christ and perform a symbolic act of religious conformity (Eusebius, *HE* 5.1.33–35). The emperor's rescript to the governor ordered that such persons should be set free in accordance with the principles established by Trajan (*HE* 5.1.47). But at Lyon there was prima facie evidence that some Christians had indulged in 'Thyestean banquets and Oedipodean intercourse,' as the orator Fronto had recently insinuated

---

JTS, N.S. 19 (1968), 518–519; Les martyrs de Lyon (Paris, 1978), 137–141.

[41] *Martyrdom* 22.2, cf. Eusebius, *HE* 5.4.1–2.

[42] The role played by popular acclamations in the condemnation of Maturus and Sanctus (*HE* 5.1.38) led Colin, Les villes libres (n. 38), 130–132, to transfer the whole episode from Gaul to Galatia in Asia Minor.

in a famous speech:[43] their slaves had made such allegations under torture or the threat of torture (*HE* 5.1.14).

Both letters describe trials conducted in public before a large audience. It must be presumed, therefore, that their accounts derive either from autopsy or from the accounts of those who witnessed them. There also survive *acta martyrum* that have earned the right to be regarded as reproducing a transcript of the trials of Christians with little or no alteration of the court record. The earliest such text is the *Acts of Justin* from the 160s (Barnes II),[44] one passage of which shows clear derivation from a Latin original. The verdict rendered by Q. Junius Rusticus, who presided over the trial in his capacity as *praefectus urbi*,[45] is reported in the authentic version of the *acta* as follows:

Οἱ μὴ βουληθέντες ἐπιθῦσαι τοῖς θεοῖς, φραγελλωθέντες ἀπαχθήτωσαν τῇ τῶν νόμων ἀκολουθίᾳ.

Let those who have refused to sacrifice to the gods be scourged and beheaded in accordance with the laws.

The Greek word ἀπαχθήτωσαν, translated here as 'let them be beheaded,' is only comprehensible as a literal translation of the Latin technical term *ducantur*, which means 'let them be led out to execution:' Pliny, for example, uses it of his

---

[43] E. J. Champlin, Fronto and Antonine Rome (Cambridge, MA, 1980), 64–66.

[44] The contrary is argued by G. A. Bisbee, Second Century 3 (1983), 129–157; Pre-Decian Acts of Martyrs (n. 29), 95–118, who admits that the Acts of Justin are 'ultimately derived' from the court record, but argues that they 'have been edited to a greater or lesser extent throughout' and voices 'the suspicion that entire sections of the acts have been interpolated or substantially edited.' He does not comment on the word ἀπαχθήτωσαν or its possible implications.

[45] PIR² J 814: Rusticus probably became *praefectus urbi* in 160 and held office until 168 (Chapter I nn. 47, 50).

action in regard to the Christians accused before him who pleaded guilty (*Ep.* 10.96.3: *perseverantes duci iussi*). Most Roman Christians of the 160s were Greek-speakers. They knew perfectly well what *ducantur* meant in the mouth of a Roman magistrate, but they would surely not have chosen this word to mean 'let them be beheaded' if they were composing in Greek. Whoever wrote the *Acts of Justin* in Greek was surely translating a Latin text, which can hardly have been anything other than a copy of the official record of the trial of Justin and his companions. According to Tatian the accusation against Justin was instigated by the philosopher Crescens, who also tried to encompass his death too (Tatian, *Oratio ad Graecos* 19).[46] Justin had earlier named Crescens 'the lover of noise and boasting' (*Apol.* 2.3.1: Κρίσκεντος τοῦ φιλοψόφου καὶ φιλοκόμπου)[47] as an enemy who was likely to make a capital charge against him, but there is no reference to him in the *Acts*, which suggests that Rusticus may not have insisted on a formal accusation in court before trying Justin.

Next in date are the *Acts of the Scillitan Martyrs*, the record of the trial of a group of humble Christians from the small town of Scilli (or Scillium) by Vigellius Saturninus, the proconsul of Africa, in Carthage on 17 July 180. Since the trial was held *in secretario* and those on trial were immediately executed, it must be inferred that the extant *acta*,

---

[46] When Eusebius quotes the passage, he omits the words καθάπερ καὶ ἐμέ (*HE* 4.16.8–9).

[47] The pun on φιλόσοφος appears to be Justin's invention, though it was soon copied by Tatian, *Oratio ad Graecos* 3.3: αἱ τῶν φιλοψόφων καὶ οὐ φιλοσόφων πανηγύρεις, and the Thesaurus Linguae Graecae registers no earlier occurrence of φιλόκομπος.

if authentic (as they certainly appear to be), must be based upon a documentary record of the proceedings.[48]

Saturninus the proconsul said: You can earn the pardon of our lord the emperor, if you return to good sense.

Speratus said: We have never done wrong, we have not lent aid to wickedness, we have never cursed \<anyone>; but when we have been ill treated, we have given thanks because we respect our emperor.

Saturninus the proconsul said: We too are religious: our religion is simple and we swear by the genius of our lord the emperor and we make offerings (supplicamus) for his well-being, as you too ought to do.

Speratus said: If you lend me your ears calmly, I shall tell you a mystery of simplicity.[49]

Saturninus said: As soon as you start to insult our sacred rites, I shall not listen to you; instead, swear by the genius of our lord the emperor.

Speratus said: I do not recognise the empire of this world. Rather, I serve that God whom no man has seen nor can see with these eyes. I have not committed theft, but I pay the tax on whatever I buy because I recognise my Lord, the emperor over kings and all nations.

Saturninus the proconsul said to the rest: Cease to be of this persuasion.

Speratus said: It is an evil persuasion to commit murder, to bear false witness.

Saturninus the proconsul said: Do not have any part in this man's madness!

Cittinus said: We no not have anyone else whom we should fear except our Lord God who is in heaven.

Donata said: Pay honour to Caesar as Caesar, but fear God.

Vestia said: I am a Christian.

Secunda said: What I am, that I wish to be.

Saturninus the proconsul said to Speratus: Do you persist in being a Christian?

---

[48] Contrast Geffcken, *Archiv für Stenographie* 57 (1906), 89: 'kein Aktenstück aus stenographische Feder, sondern entstammt der Erinnerung, worauf auch ihre Kürze führt.'

[49] Correctly glossed as meaning 'a simple (and true) religious doctrine' by J. den Boeft & J. Bremmer, *Vig. Chr.* 35 (1981), 45–47.

Speratus said: I am a Christian. And all agreed with him.

Saturninus the proconsul said: Would you not like time for delibe-ration?[50]

Speratus said: In a matter so just there can be no deliberation.

Saturninus the proconsul said: What are those things in your case?

Speratus said: Books and letters of Paul, a just man.

Saturninus the proconsul said: Have an adjournment of thirty days and reflect.

Speratus again said: I am a Christian. And all agreed with him.

Saturninus the proconsul read his decision from a tablet: It is decided that Speratus, Nartzalus, Cittinus, Donatus, Vestia, Secunda and the rest, who have confessed that they live by the Christian rite, since they have obstinately persisted after being offered the opportunity to return to the custom of the Romans, should be executed by the sword (gladio animadverti placet).

The document continues beyond the delivery of the ver-dict. Speratus and Nartzalus give thanks, the proconsul announces in public through a herald that he has ordered Speratus and the others 'to be led away' (*duci iussi*), all the martyrs thank God and gain the crown of martyrdom at once. These final sections (15–17) are an obvious addition to the preceding transcript of the martyrs' trial.

## Two Literary Passions

The *Passion of Perpetua and Felicitas*, who were together with others martyred in Carthage on the nones of March (7 March), probably in the year 204,[51] is a composite

---

[50] On the force and tone of the interrogative *numquid*, see den Boeft & Bremmer, Vig. Chr. 35 (1981), 47–48.

[51] The day (*nonis Martiis*) is both well attested and certain: C. J. M. J. Beek, Passio Sanctarum Perpetuae et Felicitatis 1 (Nijmegen, 1936), 162*–166*. On the year, see Chapter VII.

document (K-K-R VIII; Musurillo VIII; Barnes IV). An editor or redactor who himself composed the introduction (1–2), a narrative of the martyrdoms (14–21.4) and a brief peroration (21.5) quoted two documents written by two of the martyrs in their own hand: (1) an account of her arrest and imprisonment and a description of four visions that she had in prison written by Perpetua (3–10, introduced in 2: *haec ordinem totum martyrii sui iam hinc ipsa narravit, sicut conscriptum manu sua et suo sensu reliquit*), and (2) Saturus' account of a vison that he had in prison (11–13, introduced in 11.1: *sed et Saturus benedictus hanc visionem suam edidit, quam ipse conscripsit*). That the *Passion of Perpetua and Felicitas* is indeed the contemporary document that it claims to be is powerfully confirmed by the fact that it provides the only explicit evidence that the birthday of the Caesar Geta, the younger son of the emperor Septimius Severus, which Perpetua was put to death to celebrate fell on 7 March (7.4: *munere enim castrensi eramus pugnaturi: natale tunc Getae Caesaris*).[52] After Geta was murdered by his brother during the winter of 211–212, probably on 26 December 211, all traces of his existence were assiduously removed from public monuments and official records.[53] Yet enough indirect evidence, especially literary evidence, survives to

---

[52] For the original proof, now generally accepted, that Geta was born on 7 March 189, see JTS, N. S. 19 (1968), 522–525; Tertullian (1971), 263–266. V. Saxer, Atti dei martiri dei primi tre secoli (Padua, 1984), 108; Hagiographies, ed. G. Philippart 1 (Turnhout, 1994), 34, offers a different identification of the games in which Perpetua was martyred: 'Géta étant devenu César en 198, il fêta ses quinquennalia en 203.'

[53] A. Mastino, Le titolature di Caracalla e Geta attraverso le iscrizioni (Indici). Studi di Storia Antica 5 (Bologna, 1981), 175, 177, cf. Barnes, JTS, N. S. 19 (1968), 525, adducing S. Sauneron, BIFAO 51 (1952), 111–121.

show that Geta was born on or close to 7 March 189:[54] therefore, since the *Passion of Perpetua* – and only the *Passion of Perpetua* – explicitly attests Geta's birthday, it must have been written before news arrived in Carthage early in 212 of his murder and the total abolition of his memory.[55]

Both a Latin and a Greek version of the *Passion of Perpetua* survived.[56] What is the relationship between them? It has been asserted with some confidence that both the editor and the two martyrs whom he quotes 'all wrote in Greek, and that therefore the Greek version of the text is the original.'[57] But, even apart from the fact that the heading to the Greek version of the *Passion* (Gebhardt VII) transfers the martyrdoms to the reign of Valerian and Gallienus, its framing narrative translates a reading in the extant Latin version that is demonstrably corrupt.[58] Perpetua asks the tribune who was treating other imprisoned Christians rather harshly a question which is transmitted as follows in the manuscripts of the two extant versions (16.3):

---

[54] Esp. *HA*, Carac. 4.2–3, cf. JTS, N. S. 19 (1968), 523–524.

[55] It may be noting in passing that, whereas the widely used term *damnatio memoriae* is a modern invention, the concept of *abolitio memoriae* is ancient: when the Roman Senate denounced Commodus on 1 January 193, immediately after his murder during the preceding night, their acclamations included the chants '*parricidae gladiatoris memoria aboleatur*' and '*impuri gladiatoris memoria aboleatur*' (*HA*, Comm. 19.1, quoting Marius Maximus). Lactantius has *memoria nominis eius erasa est* for Domitian (*Mort. Pers.* 3.2).

[56] Edited in parallel by J. Amat, Passion de Perpétue et de Félicité, suivi des Actes. (SC 417, 1996), 98–183, followed by an edition of the much later *acta*: these are extant in two versions (284–302 = *BHL* 6634, 6636) and their literary nature is analysed by J. W. Halporn, Vig. Chr. 45 (1991), 223–241.

[57] D. Potter, Theater and Society in the Classical World, ed. R. Scodel (Ann Arbor, 1993), 57.

[58] As noted already by E. Rupprecht, RhM 90 (1941), 178.

*Quid utique non permittis nobis refrigerare noxiis nobilissimis Caesaris scilicet et natali eiusdem pugnaturis?*

Διατί ἡμῖν ἀναλαμβάνειν οὐκ ἐπιτρέπεις ὀνομαστοῖς καταδίκοις Καίσαρος γενεθλίοις ἀναλωθησομένοις;

The Greek renders the transmitted Latin *noxiis nobilissimis*, but the transmitted Latin is surely a corruption of an original text which read *noxiis nobilissimi Caesaris*: there was no good reason for Perpetua to describe the imprisoned Christians as 'most noble,' whereas the title *nobilissimus Caesar* was the standard appellation of Geta between 198 and 209.[59] When *noxiis* is emended to *noxii* and the otiose *et* is deleted as dittography after *scilicet* (with Gebhardt), the question may be translated into English as

Why at any rate do you not permit us to take refreshment as convicted criminals who belong to the most noble Caesar, since we are going to fight on his birthday?

The editor or redactor, therefore, wrote in Latin. He has often been identified with Tertullian.[60] But the undoubted similarities of style and diction prove only that he was familiar with the writings of Tertullian, which is only to be expected of anyone writing in Carthage between 203 and 211.[61] On the other hand, when Tertullian claims that Perpetua saw only her fellow martyrs in heaven (*De Anima* 55.4), he appears to conflate a vision of Perpetua with one

---

[59] Mastino, Le titolature di Caracalla e Geta (n. 53), 155–157.

[60] As by Beek, Passio 1 (1936), 93*–95*, promising a fuller discussion in his second volume – which never appeared; J. Quasten, Patrology 1 (Westminster, MD, 1950), 181–182; L. Robert, CRAI 1982, 235 n. 35 = Opera Minora Selecta 5 (Amsterdam, 1989), 797 n. 35.

[61] Tertullian (1971), 79–80, 265, cf. now R. D. Butler, The New Prophecy & 'New Visions.' Evidence of Montanism in The Passion of Perpetua and Felicitas (Washington, 2006).

of Saturus – a mistake which the author of the *Passion of Perpetua* would hardly have made.

What then of the two documents that the *Passion of Perpetua* quotes in full? Louis Robert argued that the agonistic terminology in Perpetua's dream of a wrestling contest with an Egyptian pancratiast is more precise in the Greek version than in the Latin (10.3–7).[62] The Latin appears here to mistranslate the Greek, not vice versa as in the editor's narrative: it turns the man of gigantic stature who presides over the contest between Perpetua and the Egyptian as umpire and awards her the prize (10.12: προσῆλθον τῷ βραβευτῇ καὶ ἔλαβον τὸν κλάδον) into a *lanista*, that is, a manager or trainer of a group of gladiators.[63] However, the Greek version of what has often been called Perpetua's prison diary leaves anonymous the Caesar on whose birthday Perpetua fought the beasts (γενέθλιον γὰρ ἔμελλεν ἐπιτελεῖσθαι Καίσαρος) where the Latin has the precise *natale tunc Getae Caesaris* (7.9). Moreover, even in one of the prime passages which Robert adduced to prove its priority, the Greek text appears to be dependent on the extant Latin version. For, although the Latin twice has the erroneous *lanista*, in the first of the two passages the extant Greek version has ὡς βραβευτὴς ἢ προστάτης μονομάχων, where the first term is correct, but the second reflects the Latin mistranslation of ὡς βραβευτής as *ut lanista* (10.8). Robert preserved his theory that the Greek of Perpetua's vision is prior to the Latin by means of an *ad hoc* hypothesis: he first emended προστάτης to ἐπιστάτης, then deleted the three words ἢ ἐπιστάτης μονομάχων as a later gloss added (he surmised) in a maladroit

[62] Robert, Opera Minora (n. 60), 815–817. In refutation, see already J. Aronen, L'Africa romana 6. Atti del VI Convegno di Studio, Sassari 16–18 dicembre 1988 (Sassari, 1989), 2.643–648.

[63] Robert, Opera Minora (n. 60), 825–826.

attempt to harmonise the Greek with the Latin text.[64] But to emend a word, then claim that the word emended is part of an interpolation amounts in effect to accepting that, if Perpetua wrote in Greek, the extant Greek version does not reproduce her original text, since as transmitted it depends on the Latin version of the *Passion*, even if the translator, who was fluent in Greek, for the most part correctly restored the Greek agonistic vocabulary of the original. In contrast, a strong philological case has been made for the priority of the Greek version over the Latin in Saturus' account of his vision (11–13): this section of the Greek text differs stylistically from the rest of the *Passion*, and nowhere in this section can it be shown that the Greek version is dependent on the extant Latin.[65]

The *Passion of Perpetua and Felicitas* is exactly what it appears to be – an account of the deaths of martyrs in Severan Carthage written by a contemporary who quotes documents penned in prison by the martyrs Perpetua and Saturus. Hence it provides historical evidence that is both valuable and unimpeachable.[66] It is not surprising, therefore, that the visions of Perpetua and Saturus, which are of immense interest from many points of view, including the psychological, have attracted a large scholarly literature, or that Perpetua has of late enjoyed a particular vogue as a feminist icon, especially since she is one of the few women of the Greco-

---

[64] Robert, Opera Minora (n. 60), 829.

[65] Å. Fridh, Le problème de la Passion des Saintes Perpétue et Félicité (Gothenburg, 1968), 45–83. Disputed by Amat, Passion de Perpétue et de Félicité (n. 56), 51–66, who holds that Latin was the language in which all three elements of the text were written.

[66] Barnes, Tertullian (1971), 71–80; B. D. Shaw, Past and Present 139 (1993), 3–45.

Roman world who can plausibly be claimed to speak with her own voice.[67]

Of the many notable features of the text, the preface deserves especial emphasis in the present context. The editor introduces his account of the recent martyrdoms with passion and polemic (1.1–6):

If ancient examples of faith, which attest the grace of God and produce moral improvement in man, have been set forth in literary works precisely so that God may be honoured and man comforted by the reading of them as if this makes the events real, why should

---

[67] For a variety of recent exegeses, E. R. Dodds, Pagan and Christian in an Age of Anxiety (Cambridge, 1965), 47–53; R. Rader, A Lost Tradition: Women Writers of the Early Church, ed. P. Wilson-Kastner (Lanham, MD & London, 1981), 1–17; M.-L. Franz, Passio Perpetuae: Das Schicksal einer Frau zwischen zwei Gottesbildern (Zürich, 1983); P. Dronke, Women Writers of the Middle Ages. A Critical Study of Texts from Perpetua († 203) to Marguerite Porete († 1310) (Cambridge, 1984), 1–17; M. A. Rossi, Pagan and Chrstian Anxiety: A Response to E. R. Dodds, ed. R. C. Smith & J. Lounibosa (Lanham, MD, 1984), 53–86; T. J. Heffernan, Sacred Biography. Saints and Their Biographers in the Middle Ages (New York & Oxford, 1988), 185–230 ('The Passion of Saints Perpetua ad Felicitas and the Imitatio Christi'); J. Perkins, The Suffering Self. Pain and Narrative Representation in the Early Christian Era (London, 1995), 104–113; G. Cloke, Theology and Sexuality 5 (1996), 37–57; S. Maitland, The Martyrdom of Perpetua (Evesham, 1996); C. Trevett, Montanism: Gender, authority and the New Prophecy (Cambridge, 1996), 176–184; J. E. Salisbury, Perpetua's Passion. The Death and Memory of a Young Roman Woman (London, 1997); E. Irwin, Gli imperatori severi, ed. E. dal Covolo & G. Rinaldi (Rome, 1999), 250–260; H. Vierow, Latomus 58 (1999), 600–619; J. E. Salisbury, The Blood of Martyrs. Unintended Consequences of Ancient Violence (New York & London, 2004), 84–87, 118–123; R. S. Kraemer & S. L. Lander, The Early Christian World, ed. P. F. Esler 2 (London, 2002), 1048–1068; J. Bremmer, Märtyrer und Märtyrerakten, ed. W. Ameling. (Stuttgart, 2002), 77–120. Earlier, Bremmer, The Apocryphal Acts of Paul and Thecla, (Kampen, 1996), 43–44, had suggested that Perpetua may consciously have modelled herself on Thecla.

not new proofs which contribute equally to both aims also be set forth? For these too will one day likewise be ancient and necessary for posterity, even if they are accorded less authority in their own time because the veneration of antiquity is preferred.

Let those who consider a single manifestation of a single Holy Spirit sufficient for all ages and times look to this: more recent events should be accounted greater as being closer to the end of time because the pouring out of grace has been decreed for the last stages of the world. For, God says, this will happen in the last days: I will pour out a portion of my spirit on all flesh, and their sons and daughters will prophesy; and I will pour out a portion of my spirit on my slaves and handmaidens, and your young men shall see visions and your old men shall dream dreams (Acts 2.17–18, itself quoting Joel 2.28). Hence we too, who both recognise and honour the new prophecies and the new visions both promised to us, and who consider all other manifestations of the Holy Spirit as intended to benefit the church (to provide all gifts to which in all things the Spirit was sent, just as the Lord apportions to each individual),[68] of necessity we both record them and celebrate them to the glory of God by reading <the record>, so that no-one of weak or despairing faith should think that divine grace operated only among the ancients by bestowing martyrs or revelations, since God always fulfils what he has duly promised as a blessing for those who believe and a proof for those who do not believe.

Accordingly, what we have heard <and seen> and touched with our hands, we announce also to you, brothers and dear children, so that you who were present may recall the glory of God and you who now learn of it through hearing may have fellowship with the holy martyrs and through them with the Lord Jesus Christ, to whom belong splendour and honour for all ages (1 John 1.1, 3).

The writer thus claims that the martyrdoms of Perpetua and her companions prove the validity of the New Prophecy of Montanus. He was therefore himself a Montanist and, since Perpetua was venerated as a martyr of the Christian church, not the Montanist sect, he was writing at a time when

---

[68] With allusion to 1 Corinthians 7.17; Romans 12.3.

Montanist ideas were still acceptable within the catholic church of Carthage.[69] Equally important, long before the reading of accounts of martyrdoms is attested as a common practice,[70] he composed the *Passion of Perpetua* to be read aloud at gatherings of Christians, apparently in a liturgical context since he puts his work on a level with the ancient examples of faith which are habitually read for the spiritual benefit of Christians.

Pionius was a priest of the church of Smyrna who was put to death during the reign of the emperor Decius. The *Passion of Pionius* proves its credentials as a contemporary witness in a way similar to the *Passion of Perpetua*, by showing precise and accurate knowledge of facts that were soon forgotten. The *Passion* names the proconsul of Asia who condemned Pionius as Julius Proculus Quintilianus, who is attested epigraphically as proconsul, and it dates Pionius' death to 12 March in the consulate of the emperor C. Messius Quintus Traianus Decius Augustus for the second time and Vettius Gratus (23): not only are the names correct in detail, but the *Passion of Pionius* is the only literary text that shows awareness of the fact that Decius took the name of Trajan when he became emperor. The *Passion* also includes a cameo appearance by Rufinus, a prominent rhetor (17), who must be the sophist Claudius Rufinus, attested as *strategus* of

---

[69] On the Montanism of the Passion, which is overestimated by Butler, The New Prophecy (n. 61), see esp. Tertullian (1971), 71–80; F. C. Klawiter, Church History 49 (1980), 251–261. Somewhat surprisingly, the Montanist colouring of the Passion receives no discussion whatever in the long essay by Shaw, Past and Present 139 (1993), 3–45.

[70] First apparently in the opening sentence of the *Sermo de Passione SS. Donati et Advocati* (*BHL* 2303b = *CPL* 719): *si manifesta persecutionum gesta non otiose conscripta sint, nec inconsulte in honorem martyrum et adificationem credentium anniversaria solemnitate leguntur*, etc. (PL 8.752).

Smyrna in the reign of Gordian (238–244).[71] The *Passion of Pionius* also resembles the *Passion of Perpetua* in incorporating a document written by its hero. The *Passion* states that on his death Pionius 'left this document for our advice so that even now we should have records of his teaching' (1.2). The document that follows (2–18) has been transposed from the first person into a third person narrative, although two occurrences of the pronoun 'we' have been left unchanged (10.5, 18.13), and it contains not only a narrative of the arrest of Pionius and others, their questioning by Polemo the *neocorus* and imprisonment to await the arrival of the proconsul of Asia, who alone could order their execution (2.1–4.1, 5–11, 15–18), but also a public speech by Pionius to the people of Smyrna (4.2–24) and a speech in prison (12–14). Hence it has been aptly observed that Pionius is 'both the protagonist and the director of his own passion.'[72]

There are also two references to official transcripts. Pionius records that after informal questioning Polemo conducted a brief formal interrogation of himself and the other Christians by Polemo, which was officially taken down by a *notarius*, i. e., a shorthand writer (9.1): these formal *acta* must then have been submitted to the proconsul as the basis of further legal action. The author of the *Passion* reports the actual trial on 12 March in standard protocol style (19–20). The trial both begins and ends in the normal fashion:

When he had been set before the tribunal, the proconsul Quintilianus asked: What is your name? He replied: Pionius. The proconsul said: Will you sacrifice? He replied: No. (19.2–3) … And there was

---

[71] L. Robert, *Le martyre de Pionios prêtre de Smyrne*, revised and completed by G. W. Bowersock & C. P. Jones (Washington, 1994), 96–98.

[72] Den Boeft & Bremmer, *Vig. Chr.* 39 (1985), 124.

read from a tablet in Latin: We order Pionius, who has confessed himself to be a Christian, to be burned alive. (20.7)

The author then describes the burning of Pionius in the stadium together with Metrodorus, a priest of the heretical Marcionites: he presents it as an eye-witness account (21–22, esp. 22.3: 'we who were present saw' etc.) and dates the martyrdom very precisely to the nineteenth day of the sixth month of the Asian calendar, that is, according to the Romans 12 March 250, though that was not a Saturday as stated here (23: ἡμέρᾳ σαββάτῳ), but a Tuesday.[73] The *Passion of Pionius* is a historical document of prime value not only for understanding how Decius' requirement that all adult inhabitants of the Roman Empire (except Jews) should sacrifice to the gods was enforced,[74] but also for the topography, the cults, the civic organisation, the culture and many other aspects of Roman Smyrna in the middle of the third century.[75] Moreover, it shows its honesty as a historical witness by refusing to suppress the fact that Euctemon, the bishop of Smyrna, obeyed the imperial order to sacrifice (15.2, 18.13).

---

[73] According to the table in E. J. Bickerman, The Chronology of the Ancient World[2] (Ithaca & London, 1980), 60. The ancient Armenian translation has the correct day of the week: den Boeft & Bremmer, Vig. Chr. 39 (1985), 122, adducing M. Sarapian, Wiener Zeitschrift für die Kunde des Morgenlandes 28 (1914), 405. The Old Slavonic version, however, follows the Greek and has Saturday: A. Vaillant in Robert, Bowersock & Jones, Le martyre de Pionios prêtre de Smyrne (n. 71), 134.

[74] J. R. Rives, JRS 89 (1999), 137–138, 147–151; O. F. Robinson, Penal Practice and Penal Policy in Ancient Rome (London & New York, 2007), 111–115.

[75] See the full commentary in Robert, Bowersock & Jones, Le martyre de Pionios prêtre de Smyrne (n. 71), 49–121.

## Cyprian and his Memory

Cyprian became bishop of Carthage in the late 240s, shortly before the fiercely traditional Decius, who had remained loyal to Maximinus in 238, overthrew the emperor Philip, who had been favourably disposed to the Christians. When Decius ordered all the inhabitants of the Roman Empire except Jews to sacrifice to the traditional gods and obtain documentary proof from the relevant local authorities that they had done so, Christians had to choose between four possible courses of action: to sacrifice according to the imperial decree, to obtain by bribery or otherwise a certificate stating falsely that they had sacrificed, to do nothing and await arrest, or to withdraw to a safer place.[76] The new bishop of Carthage chose the last option and departed for the small town of Curubis, where he remained until attempts to punish Christians who had not obeyed Decius' order to sacrifice petered out, apparently some time before the emperor's death on campaign in 251 discredited his attempt to secure religious conformity.[77] Cyprian's conduct during the Decian persecution, which many in Africa viewed as cowardice, caused him severe political difficulties in dealing with the *lapsi*, that is, those Christians who had actually sacrificed, but subsequently repented of their weakness, and the confessors, who had refused to sacrifice, had then been arrested and imprisoned, but who stood firm, survived and began to use the prestige which their courage had earned them.[78] Six years later, when the emperor Vale-

---

[76] G. W. Clarke, The Letters of Cyprian 1 (New York & Ramsey, NJ, 1984), 30–39.

[77] G. W. Clarke, CAH²12 (2005), 627–628.

[78] G. W. Clarke, The Letters of Cyprian 2 (New York & Ramsey, NJ, 1984), 4–19.

rian issued new legislation affecting the Christians, Cyprian
was determined not to lose the opportunity to secure glory
on earth and reward in heaven by dying as a martyr.

Cyprian and his disciples took care to preserve accurate
details of his exile in 257 and his martyrdom a year later. On
30 August 257 the proconsul Aspasius Paternus examined
Cyprian in his *secretarium* in Carthage. He began by inform-
ing the bishop:

The most holy emperors Valerianus and Gallienus have deigned to
give a letter to me in which they have instructed that those who do
not worship Roman religion are obliged to recognise traditional
Roman rites (*Romanas caerimonias*). I am therefore asking in your
name, what do you reply to me?

In reply, Cyprian declared that he worshipped the one
true God, and Paternus invited him to go into exile in
the town of Curubis. That was not the end of the hearing.
Paternus asked Cyprian for the names of his clergy, which
he declined to provide, adding that they were forbidden to
offer themselves for arrest so that they must be sought out.
The proconsul then noted that the emperors had prohibited
Christians from assembling for worship or entering their
cemeteries upon pain of death.

A record of this apparently private hearing was soon
put into circulation either by Cyprian himself or by others
acting on his behalf who presumably had no difficulty in
obtaining an official transcript of the hearing. For a letter
written to Cyprian by four Numidian bishops before the
end of 257 praises him for giving them a model for their
own conduct through what he said *apud acta proconsulis*
(*Ep.* 77.2): on chronological grounds, the *acta* to which
the Numidian bishops refer can only be the record of the
hearing on 30 August 257, which now forms the first part of
the *Acts of Cyprian* in modern editions and in some (though

not all) manuscripts (1). This is followed by a brief narrative taking the story as far as Cyprian's trial by the next proconsul Galerius Maximus in September 258 (2.1–3.2).

The corpus of Cyprian's letters, which were collected and published soon after his death, contains two letters that he wrote after his recall from exile at Curubis. In the first, Cyprian reports to another African bishop what he has discovered from envoys whom he had sent to Rome:

Valerian has sent a rescript to the Senate, directing that bishops, priests and deacons are to be put to death at once, and that senators, high-ranking officials and Roman knights are to lose their status as well as forfeit their property, and that, if they persist in remaining Christians after being so dispossessed, then they are to suffer capital punishment also. Furthermore, that women of senatorial rank (*mat-ronae*) are to be dispossessed of their property and sent into exile, and that any members of the imperial household who either confessed earlier or do so now are to have their possessions confiscated and are to be chained and transported to the imperial estates. (*Ep.* 80.2)

Valerian was probably in the East when he wrote to the Senate about the Christians. The Persians had captured and sacked Antioch, probably shortly before he became emperor around September 253.[79] Valerian went to the East in 254 and was residing in Antioch when he wrote to the city of Philadelphia in Lydia on 18 January 255 (AE 1957.19 = SEG 17.528).[80] His presence in Antioch in May 258 is attested by two imperial rescripts preserved in the Codex

---

[79] It has often been asserted that the Persians sacked Antioch twice or even three times in the mid-third century (in 253, 256 and 260): for proof that there was only one sack, which probably occurred in 253, see ZPE 169 (2009), 294–296.

[80] The inscription of a base with fragments of the original statue of Valerian may show a town at the confluence of the Rivers Tisa and Danube making official preparations for an imperial visit in 254 and thus imply that Valerian was expected to pass through the region dur-

Justinianus (CJ 5.3.5, 9.9.18),[81] and he may have remained continuously in the East until his capture by the Persians in the summer of 260,[82] although a letter written to the city of Aphrodisias in Caria in the joint name of Valerian and Gallienus has been judged to place him in Cologne on 23 August 257.[83] Valerian attached to his communication to the Senate in Rome a copy of the circular letter which he had written to provincial governors about the Christians. The letter had not yet reached Carthage when Cyprian wrote. But persecution had already commenced in earnest in Rome itself, where the bishop Sixtus and four deacons were beheaded on 6 August 258, and Christians of status were being accused, condemned and deprived of their estates. When he received Valerian's letter, the proconsul of Africa

---

ing that year (CIL 3.3255, republished by S. Dušanić, Živa Antika 15 [1965], 91–99, 107–108, whence AE 1965.304).

[81] The rescript issued in Rome on 10 October 256 was presumably issued by Gallienus, who possessed equal legal powers (CJ 6.42.15).

[82] On the movements of Valerian and Gallienus between 253 and 260, see G. Walser & T. Pekáry, Die Krise des römischen Reiches. Bericht über die Forschungen zur Geschichte des 3. Jahrhunderts (193–284 n. Chr.) von 1939 bis 1959 (Berlin, 1962), 28–50; T. Pekáry, Historia 11 (1962) 123–128; M. Christol, ANRW 2.2 (1975), 804–821; H. Halfmann, Itinera Principum. Geschichte und Typologie der Kaiserreisen im römischen Reich (Stuttgart, 1986), 236–238; M. Christol, Cahiers du Centre Glotz 8 (1997), 243–253.

[83] A letter was sent in the joint names of Valerian and Gallienus from Cologne on 23 August in a year which must be one of the years between 254 and 257: published by J. Reynolds in C. Roueché, Aphrodisias in Late Antiquity (London, 1989), 4–8 n. 1, cf. W. Eck, Köln in römischer Zeit. Geschichte einer Stadt im Rahmen des Imperium Romanum (Cologne, 2007), 554–555, with Abb. 236. I am not convinced by the arguments of Christol, Cahiers Glotz 8 (1997), 249–252, that the letter proves that Valerian was in Cologne on 23 August 257.

sent agents to arrest Cyprian so that he could be taken to Utica and tried and executed there. Cyprian went into hiding in Carthage and awaited the return of the proconsul, determined to undergo martyrdom before his own people (*Ep.* 81).

The *Acts of Cyprian* pass over that interesting detail and depict the bishop after his return from Curubis as waiting for an official summons in his own gardens 'according to the imperial command' (*ex sacro praecepto*). The summons arrived on 13 September 258. Cyprian was taken before the proconsul Galerius Maximus[84] in the gardens of Sextus to which he had retired in order to recover his health, but his case was postponed for a day. On 14 September a large crowd assembled at the garden of Sextus, but Maximus conducted the trial in the Atrium Sauciolum. The proceedings were brief in the extreme. The proconsul verified Cyprian's identity and invited him to sacrifice to the gods; the bishop refused; the proconsul consulted his *consilium* and delivered his verdict that Cyprian, whom he castigated as sacrilegious, the leader of a conspiracy and an enemy of the Roman gods and holy religions, should be beheaded; Cyprian gave thanks to God. The bishop was then led forth to execution and, after viewing by many non-Christians, his body was triumphantly buried during the night.

The author of the second part of the *Acts of Cyprian* in modern editions could in theory have used a copy of the official record of the trial of Cyprian. But he did not need to draw on a document: since the trial of 14 September 258 was held in a public place, he could have witnessed it himself, and the *Acts* contain much narrative matter that could never have formed part of a documentary record of

---

[84] Maximus is otherwise unattested (PIR$^2$ G 28).

Cyprian's case. The simplest hypothesis, therefore, is that the second part of the *Acts of Cyprian* is not derived from an official document of any sort, any more than are those passages in the *Martyrdom of Polycarp* or the *Passion of Pionius* that are written in protocol style.

Although Cyprian died as a martyr on 14 September 258, his heroic death did not entirely or immediately still complaints about his conduct as bishop during the Decian persecution. Controversy over the dead bishop continued and it was this continuing controversy that led the deacon Pontius to compose the work which is conventionally known as the *Life of Cyprian*, but which is in fact a speech designed primarily to defend its subject against his denigrators in Carthage.[85] Admittedly, Adolf Harnack once hailed the *Life of Cyprian* as the literary model that determined the form and content of all later lives of Christian saints,[86] while Delehaye analysed it as a panegyrical biography,[87] and it can still be styled *Vita Cypriani* by a practitioner of intertextuality who casts unjustified doubts on both its early

---

[85] P. L. Schmidt, Handbuch der lateinischen Literatur der Antike 4 (Munich, 1997), § 472.10: Schmidt states clearly enough that 'es handelt sich um eine Rede,' yet the editor of the volume (K. Sallmann) supplies the traditional rubric 'Die erste christliche Biographie lateinischer Sprache.'

[86] A. Harnack, Das Leben Cyprians von Pontius. Die erste christliche Biographie (TU 39.3, 1913). Harnack's opinion is both contradicted and endorsed by V. Saxer in his survey of early African hagiography in Hagiographies, ed. G. Philippart 1 (n. 52), 25–95. According to Saxer, 'la Vie n'est pas une biographie au sens où nous l'entendons aujourd'hui, mais une thèse' (41), yet he speaks of 'la tradition biographique inaugurée par Pontius avec la Vie de Cyprien' (70) and even claims 'la biographie chrétiennne' as 'un genre hagiographique inauguré par Pontius avec la Vie de Cyprien' (86).

[87] Delehaye, Passions (n. 6), 69–77 (originally published in 1921)

date and its attribution to Pontius.[88] On analysis of its style and contents, however, the so-called 'life' reveals itself not as a biography designed to be read, but as a speech, panegyrical in form and apologetic in intent, which was delivered to a live audience, probably on the first anniversary of Cyprian's death, i.e., on 14 September 259.[89] However, Jerome may be paraphrasing the title that the speech had already acquired by 392 when he penned the relevant notice for its author: 'Pontius, the deacon of Cyprian, who endured exile with him up to the day of his passion, left a splendid volume of the life and passion of Cyprian' (*De viris illustribus* 68).[90]

Panegyric and biography belonged to the same literary genre in the Greco-Roman world, so that it is sometimes difficult to discern whether a particular work is a large-scale panegyric or a miniature biography.[91] Pontius, however, though he begins by proclaiming the biographer's intent to ensure that posterity retains the memory of a great man, continues by protesting that he is not capable of doing justice to his subject (which is a commonplace of panegyric), then makes it clear that he is addressing an audience who are listening to him:

---

[88] L. Grig, Making Martyrs in Late Antiquity (London, 2004), 31.

[89] On the very early date of the work, see Sage, Cyprian (n. 22), 96–98, 348–352, 385–394, though he analyses its literary form as a traditional 'passio with the addition of a vita' (97).

[90] H. Dessau, Hermes 51 (1916), 65–72, identified Cyprian's deacon with *C. Helvius Honoratus qui et/signo Pontius* (*CIL* 8.980: Curubis) and argued that he became a deacon after holding local magistracies. The identification could possibly be correct, but it has not found much favour with those who have subsequently written about Cyprian.

[91] T.D. Barnes, From Eusebius to Augustine (Aldershot, 1994), no. XII.3–4.

Added to these reasons is the fact that you desire to know much or, if it is possible, all about him, lusting with burning ardour to discover his actions even if his living words have for the moment become silent. In this respect, if I shall say that I am deficient in the resources of eloquence, I say too little, since eloquence herself lacks suitable power to satisfy your desire in full voice (*pleno spiritu*).[92] So I am pressed from both sides: he burdens me with his virtues, while you constrain me to address you (*vos nos auribus fatigatis*).

This initial address to the audience is matched by a formal peroration which ends with the remark that 'I must confess to you simply what you know has been my view: I exult greatly, too greatly in his glory, yet I grieve more that I am left behind' (19.4). Pontius' speech falls naturally into two parts, though it is mistaken to divide it formally into two separate parts corresponding, respectively, to *life* and *passion*:[93] the first surveys Cyprian's life down to 257, while the second describes his arrest, exile in Curubis (where Pontius accompanied him), recall, trial and martyrdom using the *Acts of Cyprian* as a source. Pontius passes over the standard topics of origin, birth and education in order to start with Cyprian's heavenly birth as a Christian convert: he practised complete chastity and sold all his goods for the benefit of the poor; he displayed exemplary virtues even as a layman; he was chosen as bishop 'by the judgement of God and the favour of the people' when he was still a neophyte; and he at once began to displayed exemplary virtues appropriate to his new status.

What of Cyprian's conduct during the Decian persecution? Pontius justifies his avoidance of martyrdom by argu-

---

[92] On the meaning of the words C. Weyman, Berl. Phil Wochenschr. 35 (1915) 1274, aptly adduced Quint., *Inst.* 11.3.55.

[93] As Harnack, Das Leben Cyprians (n. 86), 31–42; M. Pellegrino, Ponzio: Vita e martirio di San Cipriano (Alba, 1955), 95–187.

ing that, if Cyprian had died under Decius, then Christians would have been deprived of his subsequent writings, which he describes one by one in a series of rhetorical questions: it was a spiritual benefit to all that the martyrdom of 'a man so necessary for so many good things' should have been postponed. Furthermore, if Cyprian had died then, he could not have comforted the sick during the plague or aided ordinary Christians, as he did assiduously after the Decian persecution.

Pontius devotes almost half his speech to Cyprian's exile and martyrdom. Cyprian was destined to die a martyr: God revealed this to him in a dream or vision on the day on which both he and Pontius arrived in Curubis, and the deacon quotes (or claims to quote) the bishop's account of it followed by his own exegesis. Pontius' account of the trial and execution of Cyprian follows the *Acts of Cyprian* quite closely, but with some significant divergences. There is no mention of the proconsul or his illness when the hearing on 13 September is suddenly cancelled; in fact, Pontius leaves the adjournment of one day unexplained except for the observation that, while 'certain persons' believe that the proconsul was unwilling to proceed on the first day, he refuses to complain about the 'laziness or distaste of the proconsul' in matters which were divinely ordered (15.7–8). And on 14 September, when Cyprian arrives for his trial in the *praetorium*, he is not tried in the main audience hall, but in a private room where the proconsul is sitting in a sweat because of a long journey. What is the reason for the contradiction? Another hagiographical text from the year 259 may provide an answer.

## A Riot in Carthage

The text to which the earliest extant manuscript gives the rather unwieldy title *Actus et visio martyrum Luci Montani et ceterorum comitum quod est X kal. Iunii* (Barnes VIII) copies or adapts the *Passion of Perpetua* in numerous passages[94] – which has sometimes encouraged the suspicion that it is a 'deliberate forgery' inspired by the earlier text.[95] Close inspection, however, reveals that its imitation of the *Passion of Perpetua* arises from the fact that the martyrs themselves modelled their conduct on that of Perpetua. The *Actus et visio* comprises three sections. It begins with a letter from Christians in prison addressed to their *dilectissimi fratres* (1.1), which describes their arrest and experiences in prison, including a series of visions which several of them saw there, including a vision of the martyred Cyprian (1–11). The letter, which concludes with the standard salutation *optamus vos bene valere* (11.6), is followed by an eye-witness narrative of the executions of the martyrs after they had been imprisoned for many months (12.1–23.6, esp. 12.1: *cum per plurimos menses reclusi tulissent carceris poenas*) and a brief peroration (23.7). Both the letter of the martyrs and the subsequent narrative exhibit a disconcerting lack of precise detail. Nevertheless, despite its vagueness, the text contains not only a number of indications that the

---

[94] See esp. P. Franchi de' Cavalieri, RQ, Supp. 8 (Rome, 1898), 5–49 = Scritti agiografici 1 (ST 221 1962), 203–245, who argued that the author of the passion (1) both imitated Cyprian and used the Passion of Perpetua as his literary model, (2) drew on an authentic document composed by the martyrs in prison, and (3) was writing a number of years after the events described.

[95] J. Rendel Harris & S. K. Gifford, The Acts of the Martyrdom of Perpetua and Felicitas (London, 1890), 26–27.

events occurred in Carthage,[96] where the martyrs were in fact put to death on 23 May 259,[97] but a precise description of the official status of the Roman magistrate who condemned the martyrs to death.

In their letter from prison, the martyrs state that after their arrest they were taken before 'the procurator who was discharging the functions of the deceased proconsul' (6.1: *et continuo eadem die subito rapti sumus ad procuratorem, qui defuncti proconsulis partes administrabat*). This passage closely resembles what the *Passion of Perpetua* says about the official who tried Perpetua and her companions (*Pass. Perp.* 6.2: *Hilarianus procurator, qui tunc loco proconsulis Minuci Opimiani defuncti ius gladii acceperat*).[98] The literary resemblance is not, however, a reason for doubting that the proconsul of Africa for the proconsular year 258/259 had died early in his year of office. On the contrary, the *Acts of*

---

[96] Franchi de' Cavalieri, Scritti agiografici 1 (n. 94), 200 n. 2. Franchi noted that the Christians who came in throngs to see the martyrdom of Flavianus had learned their faith from Cyprian (13.1) and that Flavianus not only describes Cyprian as *episcopus noster* (21.1), but also with his dying words commended Lucianus as a suitable choice for bishop (23.4: *Lucianum presbyterum commendatione plenissima prosecutus, quantum in illo fuit, sacerdotio destinavit*). Lucianus was in fact bishop of Carthage after Cyprian, though probably not his immediate successor (Optatus 1.19 [21.11–12 Ziwsa]).

[97] The *Kalendarium Carthaginense* records the commemoration of Lucius and Montanus under 23 May (J. B. de Rossi & L. Duchesne, AASS, Nov. II.1, [lxx]; H. Lietzmann, Die drei ältesten Martyrologien[2] [Berlin, 1911], 5), while the entry for 23 May in the *Martyrologium Hieronymianum* adds several other martyrs who are named in the *Actus et visio*, but mixes them in with other groups of martyrs: H. Delehaye, AASS, Nov. II.2 (1931), 268–269.

[98] Rader, A Lost Tradition (n. 67), 31 n. 9, transforms the procurator Hilarianus into Hilarion 'mentioned as an African proconsul by Tertullian.' On the proconsul, see Chapter VII, at nn. 46–55.

*Cyprian* report that the proconsul Galerius Maximus died 'a few days' after 14 September 258, and it was normal Roman administrative practice in such a situation for a high-ranking imperial procurator to govern the province for the remainder of the deceased proconsul's year of office, that is, until the following summer.[99] Moreover, an exchange during the trial, as the *Actus et visio* reports it, confirms that the magistrate presiding over the trial of the martyrs was indeed a procurator acting in place of a deceased proconsul:

> He (sc. Montanus) was asked by the governor (*praeses*) why he falsely claimed to be a deacon when he was not; he denied that he was lying. And when the *ducenarius* said that he had been given a written submission which contained the statement that he was pretending, he replied: Is it probable that I am lying while he, who gave you a false submission, is telling the truth? (20.2–3)[100]

The text makes it clear that the *ducenarius* must be identical with the *praeses* who is conducting the trial, while epigraphical evidence establishes that the senior imperial procurator in Africa who would normally replace a proconsul who died in office held the rank of *ducenarius*, i. e., a procurator with an annual salary of 200,000 sesterces.[101] As it happens, a letter of Cyprian refers to a formal declaration made in court presided over by a *procurator ducenarius* in the Span-

---

[99] For examples, see H.-G. Pflaum, Les procurateurs équestres sous le Haut-Empire romain (Paris, 1950), 134–135.

[100] Reading *me mentiri* with some of the derivative mss. Dolbeau declares a preference for deleting *verum dicere* as a gloss.

[101] On the rank of *ducenarius* in the period 180–260, see Pflaum, Les procurateurs (n. 99), 275–290, and for an index of imperial procurators in Africa Proconsularis, H.-G. Pflaum, Les carrières procuratoriennes équestres sous le Haut – Empire romain (Paris, 1961), 1092–1095.

ish province of Tarraconensis in 250 (*Ep.* 67.6.2: *actis etiam publice habitis apud procuratorem ducenarium*).[102]

If the *Actus et visio martyrum Luci Montani et ceterorum* describes events in Carthage, then what it says about the circumstances of the arrest of the martyrs deserves very close attention. Standard modern collections of early hagiographical documents take their lead from the seventeenth century editor Thierry Ruinart and print the martyrs' account of their arrest as follows:

*post popularem tumultum quem ferox vultus praesidis in necem concitavit, postque sequentis diei acerrimam persecutionem Christianorum, praevaricata violentia, apprehensi sumus Lucius Montanus ...* (2.1)

The traditional text was translated, for once not entirely inaccurately, by Herbert Musurillo as:

There was a rising among the populace, in which the vicious governor egged the people on to massacre, and this was followed by one of the fiercest persecutions of the Christians, after which, in an outburst of spurious violence, all of us were arrested: Lucius, Montanus, etc.[103]

In the earliest and best manuscript, however, this passage is transmitted in a very different form, which François Dolbeau, who in 1983 produced the only properly critical edition of the text,[104] printed as follows:

---

[102] For elucidation of the circumstances, see G. W. Clarke, Latomus 31 (1971), 1141–1145; The Letters of St. Cyprian of Carthage 4 (New York & Ramsey, NJ, 1989), 154–156.

[103] Musurillo p. 215. In the *Acts of Cyprian*, Musurillo prints *idibus Septembris,* which he translates as 'on 1 September' (171).

[104] F. Dolbeau, REAug 29 (1983), 67–82, who reports that a lost manuscript had the very similar title '*visio et actus martyrum Luci Montani Flaviani et comitum eorum*' (67). Dolbeau's important edition unfortunately remained unknown to M. A. Tilley, HTR 83 (1990), 386–391.

*post popularem tumultum quem ferox vulgus in necem praesidis concita-
rat, postque sequentis diei in acerrimam persecutionem Christianorum
praevaricatam violentiam, adprehensi sumus Lucius Montanus …* (2.1)

We were arrested after a popular riot which a wild crowd had aroused
for the purpose of killing the governor, and after violence had been
engineered to produce a very fierce pogrom of Christians on the
following day.

It may be noted in passing that as long ago as 1909 Pio
Franchi de' Cavalieri published a series of critical observations on the text of the *Actus et visio martyrum Luci Montani
et ceterorum comitum* which corrected his edition of 1898 in
some sixty places on the basis of a newly discovered manuscript of the ninth century.[105] Franchi saw that the correct
reading in the passage quoted must be *quem ferox vulgus in
necem praesidis* and not *quem ferox vultus praesidis in necem*,
which had been printed by all editors before 1909 including
himself.[106] Unfortunately, while Franchi's edition was used
by subsequent editors, his later corrections to it were ignored
for more than seven decades.

The correct text reveals a riot of a very different nature
from that described in editions before Dolbeau: it is one
for which the Christians appear to have been blamed since
it provoked an anti-Christian riot on the very next day. For
the martyrs go on to say that, after they had been arrested
and imprisoned, they were told by the soldiers guarding
them that the governor was 'uttering threats in a rage over
the events of the previous day' and proposing to burn

---

[105] P. Franchi de' Cavalieri, Note agiografiche 3 (ST 22, 1909),
3–31.

[106] Ruinart, Acta martyrum (1689), 233 = (1713), 230; Gebhardt,
p. 146.9–10; Franchi de' Cavalieri, RQ, Supp. 8 (1898), 71 = Scritti
agiografici 1 (n. 94), 263; K-K-R p. 4.9–10; Lazzati, Sviluppi (1956),
202.8–9; Musurillo, p. 214.9–10.

them alive (3.1). They do not explain why the events of the preceding day made the governor angry with them. But a mob had tried to kill the governor, and the martyrs imply that the Christian community was attacked in reprisal. What exactly happened? Franchi de' Cavalieri, who both divined the correct reading and saw what its implications were, argued that, since Galerius Maximus died 'quietly in his bed,' he cannot be the proconsul whom the procurator in the *Actus et visio martyrum Luci Montani et ceterorum* had replaced: hence he must be the proconsul of 259/260, that is, not Galerius Maximus himself, but his successor.[107] But it seems highly improbable that two successive proconsuls of Africa died months before the end of their year of office. It is surely more plausible to infer rather that Galerius Maximus died as a result of wounds which he had received in the riot to which the *Actus et visio* alludes, that the Christians of Carthage participated in, perhaps even instigated, the riot – and that this embarassing fact has been edited out of the historical record.

The *Acts of Cyprian* present Galerius Maximus as being extremely ill. When Cyprian was arrested on 13 September, so the *Acts* state, he was taken to the villa of Sextus, where the proconsul had withdrawn 'in order to recover his health' (2.4: *bonae valetudinis recuperandae gratia*) and for this reason he postponed the trial of Cyprian for a day. On the other hand, the *Acts* do not in any way claim that the death of Galerius Maximus conformed to the traditional model of divine punishment for a persecutor of those who worship the true God, even though he died only a few days

---

[107] See Franchi's discussion of 'il magistrato persecutore' in his *Note agiografiche* 3 (n. 105), 13–16.

after executing Cyprian.[108] A year later, in a speech probably delivered on the anniversary of Cyprian's martyrdom,
Pontius makes no mention either of the death or the alleged
ill health of the proconsul. If Galerius Maximus really died
from wounds received in a riot in which Christians took
part (and might even have instigated), then the author or
redactor of the *Acts of Cyprian* has deliberately falsified the
historical record by presenting his death as if it were due to
illness.

## Epilogue

The persecution of 257–259 is also illuminated by contemporary evidence from Egypt, Spain and Numidia. Eusebius'
account of persecution under Valerian consists entirely
of three series of quotations from Dionysius, the bishop
of Alexandria: first, from his letter to Hermammon (*HE*
7.10.2–9), then from his reply to Germanus, a bishop
who had attacked him (*HE* 7.11.2–19), and finally from
his letter to Domitius and Didymus (*HE* 7.11.20–25).
Dionysius blamed the persecution on Valerian's minister
Macrianus: this 'master and ruler of the synagogue of the
Eygptian magicians' persuaded the emperor to mount an
attack on the Christian clergy (*HE* 7.10.3–4). Dionysius,

---

[108] For this paradigm, E. Nestlé, Griechische Studien. Unter-
suchungen zur Religion, Dichtung und Philosophie der Griechen
(Stuttgart, 1948), 567–596; E. Heck, *MH ΘΕΟΜΑΧΕΙΝ*, oder, Die
Bestrafung des Gottesverächters. Untersuchungen zu Bekämpfung
und Aneignung römischer religio bei Tertullian, Cyprian und Lactanz
(Frankfurt & New York, 1987). The Donatist version of the Acts of
Cyprian tries to meet the point by adding that the proconsul repented
before he died (Chapter IV n. 9).

a priest and three deacons appeared before Aemilianus, the acting-prefect of Egypt, and were invited to worship 'the gods who preserve the empire': when they refused, they were sent into exile 'in a lonely parched spot in Libya, three days' journey from Paraetonium' (*HE* 7.11.4–11, 14–16, 20–25). Dionysius must be describing events of 257, when clergy who refused to conform were sent into exile. In the second stage of the persecution under Valerian, bishops and clergy were summoned back from exile, ordered again to sacrifice and executed if they refused to do so.

The *Martyrdom of Fructuosus* records the trial of the bishop of Tarragona and two deacons on 15 January 259, followed by their immediate martyrdom in the amphitheatre of the city (K-K-R XVII = Musurillo XII; Barnes VII).[109] Although the extant version may have been retouched in the fourth century,[110] it preserves a significant detail which must surely be authentic: Fructuosus was greatly loved by pagans no less than by Christians and they began to show sympathy with him when he was taken to the amphitheatre with his deacons (3.1: *populus Fructuosum condolere coepit, quia talem amorem habebat non tantum a fratribus, sed etiam ab ethnicis*). In 157 the *Martyrdom of Polycarp* had reported general popular hostility against the Christians. As soon as the herald announced that the proconsul had found Polycarp guilty, the crowd in the stadium bayed for his blood and demanded that he be exposed to the beasts:

ἅπαν τὸ πλῆθος ἐθνῶν τε καὶ Ἰουδαίων τῶν τὴν Σμύρναν κατοικούντων ἀκατασχέτῳ θυμῷ καὶ μεγάλῃ φωνῇ ἐπεβόα· Οὗτός ἐστιν ὁ τῆς ἀθεότητος διδάσκαλος, ὁ πατὴρ τῶν Χριστιανῶν, ὁ τῶν ἡμετέρων θεῶν καθαιρέτης, ὁ

---

[109] On this text, see recently Scorza Barcellona, Hagiographies 3 (n. 3), 49–52.

[110] As persuasively argued by Grig, Making Martyrs (n. 88), 39–41.

πολλοὺς διδάσκων μὴ θύειν μηδὲ προσκυνεῖν. ταῦτα λέγοντες ἐπεβόων καὶ
ἠρώτων τὸν Ἀσιάρχην Φίλιππον ἵνα ἐπαφῇ τῷ Πολυκάρπῳ λέοντα. ὁ δὲ
ἔφη μὴ εἶναι ἐξὸν αὐτῷ ἐπειδὴ πεπληρώκει τὰ κυνηγέσια

The whole crowd of the gentiles and Jews dwelling in Smyrna cried
out in uncontrollable anger and with a great shout, 'This is the teacher
of atheism,[111] the father of the Christians, the destroyer of our gods,
the one who teaches many to neither sacrifice nor worship!' (12.2)

While the participation of the Jews, which recurs in
the *Passion of Pionius* in its account of events in 250 (4,
13–14), could be no more than a Christian projection of
the underlying antipathy between the Jewish and Christian
communities in Smyrna.[112] such pagan hostility was shown
by the inhabitants of Lyon some years later in similar
circumstances (Eusebius, *HE* 5.1.7, 1.10, 1.17, 1.31,
1.43–44, 1.50, 1.57–58). In contrast, David Potter has
drawn attention to a feature of great historical interest and
significance in the African hagiographical documents from
the Valerianic persecution. The *Passion of Marianus and
James* narrates the arrest of Christians at Muguae in the territory of Cirta, their questioning and imprisonment by the
magistrates of Cirta, their visions in prison (the martyred
Cyprian appeared to Marianus),[113] their transfer to Lambae-
sis and the execution of the clerics by the cruel governor on

---

[111] Gebhardt p. 6.22 prints Ἀσίας instead of ἀθεότητος, following
the Moscow manuscript, Eusebius, *HE* 4.15.26 and the Latin version
(BHL 6870).

[112] Such hostile action by Jews is not validly attested elsewhere than
in Smyrna: J. Lieu, Tolerance and Intolerance in Early Judaism and
Christianity, ed. G. N. Stanton & G. G. Stroumsa (Cambridge, 1998),
285–295, cf. Barnes, Tertullian (1971), 90 n. 8 (slightly modified in the
second edition for legal reasons).

[113] On the vision of Marianus (6.6–15), which draws inspiration
from the Passion of Perpetua, see J. Aronen, Wiener Studien 97 (1984),
169–186.

6 May 259 (K-K-R XV = Musurillo XIV; Barnes IX).[114] In this *Passion*, as in the *Actus et visio martyrum Luci Montani et ceterorum*, imperial officials show themselves unwilling 'to allow Christians to make a spectacle of themselves.'[115] Why? Surely because it had become politically dangerous to execute socially respectable Christians, who were technically *honestiores*, by the degrading methods used for *humiliores* such as burning alive and exposure to the beasts. The riot in Carthage which followed the execution of Cyprian showed the political power of the Christians even at a time of forcible repression. Gallienus was doing little more than bowing to the inevitable when he gave the Christian church legal recognition.

---

[114] The day is recorded in the *Kalendarium Carthagiense* (AASS, Nov. II.1 [lxx]). The cruel praeses, left unnamed in the *Passion*, is plausibly identified as C. Julius Sallustius Saturninus Fortunatianus by A. R. Birley, JTS, N. S. 42 (1991), 598–610, cf. Thomasson, Laterculi Praesidum (1984), 406 n. 75, who dated Fortunatianus 'sub Gallieno,' that is, after 260. Birley also identifies this well attested Fortunatianus with the governor who executed the martyrs Terentius, Africanus and their companions, who are registered as African martyrs from the reign of Decius in the official calendar of the church of Constantinople (*Syn. Eccl. Cpl.* 169–170, 595–596). But these martyrs were celebrated in Constantinople because their relics had been transferred to the city under Theodosius (PG 86.1.213). (This notice was printed by Valesius and Reading as Theodore Lector, *HE* 2.62, but, despite an apparent statement to the contrary in CPG 7503, it is not included in his edition by G. C. Hansen, Theodoros Anagnostes: Kirchengeschichte [Berlin, 1971], 96–151.) These martyrs were therefore probably not African at all, but of eastern origin: G. D. Gordini, Bibliotheca Sanctorum 12 (Rome, 1969), 377–378; T. D. Barnes, JTS, N. S. 25 (1974), 111. The *Martyrium Terentii* BHG 1700), it may be noted, reports the name of the governor who executed Terentius, Africanus and their companions as Fortunatus, not Fortunatianus (PG 105.95–106).

[115] Potter, Theater and Society (n. 57), 61–63.

# The 'Great Persecution' (303–313)

Christianity was recognised as a lawful religion by the emperor Gallienus in 260. His action marks and symbolises the decisive transition from the Roman Empire as it had been organised by Augustus, reorganised by Vespasian and superficially remodelled by Septimius Severus to the Later Roman Empire.[1] The fundamental step of recognising the Christian church as part of the fabric of Roman society did not occur, as has so often been assumed or asserted, in April 311 when the dying Galerius repented of initiating the 'Great Persecution' in 303.[2] Still less did it occur when Constantine and Licinius met in Milan in February 313 for the marriage of Constantine's half-sister Constantia to Licinius and conferred about how they would govern their two halves of the Roman Empire after Licinius defeated Maximinus, who still ruled the East and was expected to

---

[1] D. Potter, The Roman Empire at Bay AD 180–395 (London & New York, 2004), 85–172, 217–262, cf. T. D. Barnes, NECJ 33 (2006), 161–165; 35 (2008), 251–253; (2009), 3–19. The traditional perspective is retained by S. Mitchell, A History of the Later Roman Empire, AD 284–641: The Transformation of the Ancient World (Maldon, MA & Oxford, 2007), whose index lacks an entry for Gallienus.

[2] This mistaken view is perhaps stated most clearly by J. Bleicken, Constantin der Grosse und die Christen: Überlegungen zur konstantinischen Wende (Munich, 1992), 6: 'Ich beginne mit einer Interpretation des ersten Aktes der Christianisierung der römischen Welt, mit dem Edikt des Kaisers Galerius vom 30. April 311, durch das er … das Christentum zu einer *religio licita* erklärte.'

invade Europe.[3] Incalculable damage has been done to modern understanding of both Constantine himself and the whole 'age of Constantine' by the widespread use of the bogus, improper and dangerously misleading term 'Edict of Milan,' which encapsulates an entirely false historical perspective.[4] And this false perspective has naturally been applied to the analysis of early Christian hagiography.[5] In reality, the legalisation of Christianity in the Roman Empire occurred in 260, immediately after the Persian king Shapur captured the emperor Valerian, the second emperor within a decade to encounter military disaster after a persecution

---

[3] The traditional misconceptions have recently been repeated in their crudest form by C.P. Jones, Philostratus 3 (Cambridge, MA & London, 2006), 147: 'Eusebius survived the persecution of the Christians that began under Diocletian in 303 and continued over much of the empire until Constantine and Licinius issued their edict of toleration in 313, the so-called Edict of Milan.'

[4] The term 'Edict of Milan' was shown to be totally illegitimate by O. Seeck, ZKG 10 (1891), 381–386, part of whose opening salvo reads: 'Eine Urkunde, welche man mit diesem Namen zu benennen pflegt (viz., the letter of Licinius quoted by Lactantius, *Mort. Pers.* 48. 2–12; Eusebius, *HE* 10.5.1–14), ist uns zwar noch im Wortlaut erhalten; aber diese ist erstens kein Edikt, zweitens nicht in Mailand erlassen, drittens nicht von Konstantin, und viertens bietet sie nicht dem ganzen Reiche gesetzliche Duldung, welche die Christen schön längst besaßen (381).' The term has nevertheless continued to be used, as recently in CAH[2] 12 (2005), 359 (M. Corbier), 487 (C.S. Lightfoot), 674 (J. Huskinson), 784 (chronological table); M.T. Boatwright, D.J. Gargola and R.J.A. Talbert, A Brief History of the Romans (New York & Oxford, 2006), 287; The Cambridge Companion to the Age of Constantine, ed. N. Lenski (Cambridge, 2006): 22 (B. Bleckmann), 72 (N. Lenski), 121–123, 132 (H.A. Drake), 171 (A.D. Lee), 247 (G. Depeyrot), 401 (Timeline). For a protest, and on the multiple misapprehensions encapsulated in the bogus term, see T.D. Barnes, IJCT 14 (2007, pub. 2008), 186–189.

[5] F. Scorza Barcellona, Hagiographies, ed. G. Philippart 3 (Turnhout, 2001), 39.

of his Christian subjects. Moreover, the acceptance of Christianity as one of the religions of the Roman Empire and its ruler may have left its mark in the Roman imperial coinage. Antoniniani minted at Milan with the bust and name of Cornelia Salonina Augusta, the consort of Gallienus, on the obverse, have on their reverse a series of goddesses and personifications: alongside Juno, Venus and Vesta, Luna, Felicitas and Pietas the empress is depicted as Pax, the embodiment and goddess of Peace, and named in the nominative case in a large issue with the empress as Pax and the legend *AUG / AUGUSTA IN PACE* (RIC 5.1. 197–198 nos. 57–69, esp. 57–60). The phrase *in pace* appears to have an exclusively Jewish and Christian resonance.[6]

Two rescripts of Gallienus are known from Eusebius, who quotes one and paraphrases the other, which restored to the Christian church and its bishops the right to recover property confiscated under the persecuting legislation issued by Gallienus' father and senior imperial colleague Valerian in 257 and 258. Valerian was captured by the Persian king Shapur in the summer of 260 and subjected to ostentatious humiliations in captivity (Lactantius, *Mort. Pers.* 5.1–6; Petrus Patricius, frag. 14).[7] His son immediately rescinded his father's anti-Christian legislation in a way that amounted to much more than its mere cancellation. Eusebius quotes in Greek translation the full text of a rescript issued by Gallienus in Latin:-

Αὐτοκράτωρ Καῖσαρ Πούπλιος Λικίνιος Γαλλιῆνος Εὐσεβὴς Εὐτυχὴς Σεβαστὸς Διονυσίῳ καὶ Πίννᾳ καὶ Δημητρίῳ καὶ τοῖς λοιποῖς ἐπισκόποις.

---

[6] S.L. Cesano, Rendiconti della Pontificia Accademia romana di archeologia 25–26 (1951), 105–121.

[7] For a brief outline of the reigns of Valerian and Gallienus, see recently J. Drinkwater, CAH[2] 12 (2005), 41–48.

τὴν εὐεργεσίαν τῆς ἐμῆς δωρεᾶς διὰ παντὸς τοῦ κόσμου ἐκβιβασθῆναι
προσέταξα, ὅπως ἀπὸ τῶν τόπων τῶν θρησκευσίμων ἀποχωρήσωσιν, καὶ
διὰ τοῦτο καὶ ὑμεῖς τῆς ἀντιγραφῆς τῆς ἐμῆς τῷ τύπῳ χρῆσθαι δύνασθε,
ὥστε μηδένα ὑμῖν ἐνοχλεῖν. καὶ τοῦτο, ὅπερ κατὰ τὸ ἐξὸν δύναται ὑφ᾽ ὑμῶν
ἀναπληροῦσθαι, ἤδη πρὸ πολλοῦ ὑπ᾽ ἐμοῦ συγκεχώρηται, καὶ διὰ τοῦτο
Αὐρήλιος Κυρίνιος, ὁ τοῦ μεγίστου πράγματος προστατεύων, τὸν τύπον
τὸν ὑπ᾽ ἐμοῦ δοθέντα διαφυλάξει.

Imperator Caesar Publius Licinius Gallienus Pius Felix Augustus to
Dionysius, Pinnas, Demetrius and the other bishops.

I have ordered that the benefits conferred by my gift should be
spread throughout the whole world, so that they withdraw from
the places of worship. Consequently you too can also use the ruling
in my rescript so that no-one harasses you. This was granted by me
long ago, as far as it is possible to be fulfilled by you, and therefore
Aurelius Quirinius, the *magister summae rei*, will observe the ruling
given by me. (*HE* 7.13)[8]

Eusebius also reports the gist of a similar ordinance of Gallienus addressed to other bishops allowing them to recover
'the lands of the so-called cemeteries' (*HE* 7.13: τὰ τῶν
καλουμένων κοιμητηρίων ... χωρία). What exactly is Gallienus
saying in the rescript that Eusebius quotes? Two of the
three standard English translations unfortunately replace
the active verb in the clause 'so that they depart from the
places of worship' (ὅπως ἀπὸ τῶν τόπων τῶν θρησκευσίμων
ἀποχωρήσωσιν) with a passive verb, which has the effect of
obscuring the circumstances in which the document was
issued.[9] What Eusebius quotes is the emperor's reply to a

---

[8] I have modified the translation by F. Millar, The Emperor in the
Roman World 31 BC – AD 337 (London, 1977), 572, who supplies
'[other] people' as a grammatical subject for the verb ἀποχωρήσωσιν and
glosses '[Christian] places of worship.'

[9] H. J. Lawlor & J. E. L. Oulton, Eusebius: The Ecclesiastical History and the Martyrs of Palestine 1 (London, 1927), 229: 'to the intent
that the places of worship should be given up;' G. A. Williamson, rev.
A. Louth, Eusebius: The History of the Church from Christ to Con-

petition, as he states in the introduction to his quotation (*HE* 7.13: δι᾽ ἀντιγραφῆς), and Gallienus himself describes it as 'my rescript' (τῆς ἀντιγραφῆς τῆς ἐμῆς). Since the early part of Book Seven of the *Ecclesiastical History* is largely based on the letters of Dionysius of Alexandria, it is an irresistible inference that Eusebius took the rescript from Dionysius and hence that the petitioners were the bishop of Alexandria and other bishops from Egypt.[10] Moreover, if this petition was presented in the normal way (and it is unlikely to have been forwarded by the prefect of Egypt), then at least one member of the group will have presented a *libellus* to Gallienus in person:[11] this may have happened in Rome,

---

stantine (London, 1989), 231: 'all places of worship shall be restored to their owners.' In the revised version published in the Loeb series Oulton reinstated the active voice of the Greek verb and translated 'to the intent that they should depart from the places of worship' (J. E. L. Oulton, Eusebius: The Ecclesiastical History 2 (London & Cambridge, MA, 1932), 169).

[10] Pinnes was an originally Illyrian name, but in the Roman imperial period it is attested only in Egypt. The only pre-imperial bearer of the name registered in either literary sources or the volumes so far published of the Lexicon of Greek Personal Names, ed. P. M. Fraser & E. Matthews (Oxford, 1987–2005), which do not cover Egypt, is the husband of Teuta, who ruled the Dalmatian coast of the Adriatic in 230 B. C. (Dio 12, frag. 49; 55.34; Appian, *Illyrike* 19, 21, 24). But a Pinnes was abbot of a Meletian monastery in the 330s A. D. (Athanasius, *Apol. c. Arianos* 67.1, 2), and a Πι(ν)νᾶς is named in a document with the date of 498 (Sammelbuch 12050.29, cf. 5665, 10948.30 for other names beginning Πιvv-).

[11] These two fundamental points were first made by F. Millar, JRS 61 (1971), 61, now reprinted in his Rome, the Greek World, and the East 3 (Chapel Hill, 2006), 269, and developed in his Emperor (n. 8), 571–572, to which the exegesis of Gallienus' rescript offered here is greatly indebted. I believe, however, that Gallienus' actions go well beyond the mere 'abandonment of persecution' in the same way as Constantine's actions in 306 and those of Licinius in 313 go signifi-

where Gallienus celebrated his *decennalia* in the summer of 262, and the petition may well have been presented by an Italian bishop who is lurking here anonymously among 'the other bishops.'[12] The absence of either an initial salutation or a closing formula of farewell indicates that the document is a *subscriptio* to the petition of the bishops rather than a formal letter.

The rescript reveals why the bishops had approached Gallienus. Some time earlier ('long ago' is presumably an exaggeration), the emperor had issued an edict or general ruling that ordered the restitution of confiscated property to the Christian churches and their bishops. That is a secure deduction from Gallienus' own words, even though Eusebius may have had no independent evidence for his statement that Gallienus stopped the persecution by means of public announcements posted up in the provinces, but simply drew an inference from the two rescripts.[13] In the rescript which he quotes, Gallienus replies to a petition which complained

---

cantly beyond Galerius' grant of mere toleration of Christian worship in 311 (Table 1).

[12] About a decade later, the emperor Aurelian expelled the deposed bishop of Antioch, Paul of Samosata, from 'the house of the church' after replying to a petition from Syrian bishops presented by Italian bishops: his rescript orders the church still occupied by Paul to be awarded to 'those whom the bishops of the belief (τοῦ δόγματος) in Italy and the city of Rome may send' (Eusebius, *HE* 7.30.19, cf. Millar, *Emperor* [n. 8], 572).

[13] Williamson and Louth seriously misrepresent Eusebius' meaning when they make him say both 'one of his first acts was to issue edicts ending the persecution' and 'this is the wording of the decree' (Eusebius: *History* (n. 9), 231). It is unfair of the translators to attribute their own confusion of the two documents to Eusebius, who carefully distinguishes between the rescript which he quotes (δι' ἀντιγραφῆς) and his earlier statement in his own voice that Gallienus ἀνίησί τε αὐτίκα διὰ προγραμμάτων τὸν καθ' ἡμῶν διωγμόν.

that some persons, who must have been identified in some way in the petition, had prevented and were perhaps still preventing the restitution of church property ordered by the emperor by continuing to occupy it. That is why the subject of the verb in the clause 'so that they withdraw from the places of worship' is left unspecified: the anonymous 'they' were surely identified in the petition which the emperor is answering.

It seems probable on a priori grounds, whether or not Eusebius had any evidence that it happened 'at once' (αὐτίκα), that Gallienus put an end to the persecution initiated by his father in 260 very soon after he heard of his father's capture. The rescript must be some time later, since it was issued in response to a petition delivered by bishops who should be supposed to have approached the emperor. The identity of those who prevented the Christians from recovering their property may plausibly be deduced from the political history of Egypt between the summer of 260 and the spring of 262. Gallienus lost control of Egypt in the summer of 260, when the capture of his father immediately provoked revolt and usurpation. For the whole of the Egyptian year which commenced on 29 August 260 and for part of the following year (261–262) the rulers of Egypt were the young brothers Macrianus and Quietus, proclaimed emperor by their father Macrianus, who declined to claim the imperial purple for himself.[14] Macrianus had been in charge of funds and the supply of food for Valerian's ill-fated Persian campaign, and before that had held an office which Dionysius described as if it was chief financial officer of the emperor (Eusebius, *HE* 7.10.5: ἐπὶ τῶν καθόλου λόγων

---

[14] For the ancient literary evidence for the three, see PIR² F 549 (the father), 546 (the usurper Macrianus), 547 (Quietus).

λεγόμενος εἶναι βασιλέως). According to Dionysius, it was
Macrianus who had impelled Valerian to persecute the
Christians (Eusebius, *HE* 7.10.7), and he appears to have
exercised the real power while his sons were the nominal
emperors recognised in Egypt from the late summer of 260
to the spring of 262.[15] Now Dionysius, in his festal letter for
Easter 262 (which was celebrated on 23 March), contrasted
Gallienus with earlier emperors:

ὁρῶ γὰρ ὡς ὀνομασθέντες μὲν οἱ ἀσεβέστατοι μετ' οὐ πολὺ γεγόνασιν
ἀνώνυμοι, ὁ δὲ ὁσιώτερος καὶ φιλοθεώτερος ὑπερβὰς τὴν ἑπταετηρίδα, νῦν
ἐνιαυτὸν ἔνατον διανύει, ἐν ᾧ ἡμεῖς ἑορτάσωμεν

I observe that the names of <the most> impious who were renowned
have vanished after a brief period, whereas the one who is more
holy and more God-loving has passed his seventh anniversary and is
now traversing[16] his ninth year, in which let us celebrate the festival.
(Eusebius, *HE* 7.23.4)

---

[15] There are papyri from the seventh year of Valerian and Gallienus,
which began on 30 August 259 (P. Lond. 211; P. Oxy. 1273; 2186;
P.Ryl. 110; Sammelbuch 776; 7290), but none from their eighth year,
while Gallienus is first attested as sole ruler in Egypt in March and
April 262 (P. Strassburg 7; P. Oxy. 2710): see Millar, Emperor (n. 8),
571 n. 29, citing P. Bureth, Les titulatures impériales dans les papyrus,
les ostraca et les inscriptions d'Égypte (30 a. C.–284 p. C.) (Brussels,
1964), 118–121, who registers no attestation of a second Egyptian
year for Macrianus and Quietus. Alexandrian coins were minted for
the eighth year of both Valerian and Gallienus, which began on 29
August 260: J. Vogt, Die alexandrinischen Münzen. Grundlegung einer
alexandrinischen Kaisergeschichte (Stuttgart, 1924), 1.204, 2.154.
Therefore, either the coins were minted in advance of the Egyptian
New Year or news of Valerian's capture had not reached Alexandria by
29 August 260.

[16] Not 'now completing,' as Williamson and Louth, Eusebius:
History (n. 9), 238. Since Gallienus became Augustus in September
or October 253 (PIR L 197, p. 42), Easter always fell well within one
of his regnal years, whether they were calculated from Gallienus' actual

Dionysius states the year of writing as Gallienus' ninth year of rule: the quotation comes therefore from his 'festal letter' for Easter 262.[17] When Dionysius contrasts Gallienus with impious earlier rulers, the plural is the generalising plural so common in the Greek and Latin literature of Late Antiquity. He refers specifically to Valerian, who did not complete seven years of rule on either the calendaric or Egyptian computation and who officially became an unperson after he was captured by the Persians. Moreover, Dionysius uses the subjunctive 'let us celebrate' instead of the indicative 'we celebrate' or 'we are celebrating.' Why? It may be conjectured that it was because the Christians of Easter had not been able to celebrate Easter in the normal fashion since 258, first during the Valerianic persecution and then under the usurping regime of Macrianus and Quietus. If that was the case, then the reason for the bishops' petition to Gallienus becomes clear. When Gallienus issued an edict restoring Christian property throughout the Roman Empire, the magistrates and officials who served the usurping regime of Macrianus and Quietus declined to enforce it in Egypt. After the usurpation was suppressed, Dionysius organised a petition to Gallienus requesting the enforcement of his edict of 260 in Egypt and the expulsion of those who were still continuing to occupy confiscated church property as they had under Macrianus and Quietus. It seems probable, therefore, that the petition of the Egyptian bishops was presented to Gallienus in Rome in the summer of 262.

---

*dies imperii* or according to the Egyptian computation with Gallienus' regnal years always beginning on 1 Thoth = 29 or 30 August.

[17] On these annual letters written by bishops of Alexandria from the third century until at least the eighth, see A. Camplani, *Atanasio: Lettere Festali; Anonimo: Indice delle Lettere Festali* (Milan, 2003), 15–49.

## Military martyrs?

Were any Christians executed for their religious beliefs in the last four decades of the third century? There is no reliable evidence that any Christian civilians were condemned to death for their beliefs between 260 and 303. But modern collections of *acta martyrum* include accounts of three 'military martyrs' from this period (K-K-R XVIII–XX = Musurillo XVI–XVIII). The first of these is Marinus, who was beheaded, according to Eusebius, the only evidence, 'when the churches everywhere were at peace' in a context which indicates a date between 260 and 268 (Eusebius, *HE* 7.15, cf. 28.4). In Caesarea in Palestine (Eusebius' own city), the Christian soldier Marinus was about to be promoted to the rank of centurion, which he had earned through seniority, when another claimant stepped forward and objected that Marinus could not legally receive that rank because, as a Christian, he did not sacrifice to the emperors. The governor Achaeus questioned Marinus, who 'steadfastly confessed that he was a Christian' – by which Eusebius presumably means that he refused to perform the customary sacrifice to the gods for the well-being of the emperors. When Marinus was given three hours to reconsider, Theotecnus, the bishop of Caesarea, took him into church, laid a copy of the gospels before him and bade him choose between them and the sword which he was wearing. Marinus did not hesitate, returned to the governor's court, and was condemned to death and executed.

Marinus counts as a Christian martyr because he was executed for being a Christian and refusing to sacrifice to the gods. But Eusebius may be mistaken over the date. Although he places the episode after 260, his report contains a detail that points to an earlier date. Marinus' rival complained that he did not sacrifice 'to the emperors': the plural may indicate that Marinus died during the joint rule of Valerian and Gallienus.[18] The other two 'military martyrs' come from the 290s, a period when there were Christian provincial governors, who were allowed, if Eusebius is to be believed (as he should be), to avoid the customary ritual act of sacrifice which normally inaugurated any official business (Eusebius, *HE* 8.2.4), and Christians serving in the Roman army enjoyed a similar dispensation, at least until 299 or 300, when Galerius purged his armies of Christians, presumably by ordering them to sacrifice or be discharged with ignominy (Eusebius, *HE* 8.4.3; Jerome, *Chronicle* 227[d] Helm).[19]

The *Acts of Maximilian* seem to be a heavily interpolated version of the trial and execution of the young recruit Maxi-

---

[18] Clarke, CAH[2] 12 (2005), 638 n. 123, 646.

[19] Eusebius dated the episode to the sixteenth year of Diocletian, which appears to correspond to 300 rather than 299, as had commonly been assumed: R. W. Burgess, JTS, N. S. 47 (1996), 157–158. T. Drew-Bear, La géographie administrative et politique d'Alexandre à Mahomet (Strasbourg, 1981), 93–141, published an inscription which records the military career of one Aurelius Gaius, who was a Christian from Pessinus (AE 1981.777 = SEG 31.1116: near Cotiaeum in Phrygia). Gaius served in many areas of the Roman Empire, which the inscription names in geographical order. Although some names are lost, those that survive indicate that Gaius' military service included periods not only on the Danube frontier before 293 and in southern Egypt under Galerius in 293–294, but also under Maximian in Gaul, Spain and Mauretania during his expedition to Africa in 296–298: C. Zuckerman, Ant. Tard. 2 (1994), 67. Since Gaius probably left the army shortly after 298, it seems natural to infer that he was a Christian who either resigned or was cashiered because of the purge (T. D. Barnes, JRA 9 [1996], 542–543). But if Gaius' latest datable service was in the West in 298, he may have retired before Galerius' purge, which affected only the eastern armies.

milianus by the proconsul of Africa at Theveste on 10 March 295 (K-K-R XIX = Musurillo XVII).[20] But they make it clear that Maximilianus was not executed as a Christian, but because he refused to be formally inducted into the Roman army and that his refusal was based on his firm conviction that Christians were prohibited by their religion from serving as soldiers: the proconsul sentenced Maximilianus to death on the grounds that he had 'with a rebellious mind refused the military oath' (3.1).

The *Acts of Marcellus* record the execution of the centurion Marcellus at Tingi three and a half years later, on 30 October 298 (K-K-R XX = Musurillo XVIII; Barnes XI). The textual problems of the *Acts of Marcellus* are formidable: there appear to be two recensions reflecting two independent reworkings of the text in different cities, and the manuscripts present many obviously corrupt readings.[21] But the outline of events seems clear. Marcellus' offence was that on the preceding 21 July, during the celebration of an imperial anniversary, probably the *dies imperii* of Maximian,[22] he had thrown down his military belt and sword and declared that as a Christian he could not repeat any oath of allegiance to the emperors, whom he also insulted vociferously (1–2). According to one of the two recensions this preliminary episode occurred in the camp of the Legio Septima Gemina in the province of Gallaecia in northern Spain (modern León). The governor Fortunatus then sent Marcellus under

---

[20] The document seems to combine authentic details from 295 with clear anachronisms and later additions (App. 5).

[21] App. 2 n. 17.

[22] New Empire (1982), 4 n. 5. For a different view, W. Seston, Aux Sources de la Tradition chrétienne (Neuchâtel & Paris, 1950), 239–246.

guard to Tingi, where he was tried on the basis of a written report of his crime (*acta praesidis*) by Aurelius Agricolanus, whose office is stated as '*agens vice praefectorum praetorio*' (2.2).[23] In Tingi Marcellus confirmed that he had indeed done and said what was recorded in the *acta* submitted to Agricolanus by Fortunatus. Agricolanus thereupon ordered him to be beheaded on the grounds that, though a high-ranking centurion, he had set aside and polluted his military oath and uttered words of madness in the earlier hearing before the governor (5.1).

Maximilianus and Marcellus were both put to death on the grounds that they believed that military service was incompatible with their religious beliefs and asserted that it was impossible for a true Christian to serve in the Roman army. In modern parlance, therefore, they were 'conscientious objectors' and that was the crime for which they were convicted. On a strict definition, therefore, neither Maximilianus nor Marcellus counts as a Christian martyr. Their pacifist beliefs were not shared by most of their Christian contemporaries: the proconsul was able to inform Maximilianus that there were Christians soldiers fighting in the armies of Diocletian and Maximianus, Constantius and Galerius (*Acts of Maximilianus* 2.9). The two *refuseniks* nevertheless represented an important strand of opinion in the late third century. For, in 314, the Council of Arles, which had been convened to consider the Donatist schism in Africa, considered it necessary (or perhaps merely prudent) to forbid Christians from refusing to fight now that the persecutions were over (314 Arles, Canon 3: *de his qui*

---

[23] Agricolanus was anachronistically identified as the vicarius of a diocese in New Empire (1982), 145, 181, 224: on the nature of his post, see C. Zuckerman, Travaux et Mémoires 14 (2002), 627.

*arma proiciunt in pace, placuit abstineri eos a communione*).[24]
That was a formal repudiation of the reasoning used by
Marcellus: when asked 'did you throw down your arms
(*proiecisti arma*)?' Marcellus had replied 'I threw them down
because it is not fitting for a Christian who is a soldier for
Christ the Lord to serve in secular military service' (*Acts of
Marcellus* 4.3: translated from recension M).[25] At least in
the West, therefore, Christians themselves had raised the
issue of whether their religion was compatible with military
service before Galerius purged Christians from the Roman
army in the East.[26]

---

[24] C. Munier, Concilia Galliae A. 314 – A. 506 (CCSL 148 [Turn-
hout, 1963]), 9, cf. J. Gaudemet, Conciles gaulois du IV siècle (SC
241, 1977), 48; J. Helgeland, ANRW 2.23.1 (Berlin, 1979), 805–806.

[25] Recension N has slightly different wording.

[26] G. W. Bowersock, Martyrdom and Rome (Cambridge, 1995),
41–42, states that 'the spread of Christianity into the rank and file of
the Roman army … led to the first group of soldier-martyrs, as reflected
in the martyrdom at Durostorum on the Danube.' Bowersock does
not annotate this allusion, but he presumably refers to the *Passion of
Julius the Veteran* (K-K-R XXVII = Musurillo XIX), whose martyrdom
is conventionally dated to 27 May 304 (Comm. Mart. Rom. [1940],
212). But this passion is not a reliable document, and the *praeses*
Maximus who tries and condemns Julius has no claim to be regarded
as a historical character: Barnes, New Empire (1982), 188. What the
Passion says about Julius' military service combines plausible precision
with irritating vagueness: Julius served in the Roman army for twenty
seven years (which could well be true), but, when asked what his military service was, instead of naming the units and capacity in which he
served, he replies merely: 'I was in the army and I retired as a veteran'
(2.3). Musurillo, p. 263 mistranslates the phrase *ordine meo egressus
veteranus* as 'I re-enlisted as a veteran.'

## Emperors and Persecutors (303–313)

The so-called 'Great Persecution' began in earnest on 23 February 303 when soldiers destroyed a church facing the imperial palace in Nicomedia and an imperial edict posted up on the following day made the holding of Christian assemblies illegal, ordered the destruction of Christian places of worship and the confiscation of the scriptures and all property, real and movable, owned by churches, deprived persistent Christians of their legal status and required that everyone, including Christians, perform a symbolic act of sacrifice before conducting any official or legal business of any sort (Lactantius, *Mort. Pers.* 12–13; Eusebius, *Mart. Pal.* [S] pr. 1; *HE* 8.2.4).[27] Already by the winter of 303/304, however, the policies of the eastern and the western emperors towards the Christians of their territories began to diverge significantly.[28] In the West,

---

[27] For fuller details and other evidence, see G. E. M. de Ste Croix, HTR 47 (1954), 75–76; Christian Persecution, Martyrdom, and Orthodoxy, (Oxford, 2006), 35–36; S. Corcoran, Empire of the Tetrarchs. Imperial Pronouncements and Government AD 284–324 (Oxford, 1996), 179–181 (no. 12). A letter has survived on papyrus in which the Christian Copres informs his 'sister' Sarapias that, since he has discovered that 'those who present themselves in court are being made to sacrifice,' he has 'made a power-of-attorney in favour of [his] brother' to appear in court in his place and that together they have instructed an advocate so that 'the case about the land' can proceed (P.Oxy. XXXI 2601: quotations from the translation of P. J. Parsons).

[28] de Ste Croix, HTR 47 (1954), 84–96 = Christian Persecution (n. 27), 46–59; Corcoran, Empire of the Tetrarchs (n. 27), 181–182 (nos. 13–15). K. H. Schwarte, E fontibus haurire, ed. R. Günther & S. Rebenich (Paderborn, 1994), 203–240, contended that the edict of 23 February 303 should be regarded as 'die alleinige Rechtsgrundlage der gesamten diokletianischen Christenverfolgung' (229). But Eusebius, *Mart. Pal.* 3.1, states explicitly that new imperial edicts arrived in

persecution petered out during 304, and it was quite soon officially brought to an end. Immediately after his proclamation as Augustus at York on 26 July 306, Constantine not only granted the Christians of Britain, Gaul and Spain full freedom of worship, but restored Christian property confiscated under the persecuting edict of February 303 (Lactantius, *Mort. Pers.* 24.7).[29] During the following winter Maxentius, the son of Maximian, who staged a coup in Rome in October 306, formally ended persecution in Italy and Africa (Eusebius, *Mart. Pal.* [S] 13.12–13; *HE* 8.14.1; Optatus 1.18, App. 1 [194.12 Ziwsa]), but he did not restore confiscated Christian property in the city of Rome until after Miltiades had become bishop on 2 July 311 (Augustine, *Brev. Coll.* 3.18.34; *Contra partem Donati post Gesta* 13.17 [CSEL 53.84, 113–114], cf. Chr. Min. 1.76),[30] and in Africa the process of restitution was still incomplete at the time of his defeat by Constantine (Eusebius, *HE*

---

Palestine in spring 304 requiring that the people of each city in a body should 'sacrifice and make libations to the idols.'

[29] In defence of Lactantius' report, which has often been called into question, JRS 63 (1973), 43–46; Constantine (1981), 28. One important aspect of Constantine's action has sometimes been overlooked: by issuing this law, he asserted his status as an Augustus before he made the wise political compromise of accepting appointment as Caesar from Galerius. It is unfortunately omitted from the list of imperial enactments relating to the Christians between 303 and 313 in S. Mitchell, JRS 78 (1988), 111–116, but correctly included by Corcoran, Empire of the Tetrarchs (n. 27), 185 (no. 21a).

[30] Augustine, who was writing after the Conference of Carthage in 411, drew his information from the so-called 'dossier of Donatism,' much of which survives as Optatus, App. 1–10: see L. Duchesne, Mél. d'arch. et d'hist. 10 (1890), 589–650; J.-L. Maier, Le dossier du Donatisme 1. Des origines à la mort de Constance II (303–361) (TU 134, 1987), 11–17.

10.5.15–17).[31] In the Balkans, persecution continued until April 311, when the dying Galerius, who had intensified persecution in both the Balkans and Asia Minor when he became Augustus of the East on 1 May 305 (Gregory of Nazianzus, *Orat.* 4.96), decreed toleration for the whole of the Roman Empire east of Italy (Lactantius, *Mort. Pers.* 33–35; Eusebius, *HE* 8.app. 1–4, 16–17).

In the remaining parts of the Roman Empire, however, the 'Great Persecution' continued for two more years (Lactantius, *Mort. Pers.* 36–41, 45–49; Eusebius, *HE* 9.1–10). In the areas which he controlled Maximinus first promulgated, then set out to nullify Galerius' edict of toleration and in November 311 recommenced the harrying and execution of Christians. Maximinus had received the Syrian region and Egypt as his portion of the empire to rule on his appointment as Caesar in 305, and he seized control of Asia Minor during the summer of 311 after Galerius died. The 'Great Persecution' thus lasted for a full decade in Asia Minor, the Syrian region and Egypt. In these areas it finally ended in 313 when Maximinus invaded Europe to attack Licinius, but was heavily defeated near Adrianople, fled southeastwards across Asia Minor, and committed suicide at Tarsus around midsummer. After his defeat Maximinus issued an edict of toleration which fails to disguise his insincerity (Eusebius, *HE* 9.10.7–11). Treating this edict as legally void, the victorious Licinius extended both toleration and the restitution of property to the Christians of each province formerly ruled by Maximinus as he took it over. This he did

---

[31] For a full discussion of Maxentius' policy towards the Christians, see B. Kriegbaum, Archivum Historiae Pontificiae 30 (1992), 7–54. He was motivated, it seems, by political considerations and acted in both 306/307 and 311/312 in response to the prior actions of Constantine: Barnes, Constantine (1981), 38–39.

in accordance with an agreement reached with Constantine in Milan in the late winter,[32] whereby he agreed to give to the Christians of the Balkans and the East the rights which Constantine had bestowed on the Christians of Britain, Gaul and Spain at one stroke on his accession in 306 and which Maxentius had also granted to the Christians of Italy and Africa in two stages (in 306/307 and 311).

The 'Great Persecution' is far better documented than either the sporadic outbreaks of persecution between 110 and

---

[32] Lactantius, *Mort. Pers.* 48.2–12, quotes the letter of Licinius to the governor of Bithynia posted up in Nicomedia on 13 June 313, Eusebius, *HE* 10.5.2–14, a Greek translation of a virtually identical letter posted up in Caesarea in Palestine and presumably addressed to the governor of Palaestina. Both versions refer to the meeting and mention Christianity as one of the subjects on which the two emperors agreed:

*cum feliciter tam ego Constantinus Augustus quam etiam ego Licinius Augustus apud Mediolanum convenissemus atque universa quae ad commoda et securitatem publicam pertinerent, in tractatu haberemus, haec inter cetera quae videbamus pluribus hominibus profutura, vel in primis ordinanda esse credidimus, quibus divinitatis reverentia continebatur, ut daremus et Christianis et omnibus liberam potestatem sequendi religionem quam quisque voluisset*, etc.

ὁπότε εὐτυχῶς ἐγὼ Κωνσταντῖνος ὁ Αὔγουστος κἀγὼ Λικίννιος ὁ Αὔγουστος ἐν τῇ Μεδιολάνῳ ἐληλύθειμεν καὶ πάντα ὅσα πρὸς τὸ λυσιτελὲς καὶ τὸ χρήσιμον τῷ κοινῷ διέφερεν ἐν ζητήσει ἔσχομεν, ταῦτα μεταξὺ τῶν λοιπῶν ἅτινα ἐδόκει ἐν πολλοῖς ἅπασιν ἐπωφελῆ εἶναι, μᾶλλον δὲ ἐν πρώτοις διατάξαι ἐδογματίσαμεν, οἷς ἡ πρὸς τὸ θεῖον αἰδώς τε καὶ τὸ σέβας ἐνείχετο, τοῦτ᾽ ἔστιν, ὅπως δῶμεν καὶ τοῖς Χριστιανοῖς καὶ πᾶσιν ἐλευθέραν αἵρεσιν τοῦ ἀκολουθεῖν τῇ θρησκείᾳ ᾗ δ᾽ ἂν βουληθῶσιν, κτλ.

The precise date is fixed by the fact that Licinius left Sirmium shortly after the beginning of February: Theomnestus, *Hippiatrica Berolinensia* 34.12, cf. New Empire (1982), 81. C. Zuckerman, Travaux et Mémoires 14 (2002), 617–637, has convincingly argued that the so-called Verona List of Roman provinces, datable to 314, reflects a division of the Empire into twelve dioceses, six under each Augustus, on which Constantine and Licinius agreed in Milan.

250 or the attempts of the emperors Decius and Valerian to secure religious conformity in the 250s.[33] Narrative accounts of the persecution survive from two contemporary authors who wrote from two very different perspectives. Lactantius wrote his *On the Deaths of the Persecutors* in Nicomedia in 314/315, that is, as a subject of the eastern emperor Licinius while he and Constantine were still on good terms with each other: the work was finished and published more than a year before the two Augusti went to war with Constantine invading Licinius' territory in early October 316.[34] Lactantius' tract may be regarded as a work of anti-hagiography. Modern scholarship has tended to set *On the Deaths of the Persecutors* in the framework of classical rhetoric, since in certain respects it resembles a formal *vituperatio*, comprising as it does the systematic denigration of a series of emperors obeying the same formal rules as are exemplified in a long series of encomia and panegyrics of Greek kings and Roman emperors.[35] Moreover, Lactantius' selection of facts and his wording owe much to the second book of Maccabees, with its insistence that the detailed historical record reflects divine judgement and God's intervention in human history.[36] Neither of these two literary models, however, completely explains what Lactantius actually wrote. No classical Greek or Latin work contains the same 'triumphant celebration of divine judgement' and, whereas 2 Maccabees is a narrative of national struggle and salvation, *On the Deaths of the Persecutors* concentrates on the conduct of individual emperors who persecuted the Christians and God's punish-

---

[33] Chapter II.

[34] JRS 63 (1973), 36–39.

[35] J.L. Creed, Lactantius, De Mortibus Persecutorum (Oxford, 1984), xxxvii–xxxviii.

[36] J. Rougé, SP 12 (1976), 135–143.

ment of them.[37] Lactantius, therefore, may have composed
his tract as a conscious counterpart to the acts and passions
of martyrs: whereas Christian hagiography recorded the
heroic deaths of martyrs, Lactantius set out to chronicle
the gruesome deaths of the emperors on whose orders the
martyrs of his own day were executed.

The persecutors whose deaths Lactantius describes in his
*On the Deaths of the Persecutors* are the persecuting emperors
Diocletian, Galerius and Maximinus in the East and Maximian in the West. He inserts his account of the death of
each of them into what is in effect a political history of the
Roman Empire from the winter of 302/303 to the summer
of 313 which delights in narrating civil wars, but virtually
ignores most of the known imperial campaigns against
external enemies in these years.[38] Lactantius did not intend
*On the Deaths of the Persecutors* to be an impartial history
of the early fourth century. It is rather political satire. But
Lactantius has taken great care to be factually accurate, no
matter how tendentious or misleading may be his presentation or how great the suppression of particular facts.[39] For
example, Maximinus was Galerius' nephew, the son of his
sister (*Epitome* 40.1, 18; Zosimus 2.8.1), but Lactantius
mentions only that he was related to Galerius by marriage,
when he makes the latter call him his *adfinis* when recom-
mending him to Diocletian as a suitable choice for the
imperial purple (*Mort. Pers.* 18.14: *meus, inquit, adfinis*).
This discrepancy has been pounced upon as a demonstrable

[37] These significant differences are duly noted by Creed, Lactantius
(n. 35), xxxviii.
[38] Documented in Phoenix 30 (1976), 188–193; New Empire
(1982), 61, 64, 66, 69–70, 81.
[39] J. Moreau, Lactance: De la mort des persécuteurs (SC 39, 1954);
Barnes, JRS 63 (1973), 29–46.

example of Lactantius' unreliability as a historical witness.[40] That is neither a necessary nor a plausible hypothesis: the contradiction may only be apparent: since the identity of Maximinus' wife, who bore him a son and a daughter between 304 and 308 (Lactantius, *Mort. Pers.* 50.6; Zonaras 13.1), is not known, she could be a daughter of Galerius.[41] Lactantius' silence about Maximinus' blood relationship to Galerius is deliberate and designed to diminish his dynastic claim as Galerius' nearest male relative to be appointed to the imperial college. Similarly, Lactantius presents Severus, appointed Caesar of the West in 305, as a drunkard who caroused through the night and whose main talent was his skill at dancing (*Mort. Pers.* 18.12: *illumne saltatorem temulentum ebriosum, cui nox pro die est et dies pro nocte?*). Severus must in fact have been an experienced general, as Lactantius tacitly admits when he makes Galerius justify his appointment on the grounds that he had commanded soldiers with loyalty (*Mort. Pers.* 18.12: *militibus fideliter praefuit*). Moreover, for all that Lactantius says, Severus too could have been related to Galerius by blood or marriage.[42] Though often satirical and misleading because of what it leaves out, *On the Deaths of the Persecutors* rates highly for factual accuracy in what it does say. Only in one case is Lactantius' narrative demonstrably false and fictitious. That is his account of the end of Maximian. According to Lactantius, Constantine pardoned Maximian after his attempted coup and seizure of Massilia in 310, but the ingrate then tried to assassinate him in his palace at Arles as he slept (*Mort. Pers.* 29.3–30.6). The attempted assassination is an

---

[40] C. S. Mackay, CP 94 (1999), 201–207.

[41] T. D. Barnes, CP 94 (1999), 459–460.

[42] Severus' career before 305 seems be completely unknown (PLRE 1 [1971], 837–838, Severus 30).

invention of Constantine's propaganda,[43] not of Lactantius' imagination: he uncritically accepted an official story which was being circulated at the court of Constantine in Trier between 310 and 312.[44] Constantine's propaganda machine, which blackened his father-in-law Maximian's name after his attempted coup in 310, reversed itself immediately after the Battle of the Milvian Bridge: Maxentius' mother was persuaded (or compelled) to acknowledge, probably in public, that her son had been conceived in adultery and that Maximian was not his father,[45] after which the memory of Maximian was rehabilitated to such an extent that within a few years he was being celebrated as Divus Maximianus on the coinage of Constantine, which implies an official apotheosis certified by the Roman Senate.[46] With this exception (which confirms that Lactantius cannot have been writing when he did at the behest or in the service of Constantine),[47] *On the Deaths of the Persecutors* provides a mass of detail without which it would be impossible to write a political history of the decade of persecution that began in February 303.

---

[43] There is no hint of it in *Pan. Lat.* 6 (7) delivered before Constantine in 310 shortly after Maximian's failed coup against him.

[44] JRS 63 (1973), 41–43.

[45] Origo Constantini Imperatoris 12: *de cuius origine mater eius cum quaesitum esset, Syro quondam genitum esse confessa.* The theme is taken up and elaborated by the orator of 313 (*Pan. Lat.* 12[9].4.3: *Maximiani suppositus … filius, … despectissimae parvitatis, detortis solutisque membris,* etc.).

[46] For the evidence, which principally comprises coins from the mints of Trier, Arles, Rome, Aquileia, Siscia and Thessalonica with the legend *DIVO MAXIMIANO* followed by *OPT(IMO) IMP(ERATORI)* or *SEN(IORI) FORT(ISSIMO) IMP(ERATORI)* and variations thereon, see New Empire (1982), 35. Athanasius, *Contra Gentes* 9.50–53, appears to allude to the consecration.

[47] JRS 63 (1973), 43; Constantine (1981), 13–14, 291–292.

Diocletian had invited Lactantius to come from his native Sicca in Africa some time before 303 to hold the chair of Latin rhetoric in his imperial residence of Nicomedia. In Bithynia Lactantius was at the fringes of the court and in contact with Constantine, who was being groomed for appointment to the imperial college. It was perhaps from Constantine himself that Lactantius gleaned gossip about secret deliberations in the palace both in the winter of 302–303, as Galerius impelled Diocletian to issue legislation against the Christians, and during the long months preceding the abdication of the two Augusti and the appointment of two new Caesars on 1 May 305, when Constantine and Maxentius were set aside in favour of Galerius' nominees. In 305 Galerius became the effective ruler of Asia Minor. Lactantius left Bithynia and returned to his native Africa. But it seems that around 310, after the suppression of the usurpation of Domitius Alexander, who sought alliance with Constantine against Maxentius, he migrated to the court of Constantine at Trier, where he remained until Licinius' defeat of Maximinus in the spring of 313 enabled him to resume possession of the chair in Nicomedia of which he had been deprived by the edict of 24 February 303.

Lactantius began to write his *On the Deaths of the Persecutors* in Nicomedia shortly after his return and completed the postscript on the deaths of the relatives of Galerius and Maximinus in the winter of 314–315. His tract or pamphlet was thus the work of one who was well placed to gather information on imperial politics at the highest level and the enforcement of persecution in Nicomedia. In contrast, the *Martyrs of Palestine* of Eusebius of Caesarea offers a purely provincial perspective.[48] In this work Eusebius does not

---

[48] In what follows, I have used, though sometimes modified, the

record, as has too often been assumed, all the Christians
who were executed in the Roman province of Palestine, of
which his city of Caesarea was the capital.[49] The *Martyrs of
Palestine* is rather a memoir of Eusebius' Palestinian friends
and acquaintances who suffered martyrdom in the years
303–311, a sort of record of his friends pictured therein.

Eusebius begins with Procopius, a native of Aelia (Jerusalem) who lived in Scythopolis, where he served the
church as lector, exorcist and Syriac interpreter. Procopius
was sent with others from Scythopolis to Caesarea, where
the governor Flavianus sentenced him to be beheaded. The
martyrdom of Procopius on 7 June 303 was the first of
the 'Great Persecution' in Caesarea (1.1–2). It is typical of
the personal emphasis throughout the *Martyrs of Palestine*
that Eusebius mentions in passing others who were sent
to Caesarea with Procopius ([L] 1.1: he was sent with his
companions), but does not record their fate. The next pair
of martyrs recorded by Eusbius are Zacchaeus, a deacon
of the church of Gadara, and Alpheus, who came from an
illustrious family in Eleutheropolis, but was a lector and
exorcist in the church of Caesarea: they were beheaded on
17 November 303 (1.5). On the same day, Romanus was
strangled in prison in Antioch: he was a deacon and exorcist
in the church of Caesarea who had gone to Antioch when
Diocletian was in the city (hence in the summer or autumn

---

English translation of Lawlor & Oulton, Eusebius 1 (n. 9), 327–400.
The Bollandists include the short recension in their bibliographical
guide to hagiographical texts (BHG 1193: Martyres Palaestinenses); for
what they call *Eusebii libellus prolixior* they have entries for Apphianus
and Aedesius (BHG 161), Pamphilus (BHG 1405), Procopius (BHL
6949) and Theodosia (BHG 1775).

[49] App. 6.

of 302)[50] and interrupted official sacrifices, for which Diocletian ordered his tongue to be cut out. Procopius survived
the mutilation and was kept in prison in chains for many
months until he was strangled (2).[51] Although he died in
Antioch, he was a Palestinian and Eusebius counted him
as one of the martyrs of his province. Eusebius' *Martyrs of
Palestine* thus records precisely three Christians who were
executed in the province of Palestine during the first year
of the persecution (Procopius, Zacchaeus and Alpheus),
though he refers in passing to other martyrs. Nothing could
show more clearly that he cannot have set out to provide a
full record of all the martyrs in Palestine who were put to
death in the 'Great Persecution.'

Eusebius divides his narrative into successive 'years of persecution:' he counted from the promulgation of the edict of
24 February 303 in Caesarea, so that these years begin and
end shortly before each Easter.[52] At the start of the second
year of the persecution, that is, during March 304, the persecution increased in intensity when 'imperial edicts arrived
again for the second time, much worse than the first,' whose
content Eusebius summarises: they compelled 'all the people
in all the cities in a body, men, women and children, to sacrifice and offer libations to lifeless idols' (3.1). After describing the martyrdoms of Timothy of Gaza, who was burned
alive (3.1), of Agapius and Thecla, who were exposed to the
beasts (3.2–4), and of eight men who were all beheaded at

---

[50] Constantine (1981), 20–21; New Empire (1982), 55–56.
[51] The story that Romanus miraculously retained the power of
speech and continued to preach the word of God, which occurs in
the long recension of the *Martyrs of Palestine* ([L] 2.3), but not in the
short, may be a post-Eusebian addition to the original text of 311
(App. 6 n. 10).
[52] G. W. Richardson, CQ 19 (1925), 96–100.

Caesarea on 24 March 304 (1.4), Eusebius spreads himself at length on Apphianus (4.2–15). Apphianus was a young man from Lycia who studied in Berytus and returned home before coming to Caesarea to study with Pamphilus where he met Eusebius:

> When he had been in our company, and had received training in the divine studies and been instructed in the sacred scriptures by Pamphilus the great martyr, he acquired from him a moral state of virtue by no means ordinary. (4.5)

As a postscript to the martyrdom of Apphianus, Eusebius adds that of his brother Aedesius who 'had for a long time enjoyed the instruction of Pamphilus.' Aedesius was sent to the copper mines in southern Palestine, then went to Alexandria (presumably having escaped), where he assaulted Sossianus Hierocles, an enthusiastic persecutor and prefect of Egypt (where he is attested in 310–311),[53] who was condemning Christian virgins to the brothel: he was tortured and flung into the sea (5.1–3). Other martyrdoms which receive extensive treatment also reflect Eusebius' personal knowledge of the martyrs. Agapius of Gaza was exposed to the beasts before Maximinus himself in Caesarea on 20 November 306: he was savaged by a bear, but survived until the following day in prison (where Eusebius may perhaps be conjectured to have visited him), then thrown into the sea weighted down with stones (6). As is appropriate, it is Eusebius' mentor and adoptive father Pamphilus and his companions in martyrdom who receive the fullest treatment (11a–28).

The *Martyrs of Palestine* also records the role and character of successive governors of Eusebius' province. Eusebius names three governors of Palestine between the publica-

---

[53] Barnes, New Empire (1982), 150.

tion of the edict of 24 February shortly before Easter 303 and Galerius' edict of toleration in 311. Flavianus was governor when the edict arrived (*Mart. Pal.* [S] pr. 1); he subsequently executed Procopius on 7 June 303 and Zacchaeus and Alpheus on 17 November, on both occasions in Caesareae (*Mart. Pal.* [L] 1.1–2, 1.5b-k). In 304 Flavianus was succeeded by Urbanus, who held office for several years and showed himself an enthusiastic persecutor. According to Eusebius, Urbanus was cruel by nature and took pleasure in torturing Christians ([L] 4.11): early in his tenure condemned Agapius and others to fight wild beasts during festival games at Caesarea in order to court popularity with the crowd, later he castrated young male Christians and sent virgins to the brothel ([L]3.3, 7.4). In 308, however, for offences whose nature Eusebius does not explain, the emperor Maximinus, who had come to Caesarea, suddenly and unexpectedly dismissed Urbanus and executed him at once (7.7–8). Urbanus was replaced by Firmilianus, an experienced solder who surpassed his predecessor in ferocity ([L] 8.1). A dedication made by him to Galerius through the magistrates of the *colonia* of Scythopolis names him as Val(erius) Fermilianus and opens the possibility that he continued in office beyond the year 310 (SEG 43.1073, revising AE 1964.198 = SEG 20.455: Scythopolis).[54] Like Urbanus, Firmilianus enthusiastically enforced the anti-

---

[54]  From R. Last, A. Laniado & P. Porath, ZPE 98 (1993), 229–237. The inscription had earlier been read as showing that Firmilianus was replaced by one Valentinianus as governor in 310: PLRE 1 (1971), 932, Valentinianus 1; Barnes, New Empire (1982), 152. PLRE 1 (1971), 1108, also entered 1025, Anonymus 130, as governor of Palestine in 310 and 'presumably the successor of Firmilianus.' This anonymous governor in Eusebius, *Mart. Pal.* 13.1, must in fact be Firmilianus, as suggested in New Empire (1982), 152 n. 32.

Christian policies of Maximinus. He was still governor of Palestine in early March 310 when he executed the last Christians to suffer martyrdom in Caesarea before the death of Galerius (11.25–30) and it appears that Firmilianus must be the governor who subsequently inspected the mines at Phaeno, where many Christians had been sentenced to hard labour (*Mart. Pal.* 13.1).[55]

Book Nine of Eusebius' *Ecclesiastical History* offers a contrast both to his *Martyrs of Palestine* and to Lactantius' *On the Deaths of the Persecutors* in its scope and coverage: it is a primary account of the resumption of persecution by Maximinus in 311–313, which concentrates on imperial policy as illustrated by the imperial edicts and letters posted up in public in the cities of Caesarea and Tyre which Eusebius quotes entire.[56]

## The Enforcement of Diocletian's Legislation in the West

Before the onset of the 'Great Persecution' the western Augustus had already shown that he did not automatically replicate the policies of his senior colleague in the East. For it seems certain that he never promulgated, still less attempted to enforce, the edict fixing maximum prices for a vast range of goods and services which Diocletian issued from Egypt in late November or early December 301, even though the preamble to the edict declared that it was valid for the whole world and for all time (*ILS* 642).[57] In the

---

[55] JRA 9 (1996), 551.
[56] Barnes, New Empire (1982), 67–68.
[57] SCI 21 (2002), 190–192.

spring and early summer of 303 Maximian promulgated Diocletian's edict of 24 February 303 and circulated it to the governors of the Italian, Spanish and African provinces which he administered directly. In Gaul and Britain, however, his Caesar Constantius carefully avoided creating martyrs by confiscating the scriptures and Christian property, but avoiding executions (Lactantius, *Mort. Pers.* 15.7–16.1), though it is possible that some of his subordinates did put Christians to death in some areas without his authority.[58]

In Italy, Africa and Spain there were martyrs in 303 and 304, since Maximian both promulgated and ordered the enforcement of the edict of 24 February 303, and the list of African martyrs in the 'Great Persecution' whose names are recorded epigraphically or in liturgical evidence is a very long one.[59] But Maximian did not promulgate any of Diocletian's subsequent anti-Christian legislation. The latest validly attested execution of a Christian in the territories of Maximian is that of Crispina at Theveste on 3 December 304 (K-K-R XXIX = Musurillo XXIV; Barnes XVII), and it seems clear that here persecution had effectively ceased some months before Maximian abdicated on 1 May 305. Although the proconsul of Africa and the *praeses* of Numidia, and perhaps some other zealously anti-Christian governors, exceeded the terms of the edict of 24 February 303 and issued orders on

---

[58] C. Jullian, REA 23 (1925), 367–378, drew attention to the cycle of passions of Christians who are alleged to have suffered martyrdom in northern Gaul under the *praefectus* Rictiovarus. However, 'Rictiovarus' is dismissed as an invented person in New Empire (1982), 190.

[59] See the two lists compiled by P. Monceaux, Histoire littéraire de l'Afrique chrétienne 3 (Paris, 1905), 530–535 (more than 150 African martyrs mentioned in epigraphy), 536–551 (alphabetical list of African martyrs in *acta*, the calendar of the church of Carthage and martyrologies).

their own authority that everyone should sacrifice, there is no valid evidence that Diocletian's edict of February 304 requiring universal sacrifice was ever even promulgated by Maximian, still less enforced in Italy, Africa or Spain. And on 1 May 305 Constantius became Augustus of the West and in this capacity could ensure de facto toleration for Christians throughout the western provinces of the Roman Empire. In the following year Constantius' son Constantine was proclaimed Augustus at York on 25 July 306 and as Augustus felt himself entitled to issue edicts and general laws: very shortly after his proclamation he formally rescinded Diocletian's edict of 24 February 303 and restored confiscated Christian property in the territories that he controlled – before he accepted the lower rank of Caesar from Galerius and thereby forfeited the right to legislate. In the West, therefore, the 'Great Persecution' was a relatively brief affair, and it probably claimed relatively few martyrs except in Africa.

While Christians were certainly executed in Italy and Spain for refusing to comply with the edict of February 303, and the destruction of churches appears to be attested by the fragment of an epitaph from the small town of Ferentinum 75 kilometres south-east of Rome (AE 1982, 324 = Supplementa Italica 1.59: —]sima persecutione deruta de suis pro[—),[60] only one authentic record of the trial of a Christian survives from these areas. The Acts of Euplus have been heavily interpolated, although part of the Greek version appears to be an authentic transcript of the court record (K-K-R XXV A, pp. 100.7–101.5 = Musurillo XXV A, pp. 310.4–312.15; Barnes XVI).[61] These acta do not con-

---

[60] On proposed supplements, see ZAC 2 (1998), 286 n. 40.

[61] Only the Greek version of the Acts of Euplus edited by Franchi de' Cavalieri, Note agiografiche 7 (ST 49, 1928), 47–48 (BHG 629), has any historical value, and the authentic text breaks off suddenly at

form to any of the normal patterns of the arrest and trial of Christians during the 'Great Persecution.' Calvisianus, the *corrector* of Sicily, was busy with judicial duties at Catania on 29 May 304 when someone shouted out: 'I want to die because I am a Christian.' When Calvisianus replied 'Enter the man who shouted,' Euplus entered the *secretarium* carrying a copy of the gospels. Maximus, a *vir clarissimus* who was presumably a member of the governor's *consilium*, observed that possessing such an object was 'contrary to the orders of our emperors.' Calvisianus then questioned Euplus about what he was carrying and where he got it, and finally declared: 'Since his confession has been made clear to us, let it be posted up in public.' Euplus was presumably arrested and imprisoned. For the *Acts of Euplus* resume with a formal restatement of the resumption of the case several months later:

Our lords Diocletian and Maximian being consuls for the ninth and eighth time respectively, on the day before the ides of August (i. e., 12 August 304), in the city of Catane before the tribunal, [the blessed] Euplus standing in the middle:-

Calvisianus the corrector said: What you admitted has been published in writing: reveal to us what you intend to say today.
Euplus said: What I said then, see, I confess the same to you now.
Calvisianus the corrector said: You have in your possession the prohibited reading-matter.
[The blessed] Euplus said: Yes, I have them.

---

K-K-R, p. 101.6 = Musurillo, p. 312.15. On other versions of the *acta*, see Franchi, ST 49 (1928), 21–46, who shows that the Latin version printed as K-K-R XXVB = Musurillo XXV (BHL 2728) is a confection of Baronius, whose forgery of evidence has sometimes deceived modern scholars: for some examples, see Barnes, Tertullian (1971), 262 n. 3, 269 n. 1; JTS, N. S. 25 (1974), 111; G. W. Bowersock, St. Peter's in the Vatican, ed. W. Tronzo (Cambridge, 2005), 14–15 nn. 36, 38.

The authentic text of the *Acts of Euplus* breaks off suddenly after another three brief exchanges, but it is clear that the charge on which Euplus was executed on 29 August 304 was his possession of and refusal to surrender the copy of the gospels that he had carried into court on 29 April 304. Euplus was therefore executed under the terms of the edict of 24 February 303. This shows that the persecuting edict of February 304, which ordained sacrifice for all, had not been promulgated in Sicily by the end of August 304.[62]

In Africa, the normal mechanism for the enforcement of the edict of February 303 is well attested. The *Acts of Felix* (K-K-R XXII = Musurillo XX; Barnes XII) intersperse sections in protocol style with linking narrative. The edict requiring the *principes* and magistrates of each city to seize the scriptures from bishops and priests was published everywhere. Immediately after it was posted in a small city not far from Carthage, whose name appears to be Thibiuca,[63] the *curator* Magnilianus ordered the *seniores plebis*, a priest and two lectors to appear before him, since the bishop had departed for Carthage. The proceedings against Felix fall into several distinct episodes. First, on 3 June Magnilianus questioned the Christians whom he had summoned. When the priest said that the bishop kept the sacred books at home, but was absent, Magnilianus ended the enquiry by stating: 'You will therefore be under arrest until you explain your-

---

[62]   de Ste Croix, Christian Persecution (n. 27) 56.

[63]   H. Delehaye, AB 39 (1921), 268–270, printed the name of the town, which occurs a dozen times, as *Thibiuca*. But Magnilianus is attested at Henchir Bou Cha, whose ancient name is unknown (CIL 8.23964, 23965). R. Duncan-Jones, JTS, N.S. 25 (1974), 106–110, therefore, questioned whether Felix was bishop of Thibiuca. Delehaye's reading and identification are vindicated by Maier, Dossier (n. 30), 50 n. 15.

selves to Anullinus the proconsul.' When Felix returned on the following day, Magnilianus urged him to hand over for burning the books and parchments that he acknowledged to be in his possession. Felix persistently refused to surrender them and Magnilianus gave him two days to reconsider. On the third day (6 June), Magnilianus summoned Felix again: when the bishop again refused to comply with the imperial order, he sent him to the proconsul under the escort of Vincentius Celsinus, a decurion of the city. Felix left Thibiuca on 13 June for Carthage, where he was delivered to the legate of the proconsul, who put him in prison overnight, then urged him to surrender the scriptures. When he again refused, he was put back in prison, where he remained for sixteen days until he was dragged before the proconsul in chains 'at the fourth hour of the night.' When Felix yet again refused to surrender the scriptures, Anullinus ordered him to be executed on 15 July. After Felix had uttered a short prayer of thanks to God, he was beheaded and buried on the estate of Faustus on the Via Scillitanorum (31).[64]

A thirteenth century manuscript in the Episcopal Seminary at Gorizia near Udine in northern Italy preserves a documentary record of the trial of two groups of Christians by Anullinus in 303: the first part of the *Acts of Gallonius*, which were published in 1996, appear to be an authentic record of the trial of Christians at Timida Regia, to which has been added a second part of dubious authenticity (Barnes XIII).[65] In the first part of the *Acts* (1–40) the proconsul tries Christians whom he had summoned to appear before him because they had gathered together for Sunday worship in

---

[64] The words *in via quae dicitur Scillitanorum* were presumably added before *in Fausti* some years after 303.

[65] P. Chiesa, AB 114 (1996), 251–258; Scorza Barcellona, Hagiographies 3 (n. 5), 85–88.

defiance of the imperial edict, and the documents read out
in court contain a statement by inhabitants of Timida Regia
that recently arrived Christian *magi* had organised these
conventicles. Anullinus questioned Gallonius, partly under
torture, and urged him to surrender the scriptures which he
had hidden away. He also questioned the other Christians,
whom he sentenced to death for holding illegal gatherings: while some twenty four were beheaded because 'they
met contrary to the imperial order,' two were burned alive
because they had also shouted out 'ill-omened utterances.'
Gallonius was not sentenced, but remanded to Utina for a
further hearing (41). Here, in the second part of the *Acts*
(42–57), which shows signs of later interpolation, Anullinus
again questions Gallonius about the hidden scriptures and
again applied torture. When Gallonius persistently refused,
the proconsul ordered him to be burned alive and sentenced
other Christians to be beheaded. According to the *Acts* they
suffered martyrdom on 31 December (1, 58). That date is
wrong. The calendar of the church of Carthage records the
commemoration of martyrs from Timida Regia on 31 May
and of a martyr named Gallonius on 11 June (AASS, Nov.
2.1.[lxx]: *II kal. Iun. Ss. Timidensium; III id. Iun. S. Galloni*).
Hence the diurnal date transmitted in the *Acts of Gallonius*
should emended from *pridie kalendas Ianuarii* to *pridie
kalendas Iunii* (the abbreviation *Iun.* having been corrupted
to *Ian.*): the proconsul Anullinus held assizes in Timida
Regia on 31 May, where he conducted the trial described in
the first part of the *Acts of Gallonius*, remanded Gallonius
in custody and executed him at Utina on 11 June.[66] Since

---

[66] Chiesa, AB 114 (1996), 242–251. Note, however, that there is
a lacuna in the *Kalendarium Carthaginiense* for the days between the
middle of December and 13 January (AASS, Nov. 2.1.[lxxi]).

the proconsul's edict proclaiming the imperial edict of 24 February 303 only reached Thibiuca, a town about fifty kilometres from Carthage on 3 June 303, the year must be 304.

The fullest evidence for the enforcement of the edict of 24 February 303 in Africa (or anywhere else) comes from the partially preserved record of two official enquiries which Constantine ordered into the conduct of African and Numidian bishops during the persecution. The two documents are the first two in a dossier of ten items relating to the origins of the Donatist schism that Optatus of Milevis appended to his work aganst the Donatist Parmenianus c. 370. The *Proceedings before Zenophilus* (*Gesta apud Zenophilum*) record a hearing conducted by Domitius Zenophilus, the *consularis* of Numidia, in Cirta on 15 December 320, which found that Silvanus and other bishops who ordained Maiorinus bishop of Carthage in opposition to Caecilianus were *traditores* who had surrendered copies of the holy scriptures in 303 (Optatus, App. 1 = Gebhardt XX).[67] The *Gesta* break off in the middle of a sentence after twelve and a half pages in the standard modern edition of Optatus (p. 197.13 Ziwsa). The end is lost, and a lacuna supervenes of completely indeterminate length, since it envelops both the beginning and probably a large part of the second document. This is the *Acts of the Exculpation of Felix* (*Acta purgationis Felicis*), which are a verbatim record of a hearing held by the proconsul Aelianus in Carthage on 15 February 315.[68] This hearing pronounced Felix,

---

[67] For what the *Gesta* reveal about the Christian community in Cirta between 303 and 320, see the long and careful discussion by Y. Duval, Chrétiens d'Afrique à l'aube de la paix constantinienne. Les premiers échos de la grande persécution (Paris, 2000), 21–209.

[68] Augustine, *Contra partem Donati post gesta* 33.56, reports the date as *Volusiano et Anniano consulibus XV Kal(endas) Mart(ias)* that

the bishop of Abthungi, who had consecrated Caecilianus
as bishop of Carthage, innocent of the charge of *traditio*
which the Donatists alleged against him and which (so
they argued) invalidated his consecration of Caecilianus,
whom Constantine had recognised as the catholic bishop
of the city in the winter of 312/313 very shortly after he
gained control of the African provinces (Optatus, App. 2 =
Gebhardt XXI, cf. Eusebius, *HE* 10.6.1–5, cf. 10.5.15–17;
Augustine, *Ep.* 88.3). The schism originated in a disputed
episcopal election in Carthage after the end of the persecution (probably in 307) in which the Numidian bishops
took the part of Maiorinus, the rival of Caecilianus, who
soon died and was replaced by Donatus.[69] In the present
context, there is no need to review the tortuous course of
the schism except to note that after Constantine definitively decided in favour of the Catholics in 316, he tried
repression between 317 and 321. Executions occurred and
Donatist martyrs began to be celebrated in a distinctively
Donatist hagiography.[70] What is relevant in the present
context is what the two documents preserved for posterity

---

is, 15 February 314, but it is clear that the year must be 315, since
the *acta* refer back to 18 August 314 (p. 198.19 Ziwsa = Gebhardt,
p. 206.23–24). On their historical content, Duval, Chrétiens d'Afrique
(n. 67), 215–346.

[69] The dates of the death of Mensurius, the election of Caecilianus
and the consecration of Maiorinus in opposition to him are not firmly
attested: in favour of the chronology assumed here, see JTS, N.S. 26
(1975), 18–20. A different (and lower) chronology is argued by B.
Kriegbaum, Kirche der Traditoren oder Kirche der Märtyrer. Die Vor-
geschichte des Donatismus (Innsbruck & Vienna, 1986), 130–149,
who assumes that Maxentius' edict of toleration only reached Africa in
late April or early May 308 – which seems much too late.

[70] Chapter IV.

by Optatus reveal about the enforcement of the persecuting edict of 24 February 303.[71]

On 13 December 320 there was read into the *Proceedings before Zenophilus* an extract from the *acta* of Munatius Felix, a local magistrate of Cirta, for 19 May 303 (p. 186.18–188.32 Ziwsa = Gebhardt XX.2.2–25). On this day Felix went to the house where the Christians gathered and said to the bishop Paul: 'Produce the writings of the law and anything else that you have here, as is commanded, so that you comply with the edict.' Paul replied that 'the readers have the codices, but we surrender what we have here,' but refused to name the readers. Felix ordered Paul to identify the readers or send a message to them, and had a careful inventory compiled by Paul's clergy of what the bishop handed over. When empty chests were then discovered in one room and four jars and six pots in another, and these too had been confiscated, Felix reiterated his initial demand: 'Bring forth the scriptures that you have, so that you comply with the bidding of the emperors and their edict.' One large codex was then produced. Felix then went to the houses of the lectors who were said to have copies of the scriptures in their possession. One produced four codices, another five, a third eight, a fourth seven, and a fifth two codices and four *quiniones*, while the wife of yet another lector produced six. Felix had his house searched and duly cautioned Victorinus and the subdeacons Silvanus and Carosus, who had identi-

---

[71] There is a later edition of the two documents by H. von Soden, Urkunden zur Entstehungsgeschichte des Donatismus (Bonn, 1913), 37–50 no. 28, 25–32 no. 19, which includes some textual improvements, which I have incorporated in my translation and paraphrase. For a full modern English translation (unfortunately not always accurate) of the passages summarised and quoted here, see M. J. Edwards, Optatus: Against the Donatists (TTH 27, 1997), 153–156, 170–178.

fied the lectors' houses for him, that they were in legal
jeopardy if anything had been missed.

Some years earlier there were read into the *Acts of the
Exculpation of Felix* extracts from a deposition made on 19
August 314 before Aurelius Speretius, a priest of Jupiter
and *duovir* of Carthage, by Maximus, who claimed to
speak in the name of the *seniores* of the 'catholic' Christians
(pp. 198.17–200.13 Ziwsa = Gebhardt XXI.3.3–4.20).
Maximus declared that a case would be brought against
Felix of Abthungi and Caecilianus before the emperors and
that records of the crime of Felix were being sought out:

> For when the edict of persecution had been issued against the Chris-
> tians, that is, that they should sacrifice or hand over to the flames
> whatever scriptures they possessed, Felix, who was then bishop of
> Abthungi, had given his consent that the scriptures should be handed
> over by the hand of Galatius to be burnt by fire. At that time the
> magistrate was Alfius Caecilianus, whose presence may it please you
> to notice. Since at that time the duty was laid on him of ensuring
> that all should sacrifice in accordance with the proconsul's edict,
> and that they should offer whatever scriptures they had according to
> the imperial law (*quoniam eius temporis officicum incumbebat, ut ex
> iussione proconsulari omnes sacrificarent et si quas scripturas haberent,
> offerrent secundum sacram legem*), I request, since he is present and you
> see that he is an old man who cannot travel to the imperial court, that
> he may testify on the record whether he gave a letter concerning the
> agreement, which according to the record was made by the same, and
> whether what he put in the letter is true, so that a certified record of
> these matters may be disclosed at the hearing before the emperor (*ut
> horum actus et fides in iudicio sacro detegi possit*).

Alfius Caecilianus had gone with Saturninus, the *curator*
of Abthungi, to Zama to buy linen[72] when the edict of
24 February 303 was being circulated to local magistrates

---

[72] I suspect that a noun may have fallen by haplography in the phrase
*propter lineas comparandas* (p. 199.8 Ziwsa = p. 207.20 Gebhardt).

in Africa. He testified that as they were returning[73] the Christians sent messengers to the *praetorium* to enquire whether he had received the imperial order. He replied that he had not yet received it, although he had seen copies and had witnessed the destruction of Christian basilicas and the burning of scriptures in Zama and Furni. He then at once began to comply with the imperial order: men were sent to the house of Felix to seize copies of the scriptures, while Caecilianus went to the church with Galatius, where they took the bishop's throne and letters of greeting and burned everything in front of the doors of the building 'in accordance with the sacred command.' The *Acts of the Exculpation of Felix* continue with the reading of a letter of Caecilianus to Felix written in response to a query from Augentius, Caecilianus' colleague as aedile in 303, asking whether any scriptures had been burnt in the year of his duovirate. Caecilianus immediately disputed the authenticity of the latter part of the letter, which was damaging to Felix.

The *Acts of the Exculpation of Felix* and the *Proceedings before Zenophilus* are documents that require a critical, even sceptical assessment. In such an assessment it helps to be aware, whether from observation or experience, that the purpose of official enquiries is normally not to discover the truth about the matters under investigation, but to vindicate the honesty and probity of the government (or for that matter of the university administration) that has felt itself compelled to establish an offical enquiry. In any such enquiry, therefore, much of the evidence given under oath is unlikely to comprise 'the truth, the whole truth and

---

[73] As transmitted, Caecilianus' statement *cum veniremus illo* = 'when we came there,' i.e., to Zama (p. 199.9–10 Ziwsa = p. 207.21 Gebhardt) makes no sense: he must surely mean 'as we were returning to Abthungi.'

nothing but the truth' and the person carefully chosen to
preside over the enquiry, which must pronounce in favour
of the Prime Minister who set it up, may sometimes render
a verdict at variance with the evidence that he has heard. The
two official enquiries into the charge of *traditio* ordered by
Constantine greatly resemble modern official enquiries, and
in this case there is a strong suspicion that evidence has been
falsified in order to convict Numidian bishops of the offence
that they alleged against their ecclesiastical opponents.[74] But
the truth about their conduct and that of Felix of Abthingi
does not need to be decided in the present context. What
is both relevant and indisputable here is, first, that the proconsul of Africa and his counterpart the *praeses* of Numidia
added a requirement for universal sacrifice, which was not in
the imperial edict of 24 February 303, and second, that the
initial stage of the enforcement of their enhanced version
of the edict of 24 February 303 lay in the hands of local
officials, who recorded their own actions in regard to the
Christians – doubtless out of a sense of self-preservation.

The latest account of a Christian martyrdom in the
West is provided by the *Acts of Crispina* (K-K-R XXIX;
Musurillo XXIV; Barnes XVII). Crispina was tried at
Theveste on 3 December 304 by the proconsul Anullinus
who, as Maximus testified in his deposition of 19 August
314 (Optatus, p. 198.31–32 Ziwsa = Gebhardt XXI.4.4),
had added a requirement that everyone sacrifice when he
published the imperial edict of 24 February 303. In the *Acts
of Crispina* Anullinus puts his own order on the same legal
level as the imperial edict. At the start of the trial, as soon
as Crispina was led in,

---

[74] See JTS, N. S. 26 (1975), 14–16, on the suspicious role played
by Nundinarius.

Anullinus said: Do you know the meaning of the sacred order, Crispina?

She replied: I do not know what has been ordered.

Anullinus said: That you sacrifice to all our gods for the safety of the emperors, accoring to the law given by our lords Diocletian and Maximian the pious Augusti and Constantius and Maxim<ian>us the most noble Caesars. (1.1)

And the verdict which Anullinus reads out runs as follows:

Because Crispina persists in unworthy superstition and has refused to sacrifice to our gods, I have ordered her to be executed by the sword in accordance with the heavenly instructions of the law of the Augusti. (4.1)[75]

Anullinus had added a requirement to sacrifice to Diocletian's anti-Christian legislation of 24 February 303, and it is not surprising that he appears as the persecuting magistrate in plainly fictitious hagiographical texts as active in both Africa and North Italy.[76] For Datianus, who executed the Spanish martyr Vincentius (Prudentius, *Peristephanon* 5.40, 130, 422, drawing on *acta* or a passion of Vincentius composed in the fourth century; Augustine, *Sermo* 276.4 [PL 38.1257]), is the persecuting magistrate in several cycles of Spanish passions which have no claim to authenticity.[77] Similarly, several governors of provinces in Asia Minor, who must have enforced the anti-Christian policies of the eastern emperors Galerius and Maximinus between 303 and

---

[75] On the *Acts of Crispina*, see still P. Monceaux, *Mélanges Boissier* (Paris, 1903), 383–389, who argues that, while the first part of the document (1–2) is entirely authentic and derives from 'un procès-verbal,' the second part (3–4), which includes the verdict, has been heavily interpolated.

[76] Barnes, *New Empire* (1982), 179 n. 21.

[77] B. de Gaiffier, AB 72 (1954), 378–396, cf. *New Empire* (1982), 184.

313, when they are attested epigraphically as governors, are known as persecutors only from late and unreliable hagiographical texts.[78] Eusebius' *Martyrs of Palestine* makes it clear that even in the 'Great Persecution' governors could in practice decide how rigorously to enforce imperial legislation against the Christians.

## Documents of the 'Great Persecution' from the East

In the East the 'Great Persecution' lasted much longer and fell into three distinct periods. For Asia Minor Gregory of Nazianzus records that the intensity of persecution increased on the abdication of Diocletian and again when Galerius

---

[78] For example, Aemilianus Marcianus, *praeses Ciliciae* (CIL 3.223: near Tarsus, 293/305) appears in passions of Julianus of Anazarbus (BHG 965–967e); Antistius Sabinus, *praeses* of Cyprus (J. Pouilloux, P. Roesch & J. Marcillet-Jaubert, Testimonia Salaminia 2. Salamine de Chypre 12 (Paris, 1987), 66–69 nos. 151–157: between 293 and 305) may be the Sabinus who is recorded as having executed Christians in Cyprus (*Syn. Eccl. Cpl.* 404, 502, cf. H. Delehaye, AB 26 [1907], 258); and Flavius Severianus, who honoured Galerius as Augustus while *praeses* of Isauria (AE 1972.652: Seleucia ad Calycadnum, 305/311), should be the Severianus governor of Isauria who executed the martyrs Bianor and Silvanus (PG 117.532–533; *Syn. Eccl. Cpl.* 811): on these cases, see, respectively, W. Lackner, Vig. Chr. 27 (1973), 53–55; I. Michaelidou – Nicolaou, Acta of the Fifth International Congress of Greek and Latin Epigraphy (Oxford, 1971), 381–383; D. Woods, JTS, N. S. 43 (1993), 131–132. It is, however, a gross abuse of hagiographical method for Woods, ib. 132, to transfer the martyrdom of Aquilina, who was tried by a proconsul 'Volusianus' (AASS, Iun. 3.167–171: BHG 163), from Byblos in Phoenicia to Africa just because C. Ceionius Rufius Volusianus is known to have been proconsul of Africa in 305–306 or 306–307 (ILS 1213, cf. New Empire (1982), 169).

died (*Orat.* 4.96). Until 1 May 305 Diocletian ruled Asia
Minor, the Syrian region and Egypt, while Galerius defended the length of the Danube and governed the Balkans
from the Bosporus west to the confines of Italy. On 1 May
305 Galerius added Asia Minor to his domains, while
Maximinus took the Syrian region and Egypt, and here
Eusebius' *Martyrs of Palestine* describes how the Christians
were here persecuted more vigorously than before and how
Maximinus both attempted to enforce the requirement of
universal sacrifice by using the census registers and issued
new and more coercive laws. After an interlude consequent
upon Galerius' edict of toleration, Maximinus resumed persecution both in the areas that he had controlled since 305
and in Asia Minor, which he seized in 311. Lactantius' *On
the Deaths of the Persecutors*, Eusebius' *Martyrs of Palestine*
and the ninth book of his *Ecclesiastical History* indicate that
the number of Christians executed was far greater in the East
than in the West, amounting in all to several, perhaps many
thousands. No accurate estimate of the total number of eastern martyrs in the decade of persecution is possible, though
the figure of more than 660 for the city of Alexandria alone
before the resumption of persecution by Maximinus in
November 311 looks plausible and appears to derive from
a document composed in Alexandria in 368 to celebrate
the fortieth anniversary of the election of Athanasius (*Passio
Petri* 7 [BHG, Auct. 1502a; BHL 6698b]). If that number
is even approximately correct,[79] it implies that several thousand Christians were put to death in the East between 24
February 303 and the death of Maximinus in the summer of
313. Yet, despite the fact that a high proportion of the eastern martyrs who were the object of cult in later centuries are

---

[79] As suggested in Constantine (1981), 358 n. 76.

likely to have been victims of the 'Great Persecution,' only four authentic records, apart from the *Martyrs of Palestine*, appear to survive of the trials of individual Christians in the East from these ten years – and one is of a martyr who seems to be otherwise unknown.

The *Martyrdom of Agape, Irene and Chione* is a narrative with long sections in protocol style (K-K-R XXIV = Musurillo XXII; Barnes XV). Agape, Irene and Chione were residents of Thessalonica in Macedonia who fled from the city into nearby mountains in 303 to avoid punishment under the edict of 24 February, but were arrested in the following year and together with others tried by the governor Dulcitius. The charge against them was that they refused to eat sacrificial meat (3.1). The examination of the Christians one by one is reported at some length and includes details that speak strongly for authenticity, though not necessarily for derivation from official *acta*, since Dulcitius conducts the trial in public on his tribunal (3.1): Eutychia is imprisoned, not executed, because she is pregnant (3.7) and when Dulcitius reads out his verdict that Agape and Chione are to be burned alive, he adds that several other Christians including Irene are also to be temporarily imprisoned because of their youth (4.4). On the day after the burning of Agape and Chione, Irene is brought into court again, subjected to detailed questioning by Dulcitius and finally sentenced to be burned alive (5.1–6.3). Irene then undergoes martyrdom on 1 April 304 (7). Perhaps the most interesting feature of the *Martyrdom of Agape, Irene and Chione* is that, whereas Irene still had copies of the scriptures and other Christian books in her possession (5.1), when Chione is asked whether she has 'records, manuscripts or books of the unholy Christians' in her possession, she replies that the emperors have taken them all away (4.2). Christian attitudes towards the surrender of the scriptures were very different in the East from those in Africa: there *traditio* was treated as tantamount to apostasy, whereas in the East no blame at all attached to this measure of voluntary compliance with the edict of 24 February 303.

A single damaged leaf of a papyrus written in the second half of the fourth century, which is now in the possession of Duke University (P. Duk. inv. 438), was identified some years ago by Peter van Minnen as preserving a record of the the trial of the priest Stephanus from a village in the Antinoite nome by Satrius Arrianus, governor of the Thebaid, in the city of Cleopatris in the month Choiak in the second year of the emperors Valerius Severus and Maximinus, i.e., between 27 November and 26 December 305 (Barnes XVII).[80] Satrius Arrianus appears as a persecuting governor in several other hagiographical texts,[81] but this document is the first authentic record of his persecuting activities in the Thebaid, where contemporary papyri attest him as *praeses* until the spring of 307.[82] The lacunose text is in strict protocol form except for the concluding notice of Stephanus' martyrdom and it closely resembles the much earlier *Acts of the Scillitan Martyrs* (Barnes III), for Arrianus, like Vigellius Saturninus, offers Stephanus more time for reflection. In accordance with standard practice, Arrianus asks Stephanus to sacrifice three times and three times he refuses. Finally the governor delivers his verdict. In van Minnen's translation the final seven lines read as follows:

> ] who sets [     ] or plead with you so that you [listen to the] command of our lords the emperors that you should live.

---

[80] P. van Minnen, AB 113 (1995), 13–38.
[81] PLRE 1 (1971), 14, Adrianus.
[82] New Empire (1982), 148.

[                    ] you make yourself like the wild animals.
[Listen therefore to the] verdict that you deserve. And he ordered
[                    to] write his name as follows: Stephanos
[from Lenaios they will] burn alive. He fulfilled his martyrdom
[in a] blessed and noble manner. Amen.[83]

A *martyrion* of the 'holy Stephanus' stands on casual attestation in a fifth century list of Christian clergy (P. Amsterdam
81), but he was 'an unimportant priest in an unimportant village in Middle Egypt, which was unable to get its
local hero on the national list of Egyptian martyrs' and all
memory of him vanished when the village disappeared.[84]
This discovery of a martyr previously unkown among the
surviving hagiography of early Christianity further discoun-
tenances any attempt to deduce the total number of martyrs
in the 'Great Persecution' from the number of martyrs who
happen to be known to modern scholarship.

Of the trial of Phileas, the bishop of Thmuis, who was
executed on 4 February 307,[85] no fewer than three accounts
of his trial survive in protocol style. The standard collections from Ruinart to Ruhbach's revision of Knopf and
Krüger included Latin *Acts of Phileas*, which also include
the martyrdom of the military officer Philoromus, who
protested at the condemnation of Phileas and was executed
with him (Ruinart, Acta Martyrum (1689), 548–551 =
(1713), 494–496 = K-K-R XXXI: BHL 6800), though a
proper critical edition had to wait until 1963 (Musurillo
XXVIIB: BHL 6799).[86] Two Greek papyri, neither of which

---

[83] Reproduced from van Minnen, AB 113 (1995), 31.
[84] van Minnen, AB 113 (1995), 27, cf. 19, construing the mono-
gram MP as an abbreviation of $\mu(\alpha)\rho(\tau\acute{\upsilon}\rho\iota\upsilon\nu)$.
[85] On the date, see Lawlor & Oulton, Eusebius 2 (1928), 276–277;
Barnes, New Empire (1982), 182, cf. 149.
[86] F. Halkin, AB 81 (1963), 5–27, cf. RHE 58 (1963), 136–139.

can be dated later than c. 350 on palaeographical grounds,
preserve an account of Phileas' trial together with part of
the Greek Psalter. When Victor Martin published one of the
two in 1964 from the Bodmer collection, he aptly described
it as *Apology of Phileas* (P. Bodmer XX, whence Musurillo
XXVIIA).[87] Some years later, Albert Pietersma recognised
parts of the same text in a papyrus containing the Septuagint
version of Psalms 1–4 in the Chester Beatty collection and
produced a luxurious edition of the Dublin text (P. Chester
Beatty XV) with corresponding passages of the Latin *acta*
printed *en face* together with a revision by François Halkin
of his 1963 edition of the Latin *Acts of Phileas* (BHL
6799).[88] Pietersma's publication of the three texts together
clarifies the relationship between the two previously known
texts, even though Pietersma himself muddied the waters by
changing his mind while his book was being printed. In the
introduction Pietersma argues that the Latin version of the
martyrdom of Phileas derives from the Greek *acta* preserved
in the Chester Beatty papyrus, while the Greek *Apology*,
which, like the Greek *acta*, was composed in its present
form before 350, uses the same archival material, but reworks it far more extensively, adding rhetorical flourishes,
hagiographical touches and sections of outright apologia.[89]
In a footnote to his edited text of the papyrus, however,
Pietersma discards his hypothesis of 'direct dependence' on

---

[87] V. Martin, Papyrus Bodmer XX. Apologie de Philéas évêque de
Thmouis (Cologne & Geneva, 1964).

[88] A. Pietersma, The Acts of Phileas Bishop of Thmuis (Including
Fragments of the Greek Psalter. P. Chester Beatty XV (With a New Edition of P. Bodmer XX, and Halkin's Latin Acta (Geneva, 1984), 34–83
(the new text with an English translation), 87–99 (a diplomatic text of
P. Bodmer XX), 105–108 (the Latin acta).

[89] Pietersma, Acts of Phileas (n. 88), 14–29.

the grounds that it 'is contradicted by the presence of a con-
siderable amount of unrelated material in the conclusion'
of the Latin *acta*: hence he modifies his original stemma in
favour of one which shows the Greek and Latin *acta* deriving
independently from a lost exemplar.[90] Both his reasoning
and his conclusion are false.

The Greek and Latin *Acts of Phileas*, despite being closer
to the original record of Phileas' trial in form, provide
less historically valuable information than the 'Defence of
Phileas, the bishop of Thmuis,' which reworks his interrogation by Clodius Culcianus, the prefect of Egypt, far
more extensively. For it is only the *Apology* that records, by
way of introduction, that Phileas was condemned when he
appeared in court for the fifth time and makes any reference
to his four previous appearances. On his first appearance
in court, the prefect had Phileas stretched on the rack
beyond the fourth peg before he remanded him in custody
at Thmuis for two days. Phileas was then brought in chains
and bare feet to Alexandria, where, though repeatedly insulted and beaten, he did not waver at a second, third and
fourth hearing. He was upbraided for his contumacy and
informed that he had killed many by refusing to sacrifice,
whereas Pierius had saved many by submitting to the imperial command. Finally, Phileas was summoned into court
with the twenty or so clergy who were accompanying him
and interrogated by Culcianus. There follows a lengthy
interchange between the bishop and the prefect, which runs
closely parallel in all three versions. Phileas is urged by the
prefect to take pity on his wife, brother and other relatives
to sacrifice, after which the lawyers present in court claimed
that Phileas had already sacrificed in the *secretarium*, so

---

[90] Pietersma, Acts of Phileas (n. 88), 76 (note on frag. 14.1 ff.).

that he did not need to do so again to comply with the law. When Phileas denied that he had sacrificed, the lawyers, the court officials, Phileas' relatives and even the *curator* (apparently of the city of Alexandria) requested an adjournment, which Phileas spurned, then begged him to yield until they saw that he could not be persuaded.

Here the *Apology* ends with the colophon 'Peace to all the saints!' (Ephesians 6.23). The Greek and Latin *Acts of Phileas* continue with the bishop's brother, who was one of the lawyers, asking the prefect to pardon him and Phileas' repudiation of his intercession. After this the Greek *acta* become fragmentary, but there is no sign that they ever went on to record the martyrdom of Philoromus. For the Latin *acta* not only conclude with the beheading of both Phileas and the tribune Philoromus, but also bring the latter into the story while Phileas was still in court:

There was present a tribune of the Romans by the name of Philoromus. When he saw that Phileas was surrounded by weeping relatives, but nevertheless could not be broken, he shouted out and said: 'Why do you test the man's constancy foolishly and in vain? Why do you want to make one who is faithful to God unfaithful? Do you not see that his eyes do not see your tears, that his ears do not hear your words, because his eyes behold the glory of heaven?' After he said this, everyone's anger turned against Philoromus and they demanded that he suffer the very same sentence as Phileas. The magistrate gladly agreed and ordered both to be slain by the sword. (7)

This episode has been added by a later hand. It interrupts the account in the Greek *acta* and it makes no reference to Philoromus in its account of the execution apart from a plural verb and the adjective 'both.' More important, the addition depicts a hostile audience in court where the account presents it as very well-disposed to Phileas. Furthermore, the source of the addition can be identified. For Eusebius records the martyrdom of Phileas after that of Philoromus, who served in the imperial administration of Alexandria and 'used to conduct judicial enquiries every day, attended by a bodyguard of soldiers' and he states that both were exhorted by relatives, friends, officials and the prefect to take pity on their wives and children (*HE* 8.9.6–8). The Latin *acta* derive from the Greek *acta*, but they have introduced Philoromus into the story from Rufinus' translation of Eusebius. On the other hand, Eusebius' notice of the two martyrdoms implies that behind the extant Greek *Apology* and *Acts of Phileas* lies a lost exemplar in which a redactor edited Philoromus out of an original account which included the trial of both men together.

The eighth book of Eusebius' *Ecclesiastical History* also quotes a letter of Phileas which narrates the deaths of martyrs in Egypt and is therefore another contemporary witness to the 'Great Persecution' in the East (*HE* 8.10, whence K-K-R XXX = Musurillo XXVIA, who also includes Rufinus' slightly abbreviated Latin translation as XXVIB). This letter provides contemporary evidence of the savage treatment of Christians, which hardly falls short of the tortures described in fictitious hagiography:

When all were given a free hand to insult them, some beat them with cudgels, others with rods, others with scourges, others again with straps and others with ropes. … Some <Christians> were suspended on a frame with both hands bound behind them and every limb stretched out by means of pulleys; then, when they were in this posture, torturers acting on orders began to attack their whole body, struck them with weapons not only on their sides, as is done with murderers, but also on their stomachs, legs and cheeks. Other <Christians> were suspended in midair from <the tops of> colonnades by one hand, experiencing unequalled agony from the tension in their joints and limbs. Others were bound with their face against a pillar with their feet not touching the ground, so that their bonds were drawn tight by the pressure on them of the weight of their body. (Eusebius, *HE* 8.10.4–5).

However, the fullest record of the enforcement in the East of the edict of 24 February 303 has only recently been brought to light. A dozen or so Greek manuscripts of the twelfth century or earlier preserve a passion of Athenogenes, the bishop of Pedachthoe, which differs little except in the proper names from many other passions of the type which Delehaye stigmatised as 'epic passions' (BHG 197).[91] One of these manuscripts, however, contains a much longer and more interesting *Passion of Athenogenes* than the rest (Sabaiticus 242, of the tenth century, fols. 50ʳ–78ᵛ), which Pierre Maraval published in 1992 (BHG 197b).[92] The preface and an epilogue describe the genesis of this passion:-

<The record> of the life and combat of the thrice-blessed Athenogenes, which was sought by many, I discovered with difficulty in a very old book in someone's house written in vulgar language and, to speak truly, written neither in order nor coherently, but rather with lacunae. Having read the book, I judged it necessary to <re>write it more coherently to satisfy those who hear it.
    This saint Athenogenes was born a Christian of Christian parents … (1/2)

Hilarius who was then first of the council, surnamed Pyrrhachas (the Red), the father of Hilarius the former quaestor <...>.
    I, Anysius, having found the record of the combat of the thrice-blessed martyr Athenogenes in disorder and incomplete, put it together and arranged it in order.
    The holy martyr of Christ and bishop Athenogenes was perfected on 17 July in the reign of the most impious Diocletian and Maximian, but according to us with our Lord Jesus Christ reigning, to whom glory and power for ever and ever. Amen. (42)

---

[91] Delehaye, Passions (1966), 171–226.
[92] P. Maraval, La passion inédite de S. Athénogène de Pédachthoé en Cappadoce (BHG 197b) (SH 75, 1990), 30–83.

The product corresponds exactly to what the author states about his process of composition. The framing narrative is extended and conventional: Athenogenes kills a dragon which was carrying off both animals and children from an unnamed village (4–6),[93] and performs a number of other miracles (8–10). The fictions are betrayed by an apparent anachronism: Athenogenes ransoms captives from the Goths, who were ravaging the country areas around Sebastopolis in Roman Armenia when he was ordained priest and chorepiscopus (2/3, 8). These raids belong to the 250s and 260s, which would imply that Athenogenes, who does not seem to be an old man in 303, was born in the 220s or 230s, and the author of the *Passion* is unaware that several decades elapsed between the episodes involving Goths and his hero's martyrdom. But the *Passion* includes two documents in protocol style which can be regarded as authentic records of two trials conducted by the governor Agricola or Agricolanus (the Greek has Ἀγρικόλαος) at Sebasteia in the province of Armenia Minor.[94]

## Epilogue

The authentic documents from the 'Great Persecution' show a remarkable contrast with the contemporary documents from earlier persecutions. First, eight of the ten authentic letters, passions and *acta martyrum* that survive from the period before 260 either come from the churches of Carthage and Smyrna or were preserved in those cities. For the decade

---

[93] Jerome's *Life of Hilarion* appears to provide the earliest example of this common motif in later Christian hagiography (Chapter IV).

[94] C. P. Jones, JTS, N. S. 43 (1992), 245–248.

of persecution initiated by Diocletian in 303 there is no such geographical concentration: of the six hagiographical texts in the canon used in the present work three come from Africa, none from Asia, one each from Sicily, Macedonia, Egypt and Armenia Minor.[95] Second, none of these texts describes open manifestations of popular hostility to the Christians such as Christian apologists, the letter of the Gallic churches quoted by Eusebius (*HE* 5.1.3–3.4, whence K-K-R IV = Musurillo IV) and some independently preserved hagiographical texts attest for the Antonine age, the reign of Septimius, and the persecutions of Decius and even Valerian (Barnes I, IV, V).[96] Third, and most important, whereas it is Christians who preserved all the earlier authentic records of the enforcement of persecuting legislation by Roman governors and magistrates, several of the original and authentic documents relating to the enforcement of Diocletian's edict of 24 February owe their preservation to the fact that local officials who had unwillingly enforced the edict kept documentary records of the actions which they took on receipt of orders from provincial governors. They presumably did so out of an instinct for self-preservation. After the fall of Maximinus in 313, Christians throughout the East exacted a bloody revenge on their oppressors (Eusebius, *HE* 9.11.2–11). Local magistrates who arrested Christians in 303 and sent them to their provincial governors for execution may have considered it prudent to possess and be able to produce proof that they had acted unwillingly in obeying orders that came ultimately from the emperors, should their conduct later be questioned by relatives of the

---

[95] App. 2.

[96] Observe, however, Eusebius, *Mart. Pal.* 6, on a Christian fighting beasts to entertain the people of Caesarea in games given by Maximinus on 20 November 306.

martyrs. If that hypothesis is correct, it provides yet further testimony, compelling if indirect, of the social standing and political power of the Christian church in the reign of Diocletian – which has often been denied.

*Table 1:* Toleration and Restitution, 306–313

Tabulated below are the areas in which and the dates at which different emperors rescinded Diocletian's edict of 24 February 303 by granting toleration (T) and ordering the restitution of confiscated Christian property (R)

| | | | |
|---|---|---|---|
| Britain, Gaul and Spain | T + R | 306, summer | Constantine |
| Italy and Africa | T | 306/307, winter | Maxentius |
| | R | 311 | Maxentius |
| Pannonia, Illyricum, Thrace, Greece | | | |
| | T | 311, April | Galerius |
| | R | 313, spring | Licinius |
| Asia Minor | T | 311, May | Galerius |
| resumption of persecution | | 311, November | Maximinus |
| | T | 312, December | Maximinus |
| | T + R | 313, June | Licinius |
| Oriens (the Syrian region) and Egypt | | | |
| | T | 311, May | Galerius |
| resumption of persecution | | 311, November | Maximinus |
| | T | 312, December | Maximinus |
| | R | 313, early summer | Maximinus |
| | T + R | 313, summer | Maximinus |

# IV

# The Beginnings of Fictitious Hagiography

The contemporary accounts of Christian martyrs who died at the hands of the Roman authorities provide authentic materials which modern scholars can use to write the history of the Christian church down to the end of the 'Great Persecution.' These accounts, whether they are contemporary letters, narratives closely based on court records or speeches, were of course written for the edification of the faithful, but their main purpose in every case was to preserve and to hand on to posterity the memory of martyrs and their glorious deaths. Two authentic texts from later in the fourth century have also made their way into the standard modern collections of early Christian hagiographical documents – the so-called *Testament of the Forty Martyrs*, which is in fact a letter written from prison in the name of a group of Christians awaiting execution in the last years of the reign of Licinius (Gebhardt XVI = K-K-R XXXII = Musurillo XXVIII),[1] and the *Martyrdom of Sabas the Goth*, which is a letter of 'the church of God dwelling in Gothia to the church of God dwelling in Cappadocia and to all the dioceses of the holy catholic church in every place' (K-K-R XXXIII).[2] But when persecution ceased and Christianity became the religion of the rulers of the Roman Empire, Christian hagiography on

---

[1] On this text, see esp. Franchi de' Cavalieri, Note agiografiche 3 (Rome, 1909), 64–70; Note agiografiche 7 (Rome, 1928), 155–184.

[2] C. Zuckerman, Travaux et Mémoires 11 (1991), 473–479.

the old pattern became impossible except for persecuted groups or during a recrudescence of persecution.

The schismatic Donatists in Africa endured repression for a brief period under Constantine (317–320) and again under Constans in the late 340s.[3] As Delehaye noted, the hagiography of the Donatist martyrs predictably follows the pattern of hagiography from the period of the persecution of the Christians.[4] However, in addition to authentic documents generally recognised as such, viz., (1) a sermon on the martyrdom of Donatus, bishop of Avioccala, who was put to death on 12 March during the brief period of repression under Constantine between early 317 and late 320 (PL 8.752–758; BHL 2303b = CPL 719),[5] (2) the letter of one Macrobius to the *plebs Carthaginis*, i.e., the Donatists of Carthage, describing the martyrdoms of Isaac and Maximianus in August 347, usually known as the *Passion of Isaac and Maximianus* (PL 8.767–774, from Dupin; 778–784, from Mabillon: BHL 4473 = CPL 721),[6] and (3) the *Passion of Marculus*, who died on 29 November 347 (PL 8.760–766; BHL 5271 = CPL 720),[7] the Donatists both

---

[3] The classic account, though disfigured by the author's congenital inaccuracy in detail, is W. H. C. Frend, The Donatist Church. A Movement of Protest in North Africa (Oxford, 1952), 159–162 ('The first period of repression, 317–21'); 177–187 (on the *tempora Macariana*).

[4] Delehaye, Passions (1966), 85–86.

[5] K. Schäferdiek, Oecumenica et Patristica. Festschrift für Wilhelm Schneemelcher zum 75. Geburtstag, ed. D. Papandreou, W. A. Bienert and K. Schäferdiek (Chambésy – Geneva, 1989), 175–198.

[6] Edited critically by P. Mastandrea, AB 113 (1995), 76–88. The revised versions of all three texts in J.-L. Maier, Le dossier du Donatisme 1 (Berlin, 1987), 198–211, 256–291 nos. 28, 36, 37, are translated into English by M. A. Tilley, Donatist Martyr Stories. The Church in Conflict in Roman North Africa (Liverpool, 1996), 51–87.

[7] Now edited by P. Mastandrea, AB 113 (1995), 65–75. On this

rewrote authentic documents in accordance with their own beliefs and ideology[8] and composed bogus documents. Thus a Donatist version of the *Acts of Cyprian* was produced (BHL 2039c),[9] which can be compared with the original *Acts* of the third century, while the *Passio Saturnini, Felicis, Dativi, Ampelii et sociorum*, often styled the *Acta Abitinensium*, was written specifically in order to convict Felix, the bishop of Abthungi who consecrated Caecilianus bishop of Carthage in opposition to Maiorinus, the predecessor of Donatus, of the charge of *traditio* (BHL 7492), probably more than a century after the events that it purports to describe on the basis of a documentary record.[10]

---

text, see esp. H. Delehaye, AB 53 (1935), 81–89; L. Grig, Making Martyrs in Late Antiquity (London, 2004), 54–58.

[8] On 'les passions "donatisées"', see V. Saxer, Hagiographies, ed. G. Philippart 1 (Turnhout, 1994), 60–64.

[9] Edited by R. Reitzenstein, SB Heidelberg 1913, 35–37, whose text is reprinted by Maier, Le dossier du Donatisme 1 (n. 6), 122–126 n. 9, and translated by Tilley, Donatist Martyr Stories (n. 6), 3–5. This version expands the final sentence of the original *Acts of Cyprian* (cf. Chapter II n. 108) to make the proconsul Galerius Maximus die from his illness after repenting (*paenitentiae reus decessit languore consumptus*).

[10] As argued by A. Dearn, JEH 55 (2004), 1–18. The text is translated by Tilley, Donatist Martyr Stories (n. 6), 27–49, who dates its composition 'before Caecilian's election as bishop in late 311 or early 312' on the grounds that it presents him as still a deacon and not yet bishop (26). The inference is obviously fallacious – and the disputed episcopal election at Carthage probably occurred in 307: see JTS, N. S. 26 (1975), 18–20; Constantine (1981), 56, 316 n. 129. Tilley, Donatist Martyr Stories (n. 6), 17–24, also translates the *Passio Maximae, Secundae et Donatillae* (*BHL* 5809, edited by C. de Smedt, AB 8 [1890], 107–116). Tilley dates the martyrdoms to 30 July 304 and puts the composition of the passion 'probably before the end of the persecution' (13–14), again with obviously fallacious arguments on both points.

After persecution ceased, Christian hagiography took one of two different directions. On the one hand, martyrs were replaced by monks, bishop and the holy men and women as the heroes of hagiography, while hagiographers were often more eager to instil explicit moral and theological improvement in their readers than accurately to record the actions of their heroes and heroines. On the other hand, since nothing that was both new and true could any longer be said about martyrs who were receding rapidly into the past, hagiographers who wrote about the age of persecution were compelled either to rewrite and embroider a genuine old text or resort to wholesale invention. Delehaye provided a magisterial survey of the growth of hagiographical legends and hagiographical fiction that concentrated on the development of popular beliefs, myths and legends.[11] His prime example of the growth of legend was the transformation of the humble Procopius of Eusebius of Caesarea's *Martyrs of Palestine* (1.1–2) into a prince and victorious general, one of the great Byzantine military saints, a process which was already complete before 787, when part of the fully-fledged legend was read into the minutes of the iconodule Council of Nicaea.[12] But the fictions that swamped historical fact were not always innocent. It was the emperor Constantine's propaganda machine that set in motion the process of transforming the pro-Christian Maxentius into a fearsome and bloodthirsty persecutor, a tyrant in every possible sense of the word.[13] Constantine began the metamorphosis of

---

[11] Delehaye, Légendes (1927), 12–118.

[12] Delehaye, Légendes (1927), 119–139.

[13] Constantine seems to have devised the employment of the term *tyrannus* to combine the senses of unjust ruler, usurper and persecutor at precisely this juncture: Historiae Augustae Colloquia, N. S. IV: Colloquium Barcinonense MCMXCIII (Bari, 1996), 53–63.

his brother-in-law and dead adversary immediately after the Battle of the Milvian Bridge: Maxentius' mother was induced (by what pressures or enticements is unknown) to confess on oath in a judicial setting that Maxentius was not his father's son, but the product of adultery with a Syrian, a Gallic orator elaborated on the theme in 313, and Eusebius in the East inserted the inventions of Constantine's propaganda into a revised edition of his *Ecclesiastical History* by 315 (*HE* 8.14.1–6; 9.9.2–11).[14] Thus was born, or rather created, the powerful and enduring myth that Christians were incessantly persecuted for nearly three hundred years until Constantine rescued them. Fifty years later, Julian's executions and harassment of Christians not only stimulated renewed production of authentic accounts of martyrdom in the ancient style, but encouraged the development of deliberate hagiographical fiction.

## Theodotus of Ancyra

The *Martyrdom of Saint Theodotus of Ancyra* (BHG 1782), possesses a unique importance for dating this significant development. Written in or shortly after the reign of Julian the Apostate, it both documents and exemplifies the transition from recording the actual suffering of martyrs for posterity to pious fiction. The *Martyrdom* was published by Pio Franchi de' Cavalieri 1901,[15] and two years later

---

[14] Origo Constantini Imperatoris 12: '*de cuius origine mater eius cum quaesitum esset, Syro quodam genitum esse confessa.*' The orator of 313 elaborated on the theme of the supposititious son (*Pan. Lat.* 12[9]. 3.4, 4.3, cf. Constantine [1981], 44–47).

[15] P. Franchi de' Cavalieri, I martirii di S. Teodoto e di S. Ariadne. (Rome, 1901), 9–87.

Delehaye stigmatised it as a typical epic passion.[16] Delehaye's condemnation of the text as unhistorical was widely accepted, though disputed at once by Franchi and challenged in 1951 by Henri Grégoire and Paul Orgels,[17] until 1982, when Stephen Mitchell rehabilitated the *Martyrdom* as 'a valuable and authoritative historical document,' and advanced the somewhat hyperbolical claim that it is 'one of the fullest and most reliable documents of the persecution of Maximinus.'[18] Delehaye and Mitchell reached their opposing conclusions because the *Martyrdom of Theodotus* comes from precisely the period when the literary and edificatory possibilities of fictitious hagiography were beginning to be explored.

It was Mitchell's autopsy of an inscription showing that the Byzantine church at the Turkish village of Kalecik, about forty miles east north east of Ankara, was dedicated to Saint Theodotus that led him to argue, first and correctly, that the author of the *Martyrdom* knew the topography of the ancient village of Malos, where he states that Theodotus was buried (11),[19] then to defend the historical accuracy of the *Martyrdom* on the grounds that feature after feature 'finds a parallel in authentic contemporary evidence' confirming the veracity of the main narrative and that its reliability 'is confirmed by substantial internal evidence.'[20] But the accurate topography of the *Martyrdom*, which appears to originate in

---

[16]  H. Delehaye, AB 22 (1903), 320–328.

[17]  P. Franchi de' Cavalieri, Nuovo bolletino di archeologia cristiana 10 (1904), 27–37; H. Grégoire & P. Orgels, BZ 44 (1951), 165–184.

[18]  S. Mitchell, Anatolian Studies 31 (1982), 93–113.

[19]  Mitchell, Anatolian Studies 31 (1982), 95–101, quoting the inscription published by him as RECAM 2, 212.

[20]  Mitchell, Anatolian Studies 31 (1982), 101–113.

the Montanist community of Malos,[21] shows only that its author was familiar with the area around his own village and wrote before the Persian invasion of Asia Minor in the early seventh century: in and of itself, as Delehaye emphasised in several different contexts, the fact that a hagiographer knows the topography of the place where his hero was tried and executed does not prove that he was at all close in time to the martyr's death.[22] The hagiography of Timothy and Alban illustrates the point perfectly.[23]

Although prosopography does not, as Mitchell claims, confirm the details of the narrative, shows that the author possessed genuine knowledge of or evidence for the period when Maximinus controlled Asia Minor and resumed persecution there. He does not name Maximinus, but introduces the newly appointed governor who tortured and executed Theodotus as 'a certain Theotecnus' who was violent, cruel, a thorough villain who rejoiced in killing and who had been appointed as a reward for his vices:

He had promised the emperor who was at war with the church that he would within a short time turn the Christians here to impiety, if only he was entrusted with rule over the province. This Theotecnus, even before he crossed the boundary of our homeland, so terrified the pious in advance by his announcements that the laity of the church vanished and the deserts and mountains were filled with those who fled (4, p. 63.19–23).

Theotecnus also sent specific orders before he arrived in the province: churches were to be razed to the ground, priests were to be taken to altars of the pagan gods and forcibly made to sacrifice, while those who resisted were to have their

---

[21] Grégoire & Orgels, BZ 44 (1951), 172–174; Mitchell, Anatolian Studies 31 (1982), 102–105.

[22] Delehaye, AB 22 (1903), 320–328; Méthode (1934), 37–40.

[23] Chapter VII.

property confiscated and to be imprisoned together with their children to be chained and whipped until he came to punish them (4, 63.28–35). Theotecnus is a known person and the *Martyrdom of Theodotus* adds precision to what Eusebius reports about him: Maximinus had honoured Theotecnus for his anti-Christian activities as *curator* of Antioch by appointing him to a governorship, but Licinius put him to death when he obtained control of Antioch (*HE* 9.2–3, 11.5–6; *PE* 4.2.10–11). It is only the *Martyrdom of Theodotus* that identifies Theotecnus' province as Galatia;[24] but whether in 312 the governor of Galatia had the rank and official title of *consularis* by which Theodotus addresses Theotecnus while under torture (24, p. 76.16; 27, p. 78.13: ὑπατικέ, is not at present verifiable.[25] Moreover, what the *Martyrdom* says about Theodotus himself has the stamp of truth: he owned a wineshop where he allowed Christians to take refuge from persecution (6, p. 64.26–29).

On the other hand, the *Martyrdom* has at least one of the stigmata of an epic passion. The martyr suffers tortures sufficient to kill an ordinary human being several times over, but he feels no pain and the tortures cease only after he has worn out two successive gangs of torturers; he is then sent back to prison by Theotecnus, where he recovers so that torture can be resumed on the next day. One passage will give the flavour of the whole:

None of the tools of punishment was left unused, not fire, not iron, not hooks. Surrounding him completely and tearing off his clothing, they fixed him to the wood, stood back and lacerated his ribs, everyone as strongly as he could. But they could not sustain the toil.

---

[24] Mitchell, Anatolian Studies 31 (1982), 108–110.

[25] PLRE 1 (1971), 1102; New Empire (1982), 190. The earliest governor of Galatia who is known to have had the title *consularis* appears to be Leontius in 364/365: PLRE 1 (1971), 500, Leontius 9; 1102.

The martyr smiled with pleasure at those who were striking him; he received the trial of each of the tortures in silence, neither changing the expression on his face nor giving in to the savagery of the tyrant (for he had our Lord Jesus Christ as his helper) until those who were striking him tired. When they were exhausted, others approached and took over from the first crew. The gloriously triumphant combatant surrendered his body as if it were not his own to the executioners to be wounded and torn apart and he kept his belief in the Lord of all unbending. Theotecnus ordered his ribs to be drenched in strong vinegar and torches to be applied to him. As the holy man smarted from the vinegar and his ribs were on fire, smoke arose. As a result, when he noticed the smoke from his roasting flesh, he showed displeasure by wrinkling his nose. When he saw this, Theotecnus hastily leapt from his official chair and said: 'Where is the nobility of your words now, Theodotus? For I see that you are giving in to the tortures quite quickly.' … The martyr said: 'Do not be surprised, consularis, that I wrinkled my nose when I noticed the smoke. Rather instruct your bodyguard to carry out all your orders in full, as I see that they have become exhausted. Please devise tortures and attempt every device, so that you may learn the endurance of an athlete and discover that my Lord Jesus is helping me.' (27, pp. 77.23–78.17)

It thus demands faith (some might call it gullibility) to believe that the *Martyrdom of Theodotus* is what it purports to be – the first-hand account by one 'Nilus' who was in prison with the martyr and has told nothing but the truth (36, p. 84.20–22). Moreover, the fact that Theotecnus calls Theodotus 'the champion of the Galileans' (31, p. 80.15–16) proves that the *Martyrdom* was written after the emperor Julian, who became master of Asia Minor in December 361, gave that appellation of the Christians currency for polemical purposes (Ephrem, *Contra Iulianum* 3.17: 'he mocked and nicknamed the brethren "Galilaeans";'[26] Theodoret, *HE* 3.8.1; Sozomenus, *HE* 5.4.5 ).

---

[26] Translated by J. Lieu in The Emperor Julian: Panegyric and Polemic², ed. S. N. C. Lieu (Liverpool, 1989), 121.

## Author and Source in the *Life of Antony*

Fictitious hagiography had already received its initial impetus from the *Life of Antony* (BHG 140),[27] which Athanasius published very soon after Antony died, probably in 356 (Jerome, *Chronicle* 240ᵇ).[28] This imaginative composition inaugurated the fashion of presenting the monastic life as a constant battle against the devil and his army of demons.[29] During subsequent decades, the *Life* enjoyed great success in the West and came to be regarded as the avatar of a new literary genre by Latin writers. Indeed, during the fourth and fifth centuries it influenced Latin rather than Greek writers. That is not as surprising as a priori considerations might seem to imply. For Athanasius circulated the *Life* among his ecclesiastical supporters outside Egypt, who in the late 350s were predominantly western bishops, and it was very soon translated into Latin. It was in fact translated twice within a few years of its composition. The earlier translation survives in a single manuscript of the tenth or eleventh century in the Vatican Library which attributes it to Jerome (Capitulum Sancti Petri A2, fol. 69ʳ: *incipit vita sancti Antonii monachi edita a sancto Hieronymo presbytero*). It is a crude almost word-for-word translation and probably did not circulate at all widely in the ancient world, although it has been

---

[27] This entry misleadingly equates the original *Life of Antony* with the metaphrastic *Life*: it was the latter that Montfaucon published in the Benedictine edition of Athanasius (PG 26.837–976).

[28] For modern editions of the Greek text and its translations into a variety of languages CPG 2101; on the two Latin versions, J. Fontaine, Handbuch der lateinischen Literatur 5 (München, 1989), §§ 599.2, 3.

[29] On 'monastic demons' and the importance of the Life as the fountainhead of this tradition, see V. Flint, Witchcraft and Magic in Europe, ed. B. Ankarloo and S. Clark, 2: Ancient Greece and Rome (London, 1999), 306–315.

edited no fewer than three times since its discovery nearly
a century ago (BHL 609e).[30] The other Latin translation,
which is preserved in many manuscripts, but of which there
is no modern critical edition, since it has not been edited
at all since the seventeenth century, was produced c. 370
by Evagrius, the friend of Jerome (BHL 609).[31] Evagrius
was an elegant translator who explains that he has avoided
a mechanical or literal translation in order to render the
meaning of the original more faithfully (PG 26.833–834
= PL 73.125–126: *ita transposui ut nihil desit ex sensu, cum
aliquid desit ex verbis. alii syllabas aucupentur et litteras, tu
quaere sententiam*). It was undoubtedly Evagrius' version of
the *Life of Antony* that two *agentes in rebus* came across in a
peasant's hut near Trier during the reign of Valentinian (Au-
gustin, *Conf.* 8.6.15). This was also the version that Jerome
read before he decided to invent a predecessor of Antony.

The panegyric which Gregory of Nazianzus delivered
as bishop of Constantinople in 380 praised Athanasius
for composing the *Life of Antony* as a monastic rule in the
form of a narrative (*Orat.* 21.5). Twelve years later Jerome's

---

[30] By G. Garitte (Rome, 1939), H. Hoppenbrouwers (Nijmegen,
1960) and G. J. M. Bartelink (Milan, 1974). The manuscript was first
drawn to scholarly attention by A. Wilmart, Revue bénédictine 31
(1914–1919), 163–173, who edited part of the text whose value he
had recognised.

[31] The best edition is by Bernard de Montfaucon, who printed
Evagrius' version with the Greek *Life of Antony* in his classic edition of Athanasius (Paris, 1698): both are reprinted together in PG
26.833–976. Migne also reprinted the earlier text of Rosweyde in his
Latin series (PL 73.125–170). Evagrius' epilogue closely copies the
epilogue added to the *Life* by the earlier translator, while his preface
is addressed to the priest Innocentius, who was dead by 372: Jerome,
*Ep.* 3.3, cf. J. N. D. Kelly, Jerome. His Life, Writings, and Controversies
(London, 1975), 39–40.

account of Christian writers in his *De Viris Illustribus* registered Athanasius as the author of the *Life of Antony* in its entries for both men (77, 78). For more than a millennium thereafter no-one doubted Athanasius' authorship until some Protestant scholars of the Reformation denied the traditional ascription of the *Life* in order to undermine its authority.[32] This partisan challenge was routed in 1698 by Bernard de Montfaucon in his great edition of Athanasius[33] – to such effect that Edward Gibbon's hostile and sceptical account of the rise of monasticism nowhere even hints that Athanasius' authorship might be doubted.[34]

Modern scholarly discussion began in 1876 when Hermann Weingarten argued that the depiction of early monasticism in the *Life* could not have been written during the lifetime of Athanasius, who died in 373.[35] The anachronisms alleged by Weingarten were soon disproved.[36] Nevertheless, the obvious and undeniable differences between the *Life of Antony* and Athanasius' other writings continued to arouse disquiet about whether Athanasius really was its author.

---

[32] The protagonists on each side are conveniently listed by A. Robertson, Select Writings and Letters of Athanasius, Bishop of Alexandria. Nicene and Post-Nicene Fathers II.4 (Grand Rapids, 1892), 188.

[33] In the *In Antonii vitam monitum* prefixed to his text (reprinted in PG 26.823–834).

[34] Gibbon, Decline and Fall, Chapter 37 (4.59–62 Bury = 2.413–415 Womersley).

[35] H. Weingarten, ZKG 1 (1876), 1–35, 545–574; Ursprung des Mönchtums im nachconstantinischen Alter (Gotha, 1877); 'Mönchtum,' Realenzyklopaedie für protestantische Theologie[2] 10 (1882), 758–792. His thesis was enthusiastically endorsed by H. M. Gwatkin, Studies of Arianism (Cambridge, 1882), 98–103, reprinted unchanged in the second edition (Cambridge, 1900), 102–107.

[36] See esp. A. Eichhorn, Athanasii de vita ascetica testimonia collecta (Diss. Halle, 1886); C. Butler, The Lausiac History of Palladius (Cambridge, 1898), 1.215–228.

The subjective case for doubting Athanasius' authorship was stated succinctly and eloquently by Owen Chadwick in 1968: since the *Life* shows the influence of a Pythagorean model and 'its strange desert atmosphere' is unlike anything else in Athanasius, Chadwick saluted the *Life* as 'a primitive document from the Egyptian desert,' but felt constrained to doubt whether it 'can have been written by St. Athanasius.'[37] Objective arguments against Athanasius' authorship began to be advanced again in 1980, when René Draguet published a critical edition of the Syriac translation of the *Life of Antony*, and argued that it rendered, not the extant Greek *Life*, but an otherwise unattested, more primitive version of the *Life* written in Copticising Greek by an unknown hand, of which the surviving Greek *Life* is an adaptation.[38] The first reaction to Draguet came from Martin Tetz in 1982, who acknowledged that the *Life of Antony* contains non-Athanasian features, and argued that the *Life* was not (or at least not wholly) an original composition by the bishop of Alexandria, but an adaptation of a written account of Antony supplied to him by Serapion of Thmuis, in which he left much of Serapion's original wording unchanged.[39]

---

[37] O. Chadwick, John Cassian[2] (Cambridge, 1968), 4–5. In the first edition (Cambridge, 1950), Chadwick had assumed without discussion that Athanasius was the author.

[38] R. Draguet, La vie primitive de S. Antoine conservée en syriaque. CSCO 418 = Scriptores Syri 184 (Louvain, 1980), 15*–112*.

[39] M. Tetz, ZNW 73 (1982), 1–30. The precise implications of the fact that Serapion refers to a written life of Antony circulating among the monks of Egypt shortly after 360 (*Ep. ad monachos* 13 [PG 40.940]) are unclear. The authenticity of Serapion's letter was denied by K. Fitschen, Serapion von Thmuis: Echte und unechte Schriften sowie die Zeugnisse des Athanasius und anderer (Berlin & New York, 1992), 79–84. His arguments are invalid: see JTS, N.S. 46 (1995), 329–330.

Tetz's theory has been slow to gain acceptance.[40] For some years, discussion focussed on the issue raised by Draguet. In 1986, a modification of Draguet's conclusions postulated a lost Coptic original translated directly into Syriac.[41] However, Rudolf Lorenz, Luise Abramowski and David Brakke demonstrated against Draguet that, despite significant textual differences, the Syriac version of the *Life* is based on the extant Greek version.[42] Moreover, Andrew Louth documented the occurrence in the *Life* of words, phrases and ideas which appear to be peculiar to Athanasius,[43] and Brakke integrated the *Life* into an analysis of the activities of Athanasius as an ecclesiastical politician, proclaiming that

[40] Although Tetz's study is listed in her bibliography, it does not seem to be cited in the text or footnotes of Averil Cameron, Greek Biography and Panegyric in Late Antiquity, ed. T. Hägg & P. Rousseau (Berkeley, 2000), 72–88, who asserts that the Life of Antony is 'fully compatible with the theology and political concerns of Athanasius.'

[41] JTS, N.S. 37 (1986), 353–368. Doubts about Athanasius' authorship were also voiced by J. Herrin, The Formation of Christendom (Princeton, 1987), 60 n. 23; P. Brown, The Body and Society. Men, Women and Sexual Renunciation in Early Christianity (New York, 1988), 213 n. 1.

[42] R. Lorenz, ZKG 100 (1989), 77–84; L. Abramowski, Mélanges Antoine Guillaumont (Geneva, 1988), 47–56; D. Brakke, Muséon 107 (1994), 29–53. The authenticity of seven letters attributed to Antony and preserved best in a Georgian translation is demonstrated by S. Rubenson, The Letters of St. Antony. Origenist Theology, Monastic Tradition and the Making of a Saint (Lund, 1990), 15–88. His comparison of the letters and the Life shows that the Life has transformed the humble monk of the letters into a saint (126–144). But that does not prove that the author of the Life must be Athanasius: see JTS, N.S. 42 (1991), 730–732.

[43] A. Louth, JTS, N.S. 39 (1988), 504–509, cf. H. Dörries, Wort und Stunde 1 (Göttingen, 1966), 145–224.

'there is no reason to remove the Greek *Life* from the corpus of authentic works by Athanasius.'[44]

It might thus seem that the repulse of recent challenges has definitively established Athanasius' authorship of the *Life of Antony*. Paradoxically, however, it has recently become easier to document the substantial presence of non-Athanasian elements in the *Life* more fully than before. For, when G. J. M. Bartelink produced the first proper critical edition of the Greek text in 1994, he compiled a full index of Greek words.[45] Hence it is now easy to make a systematic comparison of the vocabulary of the *Life* with the rest of the Athanasian corpus by collating Bartelink's 'index des mots grecs' with Guido Müller's lexicon to Athanasius.[46] The comparison tells very heavily against holding the *Life* to be an original composition by Athanasius himself.

More than two hundred Greek words used in the *Life* are not found elsewhere in Athanasius' extant writings except in documents quoted by Athanasius, though composed by another hand.[47] Admittedly, the absence of many of these words from Athanasius need prove nothing. Athanasius may never have had occasion, for example, to refer to bears (ἄρκτοι) or to measures of land such as *arourae*. Yet the occurrence in the *Life* of a common adverb like ἄγαν ('too much') and the emphasis on achieving ἀταραξία and avoid-

---

[44] Brakke, Muséon 107 (1994), 53; Athanasius and the Politics of Asceticism (Oxford, 1995).

[45] G. J. M. Bartelink, Athanase d'Alexandrie: Vie d'Antoine (SC 400, 1994), 391–425. Bartelink's text diverges from that of Montfaucon, which had been the standard text of the Life since 1698 (reprinted in PG 26.837–976) in more than four hundred places.

[46] G. Müller, Lexicon Athanasianum (Berlin, 1952).

[47] Almost sixty such words beginning with alpha are listed in JTS, N. S. 46 (1995), 330.

ing ἀκηδία, neither of which words belongs to Athanasius'
normal vocabulary, are hard to explain if Athanasius wrote
the *Life* as an original composition, as are three striking cases
of lexical divergence between the *Life* and Athanasius' undisputed writings. First, the adverb θεόθεν ('from God') occurs
twice in the *Life* (2.1, 50.1), but only once elsewhere in the
whole of the Athanasian corpus – as the Greek translation
of the Latin adverb *divinitus* in a letter of Julius, bishop of
Rome (*Apol. c. Arianos* 53.5 [134.21 Opitz]). Second, while
the neuter substantive κυριακόν is used to designate a church
building several times in the *Life*, Athanasius never uses the
word as a synonym of ἐκκλησία when he is speaking in his
own voice, although the usage was current in Alexandria
in his day, since it occurs five times in a document drawn
up by his congregation in his absence on 12 February 356
(*Hist. Arian.* 81 [228.29–230.20 Opitz]).[48] Third, whereas
the *Life* uses both μοναχός and μοναστήριον in their strict
etymological sense solely to designate a solitary ascetic and
his abode,[49] Athanasius uses both words in the conventional
senses of 'monk' and 'monastery' and applies them equally
to solitary ascetics and to cenobites and the places in which
they lived their solitary or communal lives.[50]

These lexical divergences are merely the most objective
and measurable criteria of profound differences of culture
and theology between the *Life* and the rest of Athanasius'
oeuvre. More than a century ago, the excellent Archibald

---

[48] Tetz, Athanasiana (n. 39), 176–179: Athanasius appears to have
added a passage which uses the word ἐκκλησία (2.3) into a pre-existing
story in which τὸ κυριακόν occurs three times (2.1–3.1).

[49] Bartelink, Vie d'Antoine (n. 45), 125 n. 2.

[50] Müller, Lexicon (n. 46), 922: note especially the commendations
of monks of both types in Athanasius, *Epistula ad Dracontium* 7 (PG
25.532 [306.10–26 Opitz-Brennecke]).

Robertson, though expressing himself in language which now sounds old-fashioned, gave an apt and valid summary of the theologically significant divergences: while Athanasius has very little to say about demons, the *Life* 'swarms with miraculous and demoniacal stories'; while Athanasius is surprisingly modern and rational – for example, in his letter to the monk Amoun on nocturnal emissions, which nowhere mentions demons (*PG* 26.1169–1176) –, the *Life* reveals a 'large credulity;' and nowhere in Athanasius can be found the 'anthropological tendency, shown especially in the corporeal nature attributed to demons' that permeates the *Life*.[51]

Recently, Istvan Perczel has added to the dossier of significant divergences by identifying a distinctively Origenist tinge in several passages of the *Life*.[52] While Perczel's claim that these prove the author to be 'deeply sympathetic to Origenism' is probably overstated, and his attempt to reinstate Draguet's thesis by arguing that Syriac *Life* is prior to the Greek because it more accurately reproduces material taken from the letters of Antony is unconvincing, he has significantly strengthened the case that the *Life* cannot be an entirely original composition by Athanasius.

The same conclusion can be established on yet another different front, when the level of culture and learning displayed in the *Life* is compared with Athanasius' other writings. Richard Reitzenstein showed in 1914 that the image in the *Life* of Antony emerging after twenty years of solitude

---

[51] Robertson, Select Writings (n. 32), 192, cf. Müller, Lexicon (n. 46), 271–272: δαίμονες appear far more frequently in the *Life* than in Athanasius' undisputed writings.

[52] I. Perczel, The Man of Many Devices, Who Wandered Full Many Ways, ed. B. Nagy and M. Sebök (Budapest, 1999), 197–213, on 20.2–9 and the use of τὸ νοερόν in 5.5, 45.2, 74.4/5.

'like a mystic initiate from a sanctuary, possessed by God'
(*Life* 14) is inspired by pagan depictions of Pythagoras.[53]
Athanasius, in contrast, though well schooled in the scriptures and biblical exegesis, shows virtually no knowledge
of classical Greek literature at all: his genuine writings are
totally devoid of detectable allusions to and borrowings
from the Greek poets, tragedians orators and philosophers.[54]

There is a serious and fundamental contradiction to be
resolved. The *Life of Antony* was composed almost immediately after its hero's death, and within a very few years Athanasius was universally accepted as its author. Yet the *Life*
contains much that Athanasius cannot be supposed to have
written. How can this curious state of affairs be explained?
The only hypothesis that saves all the phenomena appears
to be Tetz's theory that Athanasius edited, revised and put
into circulation a text that took and expanded a slavish transcription of an earlier written document supplied to him by
someone who knew Antony better than he did, whether or
not that person was (as Tetz argued) Serapion, the bishop of
Thmuis.[55] It is significant that one of the stoutest recent defenders of Athanasian authorship feels impelled to concede
that 'editorial work of Athanasius on previous material' is
obvious in some passages.[56] This is tantamount to accepting
Tetz's explanation of the non-Athanasian features of the *Life*

---

[53] R. Reitzenstein, SB Heidelberg 1914, 14–17: for comment on
some of his other arguments and his far-reaching conclusions, see now
G. Staab, Pythagoras in der Spätantike. Studien zu *De Vita Pythagorica*
des Iamblichos von Chalkis (Munich & Leipzig, 2002), 26, 125 n. 298,
263 n. 660, 281 n. 701.

[54] Athanasius (1993), 11. Gregory of Nazianzus, *Orat.* 21.6, felt
constrained to justify Athanasius' ignorance of the Greek classics.

[55] Tetz, Athanasiana (n. 39), 160–165, 173–182.

[56] Brakke, Athanasius (n. 42), 207.

without explicitly admitting that the prevailing scholarly orthodoxy is mistaken.

The preface to the *Life* clarifies the situation. Athanasius writes to monks outside Egypt who, after hearing news of Antony's death, have requested a fuller account of his way of life so that they may imitate it. In reply to their request, Athanasius apologises that he is pressed for time (pr. 4/5):

> When I received your letter, I wished to send for some of the monks who were in the habit of visiting him most frequently. (Perhaps if I learn more I may send you a fuller report.) However, since the sailing season is drawing to a close and the messenger is in a hurry, I have hastened to write to your piety both what I know at first hand (for I have seen him often) and what I have been able to discover from the man who was his follower for a long period and 'poured water on his hands' (2 Kings 3.11).

In this passage, the manuscripts offer two significantly different versions of the crucial phrase. The text printed by Montfaucon and translated into English by Robert Gregg in 1980 makes Athanasius himself claim to have played Elisha to Antony's Elijah.[57] But, as Ludwig von Hertling argued in 1929, the correct reading applies the Old Testament comparison, not to Athanasius himself, but to another who was his main source of information.[58] Hertling's choice of

---

[57] R. C. Gregg, Athanasius: The Life of Antony and the Letter to Marcellinus (New York, 1980), 30: 'when I followed him more than a few times and poured water over his hands.' In a note on the passage, Gregg comments that 'it is difficult to know what this statement conveys about the author's relationship to his subject' (135 n. 3) – but he does not mention the correct readings, which Montfaucon discussed and rejected in a long note on the passage (*PG* 26.839–840 n. 15). The erroneous reading is ancient: see T. Vivian, The Coptic Life of Antony (San Francisco, 1995), 30–31.

[58] L. von Hertling, Antonius der Einsiedler (Innsbruck, 1929), 7–9 n. 1.

variants was accepted by Robert Meyer when he translated the *Life* in 1950,[59] his arguments were restated by Tetz in 1982,[60] and Bartelink prints the reading which Hertling defended – and which has superior manuscript attestation,[61] David Brakke has translated Bartelink's text into English.[62]

Athanasius acknowledges that he is substantially indebted to a follower of Antony, whom he does not name and whom he implicitly (and disingenuously) represents as an oral rather than a written source. It is thus misleading either to assert or to deny that Athanasius is the author of the *Life of Antony* without making a necessary qualification. Athanasius circulated the *Life* outside Egypt and added a prefatory letter, but he transcribed much of the *Life* from a source, apparently with minimal rewriting. Hence it will remain in doubt whether Athanasius should best be described as author, editor or redactor until it is established in detail by further philological and stylistic investigation exactly how he modified the source or model which his preface explicitly states that he employed.

## Jerome

Jerome's three 'lives of the hermits' tend to be treated together as a group and are often assimilated to one another as

---

[59] R. T. Meyer, St. Athanasius: The Life of Saint Antony (Westminster, MD, 1950), 18: his note states the difference between the two versions accurately and recognises that von Hertling established which of the two must be correct.

[60] See now Tetz, Athanasiana (n. 39), 161–162.

[61] Bartelink, Vie d'Antoine (n. 45), 128, 129 n. 2.

[62] D. Brakke, in: Medieval Hagiography: An Anthology (New York & London, 2000), 1–30.

if they were fundamentally alike.[63] That procedure may do
little harm in the hands of an ironic historian like Gibbon,
who praised the three together as 'admirably told,' but added
the memorable complaint that 'the only defect of these
pleasing compositions is the want of truth and common-
sense.'[64] It becomes a serious bar to understanding when all
three are treated as if they formed three parts of a trilogy,[65]
or when they are put on exactly the same level of historicity,
whether all three are assumed to be fundamentally truthful
or all three are characterised as 'romances of monastic life.'[66]
Although the three texts all 'combine *realia* with rhetoric'
and reflect not only the world in which Jerome lived, but
also his conceptual universe,[67] nevertheless, profound differences exist between them, which Pierre de Labriolle stated
accurately and succinctly long ago.[68]

The three works were written at different times, and each
is a separate and independent composition with a character
of its own. Each of the three has a very different textual history and transmission, and only a small proportion of the
numerous medieval manuscripts that contain their Latin

---

[63] As by S. Rubenson, Greek Biography and Panegyric in Late
Antiquity, ed. T. Hägg & P. Rousseau (Berkeley, 2000), 119–124.

[64] Gibbon, Decline and Fall, Chapter XXXVII n. 17 (4.61 Bury =
2.415–416 Womersley).

[65] C. Mohrmann, Vite dei Santi 4 (Milan, 1975), xl: the Life of Hilarion is 'la terza della trilogia di vite di monaci composta da Girolamo.'

[66] So, respectively, E. Coleiro, Vig. Chr. 11 (1957), 178, cf. 161 ('a
group with particular features of its own'); H. Hagendahl, Latin Fathers
and the Classics (Gothenburg, 1958), 105, 117, 118.

[67] See the full study by S. Weingarten, The Saint's Saints. Hagiography and Geography in Jerome (Leiden & Boston, 2005), esp. 267–270.

[68] P. de Labriolle, Histoire de l'Église, ed. A. Fliche and V. Martin,
3: De la paix constantinienne à la mort de Théodose (Paris, 1936),
308–310.

text contain all three opuscules.[69] Although *the Life of Hilarion* contains some vivid invention, it is in essence a historical composition, the biography of a real holy man, compiled in large part from written and oral sources. The *Life of Paul*, in contrast, is complete fiction and the only episode treated in any detail is the death of its hero, who is himself an invention of its author,[70] while the so-called *Life of Malchus* (BHL 5190) makes no pretence to be a biography at all. Jerome stated its title as 'the captive monk' (*De viris illustribus* 135). It is has a totally different literary character from his two real essays in hagiography and it contains no miracles.[71] Moreover, although editors fail to make clear what title or titles stand in the Latin manuscripts, the Greek translation explicitly styles it a 'narration' (διήγησις) not a life.[72]

In the last chapter of his *De viris illustribus*, Jerome gives list of his writings 'as far as the present year, that is, the fourteenth year of the emperor Theodosius' (135: *usque*

---

[69] They are now conveniently edited together in the light of important manuscript studies in the twentieth century by E. M. Morales, Jérôme: Trois Vies de Moines (Paul, Malchus, Hilarion) (SC 508, 2007), with a French translation by P. Leclerc and an introduction by the two scholars already named and A. de Vogüé.

[70] Jerome himself later described the contents of the Life: *'Paulo … cuius nos exitum brevi libello explicuimus'* (*Chronicle* 240[b] Helm).

[71] M. Fuhrmann, Entretiens Fondation Hardt 23 (Vandoeuvres – Geneva, 1976), 58–68.

[72] The Greek version (BHG 1016) was published by P. van den Ven, Muséon, N.S. 1 (1900), 434–450, whose text was reprinted by H. C. Jameson, Studies in the Text Tradition of St. Jerome's Vitae Patrum, ed. W. A. Oldfather and others (Urbana, 1943), 523–532. It is a translation from Jerome's Latin: H. C. Jameson, TAPA 69 (1938), 411–422; S. Schiwietz, Das morgenländische Mönchtum 3 (Mödling bei Wien, 1938), 217–220. There is also a Syriac version, translated from the Greek (BHO 585), of which van den Ven published an excerpt (Muséon, N.S. 1 [1900], 450–455).

*in praesentem annum, id est, Theodosii principis quartum decimum, haec scripsi*), which corresponds to the calendar year 392.[73] The first item in the list, which appears to be in chronological order is the *Vita Pauli monachi*, written in the second half of the 370s.[74] Towards the end, immediately before Jerome's Latin translations of the New Testament from Greek and the Old Testament from Hebrew, come (in the accusative case, still governed by the initial *scripsi*) *captivum monachum, vitam beati Hilarionis* – in that order. The place of the two works in the list and the fact that the former calls Jerome's friend Evagrius *papa* (2) fixes their date of composition as c. 390, since Jerome must be writing after Evagrius became bishop of the old-Nicenes in Antioch in 388/389 (Theodoret, *HE* 5.23.2–4).[75] Moreover, Jerome makes it clear that the *Captive Monk* is the earlier of the pair. Hence it is perverse and mistaken to basis an analysis of the *Captive Monk* on the stated assumption that Jerome wrote it after the *Life of Hilarion*, modified views assumed there and replaced the earlier 'lengthy and rather rambling' *Life* with 'a new literary creation' that was 'more tightly controlled.'[76]

---

[73] In Tertullian (1971), 235–236, I argued that Jerome meant Theodosius' regnal year calculated from his *dies imperii*, i. e., the twelve months that ran from 19 January 392 to 18 January 393. That was mistaken. Jerome was using regnal years which corresponded to Julian calendar years: since he had equated 14 Valens with 378 in his continuation of Eusebius' *Chronicle* (7.1–5, 18.10–12, 249 Helm), he regarded the following year (379) as 1 Theodosius. P. Nautin, RHE 56 (1961), 33–35, had fallaciously equated the fourteenth year of Theodosius with the calendar year 393.

[74] The conventional date is c. 375, but Kelly, Jerome (n. 31), 60–61, dates it slightly later.

[75] Kelly, Jerome (n. 31), 170.

[76] Weingarten, The Saint's Saints (n. 67), 165.

Jerome begins the *Captive Monk* by comparing what he
is about to write to the battle-training of marines preparing
for a sea-fight. He has long been silent, his tongue is rusty,
he will write a short work to prepare himself for a projected
history of the church from the days of the apostles to the
dregs of the present (*ad huius temporis faecem*): for the
church, which grew to maturity through persecutions and
martyrdoms, declined in virtue after it gained power and
wealth under Christian emperors. Jerome reports, using the
form of a first-person narrative, what he heard as a young
man many years before from the aged Malchus in the village
of Maronia, which lies almost thirty miles east of Antioch.

Malchus was the only child of a tenant-farmer in the
territory of Nisibis.[77] He fled to the desert of Chalcis to be
a monk when his parents urged him to marry. After many
years, when his father died, he returned home to console his
mother, despite severe admonitions from his abbot that he
should remain. Between Beroea and Edessa, Malchus was
captured by marauding Arabs, enslaved and set to guard
flocks of sheep in the inner desert. His life as a shepherd
replicated that of a monk, and Malchus was happy until his
master rewarded him by giving him a fellow slave as his wife.
When Malchus refused, his master almost killed him. During the night, however, he discovered that the woman shared
his ideals and they decided to live together in a wholly chaste
marriage to appease their master.

Malchus was again entrusted with the care of flocks
and was absent for as much as a month at a time. At last

---

[77] Although Mierow, Classical Essays presented to J.A. Kleist
(1946), 37, prints *Marionati agelli colonus*, the text locates the farm
close to Roman and Persian frontier posts, and most of the mss. have
*Nisibeni*, even if sometimes in a garbled form: H.C. Jameson, Studies
in the Text Tradition (n. 72), 452, 459, 489.

he began to recall his monastery and, inspired by seeing the cooperative endeavour of ants,[78] he decided to escape. His wife agreed. So Malchus killed two goats to provide food during their flight and to make leather bags which they could inflate in order to cross the river, which was ten miles away. The two fled one evening, crossed a river (8.3),[79] then travelled by night hiding by day. On the third day, they saw two men on camels pursuing them and took refuge in a nearby cave. First a servant, then their master entered the cave to apprehend them, but each in turn was killed by a lioness as soon as he entered the cave. When the lioness saw Malchus and his wife, however, she picked up her cub and departed. In the evening, the pair mounted the camels, which were still waiting, set out across the desert and reached a Roman camp on the tenth day. They told their story to the tribune in command, who sent them to Sabinianus, the *dux* of Mesopotamia (10.2), who bought the camels.[80] Malchus then returned to his monastery, with his wife joining a nearby community of holy virgins.

Jerome concludes by pointing the moral of the tale, which is 'a story of chastity for the chaste': he instructs his readers to repeat it so that posterity will know that even among swords, deserts and beasts sexual purity cannot be taken

---

[78] The wording contains a clear reminiscence of Virgil, *Aen.* 4.402–407: *formicae … hiemis memores … calle angusto … fervet*.

[79] Perhaps the River Chaboras, cf. E. Sachau, Verhandlungen der Gesellschaft für Erdkunde zu Berlin 9 (1882), 144–148. Morales & Leclerc, Trois Vies de Moines (2007), 204–205, merely adduce Sallust, *Iugurtha* 91.1–2, as Jerome's probable literary model.

[80] The *dux Sabinianus* is identified with the Sabinianus who was appointed *magister militum per Orientem* in 359 (Ammianus 18.5.5, 6.1) by R. P. C. Blockley, East Roman Policy. Formation and Conduct from Diocletian to Anastasius (Leeds, 1992), 180, cf. PLRE 1 (1971), 788, Sabinanus (sic).

captive and that a true Christian may die, but cannot be overcome. Measured by its purpose, therefore, the *Captive Monk* is 'a paean in praise of life-long chastity.'[81] But its content, style and literary form have more in common with a novelette or adventure story than with the life of a saint,[82] and some serious scholars have regarded the work as wholly frivolous.[83]

The lives of Paul and Hilarion, by contrast, represent successive attempts to outdo the *Life of Antony*.[84] The *Life of Paul* (BHL 6596) is one of Jerome's very earliest works.[85] In it the young ascetic set out to create a literary stir, and he employed a style that is 'sometimes rather exuberant,'[86]

---

[81] Kelly, Jerome (n. 31), 171. Kelly continues with a valuable brief appreciation of the work as both a story and a historical source for conditions in fourth century Syria (172). But what Kelly calls the 'accurately observed details of locality' are mere incidentals: Jerome never names the *grandis amnis* within ten miles of which Malchus is held captive in the interior *solitudo* (6, 8). It is identified as the Euphrates by Schiwietz, Mönchtum 3 (n. 72), 223 n. 9.

[82] Hagendahl, Latin Fathers (n. 66), 118, detects reminiscences of only three classical authors, viz., Vergil, [Quintilian], *Declamatio maior* 13.2, and Seneca, *Troades* 510–512, which Jerome has restated in Christian terms: see G. E. Duckworth, Class. Bull. 24 (1947/48), 29

[83] Rubenson, Greek Biography and Panegyric in Late Antiquity (n. 63), 120: 'Jerome writes … simply to amuse.' This verdict is disputed at length by Weingarten, The Saint's Saints (n. 67), 165–192, who argues that the work 'presents the Christian takeover of the human body' (167).

[84] Fuhrmann, Christianisme (n. 71), 82–89; A. A. R. Bastiaensen, Hagiographies, ed. G. Philippart 1 (Turnhout, 1994), 107–110, 113–115.

[85] The prudish and heavily expurgated edition by I. S. Kozik, The First Desert Hero: St Jerome's Vita Pauli (Mount Vernon, N. Y., 1968), completely omits the section selected here for full discussion.

[86] Hagendahl, Latin Fathers (n. 66), 105, explaining the style as 'corresponding to the extravagancies of the tale.' Besides Jerome's com-

even though he told Paul of Concordia, to whom he sent the work for circulation in Italy, that he had laboured hard to lower the style for the benefit of less cultured readers (*Ep.* 10.3: *in quo propter simpliciores quosque multum in deiciendo sermone laboravimus*). There has been much discussion, Jerome begins, about who was the first monk to inhabit the desert. Some have adduced Elijah and John the Baptist as avatars, but it is generally agreed that Antony was the *caput* of the practice. That belief, so Jerome avers, is only true in part. For, although Antony, whose life is recorded in both Greek and Latin, inspired everyone else, his disciples Amathas and Macarius admit that he had an unacknowledged predecessor, a certain Paul of Thebes. Jerome has therefore decided to write briefly about his origin and end of his life, for no man knows how he lived his life, what attacks he endured of the devil.

Paul founded monasticism at the time when Decius and Valerian were persecuting the Christians. It was the time when Cornelius suffered martyrdom at Rome and Cyprian in Carthage, and when the Christians of Egypt and the Thebaid suffered savage maltreatment. Jerome produces two examples. One martyr, who had already endured the rack and searing metal, was bound, smeared with honey and exposed to the scorching sun to be tortured by flies. Another young man was taken into a cool, pleasant and sweet-smelling garden, where he was tied naked to a bed. A beautiful courtesan entered, caressed and fondled him, and began to arouse his desires. The soldier of Christ did not know what to do: after conquering torture, he was succumbing to pleasure. So,

---

bination of two lines from the Aeneid (9, quoting *Aen.* 2.650 + 6.672), Hagendahl identifies two other allusions to Virgil, one to Horace, *Ep.* 1.2.69–70, and a close imitation of Florus 1.40.7.

inspired by heaven, he bit off his tongue and spat it into the woman's face as she kissed him, so that the pain subdued his lust. Both these examples have a novelistic tinge.[87] While indulging his fervid imagination Jerome has drawn on his wide reading, so that his language is replete with classical allusions remembered, modified and moulded together. Can his precise inspiration be identified? The first example recalls the heroic endurance of Mark, the bishop of Arethusa, in the reign of Julian: after being beaten and pricked with styluses by schoolboys, he was covered in garum and honey and exposed to be stung by wasps and flies (Theodoretus, *HE* 3.7.8–10; Sozomenus, *HE* 5.10.11–14). But it may also owe something to Apuleius (*Met.* 8.22) or to a story told about the treatment of the followers of Epicurus in Crete (Aelian, frag. 39 = Suda E 2405 [2.364 Adler]).[88] In the second episode, the description of the garden recalls similar passages in Greek novels in language evocative of Virgil and Ovid.[89] The youth who bit off his tongue represents a deliberate inversion of one of the most familiar classical *exempla* of fortitude: a philosopher or suspected conspirator, who is being tortured to reveal the names of accomplices in an assassination or attempted assassination, bites off his tongue and spits it in the tyrant's face in order to avoid betraying the

---

[87] See K. Kerenyi, Die griechisch-orientalische Romanliteratur (Tübingen, 1927), 208; J. B. Bauer, Wiener Studien 74 (1961), 130–137.

[88] Bauer, Wiener Studien 74 (1961), 132–133.

[89] Bauer, Wiener Studien 74 (1961), 136, adduced Longus 2.3, 4.2–3; Achilles Tatius 1.15 and the Song of Songs 2.1, 2.16, 6.2, 8.13. As Jerome's probably unconscious models, note Virgil, *Aen.* 12.68–69: *mixta rubent ubi lilia multa / alba rosa*; Ovid, *Met.* 2.455–456: *murmure labens / ibat … rivus*; 7.186: *cum murmure serpit*; 12.411: *interdum candentia lilia gestet*; *Am.* 2.5.37: *quale rosae fulgent inter sua lilia mixtae*. It should be observed that '*aquarum*' after '*murmure*,' printed by Vallarsi (*PL* 23.19), has no manuscript attestation.

names. The story is variously told: in Valerius Maximus and Diogenes Laertius the hero is Anaxarchus, in Eusebius he is Zeno of Elea, in Ammianus Marcellinus Zeno the Stoic.[90] In the most common version, however, which occurs in Pliny the Elder, Tertullian, Iamblichus and Jerome's *Chronicle*, the Athenian whore Leaena spits her tongue in the face of the tyrant Hippias after the assassination of his brother Hipparchus.[91] Jerome has probably adapted Tertullian, and he later recorded Leaena's fortitude under the appropriate date in his *Chronicle* (106ᵃ Helm: *linguam suam mordicus amputavit*). Tertullian had used the example in reference to the persecution of Christians and he presented it as an act of defiance after the heroine had worn out her torturers.[92] Jerome has simply rearranged the elements of the story with the freedom of a novelist.

Paul was an adolescent of sixteen at the time of his temptation. He withdrew to a remote villa to escape persecution, but his sister's husband wished to betray him – another stock motif with no basis in the history of the 250s. Paul fled into the mountains, where he found a cave with rusted anvils and hammers which had been used to mint coins in the days of Antony and Cleopatra. There Paul fixed his abode and dwelt inconspicuously for almost a full century: when he was one hundred and twelve, he was visited by Antony, a

---

[90] Valerius Maximus 8.3 ext. 4; Diogenes Laertius 9.59; Eusebius, *PE* 10.14.15; Ammianus 14.9.6.

[91] Pliny, *NH* 7.57, 34.72; Tertullian, *Ad Nat.* 1.18.4: *tormenta mulier Attica fatigavit tyranno negans* etc.); *Apol.* 50.8; Iamblichus, *De vita Pythagorica*, p. 271 Kiessling; Jerome, *Chronicle* 106.4–7 Helm. Ambrose transformed Leaena into a virgin disciple of Pythagoras (*De Virginibus* 1.4.17 [*PL* 16.204]: *Pythagorea quaedam una ex virginibus* etc.).

[92] Tertullian, *Apol.* 50.8: *Attica quaedam meretrix carnifice iam fatigato postremo linguam suam comesam in faciem tyranni saevientis exspuit.*

mere nonagenarian. Arithmetic, if it were a valid indicator when considering the life of man who is alleged to have lived to the age of 105, points to a dramatic date of 341.

At this juncture, Jerome abruptly shifts focus. He narrates the visit of Antony to Paul as a forgotten episode in the life of Antony. It occupies two thirds of the total text (7–16) and is presented as deriving from Antony himself (7: *ut ipse asserere solebat*; 15: *referebat postea beatus Antonius*). Antony, who believed himself to be the only perfect monk, was informed in a dream that there was a much better monk, whom he ought to visit. On his way he came across a hippocentaur, crossed himself and said: 'Hey, you! In what part hereabouts does the servant of God live?' The animal emitted a barbarous sound, indicated the way with its right hand, and galloped off. As he continued on his way a little surprised, Antony met a tiny man with a hooked nose, horns and the feet of a goat, who offered him some dates. When Antony asked who he was, the creature informed him that he was a mortal, one of the inhabitants of the desert, whom pagans call fauns, satyrs and *incubi* and whom they worship, sent by his flock to ask Antony to pray for them. Antony wept for joy that animals should proclaim God while the city of Alexandria still worshipped false gods.

After the homunculus fled, Antony continued his journey and reached Paul, who was eager to learn what had happened in the world. A raven appeared with a loaf of bread instead of the half a loaf which God had sent Paul daily for sixty years. The two holy men then disputed all day long which of them should break the bread: finally they compromised with each taking hold of one end and tugging until the loaf split in two. The following day, after a night of wakeful prayer, Paul told his visitor that his own death was at hand and that God had sent Antony to bury him: accordingly, he asked him to go and bring the pallium which Athanasius had given him as his burial shroud. Antony returned to his monastery, retrieved the pallium, and hastened back to Paul. When he was three hours from his destination, he saw Paul ascending to heaven surrounded by angels, prophets and apostles. Antony hurried on and found Paul dead but kneeling in the posture of prayer. He prepared the body for burial, then realised that he had no shovel to dig a grave. Suddenly, two lions appeared, respectfully lay down at the feet of the dead man, and roared to show their grief. They then dug a grave with their paws, approached Antony and licked his hands and feet. He blessed them and motioned them to depart. When they had gone, he put Paul in the grave which they had dug and covered him with earth. He then returned to his monastery taking with him the tunic of palm leaves that Paul had made for himself, which he wore every Easter and Pentecost.

His story completed, Jerome invites the rich to contemplate the difference between them and Paul. They may live in luxurious houses, drink from jewelled goblets, wear silken clothes with gold thread, but they will go to gehenna and burn with their wealth. In his humble life of poverty, the apparently destitute Paul lacked nothing needful, and now he is in paradise destined for a glorious resurrection (17). Finally, a brief concluding paragraph requests readers to remember Jerome the sinner, who would gladly choose the tunic and virtues of Paul over royal purple and its penalties (18).

How seriously did its author intend this tissue of literary commonplaces and inventions to be taken? Is it anything more than the *jeu d'esprit* of a young man determined to make his mark in the world? Delehaye produced what he believed to be evidence that Paul of Thebes was a real person.[93] But the document that Delehaye adduced, the *libellus precum* submitted by the Luciferian priests Marcellinus and Faustinus to the emperors Valentinian, Theodosius and Arcadius speaks of a Paul who was active in Oxyrhynchus when George was bishop of Alexandria, that is between 357 and 361 (*Collectio Avellana* 2.93–94 [CSEL 35.1.33–34]). Admittedly, the petitioners assume that this Paul is identical with 'the most blessed Paul, who lived at the same period as that most famous Antony and was not inferior to the holy Antony in his life, zeal and divine grace' (CSEL 35.1.33.17–19). But that merely shows a desire to turn an obscure local hero into a famous person, specifically into the Paul whom Jerome had celebrated.[94] Jerome's invented Paul came from distant Thebes and cannot be identified with the historical Paul of Oxyrhynchus. Hence there is no evidence independent of Jerome that Paul ever existed.[95] More recently, the clerical author of a biography of Jerome, though he concedes the total lack of corroboration, asserts that he 'was obviously convinced that he was dealing with a historical figure.'[96] But what may be obvious to the believer

---

[93]    H. Delehaye, AB 44 (1926), 64–69.

[94]    F. Cavallera, Revue d'ascétique et de mystique 7 (1926), 302–305.

[95]    Severus, *Dial.* 1.17.1, need prove no more than that Severus had read Jerome's *Life of Paul* (Chapter V, at nn. 49–50). Despite F. Nau, ROC 10 (1905), 387–417, who argued the contrary, the Greek versions of the *Life of Paul* are translations of Jerome's Latin: see J. Bidez, Deux versions grecques inédites de la Vie de Paul de Thèbes (Ghent, 1900), vi–xlviii; K. T. Corey, Studies in the Text Tradition of St. Jerome's Vitae Patrum (Urbana 1943), 143–250. Jerome might nevertheless, have used some authentic sayings of the desert fathers later incorporated in the *apophthegmata patrum*, as argued by Nau, ROC 10 (1905), 395–397.

[96]    Kelly, Jerome (n. 31), 61, followed by Weingarten, The Saint's Saints (n. 67), 19–20, cf. P. Rousseau, Ascetics, Authority and the Church in the Age of Jerome and Cassian (Oxford, 1978), 133: 'the Life of Paul was not pure fiction.'

need not be so to the sceptic.[97] Ronald Syme took it for granted that Jerome invented Paul along with all the corroborative detail, and he quoted a revealing remark from the *Life*: 'these things will seem incredible to those who do not believe that all things are possible for those who believe' (6 [PL 23.22]: *haec igitur incredibilia videbuntur his qui non credunt omnia possibilia esse credentibus*).[98] And a historian of early monasticism dismissed the *Life* with the cutting verdict that most of what it contains is of such a nature that proof of its historical impossibility is otiose.[99] On the other hand, the *Life of Paul*, precisely because it is total fiction, reveals more about its author than he probably wished to disclose about himself, in particular his appropriation of Jewish *aggadah* and his adaptation of it to his own purposes.[100]

Jerome immediately despatched a copy of the *Life of Paul* to Paul of Concordia in north Italy with a covering letter (*Ep.* 10). But if Jerome's aim was to win literary renown by outdoing the *Life of Antony*, he was not entirely successful. Some contemporaries, perhaps even the majority, complained that Jerome had invented Paul, not discovered a genuine predecessor of Antony. Hence Jerome decided to supply authenticating evidence. He included an entry for Paul in the revised and expanded version of Eusebius'

[97] For a survey of modern opinions on the intellectual honesty of Jerome, Bastiaensen, Hagiographies 1 (n. 84), 110–113.
[98] R. Syme, Ammianus and the Historia Augusta (Oxford, 1968), 80, 82, 83. Earlier in the same chapter Jerome had invoked Jesus and his angels in support of his veracity (PL 23.21: *quod ne cui incredibile videatur, Jesum testor et sanctos angelos eius.*)
[99] K. Heussi, Der Ursprung des Mönchtums (Tübingen, 1936), 70 n. 2: 'Was die Vita im einzelnen zu berichten weiss, ist zumeist derartig, dass ein Nachweis der geschichtlichen Unmöglichkeit sich erübrigt.'
[100] Weingarten, The Saint's Saints (n. 67), 42–80.

*Chronicle*, which he completed in Constantinople in 380 and took to Rome in the next year:

*Antonius monachus cv aetatis anno in heremo moritur solitus multis ad se venientibus de Paulo quodam Thebaeo mirae beatitudinis viro referre, cuius nos exitum brevi libello explicuimus* (Jerome, *Chronicle* 240[b] Helm)

Antony the monk died in the desert at the age of 105. He was in the habit of talking to the many who came to see him about one Paul of Thebes, a man of remarkable blessedness whose death I have narrated in a short pamphlet.

The preface to the *Life of Hilarion* implies that even after the publication of the *Chronicle* Jerome's critics were still complaining that someone who had passed his whole life without being noticed by anyone probably never existed. Jerome therefore made a second attempt to outdo the *Life of Antony*: this time he wrote the life of a saint who was a known historical figure and for whose activities evidence still survives that is entirely independent of Jerome in an ecclesiastical historian writing in the middle of the fifth century.

Sozomenus was a native of Bethelia in the territory of Gaza. His grandfather was born a pagan, but he, all his household and the family of Alaphion embraced Christianity when the monk Hilarion cured Alaphion of a demon by invoking the name of Christ (*HE* 5.15.14–17). Epiphanius was from the village of Besanduca in the district of Eleutheropolis. From an early age Epiphanius associated with monks, and after visiting Egypt he returned to practise asceticism in Palestine, where he came under the influence of Hilarion. Subsequently Epiphanius went to Cyprus to introduce monasticism there – and was elected metropolitan bishop of Salamis (*HE* 6.32.1–6).[101] Some time later, when

---

[101]  The date must be 367 or 368, since Epiphanius had been bishop

Hilarion, who had spent several years in Egypt, Sicily and Dalmatia, came to Cyprus, Epiphanius welcomed him and encouraged him to remain (*HE* 5.10.1–4). When Hilarion died in Cyprus, apparently in 371 or thereabouts,[102] Epiphanius announced his death in a laudatory letter, which later provided the main documentary source for both Jerome and Sozomenus when they described the life of the Palestinian hermit.[103]

Jerome had not included Hilarion in his continuation of Eusebius' *Chronicle* (composed and revised in 379–381), and no specific cause can be identified to explain why he suddenly decided shortly after 390 to compose a full biography, unless it was to write a serious work of hagiography at last. The *Life of Hilarion* (BHL 3879) is both much longer than the *Life of Paul* and quite different in nature. As a recent analysis has observed, Jerome shows how 'the Christian must conquer pagan society from within, and come to terms with all aspects of power and popular culture' and he achieves this aim by appropriating 'the most popular and threatening form of classical literature – the novel:' in particular, Jerome takes and adapts phrases and images from

---

of Salamis for thirty six years when he died in 403 (Palladius, *Dialogue* 16.206–207 Malingrey = 56, p. 99.18 Coleman Norton).

[102] V. de Buck, AASS, Oct. IX (1869), 30, fixed the day of his death as 21 October 371.

[103] Sozomenus, *HE* 3.14.21–27, has close parallels to Jerome, *Life of Hilarion* 2–6, 9–11, 45–47 and *HE* 5.10.1–4 to *Life* 35–40. W. Israël, ZWT 23 (1880), 132–137, argued that Sozomenus used Jerome, not Epiphanius' lost letter: he was refuted by D. O. Zöckler, Neue Jahrbücher für deutsche Theologie 3 (1894), 146–178. However, the Greek versions of the *Life of Hilarion* (BHG 751z, 752–754) derive from Jerome's Latin: S. Schiwietz, Das morgenländische Mönchtum 2 (Mainz, 1913), 95–100; R. F. Stout, Studies in the Textual Tradition of St. Jerome's Vitae Patrum (1943), 306–448.

Apuleius' novel *The Golden Ass* or *Metamorphoses* to compose Christian hagiography as it were in counterpoint to pagan pornography.[104]

The preface to the *Life of Hilarion* presents a notorious problem of literary priority. It contains a passage so close in both thought and wording to a passage in the introduction to the *Vita Probi* (1.1–2) in the *Historia Augusta* that one author must have copied the other. In the recent age scholars have disputed the direction of derivation at some length (and with some asperity).[105] Both lives echo and adapt passages from two standard classical authors. First, Sallust is invoked to prove that the *virtus* of those who record great deeds is no less than that of those who perform them, subtly combining two passages from the *Bellum Catilinae* (2.3, 8.4).[106] They then paraphrase, without naming him, Cicero's version of what Alexander the Great said at the tomb of Achilles: 'How fortunate you were, young man, to enjoy a great proclaimer of your desserts!' (Cicero, *Pro Archia* 24). In the present context, the question of whether the *Historia Augusta* copies Jerome or vice versa can cheerfully be waived, since the direc-

---

[104] Weingarten, The Saint's Saints (n. 67), 81–154.

[105] In favour of the priority of Jerome, see B. Schmeidler, Phil. Woch. 47 (1927), 955–960; J. Straub, Heidnische Geschichtsapologetik in der christlichen Spätantike (Bonn, 1963), 81–105; Syme, Ammianus (n. 98), 80–83; A. Chastagnol, Recherches sur l'Histoire Auguste (Bonn, 1970), 12–16; T. D. Barnes, Historiae Augustae Colloquia, N. S. II: Colloquium Parisinum (Macerata, 1992), 23–27; Historiae Augustae Colloquia, N. S. VII: Colloquium Genevense (Bari, 1999), 34–35; of the priority of the *Historia Augusta*, Alan Cameron, JRS 55 (1965), 244–245; 61 (1971), 257–259; N. Adkin, Klio 79 (1997), 459–467; Alan Cameron, The Last Pagans of Rome (2011), Chapter XX.

[106] On Jerome's frequent quotations and adaptations of Sallust, see E. Lübeck, Hieronymus quos noverit scriptores et ex quibus hauserit (Leipzig, 1872), 117–122; Hagendahl, Latin Fathers (n. 66), 292–294.

tion of which borrows from the other makes little difference to understanding Jerome's use of Sallust and Cicero. He uses pagan writers in an elaborate plea for inspiration from the Holy Spirit which also serves to stake his claim to equality of esteem with his subject, and he points the comparison between Alexander and Hilarion: he is about to describe the life and conduct of one so great that even Homer would either envy Jerome his material or be unequal to it. Jerome admits that Epiphanius, the bishop of Salamis, who knew Hilarion well, praised him in a letter which is widely read (1.5). But Epiphanius' letter was a brief conventional laudation full of commonplaces: in contrast he will describe the unique achievements of Hilarion as an individual. And he will pay no attention to carping critics who will complain as much about this life as they complained about the *Life of Paul*, though for the opposite reason – just like the Pharisees of the Gospels who criticised Jesus for eating and drinking no less than they criticised John for fasting (Mt. 11.18–19).

After a preface that adapts Sallust and Cicero (whether at first or second hand), it is not surprising that the structure of the *Life of Hilarion* conforms as closely to the pattern of an ancient encomiastic biography as is consistent with its Christian subject and purpose.[107] Jerome knew much about Hilarion from Epiphanius (cf. Sozomenus, *HE* 3.14.21–27; 5.10.1–4), from whom he was able to take authentic and valuable details which Sozomenus chose to leave out,[108] and where both extant writers derive material from their common source, Jerome's version is sometimes both fuller and

---

[107] See esp. P. Winter, Der literarische Charakter der *Vita beati Hilarionis* des Hieronymus (Prog. Zittau, 1904), 18–24; Schiwietz, Mönchtum 2 (n. 103), 100–103; Kelly, Jerome (n. 31), 172–174.

[108] For a high estimate of the historical content and geographical accuracy of the *Life*, see I. Opelt, RQ 74 (1979), 154–177.

superior. According to Sozomenus, Hilarion fled to Sicily in the reign of Julian when the people of Gaza attempted to arrest him (*HE* 5.10.1). Jerome has a much more complicated story. Hilarion was in Egypt on his way to the Inner Desert, when Julian became ruler of the East in the winter of 361/362: on receipt of the news, the city authorities of Gaza destroyed Hilarion's monastery, submitted a petition to the emperor requesting the deaths of Hilarion and his associate Hesychius, and obtained an order for their arrest wherever they might be found. Hilarion returned to the city <of> Alexandria from his lodgings nearby before prefects arrived from Gaza with lictors;[109] as if forewarned, Hilarion had refused to stay in the monastery at Bruchion where he was expected to lodge, and thus escaped arrest. He withdrew to the Great Oasis, where after a year he heard of the death of Julian. Instead of returning to Gaza, however, he travelled by camel to Paraetonium, from where he boarded a ship sailing to Sicily (23.1–25.1).

The outline of Hilarion's life was simple. He came from Thabatha, a village five miles north of Gaza. His pagan parents sent him to study in Alexandria. A visit to Antony converted him to asceticism and, returning to Gaza, he established himself as a hermit in the desert inland from the coast road seven miles from Maiuma, the port of Gaza (2.1–7). There Hilarion remained for many years until the

---

[109] On the identification of the *Gazenses cum lictoribus praefecti*, where some had seen a reference to the prefect of Egypt, see Bastiaensen, Vite dei santi 4 (n. 104), 125, 310, who takes them to be the *duumviri* of Gaza accompanied by their lictors in a police function. Perhaps rather prefects acting as agents of or appointed by the chief magistrates of Gaza. The appendix on 'Dramatis Personae of the Vita Hilarionis' in Weingarten, The Saint's Saints (n. 67), 155–163, is unfortunately riddled with minor errors.

death of Antony, when he went to Egypt to spend a night in prayer at the place where he had died (19–20). After several years in Egypt, he went to Sicily and soon from there to Epidaurus in Dalmatia (the present-day Dubrovnik), where he stilled the sea during the tsunami of 21 July 365 by drawing three crosses in the sand (22–29).[110] Immediately thereafter Hilarion departed and sailed to Cyprus, where he died at the age of eighty and was buried – according to Jerome, at once before news of his death was divulged (29.7, 32). Ten months later his body was stolen by Hesychius, taken to Maiuma and reburied in the ancient monastery, the saint's clothing still perfectly preserved and his corpse smelling sweetly (32.6–7).

Two themes permeate the narrative fabric of the *Life of Hilarion*. One is Hilarion's constant search for a life of solitary prayer and contemplation. The other is his importance as the successor of Antony. Jerome continually emphasises that Hilarion was the founder of monasticism in Palestine in the same way as Antony was the founder of monasticism in Egypt (8.11). While Hilarion was studying in Alexandria at the age of fifteen, he heard of Antony, went to see him and immediately copied his way of life; after two months he returned to Palestine and took up the life of a solitary seven miles outside Maiuma, the port of Gaza, clad only in a sack-

---

[110] On the tsunami, whose epicentre lay near Crete and which caused widespread damage along the coasts of Egypt, Palestine and Greece, see now G. Kelly, JRS 94 (2004), 141–167; Ammianus Marcellinus the Allusive Historian (Cambridge, 2007), 322–331; B. Bleckmann, Ammianus after Julian. The Reign of Valentinian and Valens in Books 26–31 of the Res Gestae, ed. J. den Boeft, D. den Hengst & J. W. Drijvers (Leiden, 2007), 7–19. The passages of Theophanes, George the Monk and Michael the Syrian which confirm that the tidal wave from the tsunami reached the Adriatic are conveniently translated in parallel by Kelly, Ammianus (2007), 325.

cloth, a rustic cloak and a goatskin jacket which Antony had
given him (2.2–7, 3.1). Antony corresponded with Hilarion
and asked those who came to him from Syria in the hope of
a cure for their maladies why they had come so far instead
of going to his dear son Hilarion (15.1). Hilarion learned of
the death of Antony by supernatural means (19.5–7); three
years after Antony's death he visited the place where he was
buried and was asked by the distraught and famished inhabitants to pray for rain as Antony's successor; he prayed and
at once ended a drought which had lasted since Antony's
death (22.2–4).

The greater part of the *Life* inevitably comprises a series
of self-contained episodes in which Hilarion cures the ill,
drives out demons, foresees the future, performs miracles
and utters divinely inspired words of wisdom. Some of these
involve persons of rank and influence. After Helpidius, who
later became praetorian prefect,[111] and his wife Aristaenete
had visited Antony, they stopped in Gaza because their three
children fell ill with a fever so violent that the doctors de-
spaired of their lives. Aristaenete went to Hilarion and humbly besought his help. The monk, who had not set foot in
any house, let alone the city, for many years, agreed to come
to the children after dark. He did so, made the sign of the
cross and called on Jesus. The fever left the children at once.
When news of this miracle spread, many were converted to
Christ and to the monastic life – in fact, this was the start of
monasticism in Syria. Some years later (in 356), Aristaenete

---

[111] Helpidius was praetorian prefect of the East from the winter of
359/360 until he was dismissed by Julian at the end of 361 (PLRE 1
[1971], 414, Helpidius 4). The earlier career of Helpidius, who was of
low birth (Libanius, *Orat.* 42.24–25), is totally unknown: he presumably passed through Gaza when travelling to or from Egypt on official
business.

visited Hilarion again on her way to Antony, but Hilarion was able to tell her that Antony had died two days before (19.5–7). At a lower social level is Orion, the leading citizen of Aila, who was brought to Hilarion shackled in chains and possessed by a legion of demons. Orion broke free from those holding him and seized Hilarion, who was walking and expounding scripture. The holy man touched the head, then other parts of the body of the sufferer, who uttered sounds as if of a crowd as the demons left him. A little while later Orion returned with his wife and children with gifts, which Hilarion refused to accept, even when Orion told him to give them to the poor (10.5–15). It must remain a matter of speculation whether the Orion whom Hilarion healed is the Orion who profited from the spoliation of pagan temples under Constantius and was asked to disgorge these profits under Julian (Libanius, *Epp.* 763, 819).[112]

Jerome follows the lead of the *Life of Antony* in assigning a large role to demons. Hilarion was in the habit of healing animals as well as humans:

Dumb animals too were dragged to him every day suffering from madness, among them more than thirty men brought with great shouting a Bactrian camel of enormous size, which had already crushed many men, hauling it with very stout ropes. Its eyes were bloodshot, its mouth foamed, its noisy tongue was swollen, and in addition to every other terror a huge roaring filled the air. The old man therefore ordered it to be set free. At once both those who had brought it and those with the old man scatted in flight, every one of them. He alone advanced towards the animal, stretched out his hand, and said in Syriac: 'You do not frighten me, Devil, with such a large body: you are one and the same, whether in a fox or camel.' All the while he stood with his hand outstretched. After the mad beast came up to him as if to devour him, it suddenly collapsed, and submissively

---

[112] *L'église et l'empire au IVᵉ siècle. Entretiens sur l'Antiquité Classique* 34 (Vandoeuvres-Geneva, 1989), 328–329.

laid its head on the ground, so that all who were there marvelled at such sudden tameness after such great ferocity. (14.1–5)

Hilarion was also a dragon-slayer. An enormous snake which could swallow an ox whole was devastating the area around Epidaurus when he arrived, killing not only sheep and cattle, but also farmers and shepherds, whom it overpowered with its breath. Hilarion prepared a pyre, prayed to Christ and ordered the beast to ascend; when it did so, he lit the fire and burned it to death with the whole population of the city watching (29.3–4).[113] It would be rash to attempt to segregate fact from fiction in much of the *Life of Hilarion*: Jerome had a good written source in Epiphanius, he could add from what he himself had heard about Hilarion in Palestine, but he enjoyed invention and romance. One scholar of the late nineteenth century characterised the work as a *Tendenzroman* and even asserted that Hilarion himself was a mythical, not historical figure.[114] That was hypercritical, but the mistaken inference proceeded from a correct appreciation of the literary nature of much of the text. Jerome took much of his inspiration from Apuleius, and employed standard themes of panegyric and rhetoric, sometimes with a touch of humour:[115] just as when he wrote the *Life of Paul* and the *Captive Monk*, Jerome's main aim, whether he formulated it consciously or not, was to achieve literary renown, not primarily to record the authentic deeds of his hero.

---

[113] On the stereotypical nature of this story, see R. Reitzenstein, Hellenistische Wundererzählungen (Leipzig, 1906), 3–4.

[114] W. Israël, ZWT 23 (1880), 129–165, esp. 157.

[115] J. Rougé, Nuovo Didaskaleion 12 (1962), 64, detected in the miracle of the pirates 'un certain humeur qui laisse à penser que St Jérôme ne se prenait pas trop au sérieux quand il le racontait' (41). On the typology of storms at sea in Greek and Latin literature, see R. J. Tarrant, Seneca: Agamemnon (Cambridge, 1976), 262.

## Paulinus' *Life of Ambrose*

Paulinus, the biographer of Ambrose, had been secretary to the bishop of Milan: his *Life of Ambrose* (BHL 377)[116] records that he was writing down a commentary on Psalm 43 at the bishop's dictation a few days before his final illness when a burst of fire (which he later realised was the Holy Spirit) suddenly descended on Ambrose, thus portending his imminent death (42). But Paulinus did not write the *Life* until Ambrose had been dead for fifteen years, and he wrote in Africa. He indicates both the place and the date with deliberate precision. He was writing in the province where Mascezel won his victory over Gildo (51.2), and Johannes, who was sent by Theodosius in September 394 as a *tribunus et notarius* to guarantee safe conduct for followers of Eugenius who had taken refuge in Ambrose's church, 'is now prefect' (31.5). Johannes, who was *primicerius notariorum* in 408 and *magister officiorum* in the puppet regime of Priscus Attalus in 409,[117] is attested as praetorian prefect of Italy by seven different imperial constitutions between 6 June 412 and 12 June 413.[118]

---

[116] There are recent critical editions by M. Pellegrino, Paolino di Milano: Vita di S. Ambrogio (Rome, 1961), 50–129, and Bastiaensen, Vite dei Santi 4 (n. 104), 54–124. Pellegrino's text is translated into English by B. Ramsey, Ambrose (London / New York, 1997), 196–218.

[117] Zosimus 5.30.2; Sozomenus, *HE* 9.8.3, both deriving from Olympiodorus.

[118] For the evidence, see PLRE 1 (1971), 459, Johannes 2. Some works of reference accept a second prefecture in 422 on the strength of CTh 2.13.1 + 28.1 + 30.2 + 31.1 + 32.1 + 8.8.10): O. Seeck, Regesten der Kaiser und Päpste für die Jahre 311 bis 476 n. Chr. Vorarbeit zu einer Prosopographie der christlichen Kaiserzeit (Stuttgart, 1919), 346; PLRE 2 (1980), 594, Johannes 4; 1247. Hence the *Life of Ambrose* has often been dated to 422. But the fact that the compilers of the

Paulinus wrote, so he proclaims, because Augustine urged, even commanded him to write a life of Ambrose in the same way as Athanasius and Jerome had written lives of the desert fathers Antony and Paul, and Sulpicius Severus the life of Martin, the bishop of Tours. Paulinus protests that his eloquence cannot match theirs; yet he can compose a brief and truthful account, for which he possesses excellent sources of information: the trustworthy men who attended Ambrose before Paulinus; his venerable sister Marcellina; his own recollections when he was in constant attendance; those who saw him after his death in various provinces; what was written to the bishop while his death was still unknown (1.1–3). Paulinus also made systematic use of the letters of Ambrose, both the collection in ten books which the bishop published in his lifetime and a group of important letters which Paulinus himself probably preserved for posterity.[119]

The result is predictably panegyrical, sometimes grossly so, as in the series of attempts which Ambrose is alleged to have made in order to avoid consecration as bishop (7.1–9.2).[120] Although sometimes believed even by the critical,[121] they are as improbable as the stories told of emperors' re-

---

Theodosian Code dated the law from which all six fragments come to 11 July 422 does not guarantee that it was in fact issued in that year: the transmitted consular date of *Honorio XIII et Theodosio X* could be an error of the compilers for *Honorio VIIII et Theodosio V*, i. e., 412. In favour of dating Paulinus' Life to 412, see E. Lamirande, REAug 27 (1981), 44–55; id., Paulin de Milan et la "Vita Ambrosii." Aspects de la religion sous le Bas-Empire (Paris, Tournai & Montreal, 1983), 21–24.

[119] M. Zelzer, Sancti Ambrosii Opera 10.3. CSEL 82 (Vienna, 1982), lxxxv–lxxxvi.

[120] On which, see esp. Y. M. Duval, Ambrosius Episcopus 2 (Milan, 1976), 243–283.

[121] As by N. B. McLynn, Ambrose of Milan. Church and Court in a Christian Capital (Berkeley, 1994), 44–52.

luctance to assume power:[122] Ambrose had in fact used his
position as governor of the province of Aemilia and Liguria
to engineer his election as bishop of Milan.[123] Yet the *Life
of Ambrose* is also a valuable repository of important but
otherwise forgotten facts, actions and journeys. It is Paulinus alone who explicitly records that Ambrose was born
when his father was praetorian prefect in Gaul (3.1: *posito
in administratione praefecturae Galliarum patre eius Ambrosio
natus est Ambrosius*).[124] There is no call to interpret Paulinus
as saying that Ambrose's father was a lowly bureaucrat on the
staff of the praetorian prefect, or to disallow his clear statement by claiming that Paulinus was ignorant of Ambrose's
social standing and made a mistaken guess.[125] The fact that
Ambrose was a *nobilis* by birth on the strictest definition of
the term makes his political success all the more compre-

---

[122] On the etiquette of *recusatio imperii* and its adoption by
Christian bishops on their election, see J. Béranger, Recherches sur
l'aspect idéologique du principat (Basel, 1953), 137–142, 149–169;
U. Huttner, Recusatio Imperii. Ein politisches Ritual zwischen Ethik
und Taktik. Spudasmata 93 (Hildesheim, 2004), 36–37 n. 3. Béranger
adduces not only Ambrose (164) but also Pope Pius X (161, 167),
though without discussing the peculiar features of the papal election
in 1903 (Chapter VI n. 45), while Huttner notes that Ambrose was
following the example of Cyprian.

[123] Historia 51 (2002), 235–236.

[124] Paulinus provides the sole evidence (PLRE 1 [1971], 51, Ambrosius 2). S. Mazzarino, Storia sociale del vescovo Ambrogio (Rome,
1989), 75–82, identifies Ambrose's father with the Uranius who received CTh 11.1.5 in February 339 (office not stated).

[125] McLynn, Ambrose (n. 121), 33–38. His arguments make insuf-
ficient allowance for the fact that, if (as is commonly assumed) the
prefect was executed for treason in 340 when Constantinus invaded
Italy and was killed, then his property was presumably confiscated, with
the result that Ambrose grew up in genteel poverty and hence had to
make his career as if he had been born poor.

hensible. As an aristocrat by birth, Ambrose treated Roman emperors as the social inferiors that they were, and in the controversy over the Altar of Victory in 384 he argued with disdainful politeness against an adversary who may well have been his first cousin.[126]

It is Paulinus alone who records that Ambrose travelled to Rome (9.4–10.3) and then to Sirmium (11.1–12.1) a few years after his consecration as bishop of Milan in 374: these journeys can be dated to 378 and provide the key to interpreting the *De Fide* and Ambrose's dealings with the emperor Gratian, which he deliberately omitted from his published correspondence.[127] And it is Paulinus alone among surviving witers who mentions Fritigil, queen of the Marcomanni (36). Fritigil was converted to Christianity by an Italian and sent envoys to Milan with gifts to request instruction in the faith. Ambrose wrote 'a letter in the form of a catechism' urging the queen to persuade her husband to keep peace with the Romans. The king decided to seek formal Roman protection, but Ambrose unfortunately died before the queen reached Milan.

The *Life of Ambrose* proceeds in large part in resolutely chronological order. Paulinus owes little or nothing to the lives of Antony, Paul and Martin of Tours, which he had paraded as his implied literary models, for the structure of the *Life of Ambrose* closely follows the model of Suetonius.[128]

---

[126] As argued in Augustine: From Rhetor to Theologian, ed. J. McWilliam and others (Waterloo, ON, 1992), 7–13. On the definition of nobility in the late fourth century as descent from an ordinary consul, praetorian prefect or prefect of the city of Rome, see Phoenix 28 (1974), 444–449.

[127] Barnes, AT 7 (1999), 165–174; SP 38 (2001), 357–361.

[128] S. Cavallin, Literarhistorische und textkritische Studien zur Vita S. Caesarii Arelatensis. Lunds Universitets Årsskrift, N. F. 30.7 (Lund,

Paulinus begins with brief accounts of the birth, childhood, education and secular career of his hero (3–5). A fuller account of his election and consecration as bishop of Milan (6.1–9.3) is followed by his visits to Rome and Sirmium (9.4–11.1), which provides a transition to his conflict with Justina and the Arians in Milan (12–17). Next comes a long series of episodes, each narrated briefly in approximate chronological order: the linking phrase *per idem tempus* is employed no fewer than seven times (21.1; 25.1; 30.1; 34.4; 35.1; 36.1; 44.1), but Paulinus marks Theodosius' arrival in Milan in 388 (22.1: *exstincto itaque Maximo*), his departure from Italy in 391 (26.1), and his death, after which Ambrose lived on for almost a triennium (32.1).

Closely following Suetonius' arrangement of material in his imperial biographies, Paulinus turns from his chronological account of Ambrose's episcopal career to an enumeration of the bishop's personal qualities (38–41), an omen of his imminent end and two other episodes from his last years (42–44), and his final illness and death (45–48). Only the concluding sections of the *Life* can be claimed as a departure from strictly classical models to include something that is distinctively Christian. In these Paulinus describes various posthumous appearances by Ambrose, the first on the very day of his death, the last eventuating in the death of Muranus, the bishop of Bol, who had denigrated Ambrose in the presence of Paulinus (49–54). He then, in a double epilogue, addresses the reader (55) and Augustine (56)[129] in

---

1934), 15–17, mistakenly claimed that the structure of the *Life of Ambrose* was modelled on the *Life of Antony*. In disproof, see G. Luck, *Mullus. Festschrift für Theodor Klauser* (Münster, 1964), 239.

[129] Paulinus, who in his preface addresses *venerabilis pater Augustine* (1.1), here has *tuam etiam precor beatitudinem, pater* (56.1). Hence his reference to *beati viri Athanasius episcopus et Hieronymus presbyter* (1.1)

terms reminiscent of the conclusion of Jerome's *Life of Paul*, asking Augustine to pray for him and expressing the hope that writing the *Life of Ambrose* has earned him a release from punishment for his sins.

Did either Latin translation of the *Life of Antony* have any perceptible influence on writers who were not Christians? There is a close but suggestive parallel between the *Historia Augusta* and the the *Life of Antony*, of which a Latin translation had long been available in the West.[130] According to the *Historia Augusta*, the usurper Firmus anointed himself with crocodile fat and swam among crocodiles, drove an elephant, sat upon a hippopotamus, and rode enormous ostriches so fast that he seemed to be flying (*Quad. Tyr.* 6.2). Forty years ago, Ronald Syme compared these exploits of Firmus with that of the abbot Helles, who crossed the Nile on the back of a crocodile (*Historia monachorum in Aegypto* 12.6–9, pp. 94–95 Festugière).[131] Evagrius has something far closer: when Antony needed to cross a branch of the Nile at Arsinoe, although it was full of crocodiles and many other wild riverine animals, he waded safely across with his companions and returned from the other side unharmed (*Vita Antonii* 14 [PG 26.865–866 = PL 73.134]). If Helles rode a crocodile, both Antony and Firmus descended among the animals in the river, the one wading, the other swimming. But the Latin hagiographical writer who was most profoundly influenced by the *Life of Antony* was Sulpicius Severus.

---

cannot be taken to prove that he was writing after the death of Jerome on 30 September 420 (Prosper 1274 [Chr. Min. 1.469], cf. Kelly, Jerome (n. 31), 331).

[130] Historiae Augustae Colloquia, N.S. VII: Colloquium Genevense MCMXCVIII (Bari, 1999), 36.

[131] Syme, Ammianus (n. 98), 83.

# V

# Saint Martin of Tours:
# History and Invention

Sulpicius Severus' *Life of Martin of Tours* (BHL 5610) has engendered disquiet and unease among readers ever since he sent it forth into the world. Even some contemporary readers accused its author of deliberate invention. In the dialogue *Gallus* which supplements the *Life*, Postumianus says to Sulpicius:[1] 'I shudder to repeat what I have recently heard, that some poor wretch said that you told rather a lot of lies in your famous book' (*Dial.* 1.26.4: *horreo dicere quae nuper audivi, infelicem dixisse nescioquem, te in illo libro tuo plura mentitum*). In the twelfth century, three hundred years before Lorenzo Valla (1406–1457) exposed the *Donation of Constantine* as a forgery,[2] there was critical discussion of some of the problems presented by Sulpicius' chronology of his hero's life, including his military career, when some

---

[1] The modern convention has been to use the single name Severus, as in PLRE 2 (1980), 1006, Severus 20. But in the *Gallus* he always calls himself Sulpicius (1.1.5, 3.1; 1[2].4.1, 12.1, 13.1, 13.8): Sulpicius was therefore the name by which contemporaries knew him and is the name used here.

[2] Valla composed his *De falso credita et ementita Constantini Donatione declamatio* in 1440, but the first printed edition did not appear until 1517: the critical text of W. Setz, MGH, Quellen 10 (Weimar, 1976), is translated into English by G. W. Bowersock, Lorenzo Valla on the Donation of Constantine (Cambridge, MA & London, 2007), who includes a text and translation of the *Constitutum Constantini* itself (162–183).

readers noticed and attempted to explain the contradiction
between the *Life* and Gregory of Tours over the date of
Martin's birth that lies at the heart of the argument of the
present chapter.[3] But the time was not propitious for such
an exposure to be widely accepted, any more than it was for
the dismissal of the *Donation of Constantine* as a 'figment of
the imagination' by the Emperor Otto III (980–1002), so
that neither of these early triumphs of historical criticism
had any effect.[4] The fiercest onslaught on the historical reliability of the *Life* came early in the twentieth century when
Édouard-Charles Babut set out to show that it was an essentially fictitious composition, full of historical falsehoods
and invented stories.[5]

Babut's views were initially endorsed by some eminent
French medieval historians.[6] But the tide of scholarly opin-
ion turned decisively against him after the end of the First
World War, during which he was killed in action (on 28

---

[3] See the texts published by L. B. Mortensen, Cahiers de l'Institut
du Moyen Age grec et latin 59 (1989), 311–317; F. Dolbeau, Manu-
scrits hagiographiques et travail des hagiographes, ed. M. Heinzelmann
(Sigmaringen, 1992), 66–76.

[4] J. H. Plumb, The Death of the Past (Boston, 1970), 79–80, cf.
W. Ullmann, Medieval Political Thought (Harmondsworth, 1975),
98: Otto was secretly informed of the spurious character of the Donation by 'John the deacon without fingers,' and the Vatican (as is still
its wont) kept the embarrassing document in which Otto made this
declaration secret for centuries.

[5] É.- C. Babut, Revue d'histoire et de littérature religieuses, N. S. 1
(1910), 466–487; 513–541; 2 (1911), 44–78; 160–182; 255–272;
431–463; 513–543; 3 (1912), 120–159; 240–278; 289–329, all published together in book form as Saint Martin de Tours (Paris, n. d.,
publ. 1912).

[6] L. Halphen, Rev. hist. 112 (1913), 338–340; C. Pfister, Rev. hist.
122 (1916), 224–226; M. Bloch, Revue d'histoire et de littérature
religieuses, N. S. 7 (1921), 44–57.

February 1916). First Hippolyte Delehaye, who had already rejected Babut's thesis in a review of his book, then Camille Jullian, who had committed himself to the veracity of Sulpicius Severus before he read Babut, published long rebuttals of both Babut's arguments and his conclusions in which they systematically defended Sulpicius as a reliable historical witness.[7] For nearly ninety years an apparently impressive scholarly consensus has branded Babut as hypercritical, his methods as misguided and his conclusions as mistaken. Historians and scholars have treated the *Life of Martin* as an unproblematical text and regarded its author as a truthful biographer who merely desired to make his hero better and more widely known.[8] Some have read profound historical significance into the 'spiritual exchange' between Martin and Hilary of Poitiers before the latter departed into exile,[9] and one even claimed that 'the facts as related in the narrative of Sulpicius suggest that Martin was not only Hilary's disciple; he was virtually his creation.'[10] The *Life* has been gratefully used by all as a fundamentally accurate account of how north-western Gaul became Christian in the later

---

[7]  H. Delehaye, AB 32 (1913), 469–472; AB 38 (1920), 5–136; C. Jullian, REA 12 (1910), 260–280, reviewing A. Regnier, *Saint Martin (316–397)*[2] (Paris, 1907); REA 24 (1922), 37–47, 123–128, 229–235; 306–312; 25 (1923), 49–55, 139–143, 234–250.

[8]  See, for example, the uncritical use of the *Life* by P. Rousseau, *Ascetics, Authority and the Church in the Age of Jerome and Cassian* (Oxford, 1978), 143–165.

[9]  As J. Fontaine, *Hilaire de Poitiers. Évêque et docteur* (Paris, 1968), 61: 'le dialogue fécond, mais pour nous si mystérieux, qui s'engage en 356 entre les deux hommes;' J. Doignon, *Hilaire de Poitiers avant l'exil* (Paris, 1971), 506–511, on 'le séjour de Martin auprès d'Hilaire.'

[10]  N. K. Chadwick, *Poetry and Letters in Early Christian Gaul* (London, 1955), 116.

fourth century,[11] and few expressed any serious reservations
about its veracity.[12] Moreover, Jacques Fontaine buttressed
the prevailing view when, between 1967 and 1969, he
published a critical edition of the *Life of Martin* with a
monumental commentary of seven hundred and sixty pages
of what the French call 'analyses approfondies,' in which he
meditated eloquently and at heavenly length upon Sulpicius'
thirty four pages of Latin.[13] Although Fontaine believed
that Martin was twenty years older than the *Life* implies,
his commentary confidently and consistently asserted its
high historical value and contended that its reliability was
guaranteed by the human weaknesses which it attributes
to Martin.[14] Fontaine's assessment of the *Life of Martin* has
been very widely accepted. In an otherwise critical review of
Fontaine's edition and commentary John Matthews praised

---

[11] E. g., L. Pietri, La ville de Tours du IV^e au VI^e siècle: Naissance
d'une cité chrétienne (Rome, 1983), 36–87, 421–430; R. van Dam,
Leadership and Community in Late Antique Gaul (Berkeley, 1985),
119–140; D. von der Nahmer, Francia 15 (1987), 1–41.

[12] To his credit, J. Matthews, Western Aristocracies and Imperial
Court A. D. 364–375 (Oxford, 1975), 154–157, 159, sounded a note
of scepticism, albeit a slightly muted one: 'an account … which, if not
credible to every last detail, is convincingly located within its social
setting.'

[13] J. Fontaine, Sulpice Sévère: Vie de Saint Martin (SC 133, 1967;
134, 1968;136, 1969), with the long preliminary articles in Saint
Martin et son temps. Studia Anselmiana 46 (1961), 189–236; AB 81
(1963), 31–58.

[14] Fontaine, Sulpice Sévère: Vie 1 (n. 13), 171–210 ('La valeur
historique de la Vita Martini: Pour une nouvelle position de la "question martinienne" '), whose concluding sentence reads: 'loin de nous
inquiéter ou de nous decevoir, ils [sc. ces traits trop humains] doivent
au contraire nous rassurer sur la vérité historique d'un portrait qu'une
fidélité trop constante à soi-même nous eût mis justement un droit de
suspecter' (210).

him warmly for being 'preserved, by his sense of the literary genre of the *Vita*, from the easy but unnecessary and imperceptive scepticism of scholars like É.-Ch. Babut.[15] More recently, while acknowledging that at least one of Sulpicius' stories about Martin (*Life* 13.6–9) 'is not credible as it stands,' Richard Price has commended Fontaine for showing 'how we can discern, under the dramatization and symbolism that the miraculous elements confer, a solid bedrock of historical fact, firmly rooted in the distinctive features of Gallic paganism and of the spirituality of Martin himself.'[16]

Some years after Fontaine's commentary appeared, however, Clare Stancliffe voiced new doubts about the *Life* and its author's reliability. She rejected Fontaine's easy confidence in Sulpicius' truthfulness, and confronted the historical problems in the *Life* squarely and honestly, even though she ultimately concluded that Sulpicius' picture of Martin is basically reliable. Stancliffe waived the requirement of 'strict historical accuracy' as inappropriate for a hagiographer and allowed that the *Life* gives 'a one-sided presentation,' but she concluded that Sulpicius does not either tell outright lies or invent stories about Martin.[17] This defence of Sulpicius, however, which argues that he should be acquitted on the charge of perpetrating untruths, fails on the crucial episode from which Babut started his demolition. The *Life* asserts that, after Martin was discharged from the Roman army, he went to Poitiers and there spent some time with Hilary, the bishop of Poitiers, before the latter departed into exile in

---

[15] J. F. Matthews, JTS, N. S. 20 (1969), 641.

[16] R. M. Price, The Cult of Saints in Late Antiquity and the Middle Ages, ed. J. Howard-Johnston & P. A. Hayward (Oxford, 1999), 219, 224 n. 21.

[17] C. Stancliffe, St. Martin and his Hagiographer. History and Miracle in Sulpicius Severus (Oxford, 1983), esp. 341–359.

Asia Minor (5.1: *aliquamdiu apud eum commoratus est*). Like
Jullian and Fontaine, Stancliffe dated Martin's discharge
from the army to 356,[18] and she defended Sulpicius' credibility by postulating that Hilary, who was deposed by the
Council of Baeterrae and sent into exile in Phrygia by the
Caesar Julian in the spring or early summer of 356,[19] may
not actually have departed from Gaul until the late summer
of 356 when Martin hurried to Poitiers to meet him immediately after his discharge.[20] Correct chronology exposes the
fragility and falsity of this *ad hoc* and intrinsically improbable hypothesis. For the circumstantial details in the *Life*
date Martin's discharge to October 357.[21] Hence the *Life*
depicts Martin as being discharged from the Roman army
about eighteen months after Hilary was deposed and exiled,
and Sulpicius' credibility is equally damaged whether 357 is

---

[18]  Stancliffe, St. Martin (n. 17), 112, 114, 134, 136–138, cf. Fontaine, Sulpice Sévère: Vie 2 (n. 13), 439–440, 517, 524.
[19]  The evidence which fixes the year of Hilary's exile as 356 is
assembled by P. Smulders, Hilary of Poitiers' Preface to his *Opus Histo-
ricum* (Leiden, 1995), 126–131. Hilary makes it clear that the Council
of Baeterrae met while Julian was still in southern Gaul, i.e., before
mid-June 356 (*Ad Constantium* 2 [CSEL 65.198.5–15], cf. Ammianus
16.2.2): for an argument that the council convened between 7 April
and 17 May 356, see Vig. Chr. 46 (1992), 129–140.
[20]  Stancliffe, St. Martin (n. 17), 134–138, esp. 137: 'by pushing
Hilary's departure as late as is plausible … it is possible to accept
Sulpicius' story of Martin and Hilary meeting – albeit briefly – in 356.'
[21]  As argued in AB 114 (1996), 25–32. This precise and technical
demonstration is curtly dismissed by M. Vielberg, Der Mönchsbischof
von Tours im 'Martinellus.' Zur Form des hagiographischen Dossiers
und seines spätantiken Leitbilds (Berlin, 2006), 26 n. 83: 'skeptisch
wieder T. D. Barnes … hinsichtlich der Historizität des … Zusammen-
treffens mit Hilarius von Poitiers vor dessen Exil 356, doch wenig über-
zeugend in den weiteren Schlussfolgerungen.' In fact, if my argument
erred, it was on the side of positivism rather than scepticism.

the real or only the dramatic date of Martin's discharge as he depicts it.

## Martin's Military Career

Sulpicius Severus sets the military career of his hero into a political and military context which can be dated with unusual precision. According to Sulpicius (*Life* 2.1–6, 3.5–4.9, cf. Table 2), Martin was born at Savaria in Pannonia, but brought up in Italy at Ticinum. Since his father was a soldier and imperial legislation required the sons of veterans to enlist (2.5: *cum edictum esset a regibus, ut veteranorum filii ad militiam scriberentur*),[22] Martin was press-ganged and drafted into the army at the age of fifteen, where he served in cavalry *alae* of the imperial *scholae* under the emperor Constantius and subsequently under the Caesar Julian, first for about three years as a catechumen, then for approximately another two years after his baptism at the age of eighteen. Martin was discharged from the army when he protested that as a Christian he could not fight: the occasion was the distribution of a donative by Julian in the territory of the city of Worms on the middle Rhine, and after his discharge, although a battle was expected the next day, the enemy decided to capitulate rather than fight and sent envoys to offer the total surrender of themselves and their property – which Sulpicius claims as a victory given by God so that Martin

---

[22] The earliest evidence for the requirement cited by Mommsen, Ges. Schr. 6 (Berlin, 1910), 255; Jones, LRE (1964), 60, 615, 2.184 n. 14. 60, 615, 2.184 n. 14, is CTh 7.22.1 of 313 (Barnes New Empire [1982], 164). But the Acts of Maximilianus (K-K-R XIX = Musurillo XVII) assume that it already existed in 295 (App. 5).

did not need to fulfil his offer to enter battle unarmed and penetrate the enemy's ranks by making the sign of the cross.

The chronology of Martin's military career as it is described in the *Life* can be fixed virtually to the month. Martin was living in North Italy when he enlisted in the Roman army under Constantius, he served for five years, and he was discharged by Julian near Worms. Since Italy was ruled by Constantine from 312 to 337, by Constans from 337 to January 350 and by Magnentius from early 350 to August / September 352, Martin cannot have begun to serve *sub rege Constantio* before the late summer or autumn of 352. As for Martin's discharge at Worms, only the years 356 and 357 are theoretically open, since it was only in these two years that the Caesar Julian, whose movements are well documented, was in the area.[23] Of these two years, the later (357) better accommodates a triennium followed by a biennium (both of which are admittedly approximate rather than exact chronological designations) after enlistment in or after September 352. Moreover, evidence independent of Sulpicius Severus confirms that Martin's discharge as it is described in the *Life* must have occurred in the autumn 357.

Ammianus Marcellinus gives a detailed narrative of the campaigns which the Caesar Julian waged in Gaul in the later 350s. Julian was proclaimed Caesar at Milan on November 355 and crossed the Alps into Gaul to spend the rest of the winter in Vienne in Gallia Narbonensis (Ammianus 15.8.18–21, 16.1.1, 2.1). After the Council of Baeterrae Julian travelled north and reached Autun on 24 June 356 (Ammianus 16.2.2): from there he went by

---

[23] J. F. Matthews, The Roman Empire of Ammianus (London, 1989), 82, Map 3; Barnes, Athanasius (1993), 105–106, 227; J. F. Drinkwater, The Alamanni and Rome 213–496 (Caracalla to Clovis) (Oxford, 2007), 219–242, with Figs. 18, 19.

way of Auxerre, Troyes, Rheims and Decem Pagi (Dieuse) to Brotomagus (Brumath), close to the west bank of the Rhine slightly to the north of Strasbourg. From the vicinity of Strasbourg he passed rapidly down the Rhine to recover Cologne, which had been captured by Germans in November 355. Julian seems to have recovered Cologne in August 356, after which he retired up the Moselle valley to Trier and thence to Sens for the winter of 356–357 (16.3.3, 7.1, 11.1). Hence there was neither the occasion nor the opportunity for him to give a donative to his army at Worms during the campaigning season of 356. In 357, however, after Julian won his great victory over the Alamanni at the Battle of Strasbourg, he proceeded to the vicinity of Mainz, where he conducted a raid across the Rhine (17.1.2–3). Ammianus records that Julian concluded a peace treaty with the Alamanni some time after the autumnal equinox,[24] which corresponds closely with the surrender recorded in the *Life of Martin* once Sulpicius' hyperbolic rhetoric is discounted. On Sulpicius' showing, therefore, Martin was discharged from the Roman army not merely 'during one of Julian's campaigns in Gaul (c. a. 357)'[25] but precisely in October 357 (or possibly in the last days of September or at the very beginning of November).

Babut was thus entirely correct to claim that, if Martin was discharged from the Roman army as Sulpicius Severus describes, then the stay of several months with Hilary before

---

[24] Ammianus 17.1.10, 12: *aequinoctio quippe autumnali exacto per eos tractus superfusae nives opplevere montes simul et campos. ... quae illi* (sc. Alamanni) *maturata ad suam perniciem contemplantes metuque rei peractae volucriter congregati precibus et humilitate suprema petiere missis oratoribus pacem quam Caesar omni consiliorum via causatus veri similia plurima per decem mensuum tribuit intervallum.*

[25] As PLRE 1 (1971), 565, Martinus 3.

his exile presupposed in the *Life* must be unhistorical, from which he concluded that 'il est vain de chercher à sauver le récit de Sulpice.'[26] For correct chronology poses a sharp and inescapable dilemma. Either Martin served in the Roman army from c. September 352 to October 357, as the *Life* alleges, in which case Sulpicius Severus has invented Martin's encounter with Hilary of Poitiers before the latter left Gaul and departed into exile in Asia Minor in April or May 356, or Martin was ordained an exorcist by Hilary in Poitiers (*Life* 5.2), in which case Sulpicius has either invented a military career spanning the five years from c. September 352 to October 357 or attributed to Martin a real military career spanning these five years which in reality belonged to someone else. The *Life of Martin* thus contains at least one serious and irremovable contradiction, and it will not redeem Sulpicius' veracity or credit to postulate that he took the error over from a hypothetical source. An investigation of the literary nature of the *Life* is requisite.

## The Publication of the *Life of Martin*

The dialogue *Gallus*, which Sulpicius composed some years after the *Life of Martin*, provides important details about how Sulpicius put the *Life* into circulation, which are duly registered in standard modern treatments of the ancient book trade.[27] Sulpicius sent the manuscript of the *Life* to his aristocratic friend Meropius Pontius Paulinus, a Gallic aristocrat like himself, who had abandoned his secular

---

[26] Babut, Saint Martin (n. 5), 68–71.

[27] T. Birt, Das antike Buchwesen in seinem Verhältnis zur Literatur (Berlin, 1882), 103–104, 112, 352; Kritik und Hermeneutik nebst Abriss des antiken Buchwesens (Munich, 1913), 319–320.

career, taken ordination as a priest and settled near Nola in Campania, where he devoted himself to the cult of the local martyr Felix.[28] The letter in which Paulinus thanked Sulpicius compliments him in extravagant terms:

It would not have been granted to you to write a full account of Martin, if you had not made your mouth worthy of such sacred praise by means of a pure heart (Ephesians 2.14). So you are a man blessed before the Lord, since you have recounted, in language as apposite as your love is righteous, the history of this great priest who is clearly a Confessor of the Church. He too is blessed as he deserves, for he has merited a historian worthy of his faith and life; he is destined both for heavenly glory by his merits and for fame among men through your literary skill. (*Ep.* 11.11, modified from the translation by P. G. Walsh)[29]

Paulinus then circulated the *Life* in Rome, where it was copied and brought large profits to the *librarii*, who were able to sell a large number of copies at a high price, and purchasers took the *Life* with them from Rome all over the Roman world for companionship and comfort (*Gallus* 1.23.2–4). Paulinus was thus, in a very real sense, Sulpicius' literary agent. At the end of the *Gallus*, Sulpicius requests Postumianus, who is about to travel to Rome, to take the new work with him and present it to Paulinus so that 'through him Rome may learn of the sacred praises of the man, just as he circulated that first little book of mine not only through Italy, but also throughout the whole of Illyricum.' Moreover, Sulpicius charges Postumianus with making his new dialogue about Martin known wherever he may travel

---

[28] On his career, see briefly PLRE 1 (1971), 681–683, Paulinus 21; on his correspondence with Sulpicius, D. E. Trout, SP 28 (1993), 123–129

[29] P. G. Walsh, Letters of Paulinus of Nola 1 (Westminster, MD, 1967), 100–101.

beyond Italy – Africa, Achaea, Egypt and Palestine (*Gallus* 2[3].17.4–18.4).

The details of how the *Life* was put into circulation establish its date of composition. For, although the chronology of the letters of Paulinus of Nola presents complicated and intricate problems, it appears certain that the letter in which he acknowledges receipt of the *Life of Martin* was written during the year 397, probably in the spring.[30] Was Martin still alive or already dead? Some scholars have issued a peremptory ruling that Sulpicius cannot have composed, or at least cannot have published, a biography of Martin until he was dead.[31] That does not settle the question, since there was a clear precedent for the biography of a living person in Cornelius Nepos' *Life of Atticus*, where Nepos explicitly marks the transition from what he had written and published during Atticus' lifetime and what he added after his death (19.2: *<haec> hactenus Attico vivo edita a nobis sunt*). Nepos, whom Jerome had certainly read (*De viris illustribus*, pr.; *Contra Johannem Hierosolymitanum* 12 [PL 23.381]),[32] was surely also known to Sulpicius. Moreover, Sulpicius wrote three letters supplementing the *Life* when it was already in circulation, of which the second

---

[30] P. Fabre, Essai sur la chronologie de l'oeuvre de Saint Pauline de Nole (Paris, 1948), 23–27; D. E. Trout, SP 28 (1993), 124 n. 4; Paulinus of Nola. Life, Letters, and Poems (Berkeley, 1999), 21, 211–213, 239–241. A. D. Booth, Phoenix 37 (1983), 147–149, made a vain attempt to redate Paulinus, *Ep.* 11 to 403.

[31] Thus A. Chastagnol, BSNAF 1983, 134–140, who accepted the traditional date of 11 November 397 for the death of Martin and hence dated the *Life* to December 397 or January 398 (and Paulinus, *Ep.* 11 to spring 398).

[32] For presumed quotations from Nepos, see H. Hagendahl, Latin Fathers and the Classics. A Study on the Apologists, Jerome and other Christian Writers (Gothenburg, 1958), 31, 167.

and the third describe Martin's death. That procedure seems incomprehensible unless the *Life* itself had been written while Martin was still alive.[33] The *Life* should therefore be assessed without reference to an event which lay in the future when it was composed.

The *Life* begins with a preface in which Sulpicius stakes a claim to be superior to the two classic Roman historians.[34] The opening sentence echoes the opening words of Sallust's monograph on Catiline (1.1: *plerique mortales studio et gloriae saeculari inaniter dediti* etc.), and a later sentence echoes the opening words of Livy (1.6: *unde facturus mihi operae pretium videor, si vitam sanctissimi viri, exemplo aliis mox futurum, perscripsero*). But Sulpicius does not merely echo two famous literary models: he claims superiority over them. The great men whom Sallust lauds and holds up as examples had no interest in eternal life: what lasting benefit comes from reading about the valour of Hector or the philosophy of Socrates? And whereas Livy began the preface to his vast history of Rome hesitantly and with diffidence (*facturusne operae pretium sim ... nec satis scio nec, si sciam, dicere ausim*), Sulpicius proclaims certainty and advertises enlightenment: those who read the *Life of Martin* will be incited to true wisdom, the service of heaven, and divine virtue.

Sulpicius concludes his preface with an explicit claim to veracity. He beseeches his readers to believe him and not to think that he has written anything that he has not carefully ascertained and verified, for he would have chosen to stay silent rather than utter falsehoods (1.9: *obsecro autem eos qui lecturi sunt ut fidem dictis adhibeant, neque me quicquam nisi*

---

[33] Fontaine, Sulpice Sévère: Vie 3 (n. 13), 1119–1123.

[34] For the literary commonplaces evoked and adapted by Sulpicius here, see Fontaine, Sulpice Sévère: Vie 2 (n. 13), 393–427.

*compertum et probatum scripsisse arbitrentur: alioquin tacere quam falsa dicere maluissem*). But the preface is preceded by a letter which implicitly advances a claim that the *Life* is a scholarly work. Sulpicius informs his dear brother Desiderius that he had intended to withhold the little book that he had written about the life of Martin from the scrutiny of others, who might dislike his rather uncouth style and find fault with his rashness in tackling a subject that he ought to have left for writers of real eloquence. But he could not resist Desiderius' frequent requests (pr. 1: *sed petenti tibi saepius negare non potui*).[35] Hence he is sending the little work in the confidence that, as he has promised, Desiderius will not show it to anyone else. However, if others do read it, he should ask them to pay attention to the matter, not the style, and to forgive any inelegance of diction. Sulpicius, who is writing about a man whose *virtutes* ought not to remain hidden any longer, is not embarrassed by solecisms since he has forgotten his literary studies of long ago. On the other hand, Sulpicius makes a request in order to avoid having to defend himself: let the little work be published anonymously (pr. 6: *sed tamen ne nos maneat tam molesta defensio, suppresso si tibi videtur nomine libellus edatur. quod ut fieri valeat, titulum frontis erade, ut muta sit pagina et, quod sufficit, loquatur materiam, non loquatur auctorem*).

---

[35] Another commonplace: compare, for example, the opening words of Tacitus, *Dial de Orat.* 1.1: *saepe ex me requiris, Iuste Fabi, cur … nostra potissimum aetas … vix nomen ipsum oratoris retineat*). On Desiderius, see A. Feder, Studien zum Schriftstellerkatalog des heiligen Hieronymus (Freiburg im Breisgau, 1917), 144–147; Fontaine, Sulpice Sévère: Vie 2 (n. 13), 360–365. He appears to be the recipient of Paulinus, *Ep.* 43, which is dated to 406 by J.T. Lienhard, Paulinus of Nola and Early Western Monasticism (Cologne, 1977), 183–187, 190.

An introductory letter of this sort had a specific resonance in the Greco-Roman world. It was normal for the authors of mathematical and scientific works to protest that they were not ready for publication.[36] Galen, for example, claims that he never wished most of his writings to be published:

οὐκ ὠρέχθην οὐδεπώποτε τῶν ἐμῶν ὑπομνημάτων οὐδὲν ἐν ἀνθρώποις εἶναι· διαδοθέντων δ' εἰς πολλοὺς αὐτῶν ἄκοντος ἐμοῦ, καθάπερ οἶσθα, πρὸς τὸ διδόναι τι τοῦ λοιποῦ τοῖς φίλοις ὑπόμνημα λίαν ὀκνηρῶς ἔσχον. ἠναγκάσθην δὲ διὰ ταῦτα καὶ βιβλίον τι γράψαι περὶ τῆς ἀρίστης αἱρέσεως

I never had any ambition that my works might be valued among men. Since, however, as you know, they were widely disseminated against my wishes, I was extremely anxious at the idea of giving my friends a written version of any of the remainder. With all this in mind, I even felt compelled to write a book On the Best School of Philosophy (Galen, *The Order of my own Books* 1 [19.51 Kuhn], trans. P. N. Singer, slightly amended)

μικρὰ δ' ἐστὶ πάνυ τὰ τρία ταῦτα βιβλία φίλοις ἀξιώσασιν ὑπαγορευθέντα κἄπειτ' ἐκδοθέντα πρὸς ἐκείνων.

These are three very short books composed for friends at their request and later published by them (*The Order of my own Books* 2 [Kuhn 19.56], trans. P. N. Singer).[37]

In similar fashion, Galen gave several treatises to his friend the former consul Flavius Boethus when he left Rome and journeyed to his native city of Ptolemais to take up the

---

[36] R. Gräfenhain, De more libros dedicandi apud scriptores Graecos et Romanos obvio (Diss. Marburg, 1892), 50, also adducing Arrian's prefatory letter to L. Gellius, in which he complains that the Discourses of Epictetus, which were spoken and not intended for publication, 'have, I know not how, fallen into the hands of men against my wishes and without my knowlege.'

[37] Quoted from P. N. Singer, Galen. Selected Works (Oxford, 2002), 23, 26; I. Müller, Claudii Galeni Pergameni Scripta Minora 2 (Leipzig, 1891), 81.8–14, 86.8–10.

post of imperial legate of the province of Syria Palaestina.[38]
Among them were treatises which were published and circulated widely after Boethus died in his province, even though
Galen considered them not ready for publication (καίτοι
γ᾽ οὐ πρὸς ἔκδοσιν ἦν γεγονότα: *On Anatomical Procedures*
1.1 [2.217 Kuhn]). But perhaps the procedure by which
technical writings were normally put into circulation is best
illustrated by the letter to Eudemus which precedes the first
book of the *Conics* of Apollonius of Perge.

At the time when I was with you in Pergamum, I saw that you were
eager to get to know the conics I had composed: I am therefore sending you the first book after correcting it, and I shall despatch the rest
when I am satisfied with it. For I do not think that you have forgotten
hearing me say that I tackled the subject at the request of Naucrates
the geometer when he had come to Alexandria and was studying with
me and that after dealing with it in eight books I gave him a copy
rather too hastily because he was about to sail away without revising
thoroughly, but putting down everything that occurred to me intend-
ing to return to it later. Accordingly, using the present opportunity, I
am publishing what has been corrected. Since it happens that some
others who associated with me received copies of the first and second
books before they were corrected, do not be surprised if you come
across a different text.[39]

Sulpicius Severus thus adapted a well-known custom of
technical writers in order to enhance his trustworthiness.
Why did he feel that he needed to do so? Perhaps because
he knew full well that he had indulged in deliberate invention in order to enhance Martin's standing and status. The
*Life of Martin*, though initially published as a text complete
in itself, does not stand alone. Its reliability and Sulpicius'

---

[38] Birt, Buchwesen (n. 27), 314–315. Boethus seems to be known
only from Galen (PIR² F 220).

[39] Apollonius of Perge, ed. I. L. Hilberg 1 (Leipzig, 1891), 2 (with
a Latin translation).

purpose in composing it must also be assessed with reference
to supplementary works that reveal significant facts about
how the *Life* was received by its author's contemporaries.

## Supplements to the *Life*

The *Life of Martin* is unusual, though not unique, among
ancient biographies in that it was written while its hero was
still alive. Sulpicius had good reason therefore to add a supplement describing Martin's death after the *Life* had left his
hands and was already in circulation (*Ep.* 1.1: *studioseque
eum a multis legi libentissime audiebam*). It comprises three
letters addressed respectively to Eusebius, to the deacon
Aurelius, and to the author's mother Bassula in Trier: the
first describes Martin's narrow escape from accidentally
being burned to death as he slept; in the second, Sulpicius
dreams of seeing Martin enter heaven and receives news
of his death as soon as he awakes; and the third contains
a narrative account of the death of Martin.[40] The second
and third letters were presumably written very soon after
Sulpicius learned of the death of Martin. They may both
be earlier than the first letter, which answers a critic of the
*Life* who had asked (so it may be deduced from Sulpicius'
answer) how it was possible that a man who had recently
had a narrow escape from being burned to death through
his own carelessness could raise the dead or repel fire from
houses (*Life* 7–8, 14.1–3). Before answering the sceptic
Sulpicius accuses him of being under the influence of an
evil spirit, then rephrases his question and turns it around

---

[40] The letters are edited by Fontaine, Sulpice Sévère: Vie 1 (n. 13),
316–345; on their 'stylisation hagiographique,' ib. 3, 1177, 1263.

in order to blunt its force: why did a man who had raised the dead and repelled fires from houses allow himself to be caught in a fire and almost burnt to death (*Ep.* 1.2: *cur Martinus, qui mortuos suscitasset, flammas domibus depulisset, ipse nuper adustus incendio periculosae fuisset obnoxius passioni?*) This question Sulpicius can answer. For he recognises in the miserable fellow the perfidy and words of the Jews who mocked Jesus on the cross: had the critic been alive then, he too would have said: 'He saved others; himself he cannot save' (Matthew 27.42). After comparing Martin to the apostle Paul, who was bitten by a viper (Acts 28.4), and to Peter (*Ep.* 1.5–9), Sulpicius describes the episode as he heard it from Martin himself. The clerics of a church which Martin visited on a tour of his diocese prepared him a bed of straw in a heated room. Martin removed the straw since he wished to sleep on the bare floor, but it caught fire in the middle of the night. Martin woke up, but the Devil prevented him from resorting to prayer at once. He tried to escape, but was unable to unloose the bolt of the door. When the flames consumed his clothes, therefore, he put his trust completely in God and, as he prayed, he walked into the flames without suffering any harm until monks rescued him (*Ep.* 1.10–14). Sulpicius swears, invoking God as his witness, that Martin told him the whole story and lamented that he had been at fault for trying to escape the fire instead of seeking the protection of the Cross and prayer. The moral which Sulpicius impresses on his readers is that Martin's mettle was tested by this danger and truly proven (*Ep.* 1.14–15). The nature and tone of the first letter suggests that it was the last to be written. Although Sulpicius certainly wrote the third letter after the second, he placed the first where it is because the credibility of the *Life of Martin* was impugned as soon as it began to circulate.

The *Gallus* followed some time later, apparently in 403 or 404.[41] It is a dialogue in three parts, which observes many of the standard conventions of the ancient literary dialogue.[42] Although Sulpicius felt himself debarred from using the normal pagan setting of a banquet, even though Methodius had done so by composing a *Symposium* modelled on Plato's dialogue of the same name which depicted a banquet at which eleven women delivered discourses in praise of chastity, he includes the arrival of an unexpected guest. Just as a drunken Alcibiades arrives unexpectedly in Plato's *Symposium* (212d3–213a2) and just as Vipstanus Messala enters after Maternus' first speech in Tacitus' *Dialogus de Oratoribus*,[43] so in Sulpicius' dialogue, which spans two days, when the author, Gallus and Postumianus rise at dawn on the second day and Gallus is on the point of speaking, 'a crowd of monks bursts in' eager to hear about Martin followed by another group and, while many are excluded as having come out of curiosity, not piety, several people are allowed in to listen to the second day's discussion, among them Eucherius, a former *vicarius*, and the *consularis* Celsus (2[3].1.3–8).[44]

---

[41] Babut, Saint Martin (n. 5), 51; Fontaine, Sulpice Sévère: Vie 1 (n. 13), 38. Carl Halm's text, which gave the work the title *Dialogi* (CSEL 1 [Vienna, 1866], 152–216), has now been replaced by the excellent critical edition by J. Fontaine, Sulpice Sévère: Gallus. Dialogues sur les "vertues" de saint Martin (SC 510, 2006). For the convenience of readers, references are given according to the numeration at the top of each right-hand page in Halm's edition.

[42] Unfortunately, the standard survey by R. Hirzel, Der Dialog. Ein literarhistorischer Versuch (Leipzig, 1895), proceeds chronologically and contains no systematic discussion of the conventions of the genre.

[43] Messala immediately apologises for his interrruption (14.1: '*num parum tempestivus*' inquit '*interveni secretum consilium*').

[44] Eucherius and Celsus are otherwise unknown: their entries in PLRE 1 (1971), 288, Eucherius 1; 2 (1980), 279, Celsus 1, assume that they had both held office in the West. Although the unexpected

The three parts of the dialogue have the following contents:

I   Postumianus, newly arrived from the East, tells Sulpicius and Gallus, a disciple of Martin, about his pilgrimage to Egypt and Palestine

II  Gallus recounts his experiences of Martin to Sulpicius and Postumianus

III On the following day, the priest Refrigerius joins the three men; after a 'crowd of monks' bursts in and the audience is enlarged, and Gallus continues his reminiscences of Martin.

In the *Gallus* Sulpicius is less concerned to answer critics than he had been in the first letter. His main purpose is to show that Martin was at least the equal of and probably superior to the famous ascetics of Egypt. The dialogue makes explicit what is implicit, if not expressly stated, in the *Life* itself: Sulpicius wished to proclaim the virtues and achievements of a western ascetic who surpassed all the hermits and anchorites of Egypt, the home of asceticism.[45] After the scene has been set, the dialogue proper begins when Sulpicius asks Postumianus, who has recently returned from the East after an absence of three years (1.1.1), to report on the state of Christianity in the East:

---

arrival of an additional participant is erroneously stated to be rare by A. Gudeman, P. Cornelii Taciti Dialogus de Oratoribus[2] (Leipzig & Berlin, 1914), 64, the recent commentary by R. Mayer, Tacitus: Dialogus de Oratoribus (Cambridge, 2001), 132, correctly observes that 'the striking introduction of a new character was not uncommon in the course of dialogues' and identifies Cicero, *De re publica* 1.17 as Tacitus' formal model.

[45] Note the episode in the *Life* where the Devil appears to Martin in the guise of Christ (24), analysed at length by B. Studer, Nuovo Didaskaleion 13 (1963), 29–82.

*qualiter in Oriente fides Christi floreat, quae sit sanctorum quies, quae instituta monachorum, quantisque signis et virtutibus in servis suis Christus operetur.*

How the Christian faith flourishes in the East, what peace the saints enjoy, what are the rules of life of the monks, by what signs and powers Christ operates in his servants. (1.2.2, cf. Acts 2.22)

Postumianus gives a long and detailed account of his travels: he sailed from Narbo to Africa and thence made his way to Alexandria after being driven ashore in Cyrenaica (1.3–5). In Alexandria Postumianus found the Origenist controversy raging and so left the city to visit Jerome in Bethlehem, whose acquaintance he had made on an earlier pilgrimage (1.6–8.1). He spent six months with Jerome, then returned to Egypt where he travelled up the River Nile to the Thebaid to visit the monks of the desert (1.9.4–7). Postumianus expatiates at length on what he saw there (10–23) and as soon as he concludes Sulpicius embarks upon an extended comparison of Martin to the desert fathers of Egypt (1.24–25). This reaches the predictable verdict that no Egyptian ascetic can be compared with Martin, who operated not in the quiet of the desert, but in the midst of controversy and scandal 'among quarrelling clergy, among savagely raging bishops' so that alone and in his own person Martin combined all the achievements that the holy men of Egypt had attained collectively, while some of them lacked Martin's powers (1.25.1, 5). Postumianus immediately signals his agreement: although the monks, anchorites and hermits of Egypt truly deserve admiration, none of them matches the qualities of Martin (1.26.1).

The transition to the achievements of Martin is effected when Postumianus reports that some wretch has accused its author of the *Life of Martin* of telling a large number of

lies (1.26.4).[46] Postumianus who reports the complaint of
dishonesty, immediately goes on to stigmatise it as the doing
of the Devil. Such complaints do not demean Martin, but
impugn the veracity of the gospels: since our Lord stated
that all Christians are capable of performing the deeds
which Martin has performed (Mark 16.17–18),[47] no-one
who says that Martin did not do them can believe that
Christ said that. The degenerate sluggards who complain
are merely ashamed that they cannot do what Martin did,
and prefer to deny his power for good rather than admit
their own incapacity (1.26.4–6). Postumianus then turns
to Gallus, a disciple of Martin, and asks him to speak about
his master (1.26.7–8). Gallus agrees and begins to recount
the miracles performed by Martin which he has himself
witnessed (1.27). This recitation of miracles and other feats
occupies nearly twenty pages in Carl Halm's edition and
elicits an admission by Postumianus that Martin has indeed
surpassed all the holy men of Egypt:

Gallus, said Postumianus, you have outdone, you have truly outdone
not only me, an obvious booster of Martin who have always both
known and believed all these things about him, but you have outdone
all the hermits and anchorites. For none of them has exercised authority over death, as your, or rather our, Martin has. With justification,
therefore, our friend Sulpicius compares to the apostles and prophets[48]

---

[46] Quoted and translated at the start of this chapter.
[47] It is now generally agreed that these two verses do not belong
to the original Gospel of Mark – and there is no similar attribution of
miraculous powers to Jesus' true disciples in the corresponding passages
in the other evangelists (Matthew 28.16–20; Luke 24.36–49; John
20.19–23; Acts 1.6–8).
[48] On the 'prophetic typology' of the *Life of Martin*, see J. Fontaine,
*Mélanges offerts à Mademoiselle Christine Mohrmann* (Utrecht, 1963),
84–95. Sulpicius compares Martin to the apostles in *Ep.* 1.5: *o beatum
et per omnia similem apostolis etiam in his conviciis virum!*; *Chron.*

this man whom the power of his faith and the deeds of his powers declare to be completely similar to them in everything (1[2].5.1/2).

But Sulpicius knew that much of what he wrote about both the ascetics of Egypt and about Martin came from his own imagination, and he subtly signals the fact that he is writing fiction. Postumianus had seen an influential Egyptian ascetic who was constantly visited by imperial officials and even bishops (1.20.3). This man achieved what all can recognise as a physical impossibility: he survived for years on six dates a day without ever drinking anything, not even water. Significantly, Sulpicius makes Postumianus whisper the impossible detail into his ear so that the third interlocutor Gallus cannot hear (1.20.4: *hic ferebatur omni potu in perpetuum penitus abstinere ac pro cibo – tibi Sulpici in aurem loquar, ne Gallus hoc audiat – sex tantum caricis sustentari*). Postumianus had also visited the place where Paul the first hermit lodged (1.17.1: *ad eum etiam locum, in quo beatissimus Paulus primus eremita est diversatus, accessi*). It might be naive automatically to accept this as a genuine report that tourists to Egypt around 400 were shown what was said to be the dwelling of Paul, as many have done, even the most sceptical.[49] Since Paul was invented, it may be suspected

---

2.50.1: *Martino episcopo, viro plane apostolis conferendo*. In heaven after his death, Sulpicius claims, Martin consorts with the apostles and prophets, second to none in the company of the saints (*Ep.* 2.9: *est enim ille consertus apostolis ac prophetis, et, quod pace sanctorum omnium dixerim, in illo iustorum grege nulli secundus*). Specifically, had Martin lived when Christians were persecuted, he would have shown himself the equal of Isaiah under torture (*Ep.* 2.10: *numquam profecto inpar prophetae*). As Fontaine, Sulpice Sévère: Vie 3 (n. 13), 1223–1229, duly notes, Sulpicius here alludes to the *Martyrdom of Isaiah*, on which see A.-M. Denis, Introduction à la littérature religieuse judéo-hellénistique 1 (Turnhout, 2000), 633–657.

[49] E.g., Barnes, Constantine (1981), 196, 370–371 n. 53.

that Sulpicius is giving a wink to those readers alert and intelligent enough to understand his coded language. For he reiterates his veracity with an insistence difficult to parallel in fourth century literature except in combination with lies and invention. Like Athanasius defending himself against charges of treasonable dealings with western emperors who offered him shelter and political support, Sulpicius appeals to God for proof that he is telling the truth (*Ep.* 1.14: *verbis meis dominus est testis*).[50] Moreover, halfway through his account of the ascetics of Egypt, Postumianus proclaims that it is all true: *fides Christi* is his guarantee; he is not repeating mere rumours, only what he has ascertained as true through believers who deserve trust (*Gallus* 1.15.1: *fides Christi adest me nihil fingere, neque incertis auctoribus vulgata narrabo, sed quae mihi per fideles viros conperta sunt explicabo*).

The most interesting passage where Sulpicius tips his hand comes when Gallus chides Sulpicius for an omission. He expresses surprise that, although Sulpicius recorded two resurrections from the dead which Martin performed before becoming a bishop, he had omitted the resurrection which his hero performed after his consecration. Gallus, who had witnessed this miracle himself, proceeds to describe it (*Gallus* 1[2].4.3–9). Whether consciously or not, Sulpicius invites disbelief when he makes the alleged eye-witness raise

---

[50] Compare Athanasius' insistence on his truthfulness in his *Defence before Constantius* when giving a misleading account of his dealings with Constantius' brothers, the western emperors Constantinus and Constans: 'To defend myself I must tell the truth to your piety … I did not know, the Lord is my witness … Believe me, your majesty, this is how it happened, and I am not lying' (*Apol. ad Const.* 2–5, esp. 4.3 [282.16–283.4 Opitz-Brennecke: χρὴ γὰρ ἀπολογούμενόν με ἀληθεύειν τῇ σῇ θεοσεβείᾳ … οὐ γὰρ ἐγίνωσκον, μάρτυς ὁ Κύριος … πίστευε, βασιλεῦ, οὕτω γέγονε, καὶ οὐ ψεύδομαι), cf. Barnes, Athanasius (1993), 50–53, 102–105, 113.

the possibility that his reliability might be doubted (*Gallus.* 1[2].4.3: *cuius rei ego testis sum, si tamen nihil de idoneo teste dubitatis*). This constant emphasis throughout the *Gallus* on the value of the testimony to the miracles worked by Martin indicates that Sulpicius expected at least some of his readers to be as sceptical about his veracity here as they had been about the original *Life of Martin* some years before. For he knew that both works contain a large amount of deliberate invention.

Delehaye assigned Sulpicius Severus to 'that class of writers, possessing both literary power and the necessary information, who have undertaken to discharge the functions of a historian,' who were 'the last representatives of classical antiquity' and whose writings, 'instinct with art and life, must not be confused with the artificial productions of later periods.'[51] But classicism is perfectly compatible with intellectual dishonesty. The literary nature of the *Life of Martin* has usually been discussed with reference to the *Life of Antony* and Jerome's lives of the hermits Paul and Hilarion.[52] But Sulpicius' replies to his critics are suspiciously similar to similar protestations of honesty and veracity in the closely contemporary *Historia Augusta*, especially with the passage where the author of that work invokes *fidelitas historica* to camouflage a transparent invention of his own.[53] When

[51]  Delehaye, Légendes (1927), 57–58. I have quoted the translation by V. M. Crawford, The Legends of the Saints (London, 1907), 60/61. The later translation by D. Attwater, The Legends of the Saints (London, 1962), 49, fails to reproduce the elegance of Delehaye's French.

[52]  Fontaine, Sulpice Sévère: Vie 1 (n. 13), 17–58 ('Les coordonnées de la Vita Martini'). Fontaine's introduction adduces the *Historia Augusta* only in a different context (179).

[53]  HA, *Tyr. Trig.* 11.6/7: *hos ego versus … posui … ut fidelitas historica servaretur, quam ego prae ceteris custodiendam putavi, qui quod*

Sulpicius professes that he is devoted to *veritas historica*,[54] are his protestations necessarily more credible or more sincere? The *Life of Martin* belongs to the same intellectual milieu as the *Historia Augusta*, and Sulpicius might conceivably have been inspired to write as he does partly by reading this very recent work of largely fictitious biography.[55]

## When was Martin born?

The *natalis* of Martin, that is, the day on which he died, is abundantly certified as 11 November by liturgical and hagiographical evidence.[56] But there is no explicit evidence for the precise year earlier than Gregory of Tours, who was writing two centuries after Martin's death, and a recent encyclopedia professes uncertainty over whether Martin was born in 316/317 or 336.[57]

---

*ad eloquentiam pertinet nihil curo. rem enim vobis proposui deferre, non verba.* Sulpicius too has the cliché *res potius quam verba* (*Life*, pr. 3).

[54] *Dial.* 2(3).5.6: *etsi dialogi speciem, quo ad levandum fastidium lectio variaretur, adsumpsimus, nos pie praestruere profitemur historiae veritatem.* The author of the *Historia Augusta* too wished to avoid causing *fastidium* to his readers (Tac. 12.2).

[55] As suggested in Historiae Augustae Colloquia, N. S. VII: Colloquium Genevense MCMXCVIII (Bari, 1999), 38–40, though on the basis of the false hypothesis that the *Life of Martin* may have been written as late as 400 or 401.

[56] Comm. Mart. Rom. (1940), 510–511. This evidence was discounted by É.-C. Babut, Annales du Midi 20 (1908), 36–44, who dated the death of Martin between November 396 and the beginning of spring 397, averring that 'la date obituaire de 11 novembre ne peut être admise comme authentique.'

[57] L. Pietri, TRE 22 (1992), 194, citing Stancliffe, St. Martin (n. 17), 111–133, for the later date.

Gregory concludes the tenth and last book of his history, which is conventionally known as the *History of the Franks*, with a series of notices of the nineteen bishops of Tours ending with himself (10.31). According to Gregory, the first bishop of his city was Catianus, who was sent from Rome in the first year of the emperor Decius and died before the Diocletianic persecution after an episcopate of probably fifty years (the numeral has dropped out of the manuscripts). The see of Tours then remained vacant for thirty seven years until Litorius was consecrated as its second bishop in the first year of Constans and was bishop for thirty three years. Martin was consecrated bishop in the eighth year of Valens and Valentinian (Gregory's order) and served as bishop for twenty six years, four months and seventeen days, dying in the eighty-first year of his life. Brictius succeeded Martin twenty days after his death in the second year of the joint reign of Arcadius and Honorius. At the very end of the chapter Gregory sums up the chronology of the world as follows:

| | |
|---|---:|
| Years from the beginning to the Flood | 2242 |
| from the Flood to the crossing of the Red Sea by the children of Israel | 1404 |
| from the passage of the Red Sea to the Resurrection of our Lord | 1538 |
| from the Resurrection of our Lord to the passing of the holy Martin | 412 |
| from the passing of the holy Martin to the above-mentioned year, I mean the twenty-first year of my consecration, which is the fifth of Gregory, pope of Rome, the thirty-first of King Guntram, and the nineteenth of Childebert the younger | 197 |
| The sum of all which years is | 5792 |

Gregory's sums do not quite add up. The individual to-
tals add up to 5793, not 5792, and on any known or
possible computation the interval between the death and
resurrection of Christ 'under Pontius Pilate' and the passing
of Martin was considerably less than four centuries. The
contemporary correlations do not exactly coincide either.
Although Gregory the Great became Pope in 590, so that his
fifth year was 594, and Childebert became king of Austrasia
in 575, so that his nineteenth year was 594 too, Gregory was
consecrated bishop of Tours in 573, so that his twenty-first
year as bishop was 593 rather than 594, while Guntram,
who had became king of Burgundy in 561, died on 28
January 592. In the notes to his classic English translation,
O. M. Dalton adopted a counsel of despair: 'Gregory's figures present difficulties; and manuscripts disagree; attempts
to rectify and reconcile have been many, and the result new
discrepancies.'[58] But Gregory's computation that Martin
died 197 years before the year 594, in which he was writing,
corresponds to what he says elsewhere about the chronology
of the life of Martin.

Gregory dates the birth of Martin to the eleventh year
of Constantine, by which he means the calendar year 317,
since he dates the deaths of Crispus and Fausta, which certainly occurred in 326, to Constantine's twentieth year (*HE*
1.23/36). Gregory is even more precise about the death of
Martin: he died 'in the eighty-first year of his life and the
twenty sixth of his episcopate' on a Sunday in the second
year of Arcadius and Honorius and the consulate of Atticus
and Caesarius (1.35/48). All of this fits 11 November 397,
and no valid reason has ever been advanced for doubting

---

[58] O. M. Dalton, *The History of the Franks by Gregory of Tours* 2
(Oxford, 1927), 605.

the accuracy of Gregory's information on this point.[59] Admittedly the manuscript reading in a passage of the *Gallus* makes Martin live on for sixteen years after his second visit to the court of Maximus in Trier (2[3].13.6: *sedecim postea vixit annos; nullam synodum adiit, ab omnibus episcoporum conventibus se removit*): hence, by applying the normally valid principle that the evidence of a contemporary should outweigh that of a historian writing two centuries later (though mistakenly counting from Martin's first visit to Trier instead of his visit in 387) the death of Martin has been dated to 401[60] or even to 11 November 402.[61] But numbers in manuscripts are notoriously liable to corruption, and the transmitted reading, which is in fact *sedicem*, has been variously emended to *sed decem,* to *undecim* (*xi*), to *tredicem* (*xiii*), to *quattuordecim* (*xiv*) and even to *undeviginti* (*xix*).[62]

It is normally assumed that Gregory took his dates for the death of Martin, his age at death and the year of his consecration as bishop from the episcopal archives of Tours and hence that they must be correct.[63] Even Fontaine,

---

[59] L. Duchesne, Fastes épiscopaux de l'ancienne Gaule 2[2] (Paris, 1910), 299, cf. Les anciens catalogues episcopaux de la province de Tours (Paris, 1890), 24. In the earlier work Duchesne dated Martin's death to 11 November, in the later his death to 8 November and his burial to 11 November 397.

[60] Barnes, Historiae Augustae Colloquia, N. S. VII (n. 55), 37.

[61] Booth, Phoenix 37 (1983), 147–149.

[62] So, respectively, Fontaine, Saint Martin et son temps (n. 13), 196; Gallus (n. 42), 343 n. 5 (*sed decem*); L. Duchesne, Les anciens catalogues (n. 59), 24 n. 1; Stancliffe, St. Martin (n. 17), 119–120 (*xiii*); B. Vollmann, Studien zum Priscillianismus (St. Ottilien, 1965), 4–5 n. 6 (*xiv*); H. Chadwick, Priscillian of Avila. The Occult and the Charismatic in the Early Church (Oxford, 1976), 132–133 (*xix*).

[63] E. Griffe, La Gaule chrétienne à l'époque romaine 1 (Paris, 1964), 296, cf. Duchesne, Fastes épiscopaux (n. 59), 302/3. Fontaine,

who trumpets the historical reliability of *Life of Martin* so consistently, emphatically bases his commentary on the proposition that the date of 317 for Martin's birth is absolutely certain.[64] But if Martin was born in 317, as Gregory asserts, then he was twenty years older than Sulpicius' *Life* assumes and if he was discharged from the Roman army on the occasion which the *Life* describes, then he was aged forty, not twenty, and had served in the army for twenty five years. Sulpicius, lets slip a remark in the *Gallus* which shows that he knew that Martin was indeed born in 317. It follows that his account of the military career in the *Life* either is or contains deliberate invention.

## Martin at the Court of Magnus Maximus

Martin visited the court of Magnus Maximus in Trier at least twice, since Sulpicius records episodes from two separate visits at different dates. Delehaye saw and stated this clearly in 1920.[65] Subsequent investigators have often conflated the two visits, sometimes with, sometimes without serious consequences.[66] Conflation of the two has, moreover, produced an erroneous date for the trial and execution of Priscillian: from the fact that, when Martin

---

Sulpice Sévère: Vie 3 (n. 13), 1285 n. 2, asserts that 'la date de la mort de Martin est une des plus solidement attestées de sa biographie.'

[64] Fontaine, Sulpice Sévère: Vie 2 (n. 13), 432 n. 2: 'nous la considérons comme une "donnée absolue" de la biographie martinienne.'

[65] H. Delehaye, AB 38 (1920), 32: on the earlier occasion, Martin had left Trier before Pricillian was condemned (*Chron.* 2.50.5–6), but he came to Trier again *post Priscilliani necem* (*Gallus* 3.11.2–13.5).

[66] E. g., Matthews, Western Aristocracies (n. 12), 166–167; Barnes, Historiae Augustae Colloquia, N. S. VII (n. 55), 37.

was at the imperial court interceding for certain unnamed persons, he attended a banquet where one of the other guests of Maximus was Evodius, his praetorian prefect and ordinary consul (*Vita* 20.4: *praefectus idemque consul Evodius, vir quo nihil umquam iustius fuit*), it has been deduced that, since Flavius Evodius was ordinary consul in 386, the trial of Priscillian could not have occurred earlier than that year.[67] The inference is false. Sulpicius knew of and refers to an encounter between Martin and Maximus earlier than the one where he notes the presence of Evodius. On this earlier occasion, Martin had told the emperor that, if he invaded Italy and made war on Valentinian, he would at first be successful, but would soon perish (20:8: *eidemque Maximo longe ante praedixit futurum ut, si ad Italiam pergeret quo ire cupiebat bellum Valentiniano imperatori inferens, sciret se primo quidem impetu futurum esse victorem, sed parvo post tempore esse periturum*). Moreover, a letter of Ambrose shows that the bishop of Milan was in Trier at the time of the trial (*Ep.* 30 [24]): hence not only the embassy of Ambrose to Maximus, but also the trial of Priscillian and his associates by the praetorian prefect Evodius (Sulpicius Severus, *Chronica* 2.50.2–3) cannot have taken place later than the winter of 384/385.[68] Furthermore, Sulpicius' *Chronicle* states that there have been fifteen years of discord since the death of Priscillian (2.51.5: *iam per quindecim annos*), and although Sulpicius did not complete the

---

[67] A. R. Birley, Bulletin of the John Rylands Library 66 (1982/83), 13–43.

[68] T. D. Barnes, ZAC 4 (2000), 293–295. The execution of Priscillian had been dated to 385 by K. M. Girardet, Chiron 4 (1974), 577–608; Stancliffe, St. Martin (n. 17), 119.

*Chronicle* until 403,[69] he always reckons dates from the consulate of Stilicho in 400 (*Chr.*2.9.3: *omne enim tempus in Stiliconem consulem direxi*).[70]

Martin's first visit to Trier also finds a place in Sulpicius' *Chronicle* (2.49.3–50.2). After his condemnation by a council of bishops at Bordeaux, Priscillian appealed to the emperor, as many a bishop under Constantine and his sons had done before him. But Priscillian's status was disputed: although he claimed to be a bishop, he had been consecrated by two bishops only, not by three including the metropolitan bishop of his province, as laid down in 325 at the Council of Nicaea. By accepting the appeal, Maximus accepted the view of Priscillian's opponents that he was not a validly consecrated bishop: as a bishop he could only be tried by other bishops in conclave and he could suffer no punishment more extreme than deposition from his see; since he was not regarded as a bishop, he was tried in a secular court, condemned on charges that included the capital crime of black magic and duly executed. Martin and his biographer took the opposite view. Martin went to the court of Maximus to protest and lobby the emperor. Martin's intervention prompted one of Priscillian's accusers at Bordeaux to accuse him of heresy, but he persisted and succeeded in preventing a criminal trial as long as he

---

[69] The *Chronicle* incorporates the legend of the finding of the True Cross by Helena, the mother of Constantine, from a letter of Paulinus of Nola (2.33.2–34.2 < Paulinus, *Ep.* 31) which (it is agreed) Paulinus sent to him in the spring of 403: P. Fabre, Essai sur la chronologie de l'œuvre de Saint Pauline de Nole (Paris, 1948), 34, 40; Lienhard, Paulinus of Nola (n. 35), 182–187, 190.

[70] Thus the *Chronicle* correctly calculates that the Crucifixion, which it dates to the consular year 29, occurred 372 years before the consulate of Stilico (2.27.2).

remained in Trier, and before he left he obtained a solemn promise from Maximus that Priscillian and his followers would not be executed (2.50.2: *a Maximo elicuit sponsionem, nihil cruentum in reos constituendem*). For reasons which have always remained unclear, Maximus reneged on his promise to Martin.

The later visit can be dated to 387 by the incidental details which the *Life of Martin* provides when introducing the story of how Maximus passed the loving cup to Martin, who had at last agreed to dine with him, as a mark of honour expecting the bishop hand it back to him after taking the first sip, but Martin passed it to the priest accompanying him:

*nam et si pro aliquibus regi supplicandum fuit, imperavit potius quam rogavit, et a convivio eius frequenter rogatus abstinuit, dicens se mensae eius participem esse non posse, qui imperatores unum regno, alterum vita expulisset*

For, although he needed <on one occasion> to intercede with the emperor on behalf of some persons, he ordered rather than requested and he avoided dining with him despite frequent invitations, saying that he could not sit at the table of one who had deprived one emperor of his sovereignty and another of his life. (20.2)

The date cannot be earlier than 387: although Gratian was killed on 26 August 383, Valentinian, whose writ never ran beyond the Alps after his brother's death, continued to reside in Milan as ruler of Italy, Africa and western Illyricum until Maximus' troops invaded Italy and he fled to Thessalonica during this year. Who were these unidentified persons on whose behalf Martin travelled to Trier a second time? The *Gallus* supplies relevant details at some length and in very tendentious terms (2[3].11–13). Martin was compelled to go to court after the death of Priscillian to prevent an official purge of suspected heretics. Maximus had given orders for armed tribunes to go to Spain with powers not only to search out heretics, but also to execute them and confiscate their property: despite fierce opposition from some bishops who accused him of heresy, Martin persuaded Maximus to rescind the order.

It was during this second visit to Trier that, as the *Gallus* records in another passage, Martin dined alone with the wife of Maximus, who ministered to him:

*videant enim, quia Martino semel in vita iam septuagenario non vidua libera, non virgo lasciviens, sed sub viro vivens, ipso viro pariter supplicante, regina servivit et ministravit edenti, non cum epulante discubuit.* (*Gallus* 2.7.4)

Let them see that only once in his whole life was Martin <approached by a woman>: he was already a septuagenarian, and the woman was not an unattached widow or a lustful girl, but an empress living in subjection to her husband, with her husband showing equal deference, who served him and waited on him as he ate, but did not recline with him as he feasted.

Gallus compares Martin to Jesus and claims that the wife of Maximus gave him the treatment that Jesus received in Bethany from the sisters from Martha and Mary and he warmly defends Martin against critics of his behaviour (2.7.5). But his defence of Martin assumes that he was 'already a septuagenarian' in 387. In this passage, therefore, Sulpicius Severus accepts Gregory's date of 317 for the birth of Martin, and it can hardly be doubted that Martin was indeed born in 317. In an unguarded moment, Sulpicius Severus has unwittingly confirmed the falsity of the account that the *Life of Martin* had given for his military career.

The consequences are serious for our estimate of the veracity of Sulpicius. As Babut saw almost a century ago, the *Life of Martin* is not the honest and authoritative memorial of the bishop of Tours that it pretends to be. The military career which it bestows on its hero contains two utter impossibilities. Martin cannot both have been discharged from the Roman army near Worms in the autumn of 357, and consorted with Hilary before the bishop of Poitiers was exiled to Phrygia in the spring of 356. And Martin was born in 317, as Sulpicius reveals in the *Gallus*, so that he was in reality twenty years older than he would have been if he had entered the army in 352 when he was fifteen. These contradictions raise fundamental questions not merely about the nature and veracity of Sulpicius' *Life of Martin*, but also about Martin himself. For, if the military career which the *Life* bestows on Martin does not belong to him, but to someone else, what valid reason remains for believing that the rustic, uncouth and hirsute bishop of Tours ever served in the Roman army?

In the technical sense of the term as defined by Ernst Bernheim in his classic textbook of historical method, the saint's military career in the *Life of Martin* is a *Fälschung*, a term which has a wider sense than the English word 'forgery.'[71] It therefore requires explicit evidence and positive arguments to show that the rest of the *Life* is not equally fraudulent, that the *Life of Martin* deserves more respect from the critical historian than Mark the Deacon's *Life of Porphyry, Bishop of Gaza*, in which the uncritical have also too often wrongly reposed equal trust.[72]

---

[71] On the meaning of the German word *Fälschung* as used in German scholarship of the late nineteenth century, see Historia 44 (1995), 497–500; Archiv für Kulturgeschichte 79 (1997), 259–267.

[72] Chapter VI.

*Table 2:* The Military Career attributed to Martin by Sulpicius Severus

Conscripted at the age of fifteen (2.5)
*cum esset annorum quindecim, captus et catenatus sacramentis militaribus implicatus est.*

Served under Constantius and Julian (2.1)
*inter scholares alas sub Constantio, deinde sub Iuliano militavit.*

Served for about three years before he was baptised (2.5 + 3.5)
*triennium fere ante baptismum in armis fuit. … cum esset annorum duodeviginti, ad baptismum convolavit. nec tamen statim militiae renuntiavit, tribuni sui precibus evictus, cui contubernium familiare praestabat.*

Served for about two years after he was baptised (3.6)
*per biennium fere posteaquam est baptismum consecutus solo licet nomine militavit.*

Discharged by Julian near Worms (4.1–3 + 4.7)
*interea inruentibus intra Gallias barbaris, Iulianus Caesar, coacto in unum exercitu apud Vangionum civitatem, donativum coepit erogare militibus, et, ut est consuetudinis, singuli citabantur, donec ad Martinum ventum est. tum vero opportunum tempus existimans, quo peteret missionem … hactenus, inquit ad Caesarem, militavi tibi; patere ut nunc militem Deo. … postero die hostes legatos de pace miserunt, sua omnia et se dedentes.*

# History and Fiction in the fifth and sixth Centuries

Lives of recently deceased Christian men and women with a reputation for holiness have continued to be composed in almost every generation since Late Antiquity in Greek and Latin, in Syriac and Coptic, in Armenian and Georgian, in Arabic and Ethiopic, in European vernacular languages, and finally in any language on any continent where Christian communities have felt the need for exemplars of holiness to emulate. The importance of such hagiographical documents for political, social and cultural history is obvious and generally acknowledged.[1] Indeed, in the early Byzantine period the lives of saints take over the role which inscriptions had played for the Greco-Roman world as the only systematic source available for writing social history.[2] Hence the historian of the Later Roman Empire gratefully uses several

---

[1] Hence the section on 'hagiography' by A.-M. Talbot in The Oxford Handbook of Byzantine Studies, ed. E. Jeffreys with J. Haldon & R. Cormack (Oxford, 2008), 862–871.

[2] F. Halkin, Thirteenth International Congress of Byzantine Studies Oxford 1966 (Oxford, 1967), 345–354; E. Patlagean, Annales 23 (1968), 106–126; T. D. Barnes, Atti dell' XI Congresso Internazionale di Epigrafia greca e latina, Roma 18–24 settembre 1997 2 (Rome, 1999), 576, cf. L. Robert, L'histoire et ses méthodes. Encyclopédie la Pléiade (Paris, 1961), 453–497, reprinted in his Opera Minora Selecta 5 (Amsterdam, 1989), 65–109, on 'les épigraphies et l'épigraphie grecque et romaine.' Earlier Robert had made this very point briefly in the peroration of his address to the international epigraphical congress

well-known hagiographical texts as evidence for an otherwise often badly attested period. A conspicuous example from the fourth century is the *Passion of Sabas* (K-K-R XXXIII),[3] whose 'dossier' (a concept which Delehaye used later, though not when publishing the only modern critical edition of the text)[4] comprises the *Passion* itself and four letters of Basil of Caesarea: three are probably addressed to Ascholius, a priest in Scythia who wrote the *Passion* (Basil, *Epp.* 154, 164, 165), while one is a request to Junius Soranus, the *dux Scythiae* and a fellow Cappadocian with relatives in Caesarea to send 'to his homeland' relics of martyrs in the persecution which is occurring outside Roman territory (155).[5] Since the latest of the four letters thanks Ascholius for sending him relics of an unnamed martyr who can only be Sabas (165),[6] it is presumably to Basil, therefore, to whom is owed the preservation of this contemporary account of village life in Gothic territory north of the Danube in the early 370s with outside pressures from the Gothic state, which 'does what the works of Caesar and Tacitus never do – it brings us for the first time into a Germanic village,'[7] it illuminates the social background of the conversion of the Goths to Christianity, especially the

---

held in Paris in 1952, where he saluted the Bollandist Paul Peeters as 'un grand érudit' (Opera minora selecta 3 [Amsterdam, 1969], 1767).

[3] Translated into English by P. Heather & J. Matthews, The Goths in the Fourth Century (TTH 11, 1991), 111–117.

[4] H. Delehaye, AB 31 (1912), 216–221, 288–291. For the notion of 'le dossier d'un saint,' see Delehaye, Légendes (1927), 119–139.

[5] PLRE 1 (1971), 848, Soranus 2.

[6] The manuscript evidence for of the recipients of the four letters is confused, but their identities have been established by C. Zuckerman, Travaux et mémoires 11 (1991), 473–479, who also showed that the author of the Passion was the Scythian priest Ascholius.

[7] E. A. Thompson, The Visigoths in the Time of Ulfila (Oxford, 1966), 64.

attempt of the central authorities of the Tervingi 'to uphold traditional religious observances' in the aftermath of Valens' Gothic campaigns of 367–369.[8]

Although hagiography was never a literary genre on the strict definition of that term, hagiographical themes and hagiographical material permeate all types of literature from the late fourth century onwards. The two Gregories (of Nazianzus and Nyssa) and John Chrysostom, who was bishop of Constantinople from 398 to 404, are the fountainhead of an enduring Byzantine tradition of Christian panegyric.[9] John Chrysostom delivered seven encomia on the apostle Paul (CPG 4344) and a large number of encomiastic homilies on martyrs and bishops, some of them while still a priest in Antioch (CPG 4319, 4345–4353, 4355, 4357, 4359–4365).[10] Gregory of Nazianzus composed rhetorically elaborate panegyrics of Athanasius (*Orat.* 21: BHG 186) and of a Cyprian who was a conflation of the historical bishop of Carthage and a legendary magician from Antioch (*Orat.* 24: BHG 457) and a long funerary oration (λόγος ἐπιτάφιος) of Basil of Caesarea, with whom he had studied

---

[8] On the various perspectives opened up by the *Passion of Sabas*, see Thompson, Visigoths (n. 7), 64–77; Z. Rubin, Museum Helveticum 38 (1981), 34–54; W. Wolfram, History of the Goths, trans. T. J. Dunlap (Berkeley, 1988), 100–107; P. J. Heather, Goths and Romans 332–489 (Oxford, 1991), 81–82, 103–107; N. Lenski, Failure of Empire. Valens and the Roman State in the Fourth Century A. D. (Berkeley, 2002), 118–120.

[9] H. Hunger, Hochsprachliche profane Literatur der Byzantiner 1: Philosophie, Rhetorik, Epistolographie, Geschichtsschreibung, Geographie (Munich, 1978), 121–128.

[10] On the liturgical context and political significance of the sermons which John preached as bishop celebrating the arrival of holy relics in Constantinople, J. N. D. Kelly, Golden Mouth. The Story of John Chrysostom – ascetic, preacher, bishop (London, 1995), 137–141.

in Athens as a young man when the future emperor Julian was also there (*Orat.* 43: BHG 245).[11] Gregory of Nyssa composed not only encomia of his brother Basil of Caesarea (CPG 3185 = BHG 244) and of various martyrs (CPG 3183, 3185–3189, 3200) and an edifying (and largely fictitious) biography of the third century Pontic bishop Gregory the Thaumaturge (CPG 3184 = BHG 715),[12] but also a *Life of Moses* in two books (CPG 3159 = BHG 2278), in which he set forth his philosophy and which ranks as one of 'the classics of western spirituality.'[13] Moreover, when his sister Macrina died, and he took the opportunity to glorify his family in a work of hagiography which is frequently styled a *Life of Macrina* (CPG 3166 = BHG 1012). Gregory himself describes its literary form as a letter, though a letter whose length comes close to turning it into something closer to history (*Vita Macrinae* 1.1: τὸ μὲν εἶδος τοῦ βιβλίου ὅσον

---

[11] On *Orat.* 43, see N. McLynn, SP 37 (2001), 178–193. For editions with excellent introductions and commentaries on these three speeches, J. Mossay with G. Lafontaine, Grégoire de Nazianze: Discours 20–23 (SC 270, 1980), 86–193; Grégoire de Nazianze: Discours 24–26 (SC 284, 1981), 9–85; J. Bernardi, Grégoire de Nazianze: Discours 42–43 (SC 384, 1992), 25–45, 116–307

[12] Edited by G. Heil, Gregorii Nysseni opera 10.1 (Leiden, 1990), 1–57. On its intellectual context and historical value, R. van Dam, Classical Antiquity 1 (1982), 272–309; S. Mitchell, Portraits of Spiritual Authority: Religious Power in Early Christianity, Byzantium and the Christian Orient, ed. J. W. Drijvers & J. W. Watt. Religion sin the Graeco-Roman World 117 (Leiden, 1999), 99–138.

[13] Edited by H. Musurillo, Gregorii Nysseni opera 7.1 (Leiden, 1964); J. Daniélou, Vie de Moïse (SC 1[bis], 2000), 44–327; translated into English by A. J. Malherbe & E. Ferguson, Gregory of Nyssa: The Life of Moses (New York, Ramsey, NJ & Toronto, 1978), in a series with the subtitle 'A Library of the Great Spiritual Masters.' Gregory divided his work into two parts, an account of Moses' life and a contemplation on it (θεωρία).

ἐν τῷ τῆς προγραφῆς τύπῳ ἐπιστολὴ εἶναι δοκεῖ, τὸ δὲ πλῆθος ὑπὲρ τὸν ἐπιστολιμαῖον ὅρον ἐστὶν εἰς συγγραφικὴν μακρηγορίαν παρατεινόμενον). It adopts a hagiographical approach, consistently depicting Macrina, who had been abbess of a convent, in terms normally applied to martyrs.[14] At a lower literary level, despite his high literary aspirations, a follower who remained loyal to John Chrysostom after he had been exiled to Cucusus in 404 composed a funerary speech for him when news of his death reached the environs of Constantinople in the autumn of 407: it survived under the name of Martyrius, who was bishop of Antioch in the 460s, but it had to wait until 2007 before receiving a proper critical edition.[15] This speech consistently depicts John as a Christian martyr now in heaven, who supplicates God on behalf of the faithful. In the West not only were saints and martyrs obvious subjects for Christian hymnography,[16] but

---

[14] Edited by V. Woods Callahan, Gregorii Nysseni opera 8.1 (Leiden, 1952), 370–414; P. Maraval, Grégoire de Nazianze: Vie de sainte Macrine. (SC 178, 1971), 136–267. On this text, which for obvious reasons attracts feminist scholars, there are many recent studies from a variety of perspectives: see, for example, A. Momigliano, On Pagans, Jews and Christians (Middletown, CT, 1987), 206–220; R. W. Williams, Christian Faith and Greek Philosophy in Late Antiquity, ed. L. R. Wickham & C. P. Bammel. Supplements to Vigiliae Christianae 19 (Leiden & New York, 1993), 227–246; G. Frank, JECS 8 (2000), 511–530; F. Cardman, SP 37 (2001), 33–50; W. E. Helleman, SP 37 (2001), 86–102; J. Warren Smith, *JTS*, N. S. 54 (2003), 37–60; JECS 12 (2004), 57–84; M. Ludlow, Gregory of Nyssa, Ancient and (Post) modern (Oxford, 2007), 202–219.

[15] M. Wallraff, Oratio funebris in laudem Sancti Iohannis Chrysostomi. Epitaffio attribuito a Martirio di Antiochia (BHG 871, CPG 6517) (Spoleto, 2007). George Bevan and I have now published an English translation as TTH 60 (Liverpool, 2013).

[16] A. S. Walpole, Early Latin Hymns (Cambridge, 1922), 1–114 (hymns attributed to Hilary of Poitiers and Ambrose).

the Spanish poet Prudentius, who consciously set himself up as a Christian Virgil and Horace combined, composed a series of poems on martyrs, which in 404/405 he included in a collected edition of his works under the title *Peristephanon*, that is, 'On the Crowns <of the Martyrs>.'[17] In addition Prudentius set out his literary creed in a separate long poem of more than a thousand lines, which modern editors have mistakenly edited as if it belonged to this cycle of martyr poems (*Peristephanon* 10).[18] Prudentius chose to expound this theme dear to his heart through an imaginary speech by the Diocletianic martyr Romanus of Antioch, whom pious devotion had already endowed with the miraculous power of speaking volubly even after his tongue had been cut out.[19]

The rich field of Byzantine hagiography has been tilled, seeded and harvested by excellent scholars: alongside the philological and literary achievements of Hippolyte Dele-

---

[17]   On this cycle of poems, see esp. M. A. Malamud, A Poetics of Transformation. Prudentius and Classical Mythology (Ithaca & London, 1989); A.-M. Palmer, Prudentius on the Martyrs (Oxford, 1989); M. Roberts, Poetry and the Cult of the Martyrs. The *Liber Peristephanon* of Prudentius (Ann Arbor, 1993); on Prudentius' emulation of the Augustan poets, including Ovid, Palmer, Prudentius (1989), 98–179.

[18]   On the special place of this poem in Prudentius' œuvre, K. Thraede, Studien zur Sprache und Stil des Prudentius (Göttingen, 1965), 68–70, 122–137; R. Henke, Studien zum Romanushymnus des Prudentius (Frankfurt, 1983).

[19]   The clause 'nor was the tongue of his understanding silenced from preaching' is omitted in one of the surviving versions of the relevant passage in the Syriac translation of the long recension of the Martyrs of Palestine (2.2, p. 338 Lawlor & Oulton) and was probably not in Eusebius' original text of 311 (App. 6 n. 10). Prudentius' immediate source is identified as a lost prose Greek passion of Romanus by H. Delehaye, AB 50 (1932), 241–283; R. Henke, JAC 29 (1986), 59–65.

haye, it will suffice to name *honoris causa* the Bollandists
Paul Peeters and François Halkin and the Byzantinist Gilbert Dagron.[20] Good historians have also thoroughly in-
vestigated Latin hagiographical texts from the Late Roman
and Post-Roman periods.[21] The present chapter, therefore,
does not attempt any sort of general survey of Late Roman,
Post-Roman or early Byzantine hagiography even within a
restricted chronological field. It has the more modest aim
of illustrating the problems of analysis and interpretation
which a series of hagiographical texts of particular interest
pose for the historian of the fifth and sixth century. Of set
purpose nothing will be said about relatively straightforward
and unproblematical texts such as the *Life of Augustine*
which Possidius of Calama modelled on Paulinus' *Life of
Ambrose*,[22] and no general conclusions will be drawn from
the diverse material discussed.

---

[20] In addition to individual articles by these scholars cited in the
present work, note esp. the following volumes: P. Peeters, Orient et
Byzance: le tréfonds oriental de l'hagiographie grecque (SH 26, 1951);
F. Halkin, Recherches et documents d'hagiographie byzantine. (SH 51,
1971); Études (1973); Martyrs grecs II^e–VIII^e s. (London, 1974); G.
Dagron, Vie et miracles de sainte Thècle. (SH 62, 1978)

[21] On the problem of using Latin hagiographical texts from Late
Antiquity and the Middle Ages, see the methodological essay by F. Lotter, Hist. Zeitschr. 229 (1979), 298–356. A brief and superficial survey
of historically valuable hagiographical lives in Latin from the fifth and
early sixth centuries is given by H. Brandt, Ethnicity and Culture in
Late Antiquity, ed. S. Mitchell & G. Greatrex (London, 2000), 59–68.

[22] Edited by A. A. R. Bastiaensen, Vite dei santi 3 (Milan, 1975),
127–241): on the problems which it does pose, see esp. H. Diesner, SP
6 (TU 81, 1962), 350–365; C. Mohrmann, Anzeiger Wien, Phil.-hist.
Kl. 112 (1975), 307–331; A. Bastiaensen, SP 16 (TU 129, 1985),
480–486; B. Stoll, ZKG 102 (1991), 1–13.

## The Monk Isaac

Isaac was a Syrian monk who came to Constantinople while the anti-Nicene party was still dominant in the city. His first recorded action was in 378, when he shouted insults at Valens as the emperor passed through Constantinople during the summer of that year, warning him that as a heretic he faced defeat at the hands of the Goths: both Theodoretus (*HE* 3.34.1–3) and Sozomenus (*HE* 6.40.1) retailed the story in the 440s, and there is no compelling reason to dismiss it as 'clearly an *ex post facto* prophecy and a popular explanation of the disaster at Adrianople.'[23] For, within weeks of the battle, Ambrose was making exactly the same point that the Roman defeat was God's punishment for Valens' treatment of orthodox belief (*De Fide* 2.139–143, esp. 139: *divinae indignationis causa praecessit, ut ibi primum fides imperio Romano frangeretur, ubi fracta est deo*).[24] In the early 380s (so it seems) Isaac founded a monastery in Constantinople.[25] Twenty years later, when John Chrysostom came into conflict with the monks of Constantinople, Isaac was one of the leaders of the opposition against him:[26] he supported Theophilus of Alexandria against John and sailed with him to Egypt in the autumn of 403 when John returned from his first exile (Sozomenus, *HE* 8.9.4–6, 19.4). After John was exiled permanently in 404, Isaac returned

---

[23] R. Snee, GRBS 26 (1985), 406.

[24] AT 7 (1999), 170–171. This interpretation immediately gained wide acceptance among Nicene Christians: N. Lenski, TAPA 127 (1997), 129–168.

[25] J. Pargoire, Revue des questions historiques 65 (1899), 100–105, 120–126.

[26] On John's clashes with monks, especially Isaac, see Kelly, Golden Mouth (n.10), 123–125.

to Constantinople, where he died during the episcopate of Atticus, who was bishop of the city from February 406 until October 425 (*Syn. eccl. Cpl.* 865–866).[27] In fact, it seems that Isaac lived on until 416 or even later: a passage which appears in one manuscript of the *Life of Isaac* (BHG 956) states that Aurelianus built a *martyrion* of Saint Stephen immediately to the south of Isaac's monastery hoping to place in it the body of the protomartyr (which had been miraculously discovered in December 415), but instead placed the body of Isaac there when his plans to deposit the body of Stephen were frustrated.[28] Although the provenance of this report may be unclear, it deserves to be believed: Aurelianus, who was ordinary consul in 400, was, like Isaac, an enemy of John while he was bishop of Constantinople, and it is entirely credible that he wished to honour Isaac when the latter died during his second tenure of the praetorian prefecture of the east (from December 414 to summer 416).[29]

Two lives of Isaac were published in the *Acta Sanctorum* in 1668: the Greek text of the so-called *vita prior* from a Vatican manuscript (AASS, Mai. VII.244–253 = [1688], 247–258: BHG 956) and, from Lipomano, a sixteenth century Latin translation of a closely similar but much briefer life found in a Greek manuscript in Venice, the so-called *vita posterior*, (AASS, Mai. VII.254–255 = [1688], 258–260: BHG 955). Other early lives of Isaac existed, or at least re-

---

[27]  J. Pargoire, Échos d'Orient 2 (1898–1899), 138–145, also citing the *Vita Dalmatii* (BHG 482) and the *Life of Hypatios* (BHG 760). The day of Isaac's death, which is variously reported, was probably 30 May: F. Halkin, AB 66 (1948), 75–80.

[28]  Published by F. Nau, ROC 11 (1906), 200, from Paris, BN, Fonds grec 1453, fols. 225ᵛ–226.

[29]  Alan Cameron & J. Long, Barbarians and Politics at the Court of Arcadius (Berkeley, 1993), 72–75.

censions different from the two published lives: besides the apparently authentic information about Isaac's burial published by Nau from a Paris manuscript, a Greek synaxarium preserved in a manuscript of the twelfth century in Oxford derives either from another recension of the *vita prior* or, less probably, from a third life.[30] It seems to be generally agreed that the lives cannot be earlier than the sixth century.[31] A firm *terminus post quem* is provided by the fact that passages of the *vita prior* are copied word for word from the ecclesiastical history of Socrates (3.9 < Socrates, *HE* 5.6.2–7.1; 3.11 < 5.7.6–9; 3.12/13 < 5.8.3–10, 12, 20). The lives naturally make much of Isaac's protest to Valens in 378. They add that the generals Victor and Saturninus imprisoned Isaac for his protest on Valens' orders and later obtained his release from Theodosius after he arrived in Constantinople on 24 November 380 (*vita prior* 2.8, 3.10: the date is taken from Socrates, *HE* 5.6.6; *vita posterior* 5, 7). Letters of Gregory of Nazianzus confirm that Victor was in Constantinople in the early 380s, living in retirement (Gregory, *Epp.* 133, 134).[32] Saturninus negotiated peace with the Goths in Thrace in 382 and was rewarded by the ordinary consulate for 383; in the political crisis of 400 he was surrendered to Gainas and exiled together with Aurelianus (Socrates, *HE* 6.6.9–11; Sozomenus, *HE* 8.4.5; Zosimus 5.18.7–9).[33] In the 380s,

---

[30] F. Halkin, AB 66 (1948), 74–80.

[31] Dagron, Travaux et Mémoires 4 (1970), 231 n. 10; Snee, GRBS 26 (1985), 406–407; Cameron & Long, Barbarians and Politics (n. 29), 73.

[32] For his career, PLRE 1 (1971), 957–959, Victor 4.

[33] Also the sermon by John Chrysostom on the occasion 'when Saturninus and Aurelianus were exiled' (PG 52.413–420). For Saturninus' career, PLRE 1 (1971), 807–808, Saturninus 10.

both Victor and Saturninus continued to patronise Isaac
(*vita prior* 4.14–16), and in 404 Castricia, the widow of
Saturninus, who had recently died, was a violent enemy of
John Chrysostom (Palladius, *Dialogus* 4.89–94 Malingrey =
25 Coleman Norton).

There is nothing unusual in this medley of plagiarised narrative, edifying stories and authentic information in a sixth
century life of a much earlier holy man. But the *vita prior*
concludes with the startling statement that Isaac died while
Theodosius was emperor, shortly after his son Arcadius had
been proclaimed Augustus, in the consulate of Merobaudes
for the second time and Saturninus, i. e., in 383 (4.18: the
date is taken from Socrates, *HE* 5.10.5/6). Now Isaac had
founded the first orthodox monastery in Constantinople
only a couple of years before 383,[34] and the erroneous date
could in theory be due to the carelessness of a lazy plagiarist.
But the total silence of the *vita prior* about Isaac's role in
the fall of John Chrysostom suggests that someone has at
some stage deliberately edited out potentially embarrassing
facts. For to make Isaac die in 383 removes him completely
from the ecclesiastical scene nearly fifteen years before John
arrived in Constantinople. The misrepresentation is rather
part of a process which transformed the historical John, who
cared for the destitute, founded a hospital for lepers, and
attacked the extravagancies of the rich and their speculation
in property (*Dialogus* 5.100–166 Malingrey = 31–33 Coleman Norton),[35] into a relatively colourless hero suitable for

---

[34] J. Pargoire, Rev. quest. hist. 65 (1899), 121–122.

[35] On John's charitable works and social attitudes, see Kelly, Golden
Mouth (n. 10), 119–120, 135–137, 141–142. The two earliest and
fullest surviving accounts of John are the speech given by one of his
followers when news of his death at Cucusus on 14 September 407

conventional hagiography. The first straightforwardly hagiographical lives of John Chrysostom were not composed
until the seventh century by Theodore, bishop of Trimithus
in Cyprus, and a writer who called himself George of Alexandria (BHG 872, 873),[36] but thereafter the hagiography of
John flourished and blossomed for centuries (BHG 872d,
872e, 873b–881z, Auct., pp. 94–101: well over fifty later
items in total).

## Kallinikos' *Life of Hypatios*

The *Life of Hypatios* (BHG 760)[37] is generally held to be
a reliable document written very shortly after the death of
its subject.[38] In one important respect, however, the *Life of
Hypatios* provides at the same time both a perfect parallel
and a striking contrast to the *Life of Antony*, which it imi-

---

reached the vicinity of Constantinople and a 'historical dialogue'
defending John apparently written in the year after his death. The
first full critical edition of the former was published by M. Wallraff,
Oratio funebris (n. 15); of the latter (BHG 870) there are two modern
editions: P. R. Coleman-Norton, Palladii dialogus de vita S. Joannis
Chrysostomi (Cambridge, 1928); A.-M. Malingrey, Palladios: Dialogue
sur la Vie de Jean Chrysostome 1 (SC 341, 1988), 46–451.

[36] The former was edited by A. Mai, Nova patrum bibliotheca 6.2
(Rome, 1853), 265–290, whence PG 47.li–lxxxviii, while the latter
had already been included by Henry Savile in his edition (8 [Eton,
1612], 157–265).

[37] Edited with a French translation and commentary by G. J. M.
Bartelink, Kallinikos: Vie d'Hypatios (SC 177, 1971).

[38] Thus G. Dagron, Travaux et Mémoires 4 (1970), 231: 'celle (sc.
la vie) d'Hypatios est tenue généralement digne de foi, parce que son
auteur, Kallinikos, relate vers 447–450 des événements qui se situent
entre 366 et 446.'

tates in many passages.[39] Both lives are expanded versions of a written source, yet one bears the name of the redactor, the other the name of the source which he has reworked. Athanasius counts as the author of the *Life of Antony*, even though the greater part of the *Life* is a lightly edited version of a written account of Antony whose author he does not name.[40] In contrast, the *Life of Hypatios* is universally attributed to Hypatios' disciple Kallinikos, even though the preface states explicitly that the writer, whose name is unknown, has greatly expanded Kallinikos' original biography of his master, who was abbot of the monastery of Rufinianae near Chalcedon from c. 406 to his death in 446, by including additional material and removing linguistic asperities (pr. 2–7). Athanasius is the redactor rather than the author of the *Life of Antony*, while Kallinikos is the main source, not the author of the extant biography of Hypatios. Since the relation of final text and source is so similar in both cases, it seems absurd to present their authorship so differently.

The conventional date of composition shortly after the death of Hypatios, probably between 447 and 450, is deduced from passages which use the first person plural in describing events of 426 (23.1, 25.1).[41] But these 'we' passages are surely transcribed from Kallinikos, who was indeed a disciple of Hypatios. The author gives himself away when introducing the story of how Hypatios prevented a restoration of the Olympic Games of Chalcedon by Leontius, who was prefect of the city of Constantinople

---

[39] Bartelink, Vie d'Hypatios (n. 37), 33–38.

[40] Chapter IV.

[41] Bartelink, Kallinikos (n. 37), 11–12. Bartelink's notes on the text, however, speak of possible publication 'vers 470' (65 n. 4, on pr. 5).

in the mid-430s (33):[42] although such games were in fact still celebrated in the lifetime of Hypatios and Kallinikos, the *Life* alleges that they had been abolished by 'ancient emperors and Constantine of eternal memory' (33.1). This error locates the composition of the *Life of Hypatios* in the sixth century rather than the fifth.[43] Equally probative is its employment of the transcription ἰλλούστριος for the Latin rank or title *illustris* (47: πατρίκιοι, ἰλλούστριοι καὶ πᾶσα ἀξία μετὰ τῶν στρατιωτικῶν ταγμάτων) rather than the term which had been the normal Greek equivalent of *illustris* in the fifth century (ἐνδοξότατος). More than a century ago it was noted that, apart from its use on a single occasion by a pair of bishops at the Council of Ephesus in 431 (ACO 1.1.2.37, lines 9, 12), ἰλλούστριος is not found as the Greek equivalent of the Latin *illustris* before the sixth century.[44] Although ἐνδοξότατος long continued in use, its replacement ἰλλούστριος begins to appear in laws issued by Justinian from 535 onwards (*Novellae* 13.3; 15.3 [535]; 43, pr., 1 [536]; 71, tit., 1 [538]; 74.4 [538]; 117.4 [542]), while the earliest literary text to use ἰλλούστριος rather than ἐνδοξότατος is John the Lydian's work on Roman magistracies in the 550s (*De magistratibus* 3.57, p. 146.13–14 Wünsch).

────────────

[42]  On Leontius, see PLRE 2 (1980), 669, Leontius 9. He is attested as prefect from 27 November 434 (CTh 14.16.3) to 3 August 435 (CTh 16.5.66), but may have held office considerably longer: his last known predecessor is attested on 11 June 432 (CTh 6.24.11), his first known successor on 23 March 439 (CJ 1.2.9 = 11.18.1).

[43]  SP 37 (2001), 341–342.

[44]  P. Koch, Die Byzantinischen Beamtentitel von 400 bis 700 (Diss. Jena, 1903), 34.

## Melania the Younger

Of the Roman aristocrat Melania, a biography survives in both Greek and Latin (BHG 1241; BHL 5885):[45] the two texts appear to be independent reworkings of a lost original composed by the priest Gerontius in Greek before the Council of Chalcedon in 451, which the extant Greek life reproduces more faithfully.[46] The *Life of Melania the Younger* is a rich source for the social history of the senatorial aristocracy of Christian Rome. For Melania, who was born c. 385, belonged to the inner circle of the senatorial nobility of

---

[45] The Greek and Latin versions are edited by D. Gorce, Vie de Sainte Mélanie (SC 90, 1962) and M. Rampolla del Tindaro, Santa Melania Guiniore senatrice romana. Documenti contemporanei e note (Vatican, 1905), 3–40, who also reprinted the *editio princeps* of the Greek text by H. Delehaye, AB 22 (1903), 5–50 (41–85). Gorce's text is translated into English by E. A. Clark, The Life of Melania (Lewiston, NY, 1984), 25–82, with a commentary (83–152) and notes which discuss varients in the Latin version (189–194), and there is an abbreviated English translation of Cardinal Rampolla's book by E. Leahy, edited by H. Thurston, The Life of St. Melania (London, 1908). Except where stated otherwise, all references to the *Life* are to the Greek text in Gorce's numeration. Cardinal Rampolla (1843–1913), who had discovered the Latin text in 1880 while papal nuncio in Spain, it may be noted, was about to be elected Pope in succession to Leo XIII in August 1903 when, after the second round of voting, the Emperor of Austria interposed a veto right in the middle of the Conclave, through the agency of Cardinal Jan Puzyna de Kosielko, Prince-Archbishop of Kraków, after the Austrian Cardinal Anton Josef Gruscha had refused to deliver it: for a brief account of the conclave of 1903, see F. J. Baumgartner, Behind Locked Doors. A History of the Papal Elections (New York & Basingstoke, 2003), 201–204.

[46] A. d'Alès, AB 25 (1906), 401–450; Clark, Life of Melania (n. 45), 4–24; H. Delehaye, L'ancienne hagiographie byzantine. Les sources, les premiers modèles, la formation des genres, ed. B. Joassart & X. Lequeux (SH 73, 1991), 38–39.

Rome and at the age of thirteen she married the equally noble seventeen year old Pinianus (1).[47] The young soon produced two children – a daughter who was consecrated to a life of virginity, but died in infancy, and a son who was born prematurely, baptised and died at once (1, 3, 5–6). Melania then, at the age of twenty, persuaded her husband to join her in a life of abstinence and asceticism: they sold most of their landed property (which brought in an income of 120,000 solidi a year), left Italy in 408 and migrated to Africa, where they founded two monasteries, one for men and one for women (8–22). After seven years in Africa Melania and Pinianus sailed to Alexandria and settled in Palestine, where she lived with her mother Albina (28–36) and devoted herself to the ascetic life, though making the obligatory journey to visit the cells of the holy monks of Egypt (37–39). Melania eventually died in Bethlehem on 31 December 439 (57–58, 62–68). Melania's withdrawal to Palestine, did not, however, entirely sunder her ties with her noble relatives in Rome: towards the end of her life, she travelled to Constantinople to meet her pagan uncle, Rufius Antonius Agrypnius Volusianus, who had come to conduct negotiations concerning the forthcoming marriage of the western emperor to the daughter of the eastern emperor, and she persuaded Volusianus to be baptised shortly before his death on 6 January 437 (50–56).[48]

---

[47] See PLRE 1 (1971), 593, Melania 2; 702, Pinianus 2; 1142, Stemma 20; 1147, Stemma 30; 2 (1980), 1184–1185, Volusianus 6. It should be observed that when the *Life* refers to Pinianus as τὸν ἀπὸ ὑπάτων (1), the phrase does not have its normal meaning of 'ex- consul' or even 'le consulaire,' as Gorce, Vie de Sainte Mélanie (n. 45), 131, renders it: Clark, Life of Melania (n. 45), 28, translates correctly as 'who was from a consular family.'

[48] For Volusianus' career, PLRE 2 (1980). 1184–1185, Volusianus 6; on his conversion, A. Chastagnol, REA 58 (1956), 241–253.

The *Life of Melania* is not a straightforward biography with a hagiographical slant. It is conspicuous and unusual that the *Life* never names Melania's grandmother, even though her ascetic career prefigured her granddaughter's: the elder Melania too (who was born c. 340) married a scion of the Valerii when young, though she was soon widowed; the elder Melania too migrated to Palestine,[49] where she then lived for more than thirty years until her death c. 410, though she brought a piece of the True Cross to Rome when she was sixty.[50] Like her granddaughter too, the elder Melania founded monasteries (in Jerusalem).[51] But she had been a friend of Rufinus of Aquileia, the translator of Origen; she read Origen with enthusiasm; and she associated with Origenists like Evagrius Ponticus and Palladius:[52] hence the *Life* does not name the elder Melania; it merely alludes to her as 'a wife of a certain consul who ended her life abroad among the holy places,' but was mistakenly alleged by some to be to be a heretic (28: κοινωνοῦσα μεθ᾽ ἡμῶν τῶν ὀρθοδόξων αἱρετικὴ εἶναι παρὰ τινων ἐλέγετο).[53] The omissions and distortions appear to be theologically moti-

---

[49] In 374, according to Jerome, *Chronicle* 247[d] Helm.

[50] Paulinus of Nola, *Epp.* 29.11–13, 31.1, cf. Palladius, *Hist. Laus.* 54.3.

[51] Palladius, *Hist. Laus.* 46.3.

[52] E. A. Clark, SP 18.2 (1989), 173–174, 181 n. 53.

[53] N. Moine, Rech. aug. 15 (1980), 73–74. Gorce, Vie de Sainte Mélanie (n. 45). 181, translates as 'une femme de haut rang;' Clark, Life of Melania (n. 45), 47, as 'a certain woman of high status.' But ὕπατος normally has the specific meaning of 'consul' in the Greek of this period. Since the elder Melania's son was named Publicola (Palladius, Hist. laus. 54), her husband must have been a Valerius, and he is usually assumed to be the (Valerius) Maximus, whom Julian appointed praefectus urbi in 361 (PLRE 1 [1971], 582, Maximus 17; 1142, Stemma 20; 1147, Stemma 30). Gerontius has simply made a mistaken guess about Maximus' status: thirty years earlier Palladius, *Hist. Laus.* 46.1,

vated.[54] For Gerontius, the presumed author of the original life, was an anti-Chalcedonian who called Juvenalis the bishop of Jerusalem Judas for his betrayal in accepting the creed of the Council of Chalcedon in 451 (*Life of Peter the Iberian* § 47).[55] Gerontius presented the younger Melania as impeccably orthodox with an ardour for true faith 'hotter than fire' (p. 126.7–9 Gorce) – as orthodox as he himself was in his own eyes. To this end he concealed his heroine's constant study of Origen's biblical commentaries recorded by Palladius *Hist. Laus.* 55.3), her interview in Palestine in 418 with Pelagius, who to the disappointment of Augustine persuaded her of his orthodoxy,[56] and the fact that she must have tolerated Donatists on her estates in Africa (*Life* 21, p. 14 Rampolla: Latin version only).

## Germanus of Auxerre

Germanus of Auxerre died on 31 July after being bishop for many years, in a year which has been the subject of much

had described the elder Melania more accurately, if more vaguely, as 'the wife of some man of high rank, of whom exactly I do not remember.'

[54] E. A. Clark, Church History 51 (1982), 143–144, 153; SP 18.2 (1989), 173–174.

[55] R. Raabe, Petrus der Iberer. Ein Charakterbild zur Kirchen- und Sittengeschichte des fünften Jahrhunderts (Leipzig, 1895), 32; C. B. Horn & R. R. Phenix, The Lives of Peter the Iberian, Theodosius of Jerusalem and the Monk Romanus (Atlanta, 2008), 64–65; Cyril of Scythopolis, Vita Euthymii 45, 27; Vita Sabae 30, pp. 67, 42–44, 115 Schwartz.

[56] As is known from Augustine's reaction to the letter that Melania and Pinianus sent to him on Pelagius' behalf in response to which he immediately penned his De Gratia Christi et de peccato originali (CSEL 42.125–206), cf. C. P. Hammond, JTS, N. S. 28 (1977), 421–423.

dispute,[57] The *Life of Germanus* was not written until a generation had passed and his memory had faded (pr.),[58] and
it has been characterised 'almost a handbook for bishops in
the 470s and 480s' with its narrative analysed as primarily

---

[57] Under 31 July the *Martyrologium Hieronymianum* registers *Au-
tissiodoro depositio sancti Germani episcopi* (AASS, Nov.II.2.406), an
engraved calendar from Naples N(A)T(ALE) GERMANI EPISC(OPI)
(H. Delehaye, AB 57 [1939], 27: the calendar had previously been
published by B. Capasso, Moumenta ad Neapolitani ducatus historiam
pertinentia. Società di Storia Patria: Monumenti Storici, Serie Prima:
Cronache 1 [Naples, 1881], 335–339, and was subsequently the subject
of a full study by D. Mallardo, Ephemerides liturgicae 59 [1945],
233–294; 60 [1946], 217–292. A late local source of dubious value
alleges that Germanus was bishop of the city for thirty five years (*De
Gestis Episcoporum Autissiodurensium* [PL 138.219]). His death is dated
to 437 by E. A. Thompson, Saint Germanus of Auxerre and the End
of Roman Britain. Studies in Celtic History 6 (Woodbridge, 1984),
55–70; to either 437 or 442 by I. Wood, Gildas: New Approaches, ed.
M. Lapidge & M. Dumville (Woodbridge, 1984), 16 (pronouncing the
date of 448 'untenable'); between 440 and 442 by G. de Plinval, Pélage.
Ses écrits, sa vie et sa réforme. Étude d'histoire littéraire et religieuse
(Lausanne, 1943), 382 n. 4; to 442 by J. B. Bury, Later Roman Empire
1² (London, 1923), 250; to 445 by E. A. Thompson, AB 75 (1957),
135–138; P. Grosjean, ib. 180–185; R. Scharf, Francia 18 (1991),
1–19; to 446 by R. Mathisen, AB 99 (1981), 151–159; to 448 by E. A.
Thompson, Britannia 8 (1977), 311; T. D. Barnes, Phoenix 29 (1975),
158. The date of 445 runs into the obvious difficulty that the *Life* states
that the imperial court was residing in Ravenna when Germanus went
there shortly before his death (35–44), while the emperor Valentinian
III appears to have spent the whole of the year 445 in Rome, where his
presence is attested in January, June and July (*Nov. Val.* 16; 18; 13; 17,
cf. A. Gillett, PBSR 69 [2001], 143).

[58] The standard editions are those by W. Levison, MGH, Scrip-
tores rerum merovingicarum 7 (Berlin, 1919), 247–283; R. Borius,
Constance de Lyon: Vie de Saint Germain d'Auxerre (SC 112, 1965).
The *Life* is preceded by letters to Patiens, bishop of Lugdunum, who
received Sidonius Apollinaris, *Ep.* 6.12, and Censurius, bishop of
Auxerre: Borius plausibly dates the work to the years 475–480 (44–46).

allegorical.[59] The *Life* describes several otherwise unknown episodes in the obscure history of the Roman West in the fifth century. Germanus (the *Life* reports) visited Britain twice to combat the Pelagians (12–18, 25–27), and between the two visits, he travelled to Arles to request the praetorian prefect resident there to reduce the level of taxation on Auxerre, which its people found oppressive: Germanus cured the wife of the prefect, who then granted his request (19–24). Constantius names the prefect as Auxiliaris (24), which appears to fix the date to 435/437.[60] After his second visit to Britain, Germanus was asked by the people of the Tractus Armoricanus to protect them against the ravages of the Alans, whom Aetius had set on them as rebels: he confronted the Alan king Goar and persuaded him to make peace, provided that the arrangement was ratified by Aetius and the emperor (28).[61] Finally, when Germanus travelled to Italy to present a petition to the emperor at Ravenna, where he died (29–42), he restored to life the son of the *cancellarius* of the *patricius* Sigisvult who had just died of a fever (38).[62] The *Life* records a Gallic revolt under Tibatto

---

[59] Wood, Gildas: New Approaches (n. 57), 9, cf. W. Gessel, RQ 65 (1970), 1–14.

[60] PLRE 2 (1980), 206 Auxiliaris 1, citing ILS 806 (Arles), which attests him as *pr(ae)f(ectus) praeto(rio) Gallia[rum]* between 1 January 435 and 31 December 438. Scharf, Francia 18 (1991), 4–7, argues that Auxiliaris was also praetorian prefect of Gaul in 444, adducing the *Vita Hilarii Arelatensis* (BHL 3882) 22.22–40 (ed. S. Cavallin, Vitae Sanctorum Honorati et Hilarii [Lund, 1952], 99–100.)

[61] Dated to 442 by the *Gallic Chronicle of 452* 127 (Chr. min. 1.660, reedited by R. W. Burgess, Society and Culture in Late Antique Gaul. Revisiting the Sources, ed. R. W. Mathisen & D. R. Shanzer (Aldershot, 2001), 80, cf. PLRE 2 (1980), 514–515, Goar.

[62] On the patriciate of Fl. Sigisvultus, cos. 437, see Phoenix 29 (1975), 158–159, 164, arguing from Nov. Val. 9; 11 that he received the title between June 440 and 13 March 443. Constantius styles the

while Germanus was in Ravenna (40): since Tibatto had led a rebellion in north-western Gaul in 435 which ended with his capture in 437 (*Gallic Chronicle of 452* 117, 119) and is mentioned nowhere else, it remains uncertain whether Tibatto led a second revolt in 448 or the *Life* has made a chronological mistake.[63] The balance of probabilities may be tipped by the episode of the 'alleluia victory' which the *Life* alleges that the inhabitants of post-Roman Britain won with Germanus as their inspiration over the Saxons and the Picts, with whom they were at war, during his earlier visit, shortly before 430 (17–18).[64] Despite the robust defence of the historicity of the battle by writers who wish to cast light on the 'dark ages' of post-Roman Britain,[65] biblical allusions, stock motifs, the apparent use of Sulpicius Severus' *Life of Martin* and above all the imagined presence of Picts in the vicinity of St Albans stamp the episode as an invention.[66] However,

---

boy *Volusiani cuiusdam filius*: 'a certain Volusianus' can hardly be one of the attested noble Volusiani (so, rightly, PLRE 2.1183, Volusianus 3).

[63] The accuracy of the *Life* is defended in PLRE 2 (1980), 1118–1119, Tibatto, with appeal to Thompson, Britannia 8 (1977), 311.

[64] The visit is recorded under the year 429 by Prosper Tiro § 1301 (Chr. min. 1.472), who states that Germanus was sent as his deputy by Caelestinus, the bishop of Rome: on this visit, see Thompson, Saint Germanus (1984), 39–46, 55–56. G. de Plinval, Saint Germain d'Auxerre et son temps (Auxerre, 1950), 145–146, argued that Germanus remained in Britain for seven months from the summer of 429 until Easter 430.

[65] Thompson, Saint Germanus (n. 57), 44, comments: 'the working arrangement between the Saxons and the Picts is remarkable' as 'the only example of such cooperation to have been recorded from the age of the migrations.'

[66] Note also the utter vagueness of Constantius' account of Germanus' career before he was ordained a priest (1, cf. PLRE 2 [1980], 504, Germanus 1) – which suggests that he possessed no genuine information about it.

the fact that Constantius knew nothing about Britain c. 430 need not cast doubt on what he says about Germanus' activities in Auxerre and his final journey to Ravenna.

## Severinus of Noricum

The work which is conventionally known as the *Life of Severinus* (BHL 7655–7657) was written in a monastery near Naples in 511 by Eugippius, who gave it the title *commemoratorium* (46.6; *Ep. ad Paschasium* 1, 11; Paschasius, *Ep.* 2).[67] The work is not a biography of Severinus at all, but exactly what it presents itself as being: a scholarly record of his achievements and miracles. Eugippius composed the work almost thirty years after his subject died,[68] and he equipped it with the ancient equivalent of an index: between the exchange of letters between Eugippius and Paschasius, which serves the function of an introduction, stands a list of *capitula* – a standard element of ancient scholarly writing,

---

[67] On the literary character of the so-called *vita*, see H. Baldermann, Wiener Studien 74 (1961), 142–155. The text was edited three times in the late nineteenth century: by H. Sauppe, MGH Auct. Ant. 1.2 (Berlin, 1877); P. Knöll, CSEL 9.2 (Vienna, 1886); T. Mommsen, MGH, Scriptores rerum Germanicarum in usum scholarum ex Mon. Ger. recusi 26 (Berlin, 1898). The standard edition is now that by E. Vetter & R. Noll, Eugippius. Das Leben des heiligen Severin. Schriften und Quellen der Alten Welt 11 (1963), whose text is reprinted with some changes by P. Régerat, Vie de Saint Séverin (SC 374, 1991), 146–297.

[68] Severinus' death is conventionally dated to 482 from the historical context in which Eugippius locates his exhumation 'after the sixth year from his burial had flowed away'(44.4–6). The year might rather be 481: chronicles date the war of Odoacar against the Rugi (44.6) to 487 (Chr. min. 1.312–313; 2.159).

which Eusebius had introduced into Christian literature and used in his historical and apologetic works.[69]

Eugippius begins by setting what he is about to record against the historical background of the disintegration of Roman rule in the Danubian provinces:

At the time when Attila, king of the Huns, had died, both Pannonias and the other lands next to the Danube were in a state of disturbance and confusion. At that time the holy servant of God Severinus, arriving from eastern parts, was residing in a small town which is called Asturae close to Noricum Ripense and the Pannonias. (1.1)

The memorial of Severinus which is thus introduced comprises a series of more than forty separate and self-contained episodes, each of which is summarised or described in the prefixed list of contents. The quotation of a few of these will illustrate both the nature and the importance of the work:

How the young Odovacar, dressed in the vilest skins, was predicted by him to be destined to become a king.[70] (7)

That Feletheus, also called Feva, the king of the Rugi, son of the Flaccitheus mentioned above, forbade his evil wife to rebaptise catholics through fear of holy Severinus, and what danger she encountered concerning her small son Fredericus one day when she had rejected his intercession for certain persons.[71] (8)

How king Odovacar, asking him to request something from him, recalled a certain Ambrosius from exile by a letter of the servant of God and the same servant of God predicted to those who praised the king how many years he was going to reign. (32)

---

[69] JTS, N.S. 27 (1976), 418–420; Constantine (1981), 124, 182, 324 n. 129, 364 n. 125.

[70] The date is 'presumably soon after 469/70' according to PLRE 2.791–793 – when the *iuvenis*, who was born c. 433, was almost forty.

[71] Feletheus and Fredericus appear in other sources, but Flaccitheus is known only from Eugippius: PLRE 2.457; 484–485, Fredericus 2; 473.

About the son of one of the nobles of the king of the Rugi who was healed in the town of Comagenae by the prayer of the man of God. (33)

How a man suffering from leprosy, by the name of Teio, was cured. (34)

This method of composition recalls the pericopae of the gospels, and the stories contain a plethora of hagiographical commonplaces, stereotypical miracles, legendary themes and motifs, even doublets which Eugippius appears to have repeated without realising that he was repeating the same story in two slightly different forms. Nevertheless, Eugippius' memorial of Severinus' activities between his arrival in Noricum c. 455 and his death in 481 or 482 provides an irreplaceable record of the realities of provincial life in the middle of the fifth century as the western Roman Empire slowly disintegrated.[72]

## Two Stylite Saints

The first stylite saint Symeon became a subject for hagiography even in his lifetime.[73] In 444, while Symeon was

---

[72] For detailed investigation of all aspects of Eugippius' work, see the series of studies by F. Lotter, Deutsches Archiv für die Erforschung des Mittelalters 24 (1968), 309–339; Hist. Zeitschr. 212 (1971), 265–315; Severinus von Noricum. Legende und historische Wirklichkeit. Untersuchungen zur Phase des Übergangs von spätantiken zu mittelalterlichen Denk- und Lebensform (Stuttgart, 1976), 21–283; Von der Spätantike zum frühen Mittelalter. Aktuelle Probleme in historischer und archäologischer Sicht, ed. E. Ewig & J. Werner (1979), 27–90; Ostbayerische Grenzmarken 24 (1982), 1–23, with B. de Gaiffier, AB 95 (1977), 13–23, and the bibliographical surveys of R. Noll, Anzeiger Wien 112 (1975), 65–71; 118 (1981), 196–221.

[73] The three texts discussed here are translated into English with

still perched atop the last and highest of his four successive pillars in the Syrian mountains east of Antioch, Theodoret allotted him a chapter in his account of Syrian ascetics in his *Philotheos Historia* (26, cf. BHG 1678–1681).[74] Soon after Symeon died in 459, his disciple Antonius wrote a life of his master in Greek which depicts him as an intermediary between God and the world and as a 'source of wholeness and unity' (BHG 1682–1683e). Finally, in the year 521 of the Antiochene era, which began on 1 October 472,[75] a Syriac author, whose name is unknown, composed what he called a 'book of the heroic exploits of the blessed Mar Simeon': it is a panegyric whose scale exceeds that of most ancient biographies of holy men and women (BHO 1121).

The second famous stylite ascended his pillar outside Constantinople in 460 and died in 493: it was inevitable, therefore, that he should play a part in the contentious politics of the capital. The earliest Greek *Life of Daniel the Stylite* (BHG 489) was written by a disciple[76] The *Life of Daniel* speaks about the birth of a male heir to the emperor Leo and his wife Verina who is not recorded in any other extant narrative or literary source for the period (38). The horoscope

---

an excellent introduction and notes by R. Doran, The Lives of Simeon Stylites (Kalamazoo, 1992): on the literary nature and textual problems of the Syriac 'life,' see also A. Vööbus, After Chalcedon, Studies in Theology and Church History offered to Professor Albert van Roey for his Seventieth Birthday, ed. C. Laga, J. A. Munitz & L. van Rompay (Leuven, 1985), 478–484.

[74] Edited by P. Canivet & A. Leroy-Molinghen, Théodoret de Cyr: Histoire des Moines de Syrie (SC 257, 1979), 158–215.

[75] G. Downey, History of Antioch in Syria from Seleucus to the Arab Conquest (Princeton, 1961), 157–158.

[76] Edited by H. Delehaye, AB 32 (1913), 121–214 = Les saints stylites (SH 14, 1923), 1–94. Delehaye also edited the metaphrastic life (ib. 104–147, cf. PG 116.969–1037: BHG 490).

of this imperial infant was included by Rhetorius in his lost astrological work, who described it as the 'horoscope of a new-born child who did not survive,' stated the date of birth as 25 April 463, and commented that 'it was the child of an emperor and died at Byzantium' at the age of five months and six days, i. e., on 30 September 463.[77] Predictably and perhaps significantly, the *Life* leaves out the death of the infant who was born as a result of the prayers of Daniel.[78]

## Mark the Deacon, *Life of Porphyry, Bishop of Gaza*

The *Life of Porphyry, Bishop of Gaza* (BHG 1570) is an important and controverted text.[79] It has three main sec-

---

[77] Edited by F. Cumont, Catalogus Codicum Astrologorum Graecorum 8.4 (Brussels, 1921), 224–225. For its identification, see O. Neugebauer & H. B. van Hoesen, Greek Horoscopes (Philadelphia, 1959), 141–142 (L 463); D. Pingree, DOP 30 (1976), 146–148. The imperial infant has no entry in PLRE 2, even though the horoscope is noted in the entries for his parents, who had been married for at least six years at the time of his birth (664, Leo 6; 1156, Verina).

[78] G. Dagron, AB 100 (1982), 275. The *Life of Daniel* is analysed by R. Lane Fox in Portraits. Biographical Representation in the Greek and Latin Literature of the Roman Empire, ed. M. J. Edwards and S. Swain (Oxford, 1997), 175–225.

[79] For a succinct survey of the controversy, G. Couilleau, Dictionnaire de Spiritualité 10 (Paris, 1980), 265–267. The standard edition is that of H. Grégoire & M.-A. Kugener, Marc le diacre: Vie de Porphyre, évêque de Gaza (Paris, 1930), earlier editions of the Greek text having been produced by M. Haupt, Abh. Berlin, Hist.-phil. Kl. 1874. 171–215, and the Societatis Philologae Bonnensis Sodales, Marci diaconi Vita Porphyrii episcopi Gazensis (Leipzig, 1895), 1–82, which is translated into English by G. F. Hill, The Life of Porphyry Bishop of Gaza (Oxford, 1913). The Teubner edition of 1895 also prints the two later versions BHG 1571 (83–93) and BHG 1572 (94–109).

tions. They describe successively Porphyry's life before his consecration as bishop of Gaza and the first five years of his episcopate (3–32); a voyage to Constantinople in 400–402 to obtain imperial support for demolishing the pagan temples of Gaza (33–56); and the suppression of these pagan temples, especially the shrine of Marnas, the building of the great church of the city and the rapid conversion of its citizens to Christianity (53–93). According to the *Life* the new church was completed after five years, that is, in 407: the final chapters skim quickly over Porphyry's remaining years as bishop of Gaza until his death, which the *Life* dates to 2 Dystros in year 480 of the era of the city, which corresponds to the Julian date of 26 February 420 (94–103).

There are overwhelming reasons for believing that the *Life*, which presents itself as the work of Mark the Deacon, a close associate of Porphyry, whom the author claims to have met in Jerusalem when he was a young man, apparently in the 380s (5), is a *Fälschung* in the technical sense defined by Ernst Bernheim in his once standard handbook of historical method, since the *Life* is not in fact what it purports to be.[80] In 1930 Henri Grégoire surveyed scholarly opinions about the *Life of Porphyry* since the sixteenth century, and there is no need to rehearse again the antiquarian details of an old controversy.[81] Nevertheless, it will be salutary to emphasise that defence of the authenticity and reliability of

The recent and generally superior translation by C. Rapp in Medieval Hagiography: An Anthology (New York & London, 2000), 53–75, is unfortunately very incomplete: for fully 64 out of the 103 chapters of the *Life* it offers a bare summary of contents, not a translation.

[80] E. Bernheim, Lehrbuch der historischen Methode⁵, 6 (Leipzig, 1908), 331, cf. T. D. Barnes, Archiv für Kulturgeschichte 79 (1997) 259–267.

[81] Grégoire & Kugener, Vie de Porphyre (n. 79), vii–xxix.

the *Life* has always rested upon allowing subjective favourable impressions of the text to outweigh objective arguments against its honesty. Cardinal Baronius, who included a Latin translation of substantial extracts from the *Life of Porphyry* in his annalistic history of the church, proclaimed the narrative to be 'extremely faithful, with a simple style in which there shines the light of truth.'[82] After the French Protestant Daniel Blondel attacked the historical reliability of the *Life* in 1641,[83] its subsequent catholic defenders appeared content to rest their defence on little more than bare repetition of Baronius' subjective arguments. In 1658, when Hervet's Latin translation was reprinted from Lipomano in the *Acta Sanctorum*, the Bollandist Henschen prefixed a summary defence of the text which echoed Baronius' very words (AASS, Feb. III.649–650: *commentarius praevius*; 651–666: Latin translation). Similarly, while the great Jansenist scholar-historian Tillemont laboured hard to meet what he regarded as nine serious historical difficulties in the text, his arguments sometimes lapsed into mere apologia, and he introduced his defence of the *Life* by repeating Baronius' subjective assessment of its nature and value: 'il est impossible en effet de lire cette pièce sans y appercevoir cette lumière de verité que la simplicité et la gravité du style, avec le raport d'une infinité de faits fort bien circonstanciez y font briller de tous costez.'[84]

---

[82] C. Baronius, Annales ecclesiastici 5 (Rome, 1594), 70–74, 131–141 = Annales ecclesiastici, ed. A. Theiner 6 (Paris, 1866), 257–260, 326–339.

[83] D. Blondel, De la primauté en l'Église (Geneva, 1641), 552.

[84] L. S. Le Nain de Tillemont, Mémoires pour servir à l'histoire ecclésiastique des six premiers siècles 10 (Paris, 1705), 843–849, 703 (the passage quoted). Grégoire, Vie de Porphyre (n. 79), 117, pronounced

Tillemont's favourable assessment, which was accepted without hesitation (or acknowledgment) by Edward Gibbon,[85] seemed to be confirmed when the original Greek text of the *Life* was finally published in the late nineteenth century, and one brave young scholar set out to remove some of the major historical difficulties by the then fashionable method of conjectural emendation.[86] Moreover, in 1930 Grégoire, who edited the text with M.-A. Kugener for the *Collection Byzantine* of the Association Budé, summed up and seemed to settle the issue by a hypothesis which combined a favourable verdict with an explanation of the problems in the text far more precise and convincing than Tillemont's attempt to remove them altogether. Grégoire accepted that the preface to the *Life of Porphyry* copies the preface to Theodoret's *Philotheos Historia*, which is conventionally dated to 444, but he argued that an original, authentic and accurate biography written by his companion Mark shortly after Porphyry's death had been reworked some decades later by an editor who both added the preface copied from Theodoret and incompetently introduced into the text the historical errors which it now contains.[87]

Grégoire's *prima facie* attractive solution of the problems was accepted in a long review by the Orientalist François Nau, who refined it further and compared the progress of scholarship on the *Life* to the solution of mathematical problems through successively closer approximations to

Tillemont's attempt to meet one of Blondel's arguments 'faible et peu digne de sa réputation de savant honnête.'

[85] Decline and Fall, Chapter XXXII n. 60 (3.381 n. 60 Bury = 2.260 Womersley).

[86] A. Nuth, De Marci diaconi Vita Porphyrii episcopi Gazensis quaestiones historicae et grammaticae (diss. Bonn, 1897), 6–60.

[87] Grégoire, Vie de Porphyre (n. 79), xxxiii–xxxvii, ciii–cix.

the truth.[88] Since 1930 many historians have accordingly used the *Life* as providing contemporary evidence not only for the court of Arcadius, which Porphyry and Mark allegedly visited, but for matters of central importance in understanding the history and culture of Late Antiquity. In 1964 A. H. M. Jones confidently asserted that 'we have in the contemporary life of Porphyry, bishop of Gaza, a vivid picture of how things were done in the reign of Arcadius.'[89] This verdict is echoed and applied in much recent writing about the period, which uses the *Life of Porphyry* as contemporary evidence for the relations between John Chrysostom and the empress Eudoxia,[90] for the civic life of Gaza and for economic and social conditions there in the early fifth-century,[91] to illustrate general social conditions in the fourth century and the political role of imperial women;[92] as unique evidence for the enduring strength of paganism

---

[88]  F. Nau, ROC 27 (1929/30), 422–441. Nau averred that 'cette vie est authentique, au moins pour les neuf dixièmes de son contenu' (423).

[89]  Jones, LRE (1964), 1.344, cf. 172.

[90]  Kelly, Golden Mouth (n. 10), 168–170. Kelly also accepts the account that the *Life* gives of Mark's journey to Constantinople in 398 with a letter of Porphyry to John (26). Elsewhere he defends his use of this tainted source with the optimistic assertion that 'although doubt had been thrown on large portions of Mark's narrative, there is no reason to suspect the authenticity of this section' (142).

[91]  C. A. M. Glucker, The City of Gaza in the Roman and Byzantine Periods (Oxford, 1987), 1, 46–50, 65–68 nn. 109–153, 79–81, 84 nn. 48–56. A. J. Wharton, Refiguring the Post Classical City. Dura Europos, Jerash, Jerusamem and Ravenna (Cambridge, 1995), 100–103; S. Weingarten, The Saint's Saints. Hagiography and Geography in Jerome (Leiden & Boston, 2005), 113, 123, 138, 139.

[92]  C. Mango, Byzantium. The Empire of the New Rome (London, 1980), 40; K. Holum, Theodosian Empresses. Women and Imperial Dominion in Late Antiquity (Berkeley, 1982), 54–56.

around 400;[93] as furnishing a paradigm for interpreting how the cities of the eastern Roman Empire made the transition from paganism to Christianity,[94] and even more generally as reflecting societal attitudes c. 400.[95]

These claims are not invalidated by certain obvious and predictable fictions, such as the storm at sea which ceased immediately when the captain of the ship, who was an Arian, renounced his heresy and anathematised Arius (55–57).[96] In 1941, however, Paul Peeters published a Georgian version of the *Life*, and argued that it was not a translation of the Greek version, but that both the Greek and the Georgian versions were independently translated from a lost Syriac original composed in the seventh century, shortly after the Arab conquest, in order to bolster the claims of the Melkites to the main church of Gaza.[97] Peeters' long article had no

---

[93]  Jones, LRE (1964), 1.345; 2.943, 994; P. Chuvin, A Chronicle of the Last Pagans, trans. B. A. Archer (Cambridge, Mass., 1990), 76–78. In contrast, Mango, Byzantium (n. 92), 89, adduces the *Life* to show that Gaza was an exception at a time when 'most urban centres had accepted Christianity by the fourth century.'

[94]  R. van Dam, Viator 16 (1985), 1–20, esp 5 n. 14, where van Dam advances the remarkable argument that, though the *Life* poses 'many specific historical and theological questions,' they do not affect his analysis of the change 'from paganism to Christianity' in Gaza at all because he 'usually uses only uncontested activities of the bishop.'

[95]  Averil Cameron, The Mediterranean World in Late Antiquity AD 395–600 (London & New York, 1993), 58, quoting *Life* 78: 'this account of the building ... of the cathedral at Gaza ... conveys something of the excitement felt by contemporaries'; 70, citing *Life* 47–50, 63–70, 76 for the demolition of the temples at Gaza 'by the local bishop in AD 402 with the willing help of the soldiers.'

[96]  Note, however, the suspicions voiced by J. Rougé, Nuovo Didaskaleion 12 (1962), 58–60, who found that the storm in the *Life* (55–57) 'présente par bien des côtés des caractères inquiétants pour sa réalité.'

[97]  P. Peeters, AB 67 (1941), 65–216.

discernible impact on scholarship until 1984, when Ramsay MacMullen endorsed its conclusions.[98] Since then judicious scholars have rejected the *Life* as evidence for the early fifth century, as Alan Cameron did in 1987, when he roundly declared that 'the *Life of Porphyry* is a work of almost pure fiction dating from (at earliest) the mid-sixth century' and that 'Porphyry himself may never have existed.'[99]

Unfortunately, it was premature for Cameron and Jacqueline Long six years later to assume that credulity had been vanquished and to state that the *Life* 'is now recognized to be a forgery of the sixth century or later.'[100] Soon after this optimistic assessment, Frank Trombley took issue with the philological and historical arguments deployed by Peeters and produced a spirited defence of the basic reliability of the *Life* by postulating (as Grégoire and Nau had) a lost account of Porphyry from the early fifth century upon which he held that the much later *Life of Porphyry* which survives was based.[101] Several historians of Late Antiquity have subsequently declared themselves convinced by Trombley's arguments and hence have continued to assert that the

---

[98]   R. MacMullen, Christianizing the Roman Empire (New Haven & London, 1984), 86–89, 158 n.2.

[99]   Alan Cameron, Chiron 17 (1987), 355 n. 60. The *Life* was similarly dismissed by T. D. Barnes, SP 19 (1989), 8–12.

[100]   Cameron & Long, Barbarians and Politics (n. 29), 155.

[101]   F. R. Trombley, Hellenic Religion and Christianization c. 370–529 1² (Leiden, New York & Cologne, 1995), 187–282. His discussion of Gaza is based on acceptance of the *Life* as a thoroughly reliable and accurate source, which he argues to be 'almost completely vindicated as a near contemporary document of the episcopate of Porphyrius, and as an eyewitness account of the administrative realities of temple conversions and of Christianizing urban populations' (187). The hypothesis that the *Life* as extant represents a reworking of a 'rédaction primitive' composed shortly after 420 had been argued at length by Grégoire & Kugener and accepted by Nau, ROC 27 (1929/30), 424, 427, 441.

*Life* has an authentic kernel which may legitimately be used as contemporary evidence for the reign of Arcadius.[102] Moreover, Johannes Hahn has recently declared that the authenticity of the *Life of Porphyry* and the historicity of the events which it narrates are confirmed by a homily delivered by John of Jerusalem which appears to date from 394 and which is preserved in Armenian.[103] But the homily merely refers to a Porphyry who lives in Jerusalem and who has inspired John: what John actually says about him appears at first sight to suggest that he is already dead (§ 30: 'tu es entré avec les clefs dans le royaume des ciels'; § 41: 'je te béatifie, ô homme bienheureux').[104] In the face of such widespread scholarly credulity, it will not be otiose to essay a definitive proof that the *Life* cannot have been composed earlier than the sixth century.

As always, argument must proceed from the known to the doubtful, from what is certain or agreed by all to what is uncertain and in dispute. Any realistic assessment of the *Life of Porphyry of Gaza*, therefore, must begin from the indisput-

---

[102] For example, Z. Rubin, Sharing the Sacred. Religious Contacts and Conflicts in the Holy Land First-Fifteenth Centuries CE, ed. A. Kofsky & G. G. Stroumsa (Jerusalem, 1998), 31–66, who concludes that 'the two extant versions of the *Vita Porphyrii* show clear traces of a common Syriac source' and that 'it was the author of the Greek version who … gave rise to the needless misgivings concerning the authenticity of the *Vita Porphyrii*' (65).

[103] J. Hahn, Gewalt und religiöser Konflikt. Studien zur Auseinandersetzungen zwischen Christen, Heiden und Juden im Osten des Römischen Reiches (von Konstantin bis Theodosius II.). Klio, Beihefte, N. F. 8 (Berlin, 2004), 202–209.

[104] Quoted from the French translation by M. van Esbroek, AB 102 (1984), 115–125. In his introduction to the homily, van Esbroek proceeds from the assumption that John's Porphyry is the later bishop of Gaza and that the future bishop was *staurophylax* when John delivered the homily (109–113).

able fact that it copies the preface to Theodoret's *Philotheos Historia*, from which it follows that, at least in its present form, the *Life* cannot have been written earlier than c. 450. There are, therefore, three central questions to be answered. First, how long after 450 was the present text composed? Second, does the extant *Life of Porphyry* use and adapt an earlier life of the bishop of Gaza? And third, does the *Life* preserve any precise and authentic information about events c. 400? Trombley's recent defence of the *Life* postulates an early redaction 'compiled largely from a concatenation of documents and well-known facts.'[105] Can that be true?

The central argument against such a posited lost original or base text is that the *Life of Porphyry* does not merely make occasional historical mistakes, some of which are so serious as to be scarcely credible for anyone writing in the early fifth century, but that it exhibits a systematic discrepancy with verifiable facts of the period wherever its central narrative can be compared with contemporary evidence. This incompatibility with known historical facts is perhaps most obvious in its account of Porphyry's activities in Constantinople.

According to the *Life*, when Porphyry arrived in the imperial capital, he approached the empress, who was pregnant. When Porphyry prophesied the birth of a son who would reign for many years, Eudoxia promised to support his petition to the emperor, then a few days later gave birth to Theodosius who was proclaimed Augustus at birth (44: ἀπὸ λοχείας βασιλεὺς ἀνηγορεύθη) and baptised a little later, apparently after the lapse of between ten and twenty days (45–46). Now the emperor Arcadius, the empress Eudoxia and their infant son Theodosius are of course genuine his-

---

[105] Trombley, Hellenic Religion 1² (n. 101), 246–282, esp. 257–258.

torical characters, as are John the bishop of Constantinople, who is named in several passages (26, 27, 36–38, 43), and 'Eutropius the *cubicularius*, who then had great influence with the emperor Arcadius' and with whom the *Life* claims that John had interceded earlier when Porphyry sent Mark to the capital (26). But Theodosius, who was born on 10 April 401 (Socrates, *HE* 6.6.40; Marcellinus 401.3; *Paschal Chronicle* 567 Bonn), was not in fact proclaimed Augustus immediately after his birth,[106] but on 10 January 402, when he was nine months old (*Fasti Vindobonenses priores* 535 [Chr. min. 1.299], cf. Marcellinus 402.2). Grégoire and Kugener attempted to salvage the credit of the *Life* by suggesting somewhat implausibly that the phrase 'after a few days' is vague and imprecise enough to cover a period of nine months.[107] Moreover, although the *Life* gives what purports to be an eye-witness description of the ceremonies attending the baptism of the infant Theodosius, including a procession from the church where the baptism was performed (which is not identified) through the streets of Constantinople to the imperial palace (47–49), the author shows no awareness of the fact that the emperor Arcadius entered on his fifth ordinary consulate on 1 January 402 – and presumably celebrated his assumption of the consular fasces in the usual fashion. Admittedly, a sermon preserved in a

---

[106] The city of Attaleia honoured τὸν θεοφιλέστατον καὶ ἐπιφανέστα-τον ἡμῶν δεσπότην Φλ. Θεοδόσιον (R. Paribeni, Monumenti Antichi 23 [1915], 22 no. 8 = IGC 309ter): since the inscription is undated, this Theodosius may be the infant son of Arcadius, not his homonymous grandfather.

[107] Grégoire & Kugener, Byzantion 4 (1927/28), 346–348, re-produced in their Vie de Porphyre (n. 79), xxx–xxxii. They argue that 'Marc est ici très vague: μετ' ὀλίγας ἡμέρας n'a aucun sens précis' (348 = xxxi).

manuscript of the eight or ninth century, which attributes it to John Chrysostom (BHG, Supp. 1929 = CPG 4882),[108] has been claimed to furnish proof that the infant Theodosius was baptised on 6 January 402 and hence to vindicate the historical reliability of the *Life*.[109] That claim, however, rests on the erroneous assumption that the sermon must have been delivered in Constantinople on 10 January 402 either by John Chrysostom himself or by Severianus of Gabala. In fact, both stylistic and theological features of the sermon indicate that its author is Nestorius, and its content is entirely consistent with the hypothesis that Nestorius delivered it as bishop of Constantinople on the Sunday following Epiphany in January 430.[110]

A similar systematic discrepancy is apparent in what the *Life of Porphyry* says about the principal bishops of Palestine between 395 and 420. According to the *Life*, Porphyry was bishop of Gaza from 18 March 395 to 26 February 420 (16, 103). That could be correct. Two lists of Palestinian bishops are preserved from this period, one dated to September 400 and the other to December 415.[111] Neither list identifies the sees of the bishops, but they both begin with the names of Eulogius and John, that is, Eulogius of Caesarea in first place as the metropolitan bishop of the province of

---

[108] Published by A. Wenger, AB 95 (1977), 81–90.

[109] A. Wenger, REByz 10 (1952), 52–54; 29 (1971), 118; AB 95 (1977), 76–78; Holum, Empresses (n. 92), 55 n. 31.

[110] T. D. Barnes, SP 19 (1989), 12; 39 (2006), 3–5; S. J. Voicu, Augustinianum 43 (2003), 495–499.

[111] Viz., (1) the addressees of a synodical letter sent by Theophilus from Alexandria to the bishops of Palestine and Cyprus (Jerome, *Ep.* 92.1 [CSEL 55.147]) and (2) Augustine's report of a condemnation of Pelagius by the Council of Diospolis (*Contra Julianum* 1.32 [PL 44.663]), cf. D. & L. Stiernon, Dict. d'hist. et de géog. hist. 20 (Paris, 1984), 172.

Palestine, and John, who was bishop of Jerusalem from 387 to 417.[112] In the list from 400 a Porphyry appears in tenth place, while in 415 there are two bishops named Porphyry in the fourth and sixth places. Since the bishops other than Eulogius and John presumably appear in the chronological order of their elections, the Porphyry who is attested in 400 and in fourth place in 415 could well be a bishop of Gaza consecrated in 395, as the *Life* alleges that Porphyry was. Yet, even if Porphyry himself was bishop of Gaza between 395 and 420, the *Life* makes bad mistakes about the bishops of both Caesarea and Jerusalem. For it ignores the historical Eulogius and produces an otherwise unknown John as bishop of Caesarea from 395 to 404 (12–16, 32–33, 53, 62), and it has Praÿlius instead of John as bishop of Jerusalem in the 390s (10, 12, 14), even though the historical Praÿlius did not in fact become bishop until 417, after John of Jerusalem died. It is hard to avoid the conclusion that John, the predecessor of Porphyry as bishop of Caesarea in the *Life*, is an invented character who owes his existence to his famous namesake who was bishop of Jerusalem during most of Porphyry's tenure of the see of Gaza. There is no justification for treating the John of the *Life of Porphyry* as a historical character and squeezing him into the list of bishops of Caesarea between Gelasius, who attended councils of bishops in Constantinople in 381 and 394, and Eulogius, who is attested in 400 and 415.[113] It is hard to imagine how an early fifth century biographer of Porphyry could commit such gross errors about prominent bishops whose memory was still alive.

---

[112] D. Stiernon, Dict. d'hist. et de géog. hist. 27 (Paris, 2000), 160–163.

[113] R. Janin, Dict. d'hist. et de géog. hist. 12 (1953), 208, lists John as bishop of Caesarea in from 395 to 404, Eulogius from 404 to 417.

Prosopography not only exposes fictions in the *Life of Porphyry*, it points to a date in the sixth century for its composition. Admittedly, some other dubiously historical characters besides these Palestinian bishops have names that are or may be taken from the fifth or even the fourth century. According to the *Life*, Arcadius sent Cynegius, *vir clarissimus*, a member of the imperial consistorium and a zealous Christian, to Gaza to close the temple of Marnas (51, 54, 63, 69). This Cynegius, though otherwise unknown to history,[114] is normally accepted as a real historical person. But a strong suspicion that he is invented arises from the fact that his name and actions recall those of an earlier Cynegius who destroyed many temples in the East as praetorian prefect in the 380s.[115] Again, according to the *Life*, when Porphyry reached Constantinople, he enlisted the aid of the eunuch Amantius, *castrensis* of the empress Eudoxia, in obtaining the imperial order to close pagan temples at Gaza (36–41, 44, 49–52). This Amantius is otherwise unattested, although Zonaras records a eunuch Amantius (also otherwise unattested) who wielded improper influence over Theodosius between Antiochus, who was *praepositus sacri cubiculi* before 420, and Chrysaphius, who acquired power in the 440s.[116]

---

[114] PLRE 2 (1980), 331, Cynegius 2, noting that the *Life* wrongly gives his rank as *vir clarissimus*, instead of *vir spectabilis* (CTh 6.12.1: 25 September 399), but palliating the error with the excuse that 'these distinctions were not always strictly observed in literary texts.'

[115] On his career and rampage through the East, see esp. J. F. Matthews, Western Aristocracies and Imperial Court A. D. 363–425 (Oxford, 1975), 140–142, who accepts both the historicity of the Cynegius in the *Life of Porphyry*, whom he takes to be 'a close relative (possibly a son)' of the praetorian prefect, and Mark's description of his actions (142–143).

[116] PLRE 2 (1980), 66, Amantius 1 & 2; H. Scholten, Der Eunuch in Kaisernähe. Zur politischen und sozialen Bedeutung des praepositus

There was, however, a prominent eunuch Amantius in the early sixth century: he wielded influence at the court of Anastasius and played a role in the election of Justin as emperor in 518, who put him to death within ten days of his assumption of power.[117] The fictitious Amantius of the *Life of Porphyry* probably owes his existence to this later historical and well documented Amantius. A similar argument can be deployed to account for the names of the otherwise unattested and probably invented Aeneas, who appears in the *Life* as Porphyry's predecessor as bishop of Gaza (11), and the Rhodian hermit Procopius (34–36, 43, 55–56). Especially in combination, the two names ineluctably recall the Aeneas and his pupil Procopius who were active as sophists in Gaza in the early sixth century.[118]

That the *Life* was written after 500 is confirmed by a series of institutional anachronisms. To be sure, the lacunae in our evidence are such that many possible anachronisms cannot be proven to be such. For example, Porphyry finds the gate of the city locked (20). Did fourth century Gaza have a city wall with a gate? Although Choricius praises the bishop Marcianus for rebuilding the city walls in the early sixth century (*Orat.* 2.16, 54), and the *Life* may reflect his building activites, the available archaeological evidence seems not to provide evidence for the state of the walls in the early

---

sacri cubiculi im 4. und 5. Jahrhundert n. Chr. Prismata: Beiträge zur Altertumswissenschaft 5 Frankfurt a. M., 1995), 236–237 n. 30, cf. 228–230 n. 21 (Antiochus); 248–249 (Chrysaphius). Unfortunately, the survey of P. Guyot, Eunuchen als Sklaven und Freigelassene in der griechisch-römischen Antike (Stuttgart, 1980), does not go beyond the fourth century.

[117] PLRE 2 (1980), 67–68, Amantius 4.
[118] PLRE 2 (1980, 17, Aeneas 3; 921–922, Procopius 8.

fifth century.[119]. Moreover, while it is true that many officials and institutions existed both in the late fourth and the sixth centuries, such as *duces* and *consulares* of Palestine[120] or *defensores civitatis* with irenarchs under their command (25),[121] some passages in the *Life* nevertheless contain clear institutional anachronisms.

A careless slip betrays the fact that the author was writing at a time when there was no longer a western Roman emperor. For the *Life* describes how the *quaestor sacri palatii* prepares an imperial letter 'written in the name of the two emperors', by which he means that it was written in the name of Arcadius and the new-born Theodosius II (50). In 402 there were three emperors in the imperial college and an official letter by any one of them was issued in the name of all three.[122] Now, except during usurpations like that of Johannes in 423–425, western emperors were recognised in the East continuously until the death of Valentinian III in 455, and sporadically thereafter, though often as Caesar rather than Augustus, for at least another twenty years.[123] This mistake points to a date long after the death of the last Roman emperor in the West in 480.

Again, according to the *Life*, before Porphyry became bishop of Gaza, the bishop of Jerusalem entrusted him with

---

[119] Glucker, City of Gaza (n. 91), 55–57.

[120] PLRE 1 (1971), 1108; 2 (1980), 1286.

[121] Jones, LRE (1964), 144–145, 279–280, 479–480, 496–497.

[122] For the principle, New Empire (1982), 3–8.

[123] The last western emperor recognised in the East was Julius Nepos (PLRE 2 [1980]), 777–778, Nepos 3). He was sent by Leo to Italy with an eastern army to overthrow Glycerius and was proclaimed Augustus in Rome on 19 or 24 June 474. Nepos was forced to leave Italy in August 475, after which he resided in Dalmatia, where he was murdered on 9 May 480: it seems probable that the emperor Zeno recognised him as his imperial colleague until his death.

the care of the precious wood of the cross (10). Grégoire observed that 'this passage is the first mention of the post of *staurophylax* or guardian of the holy cross, which was one of the most important posts in the church of Jerusalem in the sixth century.'[124] That revealing observation does not go far enough. The first secure attestation of the post comes from the reign of Justinian, when Cyril of Scythopolis, who was writing in the 550s, records *staurophylakes* from the middle of the fifth century (*Vita Euthymii* 33, 35, 48, 49, 52, 55, 60, 69).[125] Auguste Frolow, who collected the early evidence for the post of *staurophylax*, discounted the *Life of Porphyry* precisely on the grounds that its reference to a *staurophylax* in the late fourth century is a sixth century anachronism.[126]

Another passage points equally emphatically to a date in the sixth century. Mark describes a procession in Constantinople in 402 led by 'patricians, *illustres* and every rank, together with military regiments,' all carrying candles (47: προηγοῦντο δὲ πατρίκιοι, ἰλλούστριοι καὶ πᾶσα ἀξία μετὰ τῶν στρατιωτικῶν ταγμάτων, πάντες κηροὺς βαστάζοντες). This is a sixth century procession. In 402 there were at most three *patricii* in the eastern empire, perhaps only one. Constantine had revived the ancient title of *patricius*, which under the late Republic and early empire had designated membership in an identifiable group of families, but he transformed the title into a personal badge of honour that did not pass to a

---

[124] Grégoire, Vie de Porphyre (n. 79), 10 n.1.

[125] A. Frolow, La relique de la vraie croix. Recherches sur le développement d'un culte. Archives de l'orient chrétien 7 (Paris, 1961), 171–172 no. 18, 173 no. 22.

[126] Frolow, La relique de la vraie croix (n. 125), 172: 'le texte ne semble pas toutefois d'avoir été rédigé avant le VIᵉ siècle, et il n'est pas certain que son auteur ait été au courant de l'organisation ecclésiastique en usage deux cent ans auparavant.'

man's descendants on his death.[127] The first new-style *patricius* was Flavius Optatus, consul in 334 (Zosimus 2.40.2), who was almost immediately joined by Julius Constantius, consul in 335 and a half-brother of Constantine.[128] During the rest of the fourth century, the title or rank of *patricius* was granted very sparingly. Only a half-dozen *patricii*, all close to the reigning emperor, are attested between 337, when Optatus and Julius Constantius were both killed, and the summer of 399, when the eunuch Eutropius, eastern consul of the year and *patricius*, fell from power and was put to death.[129] After the fall of Eutropius, his position as Arcadius' chief minister passed to the praetorian prefects of the East. Between August 399 and 405, this office was successively occupied by Aurelianus, Caesarius and Eutychianus, the ordinary consuls of the years 400, 397 and 398 respectively.[130] Of these three men, Euthychianus is not attested as *patricius*, though that does not necessarily entail that he never acquired the title. Caesarius was honoured by the city of Tralles as *patricius*, proconsul and praetorian prefect (*Inschriften von Tralleis und Nysa* 56), and he may have received the title before 400.[131] Aurelianus is also attested as *patricius*, but not before his long-delayed return to power and office as praetorian prefect in December 414 (*CTh* 7.7.4: 5 September 415; Chr. min. 2.71; *Anth. Gr.* 16.73). In 402 there was no-one else in Constantinople

---

[127] W. Heil, Der konstantinische Patriziat (Basel, 1966), 11–27.

[128] PLRE 1 (1971), 226, Constantius 7.

[129] Listed at Phoenix 29 (1975), 169.

[130] On the complicated problem of determining exactly when each of the three held the prefecture, which is not germane to the question at issue here, see Cameron & Long, Barbarians and Politics (n. 29), 149–161; T. D. Barnes, CP 90 (1995), 93–95.

[131] PLRE 1 (1971), 171, Caesarius 7.

besides these three men who could have been a *patricius*, and the patriciate remained an extremely rare honour for at least another fifty years.[132] At the Council of Chalcedon in 451, of the seventeen officals and senators who presided over the Council of Chalcedon, only the most senior official Anatolius, who took the chair, one of the five other high-ranking officials and four out of the twelve other senators were *patricii* (ACO 2.1.1.55, *Actio prima* 2). By the late fifth century, however, the title had become devalued and was more widely bestowed.[133] The *Life of Porphyry* describes a procession that reflects the proliferation of *patricii* which only began after 450: the *Life* was therefore written when this process was well advanced.[134] The description of the procession also contains a clear linguistic anachronism: like the *Life of Hypatios*, it employs the transcription ἰλλούστριος for the Latin *illustris* instead of ἐνδοξότατος, which had been

---

[132] Phoenix 29 (1975) 155–170.

[133] Phoenix 29 (1975) 156–158, 163–164, drawing on J. Sundwall, Weströmische Studien (Rome, 1915); Abhandlungen zur Geschichte des ausgehenden Römertums (Helsinki, 1918), 84–170. Unfortunately neither Sundwall nor PLRE 2 (1980) provides a list of *patricii* for the period 395–527.

[134] Similar arguments apply also to the *Life of Epiphanius of Salamis* (BHG 596), which C. Rapp, Papers given at the Twenty-Fifth Jubilee Spring Symposium of Byzantine Studies, Birmingham, March 1991 (Nicosia, 1993), 178–184, dates to the fifth or sixth century. The best edition of this life is in Rapp's so far unpublished thesis, The Vita of Epiphanius of Salamis – A Historical and Literary Study (diss. Oxford, 1991). Rapp argues that the *Life of Epiphanius* has a legendary character rather than being a fraudulent composition like the *Life of Porphyry*, but it too was surely composed in the sixth century: it invents not only 'Callistus the son of Aetius, the great prefect of Rome' (40, p. 101.10 Rapp), but also a sister of the emperors Arcadius and Honorius who is stated to be 'the wife of one of the patricians' (90, p. 164.4 Rapp).

the almost invariable Greek equivalent throughout the fifth century and beyond.[135]

There is also another equally clear linguistic indicator of a date no earlier than c. 500. It is not the occurrence of the verb λησμονῶ, one of the two common verbs for 'forget' in modern Greek, on which Grégoire pounced, apparently misled by his unacknowledged reliance on a standard work of reference.[136] For, although the verb is not found in any Greek literary text of the classical, Hellenistic or Roman periods, it is found in the *Doctrina Jacobi*, which was written in the third decade of the seventh century (1.43.7, p. 135 Dagron), and in John of Damascus' *Sacra Parallela* in the first half of the eighth (*PG* 95.1513), and it appears to occur in one of the famous confession inscriptions from Phrygia inscription which was first published in 1887 (SEG 6.250 = MAMA 4.285: λημόνησα, where the editors gloss 'ἐλησμόνησα').[137] The linguistic anachronism is the

---

[135] Above, p. 248.

[136] Grégoire, Vie de Porphyre (n. 79), xliv–xlv: 'nous n'avons pas trouvé λησμονῶ en dehors de notre Vie, que dans un texte faussement attribué à Athanase, et qui paraît daté du VIII^e siècle au plus tôt.' Grégoire's learning is second-hand: he has taken the reference from E. A. Sophocles, Greek Lexicon of the Roman and Byzantine Periods (New York, 1887), 713, who cites 'Pseudo-Ath. IV 797C.' The text to which Sophocles referred is the 'Speech on a miracle at Berytus, concerning the precious and venerable image of our Lord and God'(CPG 2262, cf. BHG Auct. 780–788b): it described how the Christian who made the image left it behind when he moved from one monastic cell to another because he forgot it (PG 28.797: λησμονήσας αὐτὴν ἐν τῷ κελλίῳ).

[137] Also W. M. Ramsay, Cities and Bishoprics of Phrygia 1 (Oxford, 1895), 151 no. 48; F. S. Steinleitner, Die Beicht im Zusammenhange mit der sakralen Rechtspflege in der Antike. Ein Beitrag zur näheren Kenntnis kleinasiatisch-orientalischer Kulte der Kaiserzeit (Leipzig, 1913), 49–52 n. 24, cf. 115–119; G. Petzl, Die Beichtinschriften Westkleinasiens. Epigraphica Anatolica 22 (Bonn, 1994), 132–133 no. 112.

use of 'Byzantium' to refer to the city of Constantinople. In all literary texts written between Constantine's replacement of the ancient city of Byzantium by a new Christian city and the late fifth century, the old name Byzantium is used exclusively for the old city as it existed before 324: the contemporary city is 'the city of Constantine,' New Rome, the Second Rome, the 'ruling / royal city' or some similar periphrasis.[138] The usage is perhaps clearest in the ecclesiastical historians: Socrates, Theodoretus, Sozomenus and Philostorgius all use the old name 'Byzantium' when describing its refoundation by Constantine, but never in their narrative of events after 330.[139] The same is true of the pagan historian Zosimus, who was writing shortly after 500: his narrative of events after 324 mentions the city of Constantinople thirty three times, but never calls it Byzantium. The earliest extant author who is known for certain to have called Constantine's new city on the Bosporus 'Byzantium' was the pagan Marinus in his life of the Neoplatonist philosopher Proclus, who calls it 'the royal city' once (8.24: ἐν τῇ βασιλίδι πόλει) and 'Byzantium' three times (6.6, 9.2–3, 10.7). On the first occasion when Marinus calls the city 'Byzantium,' he does so with obvious polemical intent: he presents Proclus as being under the special protection of the goddess Athena, the protectress

---

The inscription was first published by D. G. Hogarth, JHS 8 (1887), 383–384 n. 14, but it was Ramsay, JHS 10 (1889), 220–222 n. 6, who first recognised the verb as λησμονῶ.

[138] *Akten des 21. Internationalen Papyrologenkongresses in Berlin 1995*, ed. B. Kramer, W. Luppe, H. Maehler & G. Poethke. Archiv für Papyrusforschung, Beiheft 3 (Leipzig, 1997) 1. 57–60.

[139] The apparent exceptions in Philostorgius, *HE* 2.9a, 12.13, both occur in quotations by Photius.

of the city (ἡ τοῦ Βυζαντίου πολιοῦχος).[140] This significant passage escaped the notice of Romilly Jenkins, who argued that the thirty foot high statue of Athena which stood on a column in the forum of Constantine until it was destroyed by the Crusaders was Pheidias' famous statue of Athena Promachos from the Parthenon.[141] It was presumably Constantine himself who had the statue transported from Athens,[142] and it may have been the pagan claim that Athena was the protecting deity of the city that provoked the later Christian counter-assertion that the protectress of the city was not the virgin goddess Athena, but Mary the virgin mother of God.[143]

The new name caught on with surprising speed. Although Marcellinus usually calls the city Constantinople in the chronicle which he wrote there in Latin in 518, he uses *Byzantium* twice for the city (380; 516.3) and *Byzantini* four times for its inhabitants (399.3; 472.1; 491.2; 512.2). In the 520s the pagan writer Damascius used the name Byzantium fourteen times in the fragments of his *Life of Isidore* that survive. The new designation of the city and its inhabitants oc-

---

[140] H. D. Saffrey & A.-P. Segonds, Marinus: Proclus, ou Sur le Bonheur (Paris, 2002), 78, comments that 'cette affectation d'archaïsme cache probablement des raisons idéologiques.'

[141] R. J. H. Jenkins, JHS 67 (1947), 31–33, adducing Arethas, Cedrenus, Nicetas Choniates and a Byzantine depiction of the statue in Constantinople (Plate X, reproduced from J. Strzygowski, Der Bilderkreis des griechischen Physiologus, des Kosmas Indikopleustes und Oktateuch. Byzantinisches Archiv 2 [Leipzig, 1899], 36–37, Plate XIX).

[142] Despite Zosimus 5.6.3, whose report that Alaric saw Athena Promachos and Achilles parading on the walls of Athens when he besieged the city has often been construed as proof that the statue was still there in 395.

[143] The account of this development by Averil Cameron, JTS, N. S. 29 (1978), 79–108, does not mention either Marinus or Athena.

curs thirty times in the chronicle of John Malalas, although he calls the city Constantinople one hundred and twenty six times. Procopius speaks of Byzantium and Byzantines more than three hundred times, of Constantinople only in his *Buildings* and then only seven times,[144] and Procopius' continuators Agathias and Menander the Guardsman use the new name exclusively. It follows that a Christian writer who unhesitatingly calls Constantinople 'Byzantium,' as the author of the *Life of Porphyry* does in several passages (26, 27, 36, 37), can hardly be writing before the reign of Justinian.

In sum, the *Life of Porphyry*, allegedly written by his coeval Mark the deacon,

(1) copies a text written after 440,
(2) contains serious historical errors when it writes about both bishops in Palestine and events in Constantinople in the reign of Arcadius,
(3) lapses into unconscious anachronisms which reflect political conditions of the last quarter of the fifth century or later,
(4) invents characters who possess the names of well-known persons who lived in the sixth century, and
(5) reflects at least one linguistic usage that emerged no earlier than c. 500.

---

[144] For a general survey of how writers depicted Constantinople down to the sixth century, E. Fenster, Laudes Constantinopolitanae (Munich, 1968), 14–96. An electronic search in the Thesaurus Linguae Greaecae produces the following figures for the number of occurrences of the names Βυζάντιον and Βυζαντῖνοι. 70 in authors born in the fourth century, 105 in those born in the fifth and 550 in those born in the sixth, of whom Procopius accounts for 338, Menander for 30, Agathias for 25 and Evagrius for 20. The two words occur 19 times in Zosimus, but only twice in relation to events after 330 (3.11.2, 3).

It must be concluded, therefore, that the *Life of Porphyry* is a sixth century composition. It can accordingly find its appropriate intellectual milieu in the reign of Justinian, which was receptive to fictitious hagiography glorifying the use of imperial power to root out paganism.

It is theoretically possible that an author writing a full century later had access to reliable information about events in Gaza c. 400. Is there any good reason to believe that the author of the *Life of Porphyry* in fact did so? A negative verdict must be rendered on this count too. Even if it be admitted (as is argued by Trombley and implicitly accepted here) that the Greek text is prior to the postulated Syriac version from which Peeters argued that the Georgian translation was made, that does not establish the historical accuracy of any single passage in it. Trombley's defence of the *Life*, which the arguments advanced here have outflanked, implicitly concedes most of the case against its reliability and fails to demonstrate the historical accuracy of any single specific passage in the narrative.

Trombley contends that the extant text is the revised version of a propagandistic tract composed c. 415 to bolster Porphyry's claim to episcopal jurisdiction over Maiuma, the port of Gaza, which an unscrupulous and dishonest editor rewrote between 444 and 451.[145] If that is so, then it is illegitimate to extract some parts or passages of the *Life*, as Trombley does, in order to grant them a privileged position as 'an eyewitness account' of what was happening in Gaza c. 400 and to provide a basis for a statistical analysis of how the city became Christian.[146] Since the *Life* copies

---

[145] Trombley, Hellenic Religion 1[2] (n. 101), 208 n. 102, 271–282.

[146] Trombley, Hellenic Religion 1[2] (n. 101), 223–234, starting from the proposition that 'the statistical data given in the life of Porphyrius

Theodoret's *Philotheos Historia*, it cannot be what it purports
to be, unless Mark wrote it when he was at least eighty five
years old. Hence it is a *Fälschung* in the technical sense of
that word, and it follows that the *onus probandi* lies very
heavily on any who would trust it as historical evidence for
the early fifth century. So far, no-one has produced any independent evidence to confirm the accuracy of its account of
events in either Gaza or Constantinople. Historians should,
therefore, cease to use the *Life of Porphyry* as evidence for
the culture and religion of the eastern Roman Empire c.
400 and instead use it exclusively as evidence for the culture
and intellectual environment of the period in which it was
written – no earlier than the middle of the sixth century.

---

are of the utmost importance because they permit some generalization
about the rate of Christianization' (227).

# Early Christian Hagiography and Modern Historical Scholarship

The most significant advances in scholarly understanding of the history of Christianity in the Roman Empire before the Council of Nicaea occurred during the seventeenth century. Critical hagiography was born, or at least conceived, in 1607. Lives of early Christian martyrs and saints had been collected and published by the Italian humanist Bonino Mombrizio (1424–1482/1502),[1] and by Luigi Lippomano (1500–1559), one of the presiding bishops at the Council of Trent,[2] and the German Carthusian Lorenz Sauer, who is usually known under the Latin version of his name as Laurentius Surius (1522–1578).[3] But an entirely new epoch began when the Jesuit Héribert Roswey or Rosweyde (1569–1629) published what may be called a prospectus for a new and more scholarly collection which he believed

---

[1] His Sanctuarium, probably printed in 1480, was edited by the Benedictine monks of Solesmes Abbey and published as Boninus Mombritius, Sanctuarium sue Vitae Sanctorum (Paris, 1910).

[2] Aloisius Lipomanus, Sanctorum priscorum vitae (Venice, 1551–1560).

[3] Laurentius Surius, De probatis Sanctorum histories ab Al. Lipomano olim conscriptis nunc primum a Laur. Surio emendatis et auctis (Cologne, 1570–1577). A second expanded edition was completed by Sauer's colleague Mosander and published as De vitis sanctorum omnium nationum, ordinum et temporum (Venice, 1581). An expanded version in twelve volumes was published at Cologne in 1617–18.

would comprise eighteen volumes in all.[4] Rosweyde set forth four principal aims:

(1) to recover the authentic text of genuine hagiographical documents which had been distorted by later writers who wished to improve them stylistically;

(2) to recover the full texts of documents which had been mutilated by abbreviation leading to the loss of part of the text (such as the prologues, accounts of miracles and obscure passages);

(3) to search out and publish previously unedited lives of saints;

(4) to supply commentaries to elucidate difficulties in the texts and to eliminate inconsistencies and contradictions.[5]

Rosweyde edited the oldest texts available to him of the lives of the Desert Fathers,[6] but he died in 1629 without completing any of his projected eighteen volumes, despite a life of tireless scholarship. Jean Bolland (1596–1665), who inspected Rosweyde's papers after his death, convinced his

---

[4] The following brief account, which makes no claim to originality, is based on Delehaye, L'œuvre (1959), 11–114; P. Peeters, L'œuvre des Bollandistes[2] (Brussels, 1961), 4–32; D. M. Knowles, Great Historical Enterprises (London, 1963), 3–32 (from which one of the two epigraphs of the book is taken). Fuller details for the eighteenth, nineteenth and early twentieth centuries can be found in a series of volumes by B. Joassart: Hippolyte Delehaye: hagiographie critique et modernisme (SH 81, 2000); Monseigneur Duchesne et les Bollandistes (Brussels, 2002); Von Hügel, Turner et les Bollandistes (Brussels, 2002); Érudition hagiographique au XVIIIᵉ siècle: Jean Lebeuf et les Bollandistes (Brussels, 2003).

[5] In the preface to his Fasti sanctorum quorum vitae in belgicis bibliothecis manuscriptae (Antwerp, 1607).

[6] Vitae Patrum, de vita et verbis seniorum libri X historiam eremitarum complectentes (Antwerp, 1615).

Jesuit superiors that the project could be carried to completion within a reasonable period of time – a misjudgement (if indeed it was an innocent misjudgement) which proved to be uniquely fortunate and productive.

The first two volumes of the *Acta Sanctorum* covering the month of January appeared in 1643. Since saints are most easily identified and individuated by the annual celebration of their cult in a particular place on a particular day of each year, as Rosweyde's proposal of 1607 had clearly stated, Bolland and the society of scholars which he founded proceeded from the start to organise their collection and publication of the *Acta Sanctorum* by day and month, so that each saint is registered, documented and discussed under the day when his or her memory is celebrated, or was originally celebrated if the day has changed. Hence, since 1 January is the Feast of the Circumcision, the very first entry of the *Acta Sanctorum* tackled the ticklish question of the authenticity of relics (AASS, Jan. I.2–8). According to Bolland, two holy foreskins allegedly cut from the infant Jesus when he was eight days old were believed to have survived the Middle Ages. One had been in Antwerp until it was lost in 1566 when Calvinists destroyed the sanctuary in which it was kept. The other holy foreskin (so it was believed) had been given by the mother of Jesus to Mary Magdalene and remained in Jersusalem for some centuries until an angel carried it to Charlemagne who deposited it in Aachen. Charles the Bald then transferred it to Charroux, whence it reached Rome and was preserved in the oratory of St. Laurence in the Lateran in Rome where it met with a most unfortunate (and amusing) accident. On an unusually fine day in May 1559 this most holy of relics suffered damage in a manner which Bolland described in a passage which may be left untranslated in 'the decent obscurity of a learned language.' One of the canons who examined the holy object

*binis utriusque manus digitis Christi praeputium durumne sit an molle
pertentat, et ut esset certior, comprimens, in duas partes incautus divulsit*
(§ 21).

That will bring back memories of childhood for many readers, and perhaps no blame should attach to the priest who
carelessly split in two what was widely believed to be part of
the body of the infant Jesus, a relic of God Incarnate himself
left behind on earth for the pious to venerate. For this act
of unwitting vandalism (so Bolland reports) occasioned a
miracle and thus brought divine confirmation that the foreskin in Rome was indeed a genuine relic of the Lord's time
on earth. For the breaking of the foreskin was attended by
thunder, lightning and a mysterious darkness which covered
the earth. What then of the holy foreskin destroyed in 1566?
Bolland judiciously weighed the claims of the foreskin lost
in Antwerp and quoted four items of evidence that attested
its presence there in the fifteenth century. But he introduced
the evidence with a disclaimer:

*restat ut quae pro Antverpiensibus faciunt proponamus: quae quantam
vim habeant, alii judicent. Mihi certe probabile fit, saltem particulam
aliquam sacri praeputii hic extitisse* (§ 23)

It remains for us to set out what <considerations> count in favour of
the people of Antwerp: what force they have, let others judge. To me
personally it seems probable that at least some small piece of the holy
foreskin was preserved here.

Bolland does not explain how a piece of the foreskin cut
from the infant Jesus, which was preserved in Rome, could
have migrated to Antwerp. Was he therefore practising
deliberate irony in order to express scepticism about the
authenticity of the holy foreskin which came to light in Ant-

werp in the early fifteenth century? It is hard to tell – and
an investigator in the twentieth century was able to list no
fewer than thirteen places which claimed to possess the holy
foreskin.[7] But the fact that Bolland and his original collabo-
rator Godefroy Henschen (1601–1681) laid out evidence
carefully and discussed it in a humble and reverential manner exempted the earliest volumes of the *Acta Sanctorum*
from ecclesiastical censure.[8]

Before the end of the seventeenth century another nineteen volumes of the main series of the *Acta Sanctorum*
had appeared – three volumes for each of the months of
February (1658), March (1668) and April (1675); seven
volumes for May published in three batches in 1680, 1685
and 1688; and two volumes covering the first fifteen days of
June in 1695 and 1698.[9] But the Bollandist enterprise began
to arouse powerful opposition within the Catholic Church
because its critical approach sometimes had contemporary
relevance. In his entries for St. Berthold, the founding
prior of the Carmelite Order, who died c. 1188, and for
St. Albert of Jerusalem († 1214), a Carmelite who became
patriarch of that city, Daniel van Papenbroeck, usually
known as Papenbroch (1628–1714), drew readers' attention
to the total lack of historical evidence for the claim that the
Carmelite order could trace its origins back to disciples of

[7] A. V. Müller, Die 'hochheilige Vorhaut Christi' im Kult und in der
Theologie der Papstkirche (Berlin, 1907).

[8] Bolland's preface and epilogue emphasised that his work belonged
to the realm of human, not divine history (AASS, Jan. I.lxii: '*id tamen
ita suscipi a vobis opus meum volo … ut HISTORIAM HUMANAM*').
Moreover, he introduced his whole discussion with a disclaimer: he
would set out the evidence, but leave his readers to judge where the
truth lay (AASS, Jan. I.3 § 1: *proferam quae de eo varii auctores tradide-
runt: judicium de re tota Lectori relinquam*).

[9] Delehaye, L'œuvre (1959), 172–173.

the Old Testament prophet Elijah (AASS, Mar. III.788; Apr. I.797–799). The Carmelites took offence, and through their efforts the Spanish Inquisition condemned the *Acta Sanctorum* for March, April and May as heretical in 1695, and in 1700 the *Propylaeum Maii*, completed in 1688, in which Papebroch had discussed the sometimes irregular conduct of papal elections, was placed on the official index of forbidden books, where it remained until the pontificate of Pope Leo XIII (1878–1903).

It is not necessary to describe again in any detail the vicissitudes of the Société des Bollandistes and its scholarly enterprise during the eighteenth and nineteenth centuries.[10] After two long generations of magnificent achievement, the work of the Bollandists declined in intellectual quality as they ploughed through the saints of the second half of June in five volumes (1701–1717), then through the saints of July in seven volumes (1719–1731), of August in six (1733–1743) and September in eight (1746–1762), although excellent scholarship was still sometimes on display, as in the long discussion of John Chrysostom by Jean Stiltingh, which appeared in 1753 (AASS, Sept. IV.401–700). After the first three volumes for October had been published (1765, 1768, 1770), disaster struck. In 1773 a papal decree dissolved the Jesuit Order, to which the Bollandists belonged. The secular authorities soon expelled the Bollandists from their original quarters in Antwerp, and their valuable library, which included manuscript material for future volumes, was eventually dispersed. Although the Bollandists at first continued to labour elsewhere and produced three further volumes, two in Brussels (1780 and 1786) and one (covering the saints of

---

[10] The facts are set out clearly by Delehaye, L'œuvre (1959), 87–164; Peeters, L'œuvre[2] (n. 4), 23–102.

12–14 October) printed in 1794 at the Abbey of Tongerloo, where they had found sanctuary, work on the *Acta Sanctorum* petered out and then ceased altogether.

After the lapse of some decades, the scholarly enterprise was resurrected. The reconstitution of the Jesuit Order in 1814 and the creation of Belgium in 1830 created the political conditions in which the Société des Bollandistes could be revived, as it was in 1837, to exhibit and advertise the academic values of the new nation. Publication of the *Acta Sanctorum* resumed in 1845 with the seventh volume for October. But the scholarly standards of the glory days of the seventeenth century Bollandists were not attained again until Charles de Smedt (1831–1911), who became president of the Société in 1883, led the Bollandists back to the paths of rigorous and critical scholarship.[11] Finally, Hippolyte Delehaye (1859–1941), who entered the Société des Bollandistes in 1891 and became its president in 1912, firmly established critical hagiography as a branch of historical scholarship in its own right.

An unexpected discovery in the late seventeenth century put the critical study of the persecutions of the early Christians by Roman emperors on a new and much firmer basis while completely validating the approach of the Bollandists. The very nature of the Bollandist enterprise raised serious historical issues from its inception because critical investigation of early *acta martyrum* and passions inevitably challenged the accepted belief that the early Christians had endured nearly three centuries of almost uninterrupted savage repression from Roman emperors before Constantine.

---

[11] On the importance of de Smedt, B. Joassart, AB 110 (1992), 353–372; Sanctity and Secularity during the Modernist Period. Six perspectives on hagiography around 1900, ed. L. J. Barmann & C. J. T. Talar (SH 79, 1999), 6–11.

In 1678 the sole surviving manuscript of Lactantius' *On the Deaths of the Persecutors* was discovered in the Benedictine Abbey of Moissac and purchased by Colbert, the powerful minister of Louis XIV, for his private library, whence it passed into the Bibliothèque Royale and thence into the Bibliothèque Nationale in Paris (BN, fonds latin 2627, fols. 1ʳ–16ʳ). Étienne Baluze, who had informed Colbert of the value of the manuscript, published Lactantius' work in the following year.[12] Partly because the manuscript names the author as bare L. Caecilius, not L. Caelius Firmianus Lactantius,[13] the identity of the extant work with Lactantius' *liber unus de persecutione* recorded by Jerome (*De viris illustribus* 80), was often denied until René Pichon put Lactantius' authorship beyond all reasonable doubt in 1901.[14]

Lactantius' version of both the political history of the early fourth century and the origins of the persecution by imperial decree which began in February 303 remain controversial. But almost immediately after *On the Deaths of the Persecutors* was published, Henry Dodwell (1641–1711) proved the value of Lactantius' testimony about imperial policy towards the Christians.[15] The eleventh of Dodwell's

---

[12] On the manuscript and early editions, see esp. S. Brandt & G. Laubmann, CSEL 27.2 (Vienna, 1897), vii–xxviii; J. Rougé, Lactance et son temps, ed. J. Fontaine & M. Perrin. Théologie Historique 49 (Paris, 1978), 13–22.

[13] For an ancient example of confusion between the names Caelius and Caecilius, see the index to the third book of Pliny's letters in New York, Pierpoint Morgan Library M. 462, reproduced in E. A. Lowe & E. K. Rand, A Sixth-Century Fragment of the Letters of Pliny the Younger (Washington, 1922), 24 line 10.

[14] R. Pichon, Lactance: Étude sur le movement philosophique et religieux sous le règne ce Constantin (Paris, 1901), cf. T. D. Barnes, JRS 63 (1973), 39–40.

[15] Dodwell was used and praised by Gibbon, History of the Decline

dissertations on Cyprian is conventionally known by its abbreviated title *De paucitate martyrum*, but its full title stamps it as the first essay in truly critical hagiography, even though the *Acta Sanctorum* are nowhere mentioned:

*De Martyrum commemoratione, eaque occasione, de Martyrum paucitate in primaevis Christianorum persecutionibus, deque fide Actorum atque Martyrologiorum*

On the commemoration of the martyrs and the occasion <of their deaths>, on the small number of martyrs in the early persecutions of the Christians, and of the reliability of the records <of their trials> and of martyrologies.[16]

Dodwell wrote less as a protestant polemicist than as a historian committed to impartial research. His dissertation proved the truth of four assertions by Lactantius which provide the foundation of modern understanding of the history of Christianity in the Roman Empire in the second and third centuries. First, no Roman emperor between Domitian and Decius issued new legislation that either prescribed or entailed active empire-wide persecution of Christians (*Mort. Pers.* 3.4–4.2): from c. 100 to 250, although Christianity was a crime, the legal status of Christians remained unchanged and it was provincial governors who decided how strictly or how leniently to enforce the law during their

───────────────

and Fall of the Roman Empire 1 (London, 1776), Chapter XVI nn. 43, 90 (2. 89 n. 43, 103. n. 91 Bury = 1.531, 545 Walmersley). In contrast, with that lack of judgment that too often disfigures his literary classic, Macaulay disparaged Dodwell as one who had 'acquired more learning than his slender faculties were able to bear' and he opined that 'some of his books seem to have been written in a madhouse' (T. B. Macaulay, History of England from the Accession of James II 3 [London, 1855], 461).

[16] H. Dodwell, Dissertationes Cyprianicae (Oxford, 1682), 56–90 = (1684), 217–351. The eleventh of Dodwell's dissertations is naturally not among the three that the Abbé Migne chose to reprint PL 5.9–80).

term of office.[17] Second, after Valerian was captured by the Persians in 260, no emperor required Christians to sacrifice to the traditional gods until 300, when holders of official positions at the courts of Diocletian and Galerius and the soldiers serving under them in the eastern armies were required to sacrifice or be dismissed (5–6, 10.1–5). Third, during the 'Great Persecution,' which began in February 303 and lasted until 313 in Asia Minor, the East and Egypt, no Christian was martyred in the West after the abdication of Diocletian and Maximian on 1 May 305: Constantius, who had refused to execute Christians in Britain and Gaul in 303, now ruled Spain as well, and Lactantius never hints that Severus, who ruled Italy and Africa from 1 May 305 to the autumn of 306 when he was defeated, taken prisoner, deposed and later executed, was ever a persecutor (15.7–16.2, 26.5–27.1). Fourth, Maxentius, who ruled Italy and Africa from 306 to 312, cannot have been the persecutor of hagiographical legend and religious art since Lactantius explicitly excludes him from the group of persecuting emperors of the early fourth century despite his defeat by Constantine at the Battle of the Milvian Bridge: after Diocletian died on 3 December 311, 'only one of the adversaries of God survived' and he was Maximinus (43.1: *unus iam supererat de adversariis Dei, cuius nunc exitum ruinamque subnectam*). The testimony of Lactantius does not stand alone (Eusebius of Caesarea confirms the truth of what he reports for the period after 260), but it was Dodwell who proved him correct on these issues – and his proof has never been effectively gainsaid.[18]

---

[17] Tertullian (1971), 13–163.

[18] Unfortunately, Dodwell's work gave rise to a long and ultimately sterile controversy over the total number of early Christian martyrs. On the one hand, it is absurd to imagine (with *Des Knaben Wunder-*

When ideas are allowed to circulate freely, historical criticism cannot be suppressed. By the time of van Papenbroek's condemnation at then end of the seventeenth century, no serious scholar any longer had the temerity to deny that historical criticism could legitimately be brought to bear on hagiographical accounts of the persecution of the Christians in the Roman Empire. The Maurist Thierry Ruinart (1657–

---

*horn* and Gustav Mahler) how in heaven 'Elftausend Jungfrauen / Zu tanzen sich trauen' after being martyred at Cologne with Saint Ursula (BHL 8426–8451). On the other hand, Edward Gibbon was being deliberately tendentious when he accepted Grotius' high estimate of the number of Protestants executed in the Low Countries under the emperor Charles V in order to argue that 'the number of Protestants who were executed in a single province and in a single reign far exceeded that of the primitive martyrs in the space of three centuries and of the Roman empire' (Decline and Fall 1 [London, 1776], Chapter XVI [2.139 Bury = 1.580 Womersley]). Some recent estimates carry the process of minimising the number of martyrs to absurd extremes. Thus R. Stark, The Rise of Christianity. A Sociologist reconsiders History (Princeton, 1996), 179, states that 'only a tiny number of Christians ever were martyred.' Stark estimates, apparently in all seriousness, that a total of fewer than one thousand Christians were ever executed by the Roman authorities over the course of nearly three hundred years. He justifies this impossibly low total by alleging that W. H. C. Frend, Martyrdom and Persecution in the Early Church (Oxford, 1965), 413, estimated the total as 'only "hundreds, not thousands".' There are errors here on three levels. First, Stark seriously misreports Frend, who was talking solely about the number of Christians who were martyred under Decius and Valerian, that is, in 250–251 and 257–260. Second, Frend misreports the ancient source whom he took to be Porphyry and whom he accused of 'gross exaggeration' (435 n. 163): that source spoke not of 'thousands,' but of 'countless' (μύριοι) Christians who were burned alive or tortured and put to death in other ways (Macarius of Magnesia 4.4, whence Porphyry, *Contra Christianos*, frag. 36 Harnack. Third, while Macarius certainly derived material from Porphyry, he cannot legitimately be assumed to preserve Porphyry's actual words: JTS, N. S. 24 (1973), 428–430.

1709) had already published a collection of hagiographical texts with the significant title *Acta primorum martyrum sincera et selecta* (Paris, 1689). Ruinart was the favourite pupil of Jean Mabillon (1632–1707), whose *De re diplomatica*, published in the winter of 1681/2, also marks an important watershed in scholarship with its clear statement of objective criteria for deciding whether official documents from Late Antiquity and the Middle Ages are authentic or not.[19] Although Ruinart included many texts that have subsequently been shown to be fictitious or unhistorical, his choice of title carried a significant and unmistakable implication: if the collection included select authentic acts of the martyrs, what of those texts that Ruinart had excluded? The very act of selection implicitly denied the historicity of excluded acts of the martyrs and implicitly suggested that they might be inauthentic. Whether Ruinart intended to convey this implication or not, his implied rejection of the historical value of countless hagiographical documents purporting to describe the martyrdoms of early Christians has rarely been challenged in any general way since his collection appeared in a second expanded edition in 1713. A reprint as late as 1859 ensured that Ruinart's *Acta primorum martyrum* continued to serve as a quasi-canonical collection until the late nineteenth century. In the twentieth century, however, despite the discovery of previously unknown authentic documents, successive selections of early *acta martyrum* have pruned the number of texts included,[20] and this pruning has confirmed what Lactantius states clearly – that widespread, coordinated and imperially ordained persecution of the early

---

[19] On the intellectual context of the work, see H. Leclercq, Mabillon 1 (Paris, 1953), 154–180; on its importance and relevance to hagiography, Knowles, Great Historical Enterprises (n. 4), 45–49.

[20] App. 2.

Christians, though a stock theme in fictitious hagiography, whatever the actual or alleged date of the martyr, was in fact restricted to four brief periods, viz., 250–251, 257–260, 303–313 and 321–324.

The meticulous hagiographical researches of Delehaye, the first edition of whose classic book on the legends of the saints, first published in 1905, only narrowly escaped the condemnation visited on Papebroch two centuries before,[21] and Paul Peeters (1870–1950), who succeeded him as the head of the Bollandists, established three methodological principles as fundamental to the scholarly investigation of early Christian saints and martyrs.[22] First, the evidence for the cult of a saint or martyr after his or her death must be evaluated separately from texts describing his or her death.

---

[21] For this episode, see R. Aubert, AB 100 (1982), 743–780; Joassart, Sanctity and Secularity (n. 11), 26–32. Two other eminent Roman Catholic scholars were not so fortunate: the Histoire ancienne de l'église, which Louis Duchesne (1843–1922) published in three volumes between 1906 and 1910, was placed on the Index in 1912, and Pierre Batiffol (1861–1929) not only saw his book L'eucharistie, la présence réelle et la transsubstantiation (Paris, 1905) placed on the Index secretly in 1907 and openly in 1911, but was forced to resign the position of Rector of the Institut Catholique de Toulouse, which he had held for sixteen years. On these two condemnations, see B. Waché, Monsigneur Louis Duchesne (1843–1922), historien de l'Église, Directeur de l'École française de Rome (Rome, 1992), 525–613; B. Joassart, AB 114 (1996), 77–108.

[22] For full bibliographies of Delehaye and Peeters, see P. Peeters, AB 60 (1942), xxxviii–lii, reproduced with unchanged pagination in an appendix to the fourth edition of Delehaye, Légendes (1955); P. Devos, AB 69 (1951), xlviii–lix, both reprinted in Peeters, L'œuvre[2] (n. 4), 23–102. It was in my opinion a disservice to Delehaye's memory to print, fifty years after his death, the three lectures that he delivered at the Collège de France in May 1935, but never revised for publication: L'ancienne hagiographie byzantine. Les sources, les premiers modèles, la formation des genres, ed. B. Joassart & X. Lequeux (SH 73, 1991).

For there are martyrs who must be accepted as historical because their cult is attested very early but of whose trial and execution no authentic record survives, two prime examples being the Roman martyrs Sebastian and Agnes.[23]

Second, hagiographical legend has a typology that can be reconstructed and analysed. In some cases, enough evidence of different dates and types survives to reveal exactly how a genuine historical record, with unique individuating details, and sometimes with eccentric touches, which reproduce the humble realities of everyday life, has been replaced by predictable stereotypes. The development of legend can be followed and observed most fully in the hagiography of Procopius, who was executed at Caesarea in Palestine on 7 June 303 (BHG 1576–1582c)[24] and Theodore of Euchaïta on the north coast of Asia Minor Sea (BHG 1750–1753m: *Theodorus stratelates m. sub Licino*; 1760–1773: *Theodorus tiro m. sub Maximiano*). The real Procopius was a lector, Syriac interpreter and exorcist in the church of Scythopolis, and a contemporary account of his trial and execution in 303 survives from the pen of Eusebius, who talked to eye-witnesses, even if he did not witness the trial himself (*Mart. Pal.* [L] 1.1–2). Over the course of time, the humble lector and exorcist became one of the great Byzantine military saints, noble by birth, a son-in-law of Diocletian, who

---

[23] Comm. Mart. Rom. (1940), 29, 30. The the *Acta Sebastiani* are a fictitious composition of the middle of the fifth century (App. 7), while the earliest extant account of Agnes' martyrdom is the vividly imagined poem by Prudentius, *Peristephanon* 14 (ed. M. M. van Assendelft, Atti [1987], 358–367), cf. P. Franchi de' Cavalieri, RQ, Supp. 10 (Rome, 1899), 1–95, reprinted in his *Scritti agiografici* 1 (ST 221, 1962), 293–381.

[24] H. Delehaye, Les légendes grecques des saints militaires (Paris, 1909), 75–87, 214–233; Légendes (1927), 119–139.

was converted like Saint Paul after seeing a cross in the sky like Constantine. The young recruit Theodore underwent a similar metamorphosis: the historical Theodore refused to be inducted as a recruit into the army of Licinius, yet Byzantine hagiography transformed him into a great general who defeated the Persians.[25]

Third, authentic documents reveal their worth when subjected to literary and historical analysis. The most conspicuous proof of this is perhaps furnished by the *Passion of Perpetua*, which claims to incorporate documents which the martyrs Perpetua and Saturus penned in prison. On the one hand, investigation of the style and prose-rhythm of these documents establishes that they were indeed written by two different persons, neither of whom is identical with the author of the *Passion* who wrote the introduction and conclusion and incorporated the two documents in his narrative. On the other hand, the fact that the *Passion* appears to state the birthday of Geta, the younger son of the emperor Septimius Severus, correctly as 7 March, puts its composition very close in time to the events that it describes, since all traces of Geta's memory were assiduously effaced after he was murdered on 26 December 211.[26]

Critical hagiography no longer needs any justification, since it has so manifestly proved its value. On the contrary, there is a danger of taking it for granted and of assuming, perhaps because no volume of the main series of the *Acta Sanctorum* has appeared since 1925, when the fourth volume for November covering days 8–10 was published, that hagiography in the classic manner as practised by Delehaye

---

[25] Delehaye, Saints militaires (n. 24), 10–43, 127–201; AASS, Nov. IV (1925), 11–89.

[26] Chapter II.

has achieved all that it is potentially capable of achieving.[27] That might be the case if the date, value and reliability of all hagiographical texts had been established beyond doubt. However, the status and value of many hagiographical texts remains in dispute, and further progress can be made – if the results achieved by Delehaye and other exponents of critical hagiography are combined with other techniques used in historical investigations, such as chronology, prosopography and the analysis of institutions.[28] It will be appropriate, therefore, to conclude the present investigation of early Christian hagiography in its relation to the history of the Roman Empire between the second and the sixth centuries with a select series of examples which illustrate the mutual interdependence of critical hagiography and Roman imperial prosopography.

## Two fictitious proconsuls of Asia

In 1877, when Hermann Usener published the Greek text of the *Acta Timothei* (BHG 1847), of which a Latin

---

[27] This seems to have been the view of E. Patlagean, Annales 29 (1968), 106, who advocated recourse to 'l'analyse structurale, parce que la méthode positiviste couramment utilisée nous semblait insuffisante et gaspilleuse.' More than forty years on, it is not clear to me that models derived from Claude Lévy-Strauss have provided the desired enlightenment.

[28] F. Halkin, AB 71 (1953), 74, 75–77, 81, comments on the fact that Delehaye never referred to H. Grégoire, Receuil d'inscriptions grecques chrétiennes d'Asie Mineure 1 (Brussels, 1922), so that his discussion of the cult of Theodore in AASS, Nov. IV.11–89, failed to take account of the rereading and redating of relevant inscriptions, while his discussion of Tryphon in AASS, Nov. IV.318–383 omitted the attestation of the cult of Tryphon in the Troad (IGC 2).

translation had appeared in the second volume of the *Acta Sanctorum* in 1643 (AASS, Jan. III.150–151 = II (1643), 566: BHL 8294), he accepted as genuine both of the two proconsuls of Asia whom they name.[29] The first is Maximus, alleged to have been proconsul under Nero, when Paul made Timothy the first bishop of Ephesus. Usener identified the proconsul with Q. Allius Maximus, consul suffect in 49 (ILS 5540), who is not otherwise attested as proconsul of Asia; more recently, both Ursula Vogel-Weidemann in 1982 and Bengt Thomasson in 1984 have registered the consul of 49 as proconsul of Asia for the year 57–58 on the strength of the *Acta Timothei* alone.[30] Moreover, the latter appeals to Usener whom he claims that no-one has contradicted.[31] That assertion is false. Long before Ronald Syme banished the proconsul 'Maximus' altogether from the realm of history in 1983,[32] Theodor Zahn had disproved Usener's high estimate of the historical value of the *Acta Timothei* within a year of its publication,[33] and when Josef Keil attempted to reinstate the *acta* as a historical source in 1935,[34] Delehaye restated and amplified

---

[29] H. Usener, Acta s. Timothei (prog. Bonn, 1877), 7–13. A decade later Usener defended both names as taken from 'die offizielle Prokonsularliste der Provinz Asia' (Jahrbücher für protestantische Theologie 14 [1887], 238–240 = Kleine Schriften 3 [Stuttgart, 1912–1913], 83–85).

[30] U. Vogel-Weidemann, Die Statthalter von Africa und Asia in den Jahren 14–68 n. Chr. Eine Untersuchung zum Verhältnis Princeps und Senat (Bonn, 1982), 421–422 n. 57; B. E. Thomasson, Laterculi Praesidum 1 (Gothenburg, 1984), 213.

[31] Thomasson, Laterculi 1 (n. 30), 213: '*cui nemo quod sciam postea contradixit.*'

[32] R. Syme, Roman Papers 4 (Oxford, 1988), 361, reprinted from ZPE 53 (1983), 361.

[33] T. Zahn, Gött. Gel. Anz. 1878. 97–114.

[34] J. Keil, JÖAI 29 (1935), 82–92.

Zahn's proof that their author is unlikely to have possessed any genuine information about proconsuls of Asia during the lifetime of the evangelist John: since the text refers to Lystra as the capital of the province of Lycaonia, and Lycaonia did not become a separate province before c. 370 (it is first attested in Basil, *Ep.* 138),[35] the *Acta Timothei* can hardly have been composed before the fifth century.[36] The sole and transparent aim of this fictitious confection is to present Timothy as the first bishop of Ephesus. Delehaye acutely observed that a well-established cult of Timothy cannot have existed when the emperor Constantius transferred his presumed relics to Constantinople (*Descriptio consulum* 356), and that it was probably this removal that prompted the Christians of Ephesus to institute a proper celebration of his cult in their city.[37]

The *Acta Timothei* name Peregrinus as the proconsul of Asia in office when Timothy was executed on 22 January very shortly after the accession of Nerva, i. e., on 22 January 97. Peregrinus has had fewer modern fanciers than Maximus, even though his proconsulate is attested by exactly the same evidence. In the first edition of the *Prosopographia Imperii Romani* the alert and critical Hermann Dessau condemned Peregrinus and denied him a separate entry.[38] In the second edition, however, Peregrinus has acquired an entry of his own, though he is implicitly condemned as unhistorical

---

[35] K. Belke, with M. Restle, Galatien und Lykien. Tabula Imperii Byzantini 4 (Wien 1984), 55.

[36] H. Delehaye, Anatolian Studies presented to W. H. Buckler (Manchester, 1939), 77–84 = Mélanges (1966), 408–415.

[37] Delehaye, Mélanges (1966), 414–415, cf. Culte (1933), 55, 145–146.

[38] H. Dessau, PIR 3 (Berlin, 1898), 22–23.

by the observation that his name may derive from that of a third century senator.[39]

The unhistorical 'Peregrinus' of the *Acta Timothei* is relevant to an undoubtedly historical proconsul of Asia. The emperor Nerva was honoured by the city of Ephesus when Sex. Carminius Vetus was proconsul of Asia (AE 1899.71 = Inschriften von Ephesos 264). Since Nerva lacks the title Germanicus and the date therefore lies between October 96 and late 97, Vetus held office for one of the two proconsular years 96–97 and 97–98. Vetus' proconsulate is sometimes put in 97–98 so that the preceding proconsular year can be occupied by 'Peregrinus,' even by scholars who doubt his authenticity.[40] But if 'Peregrinus' is an invented proconsul of Asia, then he should be ignored completely, as he is in the entry for the proconsul Carminius Vetus in the second edition of the *Prosopographia Imperii Romani*,[41] and in both editions of Werner Eck's provincial fasti for the period 70–138, which totally discount the *Acta Timothei* and place Carminius Vetus in the proconsular year 96–97.[42]

---

[39] K. Wachtel, PIR² P 236 (published in 1998), citing W. Eck, Bonner Jahrbücher 83 (1983), 855. Usener, Kleine Schriften 3 (n. 29), 84, had already noted that the polyonymous M. Nonius Mucianus, who was suffect consul in 138 (PIR² N 146), has P. Delphius Peregrinus as one element in his full nomenclature (CIL 5.3343 [Brixia]; CIL 8.270 = 11451 = 23246 = Inscr. lat. de la Tunisie 395 [Saltus Beguensis]).

[40] So Thomasson, Laterculi 1 (n. 30), 219–220, admittedly with the qualification '*nisi spurius est.*'

[41] E. Groag, PIR² C 436 (published in 1936).

[42] W. Eck, Senatoren von Vespasian bis Hadrian (Munich, 1970), 84/85, 148; Chiron 12 (1982), 326, 327 n. 180.

## Proconsuls of Africa in 202–204

The *Passion of Perpetua* states that Perpetua and others were tried by the procurator Hilarianus who had taken over the juridical duties of a proconsul who had died during his year of office (6.2: *Hilarianus procurator, qui tunc loco proconsulis Minuci Timiniani defuncti ius gladii acceperat*). Hilarianus has long also been known from a passage of Tertullian written in the autumn of 212 which refers to him as if he were an ordinary provincial governor (*Scap.* 3.1: *sicut sub Hilariano praeside, cum de areis supulturarum nostrarum acclamassent: areae non sint!*). A pair of inscriptions published in 1968 discloses the additional and extremely interesting fact that Hilarianus was a conservative in matters of religion who upheld traditional cults in an age of increasing toleration of new religions.[43] At Asturica in Spain, the procurator P. Ael(ius) Hilarianus together with his children made two dedications for the safety of an emperor whose name has been erased (probably Commodus): one was addressed in conventional terms to the Capitoline triad of Jupiter Optimus Maximus, Juno Regina and Minverva Victrix (AE 1968.228), but the other has an unusual and significant formula, which is in fact unique – 'to the gods and goddesses to whom it is right and proper to address prayers in the pantheon' (AE 1968.227: *dis deabusque quos ius fasque est precari in pantheo*). Hilarianus (so it seems) came from Aphrodisias in Caria, and the phrase *in pantheo* is to be construed adverbially and as referring to a building: it follows that he objected to the strong contemporary trend towards including non-traditional gods in an overarching henothe-

---

[43] Adduced in Tertullian (1971), 163: for a full discussion, see J. Rives, JECS 4 (1996), 1–25.

istic system and hence was predisposed to treat Christians as religious innovators who were *eo ipso* criminals.[44]

The Latin version of the passion names the deceased proconsul as Minucius Timinianus, while the Greek has Minucius Oppianus: both are corruptions of an original Minicius Opimianus.[45] This man belonged to a known senatorial family: Salvius Rufinus Minicius Opimianus, procurator of Asia under Trajan was presumably his great-grandfather; T. Salvius Rufinus Minicius Opimianus, who had been consul suffect in 123 and proconsul of Africa in 138/139, his grandfather; and the Opimianus attested as consul suffect in 155 his father.[46] The precise year in which the Minicius Opimianus of the *Passion of Perpetua* was proconsul of Africa, could be either 202–203 or 203–204: although the day on which Perpetua suffered martyrdom is certified beyond doubt as 7 March by very early and unimpeachable evidence, the year of her martyrdom is not. Although it has been traditional to accept 203 from the *Fasti Vindobonenses* (Chr. Min. 1.287), Prosper Tiro, who was

---

[44] Rives, JECS 4 (1996), 8–18.

[45] So, apparently independently of each other, Barnes, Tertullian (1971), 267; A. R. Birley, Septimius Severus the African Emperor (London, 1971), 221 n. 1. The proconsul was registered as Minucius Timinianus Oppianus by M. Fluss, RE 15 (1932), 1844–1845, Minu / icius 28.

[46] On the proconsul, who must have been consul suffect shortly before 190, and his family, see G. Alföldy, Konsulat und Senatorenstand unter den Antoninen. Prosopographische Untersuchungen zur senatorischen Führungsschicht (Bonn, 1977), 167, 207, 308; W. Eck, RE, Supp. 14 (1974), 283–284; Historia 24 (1975), 324–327; PIR² M 621–623a.; P. M. M. Leunissen, Konsuln und Konsulare in der Zeit von Commodus bis Severus Alexander (180–235 n. Chr.). Prosopographische Untersuchungen zur senatorischen Elite im römischen Kaiserreich (Amsterdam, 1989), 141, 356, 371.

writing earlier and perhaps using the same source, has 204 (Chr. Min. 1.434).

Some modern works of reference register a Rufinus as proconsul of Africa for the proconsular year 203–204: they adduce the *Martyrologium Adonis*, according to which the virgin Gudden was tortured, then beheaded in Carthage by the proconsul Rufinus on 18 July 203 (PL 123.304), and identify the proconsul with the Rufinus who was consul suffect in 189 or 190 together with the future emperor Septimius Severus (*HA, Sev.* 4.4).[47] But the martyrology compiled by Ado, later bishop of Vienne, in 858 constitutes neither primary nor probative evidence for the proconsul Rufinus. Ado has copied his entry for Gudden from an earlier martyrology compiled at Lyon which survives in a manuscript of the first half of the ninth century in Paris (BN lat. 3879),[48] but he has transferred it to 18 July from its correct date of 27 June, which is guaranteed by a sermon of Saint Augustine (*Sermo* 294 [PL 1335–1348]).[49] Moreover, the lost *Passio Guddenis* on which the notice in the martyrologies appears to depend bears the stigmata of an 'epic passion.'[50] On the other hand, the Rufinus of these late martyrologies, if genuine, can without difficulty be identified with the attested Minicius Opimianus, whose full name was T. Salvius Rufinus Minicius Opimianus.[51] A recent suggestion has the

---

[47] A. C. Pallu de Lessert, Fastes des provinces africaines sous la domination romaine 1 (Paris, 1896), 240–241; E. Groag, *PIR*² A 966; B. E. Thomasson, Die Statthalter der römischen Provinzen Nordafrikas von Augustus bis Diocletianus 2 (Lund, 1960), 105–106; RE, Supp. 9 (1962), 1367; Laterculi 1 (n. 30), 385.

[48] On which, see Quentin, Martyrologes (1908), 131–221.

[49] As observed by P. Petitmengin, REAug 19 (1973), 184.

[50] Quentin, Martyrologes (1908), 174, 456, 482.

[51] Tertullian (1971), 263 n. 7, 267; PIR² M 622, cf. 623a.

corollary that his proconsular year was 203–204 rather than 202–203.[52] The vision of Perpetua in which she dreams of fighting against a swarthy Egyptian may reflect the first celebration of the Pythian Games established by Septimius Severus who spent part of the winter of either 202–203 or 203–204 in his native city of Lepcis (Philostratus, *Vit. soph.* 2.20, p. 601). Severus presumably passed through Carthage as he travelled from Rome to Lepcis, and it is reasonable to assume that he instituted the Pythian Games, which Tertullian noted as a recent imperial gift to Carthage (*Scorpiace* 6.2–3), during one of his visits to the city.[53]

## The date of the martyrdom of Alban

The earliest explicit record of the cult of St. Alban occurs in the *Life of Germanus* by Constantius of Lyons, who records that after the bishop of Auxerre and his companion Lupus of Troyes had routed the Pelagians in Britain, they went to give thanks to God at the shrine of the martyr Alban, whose intercession helped to calm the sea for their return to Gaul (*Vita Germani* 16, 18). Whatever doubts may cloud the reliability of Constantius' *Life* as a historical source, Germanus' devotion to Alban is confirmed by the fact that Auxerre was the centre from which the saint's cult spread in early medieval Gaul and Germany.[54]

---

[52] J den Boeft & J. Bremmer, Vig. Chr. 36 (1982), 390–391.

[53] Despite the denial by L. Robert, Opera Minora Selecta 5 (Amsterdam, 1989), 794–796, contradicting Barnes, JTS, N. S. 20 (1969), 125–126; Tertullian (1971), 34–35, 172.

[54] Delehaye, Culte (1933), 362; Mélanges (1966), 366–369; I. Wood, Gildas: New Approaches, ed. M. Lapidge & D. Dumville (Woodbridge & Dover, NH, 1984), 12–13.

Where and when was Alban martyred? Although the earliest explicit evidence appears to be the tract *De excidio Britanniae*, which Gildas probably wrote in the late fifth century (10), the tradition that places the martyrdom and the cult of Alban at Verulamium is both unanimous and secure.[55] The date of his martyrdom is another matter. Gildas conjectured that Alban, Aaron and Julius, who were martyred at Legio (Caerleon), and 'others of both sexes in different places' died during the Diocletianic persecution. But if the emperor Constantius did not execute any Christians in Britain, as Lactantius clearly states (*Mort. Pers.* 15.7–16.1), then Gildas' conjecture must be mistaken.

Liturgical and hagiographical evidence consistently attest the day of Alban's death as 22 June,[56] but no ancient source states the year. In 1968 John Morris advanced the hypothesis that Alban was tried and executed in 209 by the Caesar Geta, the younger son of Septimius Severus, who had been left behind to govern in Britain while his father and elder brother campaigned north of Hadrian's Wall.[57] This adventurous theory has enjoyed unusual success. Both William Frend and Sheppard Frere accepted it as probable even before it was published, while the latter incorporated it in all three editions of his standard history of Roman Britain;[58]

---

[55] W. Levison, Antiquity 15 (1941), 337–359. On the date of Gildas, see D. Dumville, Gildas (n. 54), 61–84.

[56] Comm. Mart. Rom. (1940), 250.

[57] J. Morris, Hertfordshire Archaeology 1 (1968), 1–8: he argues that Alban was a Roman citizen and one 'of the notables' of the province.

[58] W. H. C. Frend, Christianity in Britain, 300–700, ed. M. W Barley & R. P. C. Hanson (Leicester, 1968), 38; S. S. Frere, Britannia: A History of Roman Britain (London, 1967), 332 = Britannia² (London, 1974), 371 = Britannia³ (London, 1987), 321. In the first edition, Frere claims that Geta was 'governor of Britannia Superior' (Britannia

the relevant volume of the Oxford History of England accepted it on Frere's authority;[59] and Anthony Birley found a place for it in his biography of Septimius Severus.[60] Yet the arguments used by Morris for dating this 'notable and isolated happening' to 209 seriously transgress accepted canons of hagiographical method, and what little is known about Christianity in Roman Britain before Constantine suggests that Alban, like Aaron and Julius, was executed under either Decius or Valerian.[61]

The evidence adduced by Morris is a passage in what appears to be the earliest version of the *Passio Albani* (BHL 210d), which Wilhelm Meyer published from a Turin manuscript in 1904, together with another version of the same passion from a Paris manuscript (BHL 211).[62] In the Turin version, the most impious emperor Severus launches a violent persecution in Gaul, then crosses to Britain, where he orders all Christians to be executed. Alban, who had sheltered a fleeing cleric, is brought before Severus, now described as *impiissimus Caesar*, that is, 'the most impious emperor.' He first questions, browbeats and attempts to

[1967], 178), but it now seems probable that the province of Britannia was not divided until c. 213: A. R. Birley, The Roman Government of Britain (Oxford, 2005), 333–336.

[59]  P. Salway, Roman Britain (Oxford, 1981), 720.

[60]  A. R. Birley, Septimius Severus: The African Emperor (1971), 263; The African Emperor: Septimius Severus (London, 1988), 189, cf. The Later Roman Empire Today, ed. M. M. Roxan (London, 1994), 63 n. 118.

[61]  C. Thomas, Christianity in Roman Britain to AD 500 (London, 1981), 46, 48–50; W. H. C. Frend, The Archaeology of Early Christianity. A History (London, 1996), 252.

[62]  W. Meyer, Die Legende des h. Albanus des Protomartyr Angliae in Texten vor Beda. Abh. Göttingen, Phil.-hist. Kl., N. F. 8 .1 (Berlin, 1904), esp. 35–46 (diplomatic texts), 46–62 (comparison of edited texts of these two versions and Bede, *HE* 1.7, printed in parallel).

bribe Alban in a way familiar from countless epic passions,[63] then has him tortured, and finally condemns him to death. Between the tribunal and the place of execution there was a river in flood, which miraculously dried up after the emperor departed. But, when the execution party ascended a hill and Alban requested water before being beheaded, a spring gushed forth from the ground, after which Alban and the executioner who had refused to kill him were both executed. Thereupon, the most impious Caesar ordered persecution to cease *iniussu etiam principum* (20).

What is the date and historical value of the *Passio Albani*? The Turin version was composed in Gaul, and, since it plagiarises other Gallic passions, Meyer dated it to the sixth century.[64] But Victricius of Rouen, who delivered his speech or sermon *In Praise of the Saints* (*De laude sanctorum*) shortly before 400, alludes to a martyr about to be executed who ordered rivers to subside and who can only be Alban (12.104–105: *ille inter manus carnificum, ne qua mora fieret properanti, iussit redire fluminibus*).[65] It follows that the story of Alban's execution on 'a green hill far away / without a city wall' was already being told before the end of the fourth century. Does the surviving *Passio Albani* transmit authentic information about the execution of Alban? Frere, echoing Morris, argues that its 'detailed knowledge of the topography of Verulamium gives

---

[63] E. g., *Passio Albani* (Turin version) 9: *sacrifica diis nostris et eris magnus in palatio nostro. aurum et argentum a me accipe et possessiones. et senatorum nobilium filiam tibi trado in matrimonium.*

[64] Meyer, Legende des h. Albanus (n. 62), 21–24.

[65] The allusion was identified by I. Mulders and R. Demeulenaere, CCSL 64 (1985), 92, cf. G. R. Clark, JECS 7 (1999), 399. It is not noted in the translation by P. Buc, Medieval Hagiography: An Anthology (New York & London, 2000), 31–51.

it undoubted authority.'[66] But, even if the premiss of the
inference were granted, the conclusion would not follow.
For it would prove only that the author of the passion
knew, or copied a source which knew, the topography of
Verulamium in the late fourth century: it would not prove
that he knew anything about real events in the city in the
early third century any more than the accurate topography
of Ephesus shown in the *Acta Timothei* proves that their
author knew the names of proconsuls of Asia under Nero
and Nerva.[67] In fact, however, a close reading of the *Passio
Albani* fails to discover any such 'detailed knowledge' of the
topography of Verulamium.

Morris' historical reconstruction depends very heavily on
the three words *iniussu etiam principum*, whose authenticity
he holds to be guaranteed by their apparent illogicality.[68]
Meyer had argued that the Turin version was used by the
author of the Paris version, who throughout replaces the
emperor by an unnamed *iudex*, which makes sense of these
words.[69] Delehaye challenged the presumed derivation as
failing adequately to explain the divergences between the
two versions.[70] But, if the two extant texts derive independently from a lost earlier original (as Delehaye suggested),
then it is probable that the author of the Turin version
introduced the emperor to replace a magistrate in his
source.[71] Moreover, the theory advanced by Morris requires
the improbable postulate that this decisive phrase, which

---

[66] Frere, Britannia[3] (n. 58), 321.

[67] Above, at nn. 32–45.

[68] Morris, Hertfordshire Archaeology 1 (n. 57), 3.

[69] Meyer, Legende des h. Albanus (n. 62), 24–34.

[70] Delehaye, Passions (1966), 285–288.

[71] On the central role of emperors in fictitious hagiography, see
Delehaye, Légendes (1927), 21.

(so he claims) 'fits one known year in Roman history, and one only,' somehow survived through an authentic chain of transmission from Verulamium in 209 to Merovingian Gaul three centuries later when it was used by an author who otherwise shows no awareness that there was more than one Roman emperor at the time about which he wrote.

## Proconsuls of Asia under Decius

Two proconsuls of Asia are named in hagiographical texts as executing Christians during the reign of the emperor Decius (summer 249 to c. June 251). The *Passion of Pionius* names Julius Proculus Quintilianus as proconsul in February 250 (23).[72] Since an inscription at Eleusis attests Quintillianus as both a Eumolpid and proconsul of Asia (IG 2/3². 4218, 4219), it has never been seriously doubted that he was indeed proconsul of Asia in 249/250. A proconsul Optimus, whom some manuals of reference register as the immediate successor of Quintillianus,[73] is attested only by the *Acta Maximi* (Gebhardt X = K-K-R XII: BHL 5829) and the *Acta Petri, Andreae, Pauli et Dionysiae* (AASS, Mai. III.450–451; Ruinart, *Acta Martyrum* [1689], 147–149 =

---

[72] The *Passion of Pionius* is the direct or ultimate source of the notice in the Paschal Chronicle 504 Bonn.

[73] W. H. Waddington, Fastes des provinces asiatiques de l'empire romain depouis leur origine jusqu'au règne de Dioclétien 1 (Paris, 1872), no. 176; W. Hoffmann, RE 18.1 (1942), 804–805; Thomasson, Laterculi 1 (n. 30), 236; PIR² O 129 (with hesitation and much bibliography). H. Dessau, PIR¹ O 84, held Optimus to be fictitious, and suggested that his original name as an alleged proconsul of Asia was Aristus.

[1713], 158–160: BHL 6716). Even in combination, these two documents, which are both of very dubious value, do not furnish adequate proof that Optimus was proconsul of Asia in 250–251.[74] Moreover, the provenance of the name can perhaps be divined. A Fl(avius) Optimus is attested as a non-senatorial governor of Phrygia by an undated inscription in which the people of Meirus in Phrygia salute him as 'benefactor and saviour of the province.'[75] When J. G. C. Anderson published the inscription in 1897, he opined that it 'probably dates after the reorganisation of Diocletian.'[76] In the following year, however, in a postscript, Anderson bowed to the authority of Sir William Ramsay, who in a private letter assigned Optimus to the later fourth or even fifth century.[77] Subsequent epigraphical discoveries, some of them very recent, suggest that a date late in the reign of Diocletian is correct, either before or just after the combined province of Caria-Phrygia, which had been created shortly before 249, was divided into its two component parts.[78] If Optimus was a governor who executed Christians in Phrygia between 303 and 313, then he could be a historical model whose name a later hagiographer appropriated for a persecutor of his own invention.

---

[74] V. Chapot, *La province romaine proconsulaire d'Asie* (Paris, 1904), 314 n. 1, cf. P. Franchi de' Cavalieri, *Note agiografiche* (ST 8, 1902), 83–93.

[75] Best edited by C. H. E. Haspels, *The Highlands of Phrygia* (Princeton, 1971), 331 no. 87.

[76] J. G. C. Anderson, *JHS* 17 (1897), 424.

[77] Quoted by Anderson, *JHS* 18 (1898), 342. Ramsey's date is accepted by Goldfinger, *RE* 6 (1909), 2607 no. 140; *PLRE* 1.650, Optimus 2.

[78] C. Roueché, *Splendidissima Civitas*, ed. A. Chastagnol, S. Demougin & C. Lepelley (Paris, 1996), 239.

## Maximian and the prefect Hermogenianus

An inscription from Brixia, published in 1986, attests Aurelius Hermogenianus as praetorian prefect with Julius Asclepiodotus while Constantius was Caesar, i.e., between 293 and 305 (AE 1987.456). At first sight, it is tempting to infer that 'the new inscription lends credibility to the *Passio Sabini* (BHL 7451–7454), which presents Hermogenianus as a *praefectus* with Maximian when he was in Rome in 304.'[79] On more mature reflection, matters do not appear to be quite so simple. The *Passio Sabini*, which was written between c. 450 and c. 700, is a thoroughly fictitious composition.[80] It produces a 'Venustianus' unknown to history who has the unattested and impossible post of *Augustalis Tusciae*.[81] Moreover, the author assumed that Maximian promulgated Diocletian's edict ordaining universal sacrifice in the West: the Roman populace in the Circus Maximus chants *Christiani non sint*; the Senate is then consulted and Maximian orders that Christians either be compelled to sacrifice to the gods or be executed and their property confiscated.

Hermogenianus is named by the *Passio Sabini* as the *praefectus urbi* who convened and consulted the Roman Senate about the Christians. Admittedly, Baronius published a

---

[79] JRA 9 (1996), 547.

[80] On the date and nature of the passion, F. Lanzoni, RQ 17 (1903), 1–26, cf. H. Delehaye, Légendes (1927), 83–84.

[81] Not in PLRE 1 (1971), whose fasti (1094) include two equally fictitious governors of Italian provinces as holding office under Diocletian: 'Megetius,' allegedly Augustalis in Umbria, from the *Acta Firminae* (A. Dufourcq, Étude sur les Gesta Martyrum romains 3 [1907],129–132: BHL 3001b) and 'Pancratius,' proconsul of Tusciae according to the *Acta Cassiani* (AASS, Aug. III.27–30; K-K-R XXI: BHL 1637).

version of the passion which styles Hermogenianus praetorian prefect,[82] and some students of Roman jurisprudence
have defended the letter of Maximian to 'Venustianus'
beginning '*ex suggestione patris nostri Hermogeniani praefecti praetorio*,' which the *Passio Sabini* purports to quote,
and hence identified the prefect as the Diocletianic jurist
Hermogenianus.[83] But Baronius cannot be relied upon to
report manuscripts accurately,[84] and the manuscript basis
of his text of the *Passio Sabini* is unknown. Comparison of
Baronius' text with published versions of the passion that
reproduce identifiable manuscripts and which run closely
parallel to one another,[85] indicates that Baronius condensed,
paraphrased and partly rewrote a text very similar to these.
Baronius turns plain Maximian into Maximianus Herculius
and plain Hermogenianus into Eugenius Hermogenianus
and makes the latter preside in the Senate as praetorian
prefect – which was the function of the *praefectus urbi* in
late imperial Rome.[86] Moreover, as praetorian prefect c.
300 Hermogenianus is attested as *vir eminentissimus*, that
is, a non-senator.[87]

---

[82] Annales ecclesiastici 2 (Rome, 1594), 711 (A. D. 301, nn. 18, 19).

[83] D. Liebs, Hermogenians Iuris Epitomae. Abh. Göttingen, Phil.-
hist. Kl.³ 57 (1964), 34–36; Die Jurisprudenz im spätantiken Italien
(260–640 n. Chr.) (Berlin, 1987), 39–51; A. Honoré, Emperors and
Lawyers² (Oxford, 1994), 178. The letter is, however, rejected as 'almost
certainly spurious' by S. Corcoran, The Empire of the Tetrarchs. Imperial Pronoucements and Government AD 284–324 (Oxford, 1996),
136.

[84] Chapter III n. 61.

[85] Liebs, Hermogenians Iuris Epitomae (n. 83), 32–33, conveniently prints Baronius' version in parallel with those published by E. de
Azevedo (Rome, 1754) and by Baluzius in 1679.

[86] A. Chastagnol, La préfecture urbaine à Rome sous le Bas-Empire
(Paris, 1962), 68–69.

[87] A. Chastagnol, ZPE 79 (1989), 165–168.

It is imprudent, therefore, to rely upon the *Passio Sabini* as proving either that Aurelius Hermogenianus was still praetorian prefect in 304 or that he was with Maximian in Rome in April 304. Maximian may have watched games in the Circus Maximus on 21 April 304, the birthday of Rome (the text has 16 April),[88] while Hermogenianus may still have been praetorian prefect in April 304, but it should not be assumed that the author of the *Passio Sabini* possessed authentic information about Hermogenianus or the movements of Maximian.[89] He could have hit upon the truth by accident, as did the hagiographers who brought the emperor Hadrian to the north Italian city of Brixia, which he must have visited during his tour of North Italy in 127 (AASS, Feb. V.810–821, cf. BHL 2836–2840; AASS, Apr. II.520–523, cf. BHL 1528–1531; Mai. V.277–279, cf. BHL 117).[90] For what it is worth, a fictitious *Passion of Victor* locates Maximian in Milan on 8 May 304 (AASS, Mai. II.285–287: BHL 8580), which could also be true without being authentic.[91]

## Real names and invented characters

Writers of fiction often model the names of characters of their own invention on real people in the world or in the social circles in which they themselves live: hence, as a

---

[88] New Empire (1982), 60.

[89] New Empire (1982), 136–137.

[90] Hadrian left Rome on 3 March 127 for a tour of Northern Italy, returning in July or August: L. Vidman, Fasti Ostienses[2] (Prague, 1982), 49: *V non(as) Mart(ias) Augustus profe[ec]tus ad Italiam circum[padanam]*.

[91] New Empire (1982), 59–60.

master of prosopography observed, 'a name often supplies a clue to source or date.'[92] One of the best examples of the phenomenon occurs in an English novel which reproduces many stereotypical features of hagiographical fiction: Evelyn Waugh's *Helena* frequently mistakes legend for historical fact, it transforms a humbly born saint into a princess (the daughter of Old King Cole of Colchester), and its language frequently lapses into vulgarity.[93] When Waugh went up to Oxford in 1922, his tutor at Hertford College was C. R. M. F. Cruttwell: the two men took an almost instant dislike to each other and, after Waugh left Oxford, he exacted revenge by including in his early novels a series of variously disreputable characters with the rare surname of Cruttwell.[94]

---

[92] R. Syme, Emperors and Biography. Studies in the Historia Augusta (Oxford, 1971), 265. A footnote supplies a modern example: 'in the Greenmantle of John Buchan (1916), Hilda von Einem derives patently from the man who became Prussian Minister for War in 1902.'

[93] For two very different discussions of the novel, see D. L. Patey, The Life of Evelyn Waugh. A Critical Biography (Oxford, 1998), 289–297; H. W. Drijvers, Classics Ireland 7 (2000), 25–50. Patey, as a modern literary critic, is blissfully unaware that, although wood believed to be the Holy Cross was indeed found c. 325, Helena was only brought into the story some sixty years later by deliberate invention. Waugh, whose talent was essentially comic and satirical, bizarrely professed to regard this ill-written, pious, sentimental and sanctimonious romance as his best work. It contains only one truly memorable passage, though one very pertinent to hagiography: Waugh makes Lactantius insult Gibbon as 'a false historian, with the mind of Cicero or Tacitus and the soul of an animal' who set out 'to write down the martyrs and excuse the persecutors' (Chapter 6).

[94] Long after Cruttwell's death, Waugh published a cruel description of his tutor: A Little Learning. An Autobiography: The Early Years (London, 1964), 173–175. On the relation betwen the real Cruttwell and fictitious Cruttwells, see esp. S. Hastings, Evelyn Waugh. A Biography (London, 1994), 85–87, 101, 173, 209, 373, 380; J. H. Wilson,

The principle that fiction tends to reflect an author's contemporary world, was strikingly applied to an ancient text by Hermann Dessau in 1889, who first showed that the claims of the *Historia Augusta* to have been composed at various dates under Diocletian (before 305), Constantius (in 305–306) and Constantine as sole ruler (after 324) are self-contradictory and hence false; then proved that the work copies a long passage from a text written in 360; and finally argued that many of the inventions in the *Historia Augusta*, including proper names, are inspired by historical characters and real events of the closing decades of the fourth century.[95] Starting seventy five years later, a long series of articles and books by Ronald Syme expanded and deepened the arguments for a date in the late fourth century with a copious abundance of examples, but at the logical level, as he candidly conceded, Syme was reiterating a case that Dessau had proved long before.[96]

An important hagiographical example of the phenomenon can be found in the legends about George, who eventually became Saint George the dragon-slayer, the patron saint of England. These have been the object of a recent study which revives the hypothesis that Saint George was not a victim of the 'Great Persecution,' as is normally

---

Evelyn Waugh. A Literary Biography, 1903–1924 (Cranbury, N.J., 1996), 109–115. Waugh (it may be noted) was a social conformist who had affairs with other male undergraduates when it was fashionable in the Oxford of the 1920s, but carefully edited his homosexual past out of his autobiography.

[95] H. Dessau, Hermes 24 (1889), 337–392.

[96] See the opening salvoes of Syme's first paper on the Historia Augusta, delivered in 1964, published in 1966 and republished in 1971: 'Seventy-five years have passed. Much erudition was thrown into the battle, some of it in vain; … The decisive blow for freedom was struck in 1889' (Emperors and Biography [1971], 1).

believed, but was in reality the George who replaced Athanasius as bishop of Alexandria in 358 and was lynched in
December 361, apparently by a pagan mob, and whose cult
was subsequently transformed into that of an alleged martyr
under Diocletian or Maximinus.[97] In the present context, it
will suffice to acknowledge that, while the cult of George
is not attested before the reign of the emperor Anastasius
either at Lydda / Diospolis, where his body reposed in the
sixth century (Theodosius, *De situ terrae sanctae* 4 [CCSL
175.116]), or elsewhere,[98] the premiss of the new argument
is false. It assumes and asserts that the fact that Eusebius'
*Martyrs of Palestine* registers no martyr named George who
was tried and executed at Diospolis 'suffices to prove that
George did not die during the so-called great persecution.'[99]
But that is to mistake totally the nature of Eusebius' work,
which is not (and never set out to be) a complete record of
all the Christians who were martyred in Palestine between
303 and 311.[100]

The hagiography of Saint George is unusually varied
and voluminous, and its development is well-documented
(BHG 669y–691y; BHL 3363–3406g). The Byzantin-

---

[97] D. Woods, The Great Persecution, Maynooth, 2003, ed. D. V.
Twomey & M. Humphries (Dublin, 2009), 131–158.

[98] For a brief survey of the development of the cult of George, see
E. Lucius, Die Anfänge des Heiligenkults in der christlichen Kirche,
ed. G. Anrich (Tübingen, 1904), 239–242. Dated inscriptions show
that his cult had spread beyond Palestine by 515/516: Delehaye, Saints
militaires (n. 28), 45–50; F. Halkin, AB 67 (1949), 95, 98, 100–101,
103, 105, 107–108; 71 (1953), 335–336; Études (1973), Addenda to
III. 131. For early epigraphic evidence for the cult of George in Palestine itself, see Halkin, AB 69 (1951), 68, 72, 74–76; Études (1973),
Addenda to II. 72, 74.

[99] Woods, Great Persecution (n. 97), 152.

[100] App. 6.

ist Karl Krumbacher assembled the material known a century ago and established that the accounts of George in the poet Romanos, who wrote under Justinian, and later passions of Saint George, including the Latin *Passio Georgii* which falsely purports to be an eye-witness account (BHL 3363),[101] depend on a version which he described as a popular story or legend ('das alte Volksbuch').[102] This original *Passio Georgii* was committed to writing no later than c. 400: a few leaves of a palimpsest in Vienna, which preserve brief extracts (Vindobonensis lat. 954), appear to belong to the fifth century (BHG 670),[103] Many of the invented characters in it possess the names of historical persons active in the fourth century. The acuity of Paul Maas detected the inspiration of the most significant of the invented names in this story.[104] There are some surprising coincidences of name between (a) fictitious characters in the *Passio Georgii* and (b) real historical persons who were

---

[101]  Delehaye's verdict on this text, though severe, was fully justified: *cumulum ineptiarum merito dixeris, nec satis est apertissima inde mendacia tollere ut ad historiae veritatem reducatur* (Comm. Mart. Rom. 152).

[102]  K. Krumbacher, Der heilige Georg in der griechischen Über-lieferung, ed. A. Erhard (Munich, 1911), 1–105 (critical editions of relevant texts), 106–302 (the relationships between the various versions). For fragments of a passion found at Qas'r Ibrim in Nubia and its relation to other passions of St George, see W. H. C. Frend, JAC 32 (1989), 89–104

[103]  First published by D. Detlefsen, SB Wien, Phil.-hist. Kl. 27 (1858), 383–404; re-edited by Krumbacher, Der heilige Georg (n. 102), 1–3. The so-called *Decretum Gelasianum* (CPL 1676) classifies the *Passion of George* among the apocryphal books which are to be rejected, and a papyrus fragment datable c. 700 was published in 1950 (P. Nessana 6): L. Casson & E. L. Hettich, Excavations at Nessana 2: Literary Papyri (Princeton, 1950), 128–142.

[104]  Quoted by Krumbacher, Der heilige Georg (n. 102), 305: 'König Dadianos = Konsul Datianos vom Jahre 359.'

active between 345 and 361: (a) the Persian king 'Datianus' and (b) Datianus, who lived in Antioch and was ordinary consul in 358; (a) a prominent man 'Athanasius' and (b) Athanasius, who was bishop of Alexandria between 328 and 373 (with intermittent gaps); (a) 'Magnentius' and (b) Magnentius, who supplanted Constans as Roman emperor of the West in 350 and ruled in Gaul until 353; (a) the general 'Anatolius' and (b) Anatolius the *magister officiorum* of Julian from 360 to 363, who died in the same battle as the emperor. Furthermore, George himself is stated to come from Cappadocia, just like George 'the Cappadocian' who replaced Athanasius as bishop of Alexandria in the late 350s (Athanasius, *De Fuga* 6.2). The coincidences are too numerous to be accidental: since the author of the original *Passio Georgii* was writing before the end of the fourth century, he used the names of historical personages active in the middle decades of the century as characters in stories about George that he himself invented.[105]

Many further examples of real names reflected in hagiographical invention could be added. The account of the trial of the martyr Zosimus at Anazarbus in Cilicia, which is a pastiche of hagiographical clichés, names the official who tried Zosimus as Domitianus the *comes sacrarum largitionum* (BHG 2476).[106] It is hard to avoid the inference that this fictitious official is modelled on the Domitianus who had been *comes sacrarum largitionum* before Constantius appointed him praetorian prefect and sent him to Antioch in 353 (Ammianus 14.7.9, 11.17): François Halkin conjectured

---

[105] A eunuch Eutropius was added in secondary version of the *Passio* (p. 25.25 Krumbacher): he must owe his name to the famous eunuch and consul Eutropius, who fell from power in August 399 and was killed shortly thereafter (*PLRE* 2[1980], 440–444, Eutropius 1).

[106] Published by F. Halkin, AB 70 (1952), 254–261.

that the author may have taken the name and office from an inscription.[107] Again, a group of saints alleged to have been martyred in the Antonine age comprises Senator, Viator, Cassiodorus and Dominata (AASS, Sept. IV.349–350, cf. BHL 7575a). Whatever the origin of the last name, whose form is anomalous, the first three alleged martyrs owe their names (and probably their existence) to two Late Roman senators, viz., Fl. Viator, who was ordinary consul in 495, and Fl. Magnus Aurelius Cassiodorus Senator, the minister of Theodoric and consul in 514.[108] A modern and more amusing example of the phenomenon is the discovery of an ancient Saint Napoleon while Napoleon Bonaparte was Emperor of France.[109] Two manuscripts of the *Martyrologium Hieronymianum* record that a Neopolis died in prison in Alexandria together with the martyr Saturninus, who is well attested as an Alexandrian martyr (AASS, Nov. II.2.225). Neopolis secured admittance to the so-called historical martyrologies of the Middle Ages and thence to the Roman martyrology.[110] Shortly after 1800, celebration of the anniversary of his martyrdom was moved from 2 May to 15 August in order to coincide with the birthday of the emperor Napoleon and the Assumption of the Virgin, and Cardinal Caprara issued a document which explained that, through a perfectly normal linguistic evolution, the name of the supposed Alexandrian martyr became Napoleo in

---

[107]  Halkin, AB 70 (1952), 254 n. 1, noting that a persecuting official 'Domitianus' appears at a variety of dates in a variety of posts – *vicarius* at Ancyra in Galatia, *comes* at Corycus in Cilicia, *comes Lycaoniae* (whence PLRE 1 [1971], 262, Domitianus 2), *comes* at Iconium and governor at Pisidian Antioch.

[108]  Delehaye, Mélanges (1966), 179–188.

[109]  Delehaye, Mélanges (1966), 318–325.

[110]  Quentin, Martyrologes (1908), 212, 426, 452 482.

medieval Italy, which was the equivalent of Napoleone in modern Italian.[111]


# Epilogue

Eusebius of Caesarea prefaced his account of the 'Great Persecution' by stating explicitly that his aim was to preserve the memory of events in his own day and hand it on to future generations (*Mart. Pal.* [L] 1.8).[112] Such too had been the aim of those who before Eusebius preserved documentary records of early martyrdoms. Hagiography on the model of Eusebius' *Martyrs of Palestine*, which seeks to transmit honest, truthful and accurate accounts of the suffering and death of martyrs and confessors, has continued to be written by the survivors and contemporary witnesses of persecution ever since – and will asssuredly continue to be written whenever and wherever men and women are persecuted, tortured and put to death for their religious beliefs. The 'book of martyrs' by John Foxe (1516–1587) in sixteenth century England[113] and the memoirs of Jewish survivors of

---

[111] It is either fortunate or regrettable according to one's point of view that no suitable saint was available for a later dictator and conqueror named Adolf to exploit: clearly neither Adulfus, the English bishop of the seventh or eighth century (AASS, Iun. IV.427–428; BHL 1428) nor the Adulfus who was martyred by a Muslim ruler at Corduba c. 825 (AASS, Sept. VII.478: BHL 84) would have served the necessary purpose.

[112] Chapter III; App. 6.

[113] The title page of the first edition reads as follows: Actes and monuments of these latter and perillous dayes, touching matters of the Church, wherein ar comprehended and described the great persecutions & horrible troubles, that haue bene wrought and practised by the Romishe Prelates, speciallye in this realme of England and Scotlande,

the holocaust during the Second World War[114] are only the
most obvious and famous modern examples of such commemoration of genuine martyrs.

Fictitious hagiography, however, has flourished alongside
the genuine article and bogus saints have been invented at
least since Jerome created Paul the proto-hermit out of his
own imagination.[115] There is, for example, a conspicuous
lack of early attestation of the great Byzantine military saint
Demetrius, the patron and defender of Thessalonica: the
explanation (so it is plausibly argued) is that Demetrius owes
his existence to the fifth century misreading of the name of
the martyr Emeterius in a shrine dedicated to the Spanish
martyrs Emeterius and Chelidonius from Calagurris celebrated by the poet Prudentius (*Peristephanon* 1.1–120).[116]
A praetorian prefect named Leontius, it is recorded, restored
the shrine of Demetrius, which was deserted and in disre-
pair.[117] Now a Leontius is attested as praetorian prefect of

---

from the yeare of our Lorde a thousande, unto the tyme nowe present.
Gathered and collected according to the true copies & wrytinges
certificatorie, as wel of the parties them selues that suffered, as also
out of the Bishops Registers, which wer the doers therof, by Iohn Foxe
(London, 1563). Foxe registered more than 280 martyrs in England
and Wales between 4 February 1555 and the death of Queen Mary on
17 November 1558.

[114] A motivation identical to that of Eusebius was stated in the entry
in his diary for 30 July 1943, which Avraham Tory (né Golub) wrote
in Yiddish, hid for preservation and later recovered: 'It is incumbent
upon us to hand down to future generations the story of what befell
Lithuanian Jewry' (Surviving the Holocaust: the Kovno Ghetto diary,
trans. by J. Michalowicz, ed. M. Gilbert, with textual and historical
notes by D. Porat [Cambridge, MA, 1990], 446).

[115] Chapter IV.

[116] D. Woods, HThR 93 (2000), 226–234.

[117] The relevant evidence is translated and discussed by J. C. Ske-

Illyricum in 412–413 (*CTh* 7.4.32; 12.1.177; *I. Creticae* 4.325 [Gortyn: undated]). It is therefore a reasonable hypothesis that a Spaniard in the entourage of Theodosius brought alleged relics of Emeterius and Chelidonius from his home province to Thessalonica while the newly appointed emperor was residing there in 379–380 and built a shrine for them, but took them with him when the imperial court moved to Constantinople, with the result that the shrine of these Spanish martyrs, who had no local devotees, was abandoned for more than thirty years until Leontius restored it.

A more recent example may be provided by Lord Macaulay, whose history of England from 1685 to 1697 waxed eloquent over Margaret Maclachlan (or Lauchlan) and Margaret Wilson who (so Macaulay believed) 'suffered death for their religion' by being tied to stakes in the Solway Firth and drowned by the incoming tide on 11 May 1685 for refusing to 'abjure the cause of the insurgent Covenanters, and to attend to the Episcopal worship.' Macaulay's account of the death of Margaret Wilson, 'a maiden of eighteen' who 'was sustained by an enthusiasm as lofty as any that is recorded in martyrology,' incorporates at least one cliché familiar from Late Roman, medieval and Byzantine hagiographical fiction:

She saw the sea draw nearer and nearer, but gave no sign of alarm. She prayed and sang verses of psalms till the waves choked her voice. When she had tasted the bitterness of death she was, by a cruel mercy, unbound and restored to life. When she came to herself, pitying friends and neighbours implored her to yield. ... 'Will she take the abjuration?' [the presiding officer] demanded. 'Never!' she exclaimed. 'I am Christ's; let me go!' And the waters closed over her for the last time.[118]

Macaulay quotes 'the epitaph of Margaret Wilson, in the churchyard at Wigton' from a hagiographical collection published in 1714,[119] and he names as his source for his narrative of the episode a work of hagiography published eight years later.[120] But where Macaulay envisages a death and miraculous restoration to life, the *Cloud of Witnesses* has a plain statement of alleged fact ('being put oft into the Water, and when half dead, taken up again, to see if she would take the oath, which she refused to her last breath'),[121] while the document of 19 February 1711 which can be identified as the main source of this work of hagiography has something equally prosaic and unremarkable.[122] More serious, in 1863 the Scottish lawyer Mark Napier dismissed the account published in 1722 as 'a calumnious tissue of monstrous fables' which had 'poisoned the history of Scotland to an extent that is now perhaps irremediable:' he claimed not only that

---

[118] Macaulay, History of England 1 (London, 1849), 501–502 (Chapter IV).

[119] A Cloud of Witnesses, for the Royal Prerogatives of Jesus Christ or, The Last Speeches and Testimonies of those who have suffered for the Truth, in Scotland, since the year 1680 (Edinburgh, 1714). Macaulay does not specify which edition of the Cloud of Witnesses he has used: the epitaph which he quotes cannot be found among those printed in the appendix of inscriptions in the first edition (285–290).

[120] R. Wodrow, The History of the Sufferings of the Church of Scotland from the Restauration to the Revolution 2 (Edinburgh, 1722), 505–507 = 4 (Glasgow & Edinburgh, 1830), 246–249.

[121] Cloud of Witnesses (n. 119), 246.

[122] The Session Book of Penninghame 1696–1724, ed. H. Paton (Edinburgh & London: privately printed, 1933), 284: 'before her breath was quite gone, they pulled her up and held her till she could speak and then asked her if she would pray for the king.'

Macaulay had placed credit in a fictitious story invented by Alexander Shields in 1690,[123] but also that he had seriously misrepresented his named source by suppressing any mention of a significant document there discussed, even if discounted, namely, a reprieve *sine die* of the two women granted by the Privy Council of Scotland and entered in the records in Edinburgh on 30 April 1685.[124] Napier also published the text of Margaret Maclachlan's petition for pardon and drew the reasonable inference that both women were in fact pardoned, not executed.[125] Napier reiterated his thesis seven years later after Archibald Stewart had defended Wodrow's account of 1722 as historically accurate in a book to which the pious have continued to appeal.[126] A recent investigator reports that, like Napier before him, he failed to find any trace of the written attestations of witnesses to the martyrdoms which Wodrow claimed to possess.[127]

---

[123] The drowning of the two women first appears in A Short memorial of the Sufferings and Grievances, Past and Present, of the Presbyterians in Scotland: Particularly of those called by the Nick-name Cameronians, which Shields published anonymously (Edinburgh, 1690), 35–36.

[124] M. Napier, The Case for the Crown in re The Wigtown Martyrs proved to be Myths versus Wodrow and Lord Macaulay, Patrick the Pedler and Principal Tulloch (Edinburgh & London, 1863), v, 64–87.

[125] Napier, Case for the Crown (n. 124), esp. 15–71.

[126] M. Napier, History Rescued in Answer to History Vindicated (Edinburgh, 1870), answering A. Stewart, History Vindicated in the Case of the Wigtown Martyrs (Edinburgh, 1867; 2nd edition 1869), cf. H. MacPherson, Records of the Scottish Church History Society 9 (1947), 175.

[127] A. M. Starkey, Church History 43 (1974), 496, cf. Wodrow, History of the Sufferings 4 (1830), 247: 'I shall mostly give my narrative of it from an account I have from the forementioned Mr. Rowan, now with the Lord, late minister of Penningham, where Margaret Wilson lived, who was at pains to have its circumstances fully vouched by

The need for critical hagiography will abide until oppression vanishes from the face of the earth and there are no more victims of religious persecution.

---

witnesses, whose attestations are in my hand.' Starkey ascertained that Rowan's version consists of a verbatim extract from the Penninghame minute-book of 1711, though he acquits Wodrow of knowingly perpetrating a falsehood on the grounds that for him 'truth came before faith,' so that he merely failed to scrutinise his sources critically enough.

Appendices

# 1

# Were Early Christians crucified?

It is widely believed that the followers of Jesus who were put to death by the Roman authorities included many who were crucified like their master.[1] The ancient evidence does not bear out this modern supposition.

## Nero's entertainments

After the great fire of Rome in July 64, the emperor Nero executed a large number of Christians in an attempt to fix blame on them for starting the fire. To this aim he devised novel punishments designed to make the punishment fit the alleged crime. Tacitus, who is the only detailed surviving

---

[1] So M. Hengel, Crucifixion in the Ancient World and the Folly of the Message of the Cross (London, 1977). On various aspects of crucifixion as a penalty in Roman law, P. Garnsey, Social Status and Legal Privilege in the Roman Empire (Oxford, 1970), 126–129; W. Kuhn, ANRW 2.25.1 (1982), 685–775; J. & L. Robert, Fouilles d'Amyzon en Carie 1. Exploration, Histoire, Monnaies et Inscriptions (Paris, 1983), 259–263; J.-J. Aubert, Speculum Iuris. Roman Law as a Reflexion of Social and Economic Life in Antiquity, ed. J.-J. Aubert and B. Sirks (Ann Arbor, 2002), 110–130. It should be noted that the classic discussion of crucifixion by T. Mommsen, Römisches Strafrecht (Leipzig, 1899), 918–921, adduced only one passage relating to Christians and that in this passage it is not the Christian martyr who is crucified, but his accuser, who was presumably a slave punished for accusing his master (Eusebius, HE 5.21.3).

source for the whole episode, described Nero's novel punishments in a typically brief and allusive fashion in a passage which has been corrupted in transmission (*Annals* 15.44.4). The so-called second Medicean manuscript of Tacitus of the eleventh century, which was written at the monastery of Monte Cassino between 1038 and 1058 (Laurentianus LXVIII 2) presents it as follows:-

*et pereuntibus addita ludibria, ut ferarum tergis contecti laniatu canum interirent aut crucibus adfixi aut flammandi atque ubi defecisset dies in usu nocturni luminis urerentur.*

There is also an ancient indirect witness to the text. Tacitus was one of the sources used by Sulpicius Severus in the brief chronicle of the history of the world that he composed nearly three hundred years later.[2] Sulpicius possessed the full text of both *Annals* and *Histories*: he used Tacitus both for Nero's persecution in 64 and for the sack of the temple in Jerusalem in A.D. 70, and he incorporated Tacitean turns of phrase in his account of the death of Nero in 68 which he presumably found in Tacitus' account of the revolt of Vindex, the proclamation of Galba and the fall of Nero in the lost *Annals* XVIII.[3] He describes Nero's killing of Christians in 64 as follows:

*igitur vertit invidiam in Christianos, actaeque in innoxios crudelissimae quaestiones: quin et novae mortes excogitatae, ut ferarum tergis contecti laniatu canum interirent, multi crucibus affixi aut flamma usti, plerique in id reservati, ut cum defecisset dies, in usum nocturni lumini urerentur* (*Chronica* 2.29.2).

Sulpicius is relevant to deciding what Tacitus wrote at two points in his account of how Christians perished in 64.

---

[2] On the precise date of Sulpicius' *Chronicle*, Chapter V at nn. 69–70.

[3] T.D. Barnes, CP 72 (1977), 224–231.

First, he read *in usum* where the Medicean manuscript of
Tacitus has *in usu*: that is clearly the correct reading, since
*in usu* would imply previous use. It may be noted that,
without knowledge of Sulpicius Severus, a humanist of the
fifteenth century saw that *in usu* cannot be what Tacitus
wrote and emended it to *in usum*, the reading to be found in
a manuscript now in Zaragoza (Caesaraugustensis 9439 = Z
in Heubner's edition).[4] Second, he appears to have read *aut
flammandi atque*, since he agrees with the Medicean manuscript in stating that Nero employed three separate methods
of punishment – mauling by wild beasts, crucifixion and
being set alight as human torches. But it has long been
recognised that the transmitted text, although supported by
Sulpicius, cannot be correct. Many emendations have been
essayed, but the most convincing is Georg Andresen's deletion of the words *aut flammandi atque*,[5] though these words
are less likely to be an interpolation from Sulpicius Severus
(as Andresen supposed) than to arise from an intrusive gloss
that predates the end of the fourth century.[6] Two recent editors of the *Annals* have rightly accepted Andresen's deletion
and print the passage as follows:

[4] For proof that all the correct readings in the *recentiores* of *Annals*
XI–XVI and *Histories* I–V are the product of humanist conjecture and
not derived from a lost manuscript independent of M, see F. R. D.
Goodyear, CQ 15 (1965), 299–322; 20 (1970), 365–370; F. Römer,
P. Corneli Taciti Annalium libri XV–XVI (Vienna, Cologne & Graz,
1976), xxix–lxviii; R. J. Tarrant, Texts and Transmission. A Survey of
the Latin Classics, ed. L. D. Reynolds (Oxford, 1983), 407–409.
[5] G. Andresen, Jahresberichte des Philologischen Vereins zu Berlin
39 (1913) 165–166; 40 (1914), 75. In his revision of the fifth Teubner
edition of C. Halm's text of the *Annals* (Leipzig, 1913), Andresen
bracketed the words *aut flammandi atque* as an interpolation.
[6] R. Hanslik, Wiener Studien 76 (1963), 106–107.

*et peruntibus addita ludibria, ut ferarum tergis contecti laniatu canum interirent aut crucibus adfixi [aut flammandi atque], ubi defecisset, dies in usum nocturni luminis urerentur.*[7]

And, as they perished, mockeries were added, so that, covered in the hides of wild beasts, they expired from mutilation by dogs, or were burned fixed to crosses for use as nocturnal illumination on the dwindling of daylight.[8]

Tacitus refers to novel punishments added as mockeries to normal modes of execution (*pereuntibus addita ludibria*). In what precisely did Nero's innovations consist?

Ted Champlin's recent study of Nero explains the first perfectly: instead of the normal exposure to wild beasts (*damnatio ad bestias*),[9] the criminals 'have themselves become the beasts, and are attacked by hunting dogs.'[10] Champlin has also illuminated the burning of Christians

---

[7] F. Römer, P. Corneli Taciti Annalium libri XV–XVI (n. 4), 67; H. Heubner, P. Corneli Taciti libri quae supersunt 1[2] (Stuttgart & Leipzig, 1994), 369. Both appeal to H. Heubner, Hermes 87 (1959), 223–230; Hanslik, Wiener Studien 76 (1963), 107.

[8] Modified from the translation by A. J. Woodman, Tacitus: The Annals (Indianapolis & Cambridge, 2004), 326. Woodman reads *crucibus adfixi ac flammandi, [atque] ubi* etc. stating that he does so 'after Weyman / Linck' (388). In fact, both C. Weyman, Festgabe für Martin von Schanz (Würzburg, 1912), 172, and K. Linck, De antiquissimis veterum quae ad Iesum Nazarenum spectant testimoniis. Religionsgeschichtliche Versuche und Vorarbeiten 14.1 (Giessen, 1913), 61–62, 89–91, 98, preferred *et* in place of the *aut* of the manuscript, though Weyman believed that *ac* and *atque* had almost equal claims to be regarded as what Tacitus wrote. A much more radical change in the transmitted text was made by H. Fuchs, who posited a lacuna and printed *crucibus affixi et flammandi <alimenta ignium induerent> atque, ubi* etc.: P. Cornelius Tacitus: Annalium ab Excessu Divi Augusti quae supersunt 2 (Frauenfeld, 1949), 134, cf. *Vig. Chr.* 4 (1950), 87–93.

[9] On which, see Garnsey, Social Status and Legal Privilege (n. 1), 129–131.

[10] E. Champlin, Nero (Cambridge, MA & London, 2003), 122.

as torches by interpreting it as Nero's revenge for the burning of the Temple of Luna Noctiluca on the Palatine, that
is, 'Luna Light of the night, which was probably lit up at
night.'[11] Tacitus' *in usum nocturni luminis* carries a precise
allusion to the circumstances of 64: the burning Christians
supplied the light at night formerly supplied by the Temple
of Luna Noctiluca which they were alleged to have burned
down. The punishment meted out to Christians in Rome
in 64 was thus not a modified form of crucifixion, but a
modified form of burning at the stake.[12] The victims in this
'fatal charade' were presumably clad in easily combustible
tunics, a punishment described by Seneca when he invites
Lucilius to contemplate various methods of execution and
deadly torture:

*cogita hoc loco carcerem et cruces et eculeos et uncum et adactum per
medium hominem, qui per os emergeret, stipitem et distracta in diversum
actis curribus membra, illam tunicam alimentis ignium et inlitam et
textam, et quicquid aliud praeter haec commenta saevitia est.*

Picture to yourself under this head strangulation in prison, the cross,
the rack, the hook, the stake driven right through a man to protrude
from his mouth, limbs torn apart by chariots set in motion in different directions, that tunic smeared and interwoven with inflammable
materials, and whatever else besides these that savage cruelty has
devised. (*Ep.* 14.5: modified from the Loeb translation of R.M.
Gummere)

---

[11] Champlin, Nero (n. 10), 122–123, 302 n. 29, cf. J. Aronen,
'Noctiluca, Templum,' LTUR 3 (Rome, 1995), 345. The temple is
attested only in Varro, De lingua latina 5.68: *itaque ea [sc. Luna] dicta
Noctiluca in Palatio : nam ibi noctu lucet templum.*

[12] Compare the execution of Laureolus described by Martial, *Spect.*
9(7).3–4: J.-J. Aubert, Speculum Iuris (n. 1), 111, correctly charac-
terises it as 'a fake crucifixion, as the victim was ultimately gutted by
a bear.'

Seneca composed this letter at a date very close to Nero's spectacular executions. There are few precise indications of date in his *Epistulae Morales*, but it seems almost certain that the fourteenth letter was written before the Great Fire of Rome.[13] The incendiary tunic belongs to normal Roman judicial practice which incorporated a variety of 'cruel and unusual punishments': some decades after Seneca, the poets Martial and Juvenal allude to the same punishment as *tunica molesta* (Martial 4.86.8, 10.25.5; Juvenal 8.235: *tunica punire molesta*).

Erich Koestermann's commentary on the passage is partially vitiated by his belief that a fifteenth century manuscript of *Annals* XI–XVI and *Histories* preserved in the public library at Leiden (Leiden, PL 16B) preserves a textual tradition independent of the Medicean manuscript.[14] Hence he treated the reading *flammati* in the Leidensis as having equal authority with M's *flammandi* and printed it in his Teubner edition of 1960 as what Tacitus wrote, and it was unfortunately in this corrupt form that Martin Hengel quoted the passage in his classic study of crucifixion in the ancient world, where he assumed that in 64 'crucifixion was the basic punishment to which the *addita ludibria* were added.'[15] Nevertheless, Koestermann's defence of the incorrect reading *aut crucibus adfixi atque flammati, ubi* etc. points the way to a proper understanding of both Tacitus' meaning and Nero's innovation. Koestermann argued that the reading *flammati* gives good sense, but that it labours

---

[13] M. Griffin, Seneca. A Philosopher in Politics (Oxford, 1974), 396, 400.

[14] As he asserted categorically in the preface to his second Teubner edition: E. Koestermann, P. Corneli Taciti libri qui supersunt I$^2$ (Leipzig, 1960), xii–xvi.

[15] Hengel, Crucifixion in the Ancient World (n. 1), 26–27.

under the disadvantage that the Christians ought to have been bound to stakes, not crosses.[16] As Koestermann realised, Tacitus describes not a crucifixion, but a *Verbrennungstod*, a burning alive.[17] The mockery that was added consisted in the substitution of a cross for the normal stake in order to parody the Crucifixion. These followers of Christ were not suspended from a cross as in a real crucifixion: they were bound with ropes to a stake, with their arms tied to a cross-piece and extended in the posture of crucifixion; they were not suspended by their hands or wrists as they would have been in a real crucifixion, since it was never intended that they should die of exhaustion and asphyxiation as those crucified normally did in a death which was both painful and slow.[18] The Christians killed by Nero by the banks of the River Tiber were burned alive, not crucified: their cross was purely symbolic.

## Punishment for the *nomen Christianum*

The Christians of Rome so cruelly punished in 64 were executed as arsonists, not as religious deviants. After the mere profession of Christianity came to be treated as a capital crime by the Roman authorities, how many of those who were convicted as Christians were crucified rather

---

[16] E. Koestermann, Cornelius Tacitus: Annalen 4 (Heidelberg, 1968), 257: 'Das gibt gewiss einen glatten Sinn, leidet aber darunter, dass beim Verbrennungstod die Opfer nicht ans Kreuz geschlagen, sondern durch stipites an den Pfahl geheftet wurden.'

[17] So already Weyman, Festgabe Schanz (n. 8), 172.

[18] Hence the breaking of the legs of the criminals crucified with Jesus to make sure that they were dead before the Sabbath began at sunset (John 19.31–32).

than executed in other ways? It seems natural to assume that crucifixion was one of the normal punishments for the early Christian martyrs.[19] But the evidence shows a curious disparity between a plethora of general statements and a lack of specific instances. To be sure, it is easy to draw up a list of passages written before 260 which speak in general terms of the crucifixion of contemporary Christians.[20] Before the 'Great Persecution,' however, there is only one certain case of a named Christian who was crucified in the regular fashion – and he was not crucified for being a Christian.[21] Atticus, the governor of Judaea, tortured and executed Symeon, the successor of James as leader of the Christian community

---

[19] Hengel, Crucifixion (n. 1), 32: until 311 'not only were crosses set up all over the empire, but Christians themselves will either have been executed on the cross or at least will have reckoned with crucifixion or similar punishment;' Garnsey, Social Status and Legal Privilege (n. 1), 127: 'the cross was frequently used for the punishment of Christians, at least from the time of Nero.' Garnsey adduces the *Acts of Carpus, Papylus and Agathonice* (K-K-R II = Musurillo II). However, not only do the extant Greek and Latin versions contain too many obvious interpolations to be regarded as historically reliable (JTS, N.S. 19 [1968], 514–515), but this is another mock crucifixion: after being hoisted upright on a cross, both Papylus and Carpus are burnt alive (36–41 Greek = 4 Latin).

[20] Matthew 23.34; Ignatius, Letter to the Romans 5.3; Shepherd of Hermas, Vision 3.2.1 (10.1); Justin, Dialogue with Trypho 110.4; Celsus, quoted by Origen, Against Celsus 8.39.54; Tertullian, Ad Nationes 1.3.10, 1.18.10; Apologeticum 12.3; 30.7; Ad Martyras 4.2, 4.9; De Anima 1.6, 56.8; Minucius Felix, Octavius 9.4; Cyprian, De habitu virginum 6 (CSEL 3.1.192.9–10). This list excludes the more numerous references to the crucifixion of Christ himself such as Lucian, De Morte Peregrini 11.

[21] As is correctly stated by Aubert, Speculum Iuris (n. 1), 127–128, who allows that Peter might have been crucified, but rightly dismisses the alleged three day long crucifixion of his brother Andrew as a romantic invention.

in Jerusalem, in the reign of Trajan (Hegesippus, quoted by
Eusebius, *HE* 3.32.3, 6, cf. 3.11). Atticus, whose identity
is uncertain,[22] did not sentence Symeon to death for being
a Christian. Symeon was a cousin of Jesus and he was accused (Hegesippus reports) because he was a descendant of
King David, as Jesus was claimed to be (Matthew 1.1–17;
Luke 1.70, 2.4). Atticus therefore condemned him as the
potential leader or figurehead of a Jewish rebellion. As for
the apostle Peter, the only early evidence for the mode of his
execution (John 21.18) indicates that he was burned alive in
64 as part of Nero's deadly entertainments.[23]

---

[22] A. R. Birley, JRS 85 (1995), 294, proposes M. Quintius Atticus
(*PIR²* Q 40). Atticus was identified as the father of the famous Herodes
Atticus, whose name was presumably (Ti. Claudius) Atticus (Herodes),
by E. M. Smallwood, JRS 52 (1962), 131–133. Smallwood's identifica-
tion was accepted in E. Schürer, History of the Jewish People in the
Age of Jesus Christ 1, revised and edited by G. Vermes & F. Millar
(Edinburgh, 1973), 516; W. Eck, Senatoren von Vespasian bis Hadrian.
Prosopographische Untersuchungen mit Einschluss der Jahres- und
Provinzialfasten der Statthalter (Munich, 1970), 156–157, 243; Chiron
12 (1982), 334, 336, 338; 13 (1983), 221; B. E. Thomasson, Laterculi
Praesidum 1 (Gothenburg, 1984), 324. All these scholars assumed that
the father of Herodes Atticus was suffect consul in 104 and hence could
have been governor of Judaea from 100/101 to early 103. It is now
clear, however, that the consulate of Herodes Atticus' father belongs
to 132 or 133 (*CIL* 16.174; AE 1990.763, cf. A. R. Birley, ZPE 116
[1997], 209, 212, 229–237). Although Hegesippus stated Atticus' title
as ὑπατικός, the governor of Judaea was of praetorian rank: similarly, a
letter sent by an Egyptian soldier from Bostra on 26 March 107 calls the
praetorian governor of the new province of Arabia, under whom he was
serving, Κλαύδιον Σε[ουῆ]ρ[ο]ν τὸν ὑπατικόν (P. Michigan 466.26–27),
even though Severus did not become consul until 112: see A. Degrassi,
I fasti consolari dell'impero romano [Rome, 1952], 33; G. W. Bowersock, Roman Arabia (Cambridge, MA & London, 1983), 81, 83, 85.

[23] Chapter I.

The ancient evidence thus does not support the modern assumption that crucifixion was one of the normal modes of execution that the Roman authorities inflicted on Christians. In contrast to the apparent abundance of general references to crucifixion, there is a conspicuous dearth of evidence for the crucifixion of individual martyrs or groups of named martyrs, despite the frequent attestation of execution by the sword, by burning alive and by exposure to wild beasts in the arena.[24] Moreover, crucifixion is absent from a detailed list of atrocities, including the indignities inflicted on contemporary Christians, in a *Commentary on Daniel* written in the early third century probably in Asia Minor:[25]

Χρὴ οὖν ἐνορᾶν τὴν ἐσομένην τῶν ἁγίων τότε θλῖψιν καὶ ταλαιπωρίαν – δεῖ γὰρ ἡμᾶς ἐκ τῶν ἤδη μερικῶς γινομένων ἐννοεῖν τὰ ἐσόμενα –, τοιαύτης ζάλης καὶ ταράχου ἐν παντὶ τῷ κόσμῳ γενησομένης, καὶ πάντων πιστῶν πανταχοῦ ἀναιρουμένων καὶ κατὰ πᾶσαν πόλιν καὶ χώραν σφαζομένων, καὶ δικαίων αἵματος ἐκχυνομένου, καὶ ζώντων ἀνθρώπων καιομένων, καὶ θηρίοις ἑτέρων παραβαλλομένων, καὶ νηπίων ἐν ἀφόδοις φονευομένων, καὶ ἀτάφων πάντων ῥιπτουμένων καὶ ὑπὸ κυνῶν βιβρωσκομένων, παρθένων τε καὶ γυναικῶν παρρησίᾳ φθειρομένων καὶ αἰσχρῶς ἐμπαιζομένων, καὶ ἀναρπαγῶν γινομένων, καὶ κοιμητηρίων ἁγίων ἀνασκαπτομένων, καὶ λειψάνων ἀνορυσσομένων καὶ ἐν πεδίῳ σκορπιζομένων, καὶ βλασφημιῶν γινομένων (Hippolytus, *In Danielem* 4.51)[26]

It is necessary to see here (i.e., in this passage) the future oppression and suffering of the saints – for we must infer what will be then (sc. in the last days) from what is already on occasion happening –, when there will be such hail and disturbance in the whole universe, with all the faithful destroyed everywhere, butchered in every city and every

---

[24] Chapters II, III.

[25] J.A. Cerrato, Hippolytus between East and West. The Commentaries and the Provenance of the Corpus (Oxford, 2002), 134–137, 152–157, 162–165, 168–171, 230, 238–242.

[26] The Greek text and an ancient Armenian translation of the passage are printed in parallel by M. Richard & N. Bonwetsch, Hippolytus Werke 1.1. Kommentar zu Daniel[2] (Berlin, 2000), 314–317.

country district, with the blood of the just poured out, with human beings burnt alive and others exposed to wild beasts, with infants murdered in the streets, with all <of these> cast out unburied and eaten by dogs, with married and unmarried women being corrupted and foully abused with excessive freedom, with the occurrence of violent thievery, with the uprooting of the resting-places of saints and the digging up and casting out of their corpses on the plain, and with grave insults to God.

Only for the 'Great Persecution' is there reliable or contemporary evidence that anyone was crucified by the Roman authorities for being a Christian. Eusebius reports that Theodulus, 'a venerable and godly old man' whose long years of dutiful service had earned him a high position in his master's household, so infuriated his master by saluting a martyr with a kiss that he had him crucified (*Mart. Pal.* 11.24). Theodulus' master was Firmilianus, the governor of Palestine, but Firmilianus did not crucify him for defying any imperial order to sacrifice: he was surely exercising the ancient right of a master to crucify a disobedient slave.[27] Despite the lack of precedents, however, Eusebius reports that freeborn Christians were crucified during the 'Great Persecution.' He waxes eloquent on the sufferings of Christians in Egypt in Book Eight of his *Ecclesiastical History*:

One would also wonder at those of them who suffered martyrdom in their own land, where countless numbers of men, women and children, despising this transient life, endured various forms of death for the sake of our Saviour's teaching. Some of them were committed to the flames after being torn, racked and grievously scourged, and suffering manifold other torments terrible to hear, while some were drowned in the sea; others with good courage stretched forth their heads before those who were cutting them off, or died during their

---

[27]  Mommsen, Strafrecht (n. 1), 919. On the banality of the crucifixion of slaves who crossed their masters, see J. & L. Robert, Fouilles d'Amyzon en Carie 1 (n. 1), 261–262.

tortures, or perished of hunger; others again were crucified, some as malefactors usually are, but some even more brutally upside down, with their heads towards the ground, and kept alive until they starved to death hanging on the shaft of the cross. (*HE* 8.8)

Before he wrote these words, Eusebius had visited Upper Egypt, where he witnessed many martyrdoms by decapitation and burning, probably in 312–313 (*HE* 8.9.4). Hence it seems rash to dismiss his report of crucifixions during Maximinus' renewed persecution during these two years. But the fact remains that his first-hand account of persecution between 303 and 311 in his own province in his *Martyrs of Palestine* records no crucifixion except that of Theodulus. Moreover, the chronology of Book Eight of the *Ecclesiastical History* is so confused that it includes martyrdoms datable with certainty after Galerius' edict of toleration with which it explicitly ends (*HE* 8.17).[28] Eusebius can therefore safely be used only as evidence that freeborn Christians may have been crucified during the last paroxysm of violence against the Christians in the territories ruled by Maximinus, whose repression of Christians in Asia Minor from the autumn of 311 to the spring of 313 was significantly more brutal than persecution had ever been under Galerius, who ruled Asia Minor from 305 to 311 (Gregory of Nazianzus, *Orat.* 4.96). It seems probable, therefore, that no Christians had been crucified under earlier persecuting emperors.

---

[28] Constantine (1981), 156–158. The clearest example is Lucian of Antioch (Eusebius, *HE* 8.13.2): he was executed on 7 January 312 after being tried by Maximinus himself in Nicomedia (9.6.3, cf. ZAC 9 [2005], 350–353).

# 2

# Modern Collections of Early Hagiographical Documents

Thierry Ruinart published his *Acta primorum martyrum sincera et selecta*, which he claimed to include only authentic documents, in Paris in 1689. A second revised and expanded edition appeared twenty four years later in Amsterdam in 1713, the last reprint at Regensburg in 1859. Ruinart's collection continued in scholarly use for more than another century: the 1859 reprint, though riddled with misprints, was still adduced in the first volume of the *Prosopography of the Later Roman Empire* (Cambridge, 1971) as the only documentation for several dozen governors before and during the 'Great Persecution,'[1] and some of Ruinart's texts were reproduced unchanged in the much smaller selections of early *acta martyrum* produced in the twentieth century alongside texts reprinted from modern critical editions and authentic documents discovered since Ruinart's day. As an aid to readers, therefore, listed below are the editions from which each of the documents in the standard modern collections of early *acta martyrum* and passions is reprinted.[2] The contents of the following two works are not summarised:

---

[1] Listed in New Empire (1982), 185–191. The 'list of abbreviations' in PLRE 1.xi–xx includes the inaccurate entry: 'Ruin.2 = T. Ruinart, Acta Martyrum sincera, ed. 2, Ratisbon (1859).

[2] Where the text is published as or in a separate monograph with the same title, the editor's name alone is normally given.

(1) G. Lanata, *Gli atti dei martiri come documenti processuali.*
    *Studi e testi per un Corpus Iudiciorum* 1 (Milan, 1973),
    who prints only the *contenuto processuale* of fifteen docu-
    ments whose full text stands in the collections of Knopf-
    Krüger-Ruhbach and Musurillo.[3]

(2) *Atti e passioni dei martiri*, edited by A. A. R. Bastiaensen
    and others (Milan, 1987). Although Bastiaensen's collec-
    tion contains some new critical editions commissioned
    for the volume, it includes only eleven of the texts in
    the twentieth century collections listed below, but finds
    space for Prudentius' poem on Agnes (*Peristephanon* 14),
    which is an imaginative piece of unadulterated fiction
    despite the very early attestation of the cult of Agnes
    (Chr. min. 1.71).[4]

## Gebhardt (1902)

Oscar von Gebhardt's selection of documents with the double title *Acta Martyrum selecta. Ausgewählte Märtyreracten
und andere Urkunden aus der Verfolgungszeit der christlichen
Kirche* (Berlin, 1902) set out, for the most part, to print
critical texts. Gebhardt did not simply reprint earlier editions: he utilised recent manuscript discoveries and, while
modestly claiming that he had done little, made significant
improvements in most of the texts which he reproduced.

---

[3] For the *Passio Marcelli* (BHL 5254), Lanata prints (202–204) a
text based on her full critical edition in Byzantion 42 (1972), 509–522.

[4] M. Armellini, Il cimitero di S. Agnese sulla Via Nomentana
(Rome, 1880), esp. 39–39; Delehaye, Culte (1933), 276, cf. P. Franchi
de' Cavalieri, RQ, Supp. 10 (Rome, 1899), 1–95, reprinted in his
Scritti agiografici 1 (ST 221, 1962), 293–381

I       *Martyrdom of Polycarp* (BHG 1560)
        Theodor Zahn (Leipzig, 1876); J. B. Lightfoot (London, 1889)

II      *Acts of Carpus, Papylas and Agathonice* (BHG 293)
        A. Harnack, TU 3.3–4 (1888), 440–452; B. Aubé, Rev. arch. 42 (1881), 348–360[5]

III     *Acts of Justin* (BHG 973)
        J. C. T. Otto (Jena, 1879)

IV      *Acts of the Scillitan Martyrs* (BHL 7527; BHG 1645)
        Latin: J. A. Robinson (Cambridge, 1891)
        Greek: H. Usener, Index scholarum quae summis auspiciis regis augustissimi Guilelmi, Imperatoris Germaniae in Universitate Fridericia Guilelmia Rhenana per menses aestivos anni MDCCCLXXXI a die XX mensis aprilis publice privatimque habebuntur (Bonn, 1881), 3–6

V       Letter of the churches of Vienna and Lugdunum = Eusebius, *HE* 5.1.1–2.8[6]

VI      *Martyrdom of Apollonius* (BHG 149; BHO 79)
        Greek: J. van den Gheyn, AB 14 (1895), 286–294; E. T. Klette, TU 15.2 (1897), 92–131; A. Hilgenfeld, Zeitschrift für wissenschaftliche Theologie 41 (1898), 186–194
        Armenian: Burchardi's German translation from A. Harnack, SB Berlin 1893. 728–739

VII     *Passion of Perpetua* (BHL 6633; BHG 1482)
        P. Franchi de' Cavalieri, RQ, Supp. 5 (1896), 104–

---

[5] Reprinted in Aubé's L'église et l'état dans la seconde moitié du IIIe siècle (249–284)[2] (Paris, 1885), 499–506.

[6] E. Schwartz allowed Gebhardt to use his critical edition of Eusebius' Ecclesiastical History (Berlin, 1903–1909) in advance of publication.

148[7] (with the use of additional manuscripts not used by Franchi)

VIII     *Passion of Pionius* (*BHG* 1546)
O. von Gebhardt, Archiv für slavische Philologie 16 (1896), 156–171

IX     *Acta disputationis Achatii* (BHL 25) = Ruinart

X     *Acta Maximi* (BHL 5829) = Ruinart

XI     *Acts of Cyprian* (BHL 2037)
W. Hartel, CSEL 3.3 (1871), cx–cxiv

XII     *Martyrium Cononis* (*BHG* 361)
A. Papadopulus-Kerameus (St. Petersburg, 1898)[8]

XIII     *Passion of Marianus and Jacobus* (BHL 131)
P. Franchi de' Cavalieri, ST 3 (1900)

XIV     *Passion of Montanus and Lucius* (BHL 6009)
P. Franchi de' Cavalieri, RQ, Supp. 8 (1898), 71–86

XV     *Passio Irenaei* (BHL 4466) = Ruinart

XVI     *Testament of the Forty Martyrs of Sebasteia* (BHG 1203)
N. Bonwetsch, (Leipzig, 1897), cf. Neue kirchliche Zeitschrift 3 (1892), 713–721

XVII     *Martyrdom of the Forty Martyrs of Sebasteia* (BHG 1201)
Gebhardt's own text based on the edition of R. Abicht and H. Schmidt, *Archiv für slavische Philologie* 18 (1896), 144–152, and two other manuscripts

XVIII   Two *libelli* of the Decian persecution
1 C. Wessely, Anzeiger Wien, Phil.-hist. Kl. 331 (1894), 3–4;
2 E. Krebs, SB Berlin 1893. 1007–1014[9]

---

[7] Reprinted in Franchi's Scritti 1 (n. 4), 108–138.

[8] Gebhardt also prints the notice of Conon's martyrdom from a Greek menologium in Leipzig, Stadtbibliothek Cod. Rep. II. no. 25.

[9] These were the first two such *libelli* to be published: they are nos. 5

XIX CIL 3.12132 = E. Kalinka, TAM 2.3 (Vienna, 1944), no. 785
Gebhardt prints both Mommsen's text and the alternative restorations by O. Benndorf and E. Bormann, JÖAI 16 (1893), 93–94, 108

XX *Gesta apud Zenophilum* = Optatus, App. 1, pp. 185–197 Ziwsa

XXI *Acta purgationis Felicis* = Optatus, App. 2, pp. 197–204 Ziwsa

XXII *Acts of Paul and Thecla* (BHG 1713)
R.A. Lipsius and M. Bonnet, Acta Apostolorum apocrypha 1 (Leipzig, 1893), 235–272

## Knopf-Krüger (1929, reprinted in 1965 with additions by Gerhard Ruhbach)

The first two editions of Rudolf Knopf's *Ausgewählte Märtyrerakten* were published in Tübingen in 1901 and 1913 in the *Sammlung ausgewählter kirchen- und dogmengeschichtlicher Quellenschriften* edited by Gustav Krüger (Neue Folge 3). In 1929, nine years after Knopf's death in 1920, Krüger produced a reworking of his edition ('Neuarbeitung der knopfschen Ausgabe') which practically amounted to a new collection. For Krüger was able to use critical editions unavailable to Knopf and he included additional documents. Krüger's revision of Knopf's collection at once became the standard edition of the authentic early *acta martyrum* used by critical historians of early Christianity, and in 1965 Gerhard Ruhbach produced a fourth edition, comprising

and 1 respectively. in the corpus of libelli assembled by J.R. Knipfing, HTR 16 (1923), 363–390.

a photographic reprint of the 1929 edition with misprints corrected and substantial addenda, including the shortest and the longest recensions of the *Acts of Justin*. The following list notes the editions used in the 1929 and 1965 editions.

I        *Martyrdom of Polycarp* (BHG 1560)
         K. Bihlmeyer, Die apostolischen Väter 1 (Tübingen, 1924), 120–132
II       *Acts of Carpus, Papylus and Agathonice* (BHG 293; BHL 1622m)
         Greek: Gebhardt II
         Latin: P. Franchi de' Cavalieri, Note agiografiche 6 (ST 33, 1920), 43–45
III      *Martyrdom of Ptolemaeus and Lucius* = Justin, *Apol.* 2.2
IV       *Acts of Justin* (BHG 973)
         P. Franchi de' Cavalieri, Note agiografiche (ST 8, 1902), 33–36, cf. Nuove note agiografiche (ST 9, 1902), 73–75
V        *Letter of the Churches of Lyons and Vienne* = Gebhardt V
VI       *Acts of the Scillitan Martyrs* (BHL 7527) = Gebhardt IV
VII      *Martyrdom of Apollonius* (BHG 149):
         E. T. Klette, TU 15.2 (1897), 92–131; Gebhardt VI; Max, Prinz zu Sachsen, Der heilige Märtyrer Apollonius von Rom. Eine historisch-kritische Studie (Mainz, 1903); G. Rauschen, Monumenta minora saeculi secundi (Bonn, 1915), 69–88
VIII     *Martyrdom of Perpetua* (BHL 6633)
         J. A. Robinson (Cambridge, 1891);
         P. Franchi de' Cavalieri, RQ, Supp. 5 (1896), 104–148; Gebhardt VII

| IX | *Martyrdom of Potamiaena and Basilides* = Eusebius, *HE* 6.5 |
|---|---|
| X | *Passion of Pionius* (BHG 1546) = Gebhardt VIII |
| XI | *Acta Acacii* (BHL 25) |
| | J. Weber, De actis Sancti Acacii (Diss. Strassburg, publ. Leipzig-Borna, 1913), 46–52 |
| XII | *Acta Maximi* (BHL 5829) = Gebhardt X |
| XIII | *Acts of Cyprian* (BHL 2037) = Gebhardt XI |
| XIV | *Martyrium Cononis* (BHG 361) = Gebhardt XII |
| XV | *Passion of Marianus and Jacobus* (BHL 131) = Gebhardt XIII |
| XVI | *Passion of Montanus and Lucius* (BHL 6009) = Gebhardt XIV |
| XVII | *Passion of Fructuosus* (BHL 3196) = Ruinart |
| XVIII | *Martyrdom of Marinus* = Eusebius, *HE* 7.15 |
| XIX | *Acta Maximiliani* (BHL 5813) = Ruinart |
| XX | *Acts of Marcellus* (BHL 5254) |
| | H. Delehaye, AB 41 (1923), 260–267 (two recensions) |
| XXI | *Martyrium Cassiani* (BHL 1636) = Ruinart |
| XXII | *Acts of Felix* (BHL 2893s) |
| | H. Delehaye, AB 39 (1921) 268–270 |
| XXIII | *Martyrdom of Dasius* (BHG 491) |
| | F. Cumont, AB 16 (1897), 11–15 |
| XXIV | *Passion of Agape, Irene and Chione* (*BHG* 34) |
| | P. Franchi de' Cavalieri, Nuove note agiografiche (ST 9, 1902), 15–19 |
| XXV | *Acts of Euplus* (BHG 629; BHL 2728) |
| | Greek: P. Franchi de' Cavalieri, Note agiografiche 7 (ST 49, 1928), 46–48 |
| | Latin = Ruinart |
| XXVI | *Passio Irenaei* (BHL 4466) = Gebhardt XV |

XXVII    *Acta Julii* (BHL 4555)
        H. Delehaye, AB 10 (1891), 50–52
XXVIII  *Acta Claudii* (BHL 1829) = Ruinart
XXIX    *Acts of Crispina* (BHL 1989b)
        P. Franchi de' Cavalieri, Nuove note agiografiche
        (ST 9,1902), 32–35
XXX      *Letter of Phileas* = Eusebius, *HE* 8.10
XXXI     *Acts of Phileas* (BHL 6799) = Ruinart
XXXII    *Testament of the Forty Martyrs* (BHG 1203) = Geb-
        hardt XVII
XXXIII  *Passion of Sabas* (BHG 1607)
        H. Delehaye, AB 31 (1912), 216–221
Addenda (125–129)
*Acts of Justin*: short and long recensions (*BHG* 972z, 974)
from Lazzati, Sviluppi (1956), 120–127

## Lazzati, *Sviluppi* (1956)

Giuseppe Lazzati devoted his book mainly to the development of Christian hagiography as a literary genre, but
he added a long appendix of fourteen texts grouped by
literary form with a subordinate ordering by date within
each group – two ancient letters on martyrs, four 'dramatic'
readings, three 'dramatic-narrative' readings and three plain
'narrative' readings. Since Lazzati does not number the texts
that he prints, the numbers below refer to the pages of each
text: the title of each document is that assigned to it by Lazzati, translated into English where he uses Italian.

99–106    *Letter of the Church of Smyrna to the Church of*
        *Philomelium* (BHG 1560)
        K. Bihlmeyer, Die apostolischen Väter 1(Tübin-
        gen, 1924), 120–132

108–116 *Letter of the Churches of Lyon and Vienne to the Churches of Asia and Phrygia*
Eusebius, *HE* 5.1.1–2.8, 5.3–4 (Schwartz)

120–127 *Martyrium Iustini, Charitonis et aliorum* (BHG 972z; 973; 974)
(A) based on Lazzati's collation of Paris, B.N., Graecus 1470 and P. Franchi de' Cavalieri, Note agiografiche 6 (ST 33, 1920), 5–17
(B) P. Franchi de' Cavalieri, Note agiografiche (ST 8, 1902), 33–36; Nuove note agiografiche (ST 9, 1902), 73–75, with F. C. Burkitt, JTS 11 (1909), 61–66
(C) B. Latyšev, Menologii anonymi byzantini quae supersunt (St. Petersburg, 1912), XXX[10]

129–130 *Passio Scillitanorum* (BHL 7527)
J. A. Robinson (Cambridge, 1891)

132–137 *Martyrium Carpi, Papyli et Agathonices* (BHL 1622m; BHG 293)
Latin: P. Franchi de' Cavalieri, Note agiografiche 6 (ST 6, 1920), 43–45
Greek: A. Harnack, TU 3.3–4 (1888), 440–452

139–140 Maximilian: no title (BHL 5813) = Ruinart

143–146 *Passio Marcelli* (BHL 5254)
H. Delehaye, AB 41 (1923), 260–267 (two recensions)

148–150 *Passio Crispinae* (BHL 1989b)
P. Franchi de' Cavalieri, Nuove note agiografiche (ST 9, 1902), 32–35

155–159 *Passio Cypriani* (BHL 2037)

---

[10] All three texts are reprinted from G. Lazzati, Aevum 27 (1953), 490–497.

R. Reitzenstein, SB Heidelberg, Phil.-hist. Kl.
1913, Abh. 14, 12–17

162–166   *Passio Fructuosi* (BHL 3196)
P. Franchi de' Cavalieri, Note agiografiche 8
(Rome, 1935), 183–194

169–174   *Martyrium Apollonii* (BHG 149)
E. T. Klette, TU 15.2 (1897), 92–130; G.
Rauschen, Monumenta minora saeculi secundi
(Bonn, 1914), 69–88

178–189   *Passio Felicitatis et Perpetuae* (BHL 6633)
C. J. M. J. van Beek (Nijmegen, 1936), cf. Aevum
30 (1956), 30–35

191–200   *Passio Mariani et Iacobi* (BHL 131)
P. Franchi de' Cavalieri, ST 3 (1900), 47–61

202–213   *Passio Montani et Lucii* (BHL 6009)
P. Franchi de' Cavalieri, RQ, Supp. 8 (1898),
71–86, cf. Note agiografiche 3 (ST 22, 1909),
3–31

## Musurillo (1972)

Herbert Musurillo's *Acts of the Christian Martyrs* (Oxford,
1972) is very far from being the 'new critical edition of the
Acts of the Christian martyrs' promised in its preface, while
his English translations and notes abound in easily avoidable
and sometimes comic errors.[11] These facts are well known,

---

[11] F. Millar, JTS, N. S. 24 (1973), 239–243. Two examples will illustrate the general point: (1) 'Hilarianus procurator' in the *Passion of Perpetua* 6.3 is translated 'Hilarianus the governor' and his office is glossed
as 'proconsul Africae' (113), even though the text clearly states that he
was a procurator acting in place of a deceased proconsul (*qui tunc loco
proconsulis … defuncti ius gladii acceperat*); (2) a sentence in the *Passion*

and the Clarendon Press subsequently commissioned a replacement from Anthony Birley.[12] Unfortunately, Birley abandoned the task and his commission was transferred to another Roman historian, whose edition has yet to appear.[13]

For most documents Musurillo either reproduces the text of Knopf-Krüger-Ruhbach or bases his text on exactly the same modern edition or edition(s) as used in Knopf-Krüger-Ruhbach: the following list makes no attempt to distinguish between the two cases, and it gives the titles in the form which Musurillo assigns to them.[14]

I      *Martyrdom of Polycarp* (BHG 1560) = K-K-R I
II     *Acts of Carpus, Papylus and Agathonice* (BHG 293; BHL 1622m) = K-K-R II

---

*of Pionius* which means 'I shall ask for you to be condemned to <fight in> my son's gladiatorial games' is translated as 'After your condemnation I shall ask for you to compete in single combat with my son' (161). Musurillo's inaccurate translation of the *Passion of Perpetua* is reprinted in E. A. Petroff, Medieval Women's Visionary Literature (Oxford, 1986), 70–77, cf. 45–46. R. Rader, A Lost Tradition: Women Writers of the Early Church, ed. P. Wilson-Kastner (Lanham, MD & London, 1981), 19–30, provides a superior, though still imperfect translation

[12] See the verdict on Musurillo delivered by G. W. Bowersock, Martyrdom and Rome (Cambridge, 1995), 41 n. 1: 'an unreliable work, which a new edition prepared by A. Birley will soon replace.' It may not be inappropriate to record that I read Musurillo's manuscript as a referee for the Clarendon Press some years before it was published and that the Press rejected my assessment that Musurillo's texts, translations and notes all needed to be completely redone by a competent scholar.

[13] On publishers' lack of wisdom in commissioning scholars who have little or no previous experience in editing to produce critical editions of ancient texts, see the sage remarks of M. L. West, Textual Criticism and Editorial Technique (Stuttgart, 1973), 62.

[14] Musurillo rightly discards K-K-R XI and XII: for proof of their inauthenticity, see, respectively, Delehaye, Passions 2 (1966), 246–258; H. Lietzmann, Kleine Schriften 1 (TU 67, 1958), 241–243.

| III | *Martyrdom of Ptolemaeus and Lucius* = K-K-R III |
| IV | *Acts of Justin and his Companions* (BHG 972z; 973; 974), Recensions A, B, C |
| | Lazzati, Sviluppi (1956), 120–127, cf. Aevum 27 (1953), 473–497 |
| V | *Letter of the Churches of Lyons and Vienne* = K-K-R V |
| VI | *Acts of the Scillitan Martyrs* (BHL 7527) = K-K-R VI |
| VII | *Martyrdom of Apollonius* (BHG 149) = K-K-R VII |
| VIII | *Martyrdom of Perpetua and Felicitas* (BHL 6633) |
| | C. J. M. J. van Beek (Nijmegen, 1936) |
| IX | *Martyrdom of Potamiaena and Basilides* = K-K-R IX |
| X | *Martyrdom of Pionius* (*BHG* 1546) = K-K-R X |
| XI | *Acts of Cyprian* (*BHL* 2037) |
| | R. Reitzenstein, SB Heidelberg, Phil.-hist. Kl. 1913, 12–17 |
| XII | *Martyrdom of Fructuosus and Companions* (BHL 3196) |
| | P. Franchi de' Cavalieri, Note agiografiche 8 (ST 65, 1935), 183–194 |
| XIII | *Martyrdom of Conon* (BHG 361) = K-K-R XIV (abbreviated)[15] |
| XIV | *Martyrdom of Marian and James* (BHL 131) = K-K-R XV |

---

[15] On the fictitious nature of this text, see esp. A. Harnack, Chronologie der altchristlichen Literatur bis Eusebius 2 (Leipzig, 1904), 469–470; J. E. Taylor, Christians and the Holy Places (Oxford, 1993), 243. The *praefectura Pamphyliae* which the *Martyrdom of Conon* alleges in the 250s is an obvious anachronism.

XV       *Martyrdom of Montanus and Lucius* (*BHL* 6009) = K-K-R XVI

XVI      *Martyrdom of Marinus* = K-K-R XVIII

XVII     *Acts of Maximilian* (BHL 5813) = K-K-R XIX = Ruinart

XVIII    *Acts of Marcellus* (BHL 5254) = K-K-R XX

XIX      *Martyrdom of Julius the Veteran* (BHL 4555) = K-K-R XXVII

XX       *Martyrdom of Felix the Bishop* (BHL 2893s) = K-K-R XXII

XXI      *Martyrdom of Dasius* (BHG 491) = K-K-R XXIII

XXII     *Martyrdom of Agape, Irene, Chione and Companions* (BHG 34) = K-K-R XXIV

XXIII    *Martyrdom of Irenaeus Bishop of Sirmium* (BHL 4466) = K-K-R XXVI

XXIV     *Martyrdom of Crispina* (BHL 1989b) = K-K-R XXIX

XXV      *Acts of Euplus* (BHG 629; BHL 2728) = K-K-R XXV

XXVI     *Letter of Phileas* = K-K-R XXX

XXVII    *Acts of Phileas* (BHG, Auct. 1513k; BHL 6799)
         Greek: V. Martin, Papyrus Bodmer XX: Apologie de Philéas évêque de Thmouis (Coulogny-Geneva, 1964), 24–52
         Latin: F. Halkin, AB 81 (1963), 19–27

XXVIII   *Testament of the Forty Martyrs of Sebaste* (BHG 1203) = K-K-R XXXII

The existing collections mislead by reproducing texts that have no right to be regarded as either authentic or contemporary (K-K-R II, VII, XI, XII, XIV, XXI, XXIII, XXVI, XXVII; Musurillo II, VII, XIII, XIX, XXI, XXIII) and involve themselves in inconsistencies by including quotations of and paraphrases by Eusebius (K-K-R V, IX, XVIII; = Musurillo V, IX, XVI), while excluding Eusebius' quotation of the description by Dionysius, the bishop of Alexandria during the Valerianic persecution, of his court appearance before Aemilianus, the deputy prefect of Egypt (*HE* 7.11.6–11), which has at least an equal claim to be included.[16] For the purposes of the present work, therefore, I have drawn up my own canon of hagiographical documents from the period 150–313 which I regard as authentic and / or contemporary either wholly or in significant part and which are normally cited throughout the present work in the form 'Barnes I' etc.[17] My canon is divided into separate lists according to the literary form of each text, but the texts are numbered chronologically, as in the twentieth century collections, and I note recent critical editions which I have used in addition to the standard collection of Knopf-Krüger-Ruhbach.

(A) Texts in protocol form (with or without a record of the execution of the martyrs)

II          *Acts of Justin and his Companions* (K-K-R,
            pp. 125–126)
            160/168
            A. Hilhorst, Atti (1987), 52–56
III         *Acts of the Scillitan Martyrs* (K-K-R VI)
            180
            A. A. R. Bastiaensen, Atti (1987), 100–104

---

[16] Chapter II.

[17] On modern discussions of all the texts in Knopf-Krüger-Ruhbach and Musurillo (and some others), see the surveys by V Saxer, Hagiographies, ed. G. Philippart 1 (Turnhout, 1994), 29–64 (Africa); F. Scorza Barcellona, Hagiographies 3 (2001), 44–84 (other areas).

---

[18] On the various versions of the *Acts of Cyprian*, see R. Reitzenstein, Nachrichten Göttingen 1919, 177–219.

[19] For a list of editions and manuscripts, F. Masai, Scriptorium 20 (1966), 11–15. On the complicated textual problems posed by the variant readings in the two recensions as published by H. Delehaye, AB 41 (1923), 260–267, see B. de Gaiffier, Archivum Latinitatis Medii Aevi 16 (1941), 127–136; AB 61 (1943), 116–139; F. Masai, Byzantion 35 (1965), 277–290; Vivarium 3 (1965), 95–114; Scriptorium 20 (1966), 16–30; de Gaiffier, Archivos Leonenses 23 (1969), 13–23; F. Dolbeau, AB 90 (1972), 329–335. The *Acts of Marcellus* are argued to be 'une composition littéraire qu'on a tort de traiter comme un document officiel' composed towards the end of the fourth century by C. Zuckerman, Travaux et Mémoires 14 (Paris, 2002), 626–627.

## The Classification of Early Hagiographical Texts

In 1921 Hippolyte Delehaye's classic study of 'the passions of the martyrs and literary genres' drew a basic distinction between historical passions on the one hand and panegyrics, epic passions and hagiographical novels on the other.[1] Within the former category Delehaye evaluated 'les passions historiques' under the three headings of the hagiography of Smyrna, the hagiography of Carthage and a miscellaneous category of isolated texts.[2] This primarily geographical classification of the authentic and contemporary documents brings out an important fact about early Christian hagiography. For the period between the reign of Antoninus Pius and Gallienus' de facto recognition of Christianity as a legally tolerated religion in 260, the ten texts listed as wholly authentic and / or genuine in Appendix 2 comprise

(1) the *Martyrdom of Polycarp* (Barnes I) and the *Passion of Pionius* (Barnes V) from Smyrna;[3]
(2) a series of African texts which were almost certainly all preserved in Carthage, even though Marianus and

---

[1] The first four of the six chapters of Delehaye, Passions (1966), have the titles: 'les passions historiques' (15–131), 'les panégyriques' (133–169), 'les passions épiques' (171–226) and 'genres secondaires et genres mixtes' (227–258).

[2] Delehaye, Passions (1966), 15–131.

[3] In this context, Delehaye, Passions (1966), 22–26, also discussed the inauthentic *Vita Polycarpi*, which is a fifth century composition (BHG 1561).

James were executed in Numidia: the *Acts of the Scillitan Martyrs* (Barnes III); the *Passion of Perpetua* (Barnes IV); the *Acts of Cyprian* (Barnes V); the *Acts and Vision of Montanus and Lucius* (Barnes VIII); and the *Martyrdom of Marianus and James* (Barnes IX);

(3) the *Acts of Justin* (Barnes II) from Rome; the *Martyrdom of Fructuosus and his companions* (Barnes VII) from Tarragona;

(4) a speech delivered in Carthage, probably on 14 September 259 (Barnes X).

Delehaye included the *Acts of Carpus, Papylus and Agathonice* (K-K-R II = Musurillo II) among the hagiography of Smyrna, but he assigned the letter of the Gallic churches describing martyrdoms at Lyons (K-K-R V= Musurillo V), to the third, miscellaneous category.[4] Eusebius, however, found both the *Acts of Carpus, Papylus and Agathonice* and the letter of the Gallic churches in a collection of hagiographical documents that included the accounts of the martyrdoms of Polycarp, which probably occurred in 157, and of Pionius in 250 (*HE* 4.15.46–48). This letter too, therefore, belongs by right to the 'hagiography of Smyrna,' since it was preserved by its recipients in the Roman province of Asia, not in Gaul by its writer (who is often identified as Irenaeus of Lyons), and it survived because it was included in the lost collection of early martyrdoms used by Eusebius, which (it may plausibly be supposed) was compiled in Smyrna.[5]

Lazzati's study of 'the developments of the literature on the martyrs in the first four centuries' approached the earliest hagiographical texts from the standpoint of a student of Christian literature rather than that of a historian of the

---

[4]  Delehaye, Passions (1966), 89–91.
[5]  Chapter II.

Christian church.[6] Lazzati consistently looked for *un filo conduttore* that would reveal a clear path of literary development. In accordance with these evolutionary expectations, he identified the original and primary form of literature about martyrs as the letter, and he argued that what determined the subsequent development of hagiographical literature was its liturgical use, other types of hagiographical text being produced as 'dramatic readings' composed for and used in a liturgical context. Admittedly, there is very early attestation of liturgical use of hagiographical texts in the *Passion of Perpetua* (Barnes IV), whose preface refers to the reading of 'ancient examples of faith' (*si vetera fidei exempla ... propterea in litteris sunt digesta, ut lectione eorum quasi repraesentatione rerum et Deus honoretur et homo confortetur, etc.*) and whose epilogue urges that any who magnify, honour and adore the glory of Christ Jesus ought to read the *Passion* 'for the edification of the church' (21.5: *quam qui magnificat et honorificat et adorat, utique et haec non minora veteribus exempla in aedificationem ecclesiae legere debet*). But Lazzati's theory hardly does justice to the variety of the authentic material that survives from the pre-Constantinian period. It is hard to see how the Greek *Acts of Justin* from the 160s (Barnes II) and the even plainer Latin *Acts of the Scillitan Martyrs* from 180 (Barnes III) can represent any sort of literary evolution from the epistolary form of the earliest hagiographical document, the *Martyrdom of Polycarp* (Barnes I), which was written in Asia and is not known to have circulated as far afield as Rome or Africa. Nor does Lazzati even attempt to explain how Pontius' speech on the first anniversary of the martyrdom of Cyprian (Barnes X) might fit into his postulated schema of development. Moreover,

---

[6] See the statement of aims in Lazzati, *Sviluppi* (1956), 1–12.

while documents in protocol style predominate among the genuine hagiographical records of the 'Great Persecution' (Barnes XII–XIX), the only genuine hagiographical document from the brief and selective resumption of persecution by Licinius is a letter of condemned Christians from prison (Gebhardt XII = K-K-R XXXII = Musurillo XXVIII).

Perhaps more illuminating than Delehaye's observations about the geographical provenance of early Christian hagiographical documents or Lazzati's hypothesis of literary development offered by Lazzati is a simple chronological observation: the genuine early documents come from three distinct periods of persecution separated by gaps of a generation or more. The earliest Christian martyr whose death is described in an extant text is bishop Polycarp of Smyrna in the late 150s, and three more genuine texts survive from the next fifty years (Barnes I–IV). Then a gap supervenes from the early third century to the persecutions of Decius in 250, from which one authentic text survives (Barnes V) and of Valerian in 257–259, from which a cluster of five genuine hagiographical texts survive (Barnes VI–X). Then there is another gap: since no Christians were executed for their religious beliefs between 260 and 303,[7] there were no martyrs to commemorate. Moreover, the most important contemporary hagiographical text from the 'Great Persecution' that started in 303 is Eusebius' *Martyrs of Palestine*,

---

[7] Although Eusebius, *HE* 7.15, explicitly dates the martyrdom of Marinus to the sole reign of Gallienus, the charge which he reports that Marinus' rival made against him is that he was not allowed to be a centurion because 'he was a Christian and did not sacrifice to the emperors' (μὴ ἐξεῖναι μὲν ἐκείνῳ τῆς Ῥωμαίων μετέχειν ἀξίας κατὰ τοὺς παλαιοὺς νόμους, Χριστιανῷ γε ὄντι καὶ τοῖς βασιλεῦσι μὴ θύοντι, κατηγόρει). This appears to imply a date before the capture of Valerian by the Persians in 260: G. W. Clarke, CAH² 12 (2005), 638 n.123, cf. 646.

which he composed to commemorate friends and associates who had suffered martyrdom between 303 and 311 before including a revised and abbreviated version in one of the editions of his *Ecclesiastical History*.[8] It is also evident from the *Acta purgationis Felicis* of 315 and the *Gesta apud Zenophilum* from 320 (reproduced as Gebhardt XXI and XX respectively) that non-Christian local magistrates who were compelled by orders from higher authority to seize Christian property and arrest Christians in 303 kept careful records of their actions – perhaps in order to defend themselves later when the political situation changed and persecution ended.[9]

---

[8] App. 5.
[9] Chapter III.

# Two Problems in the *Martyrdom of Polycarp*

Eusebius included the *Martyrdom of Polycarp* (Barnes I) in his *Ecclesiastical History* (*HE* 4.15.1–45): after an introduction which dates the episode to the joint reign of Marcus Aurelius and Lucius Verus (1), Eusebius first quotes the heading of the letter of the church of Smyrna (2–3), then paraphrases the first part of the letter (4–14 = *Mart. Pol.* 1–7) before quoting verbatim the sections describing the arrest, trial and death of Polycarp himself (15–45 = *Mart. Pol.* 8–19.1$^a$). Comparison of the original and Eusebius' version has encouraged the speculative hypothesis that the extant *Martydom of Polycarp* has undergone substantial rewriting and interpolation.[1] A sober assessment, however, suggests that, while Eusebius' paraphrase of the first part of the letter distorts the original, it probably does so unintentionally; for when Eusebius quotes the larger part of the letter, he quotes faithfully and accurately, though there are minor verbal divergences and the transmitted text of the *Martyrdom* contains a miraculous detail which he may deliberately have omitted (the dove in 16.1) and continues for more than twenty lines beyond the point at which Eusebius ends (19.1$^b$–20).[2]

---

[1] H. Campenhausen, Aus der Frühzeit des Christentums (Tübingen, 1963), 253–301, H. Conzelmann, Nachrichten Göttinger Akademie 1978, N. 2, 41–58.

[2] As argued in JTS 19 (1968), 510–512. Subsequent arguments of a number of other scholars are assembled and summarized by W. R. Schoedel, ANRW 2.27.1 (1993), 351–354.

## The Year of the Martyrdom

In the medieval manuscripts, the text of the letter of the church of Smyrna is followed by a series of appendices. The first is a chronological notice, which has always been central to historical investigations of the *Martyrdom of Polycarp*:

Μαρτυρεῖ δὲ ὁ μακάριος Πολύκαρπος μηνὸς Ξανθικοῦ δευτέρᾳ ἱσταμένου κατὰ δὲ ῾Ρωμαίους πρὸ ἑπτὰ καλανδῶν Μαρτίων σαββάτῳ μεγάλῳ ὥρᾳ ὀγδόῃ. συνελήφθη δὲ ὑπὸ ῾Ηρώδου ἐπὶ ἀρχιερέως Φιλίππου Τραλλιανοῦ, ἀνθυπατεύοντος Στατίου Κοδράτου, βασιλεύοντος δὲ εἰς τοὺς αἰῶνας τοῦ κυρίου ἡμῶν Ἰησοῦ Χριστοῦ.

The blessed Polycarp died as a martyr on the second day from the start of the month Xanthicus (seven days before the kalends of March according to the Romans), on a great Sabbath, at the eighth hour. He was arrested by Herodes, in the year when Philippus of Tralles was high priest and Statius Quadratus proconsul, with our Lord Jesus Christ reigning for ever. (21)

It is not known when this notice was added, but whoever added it certainly possessed independent and accurate prosopographical information that cannot be gleaned from the preceding text. He knew that the proconsul of Asia who tried and condemned Polycarp, whom the letter leaves anonymous (3, 4, 9–12), was Statius Quadratus, who is independently attested as proconsul by an inscription from Magnesia ad Sipylum (IGRR 4.1339 = Inschriften von Magnesia am Sipylos 19), and he knew that Philippus the Asiarch (12.2) came from Tralles, a fact abundantly confirmed by inscriptions from that city (Inschriften von Tralleis und Nysa 51 = OGIS 499; 126–131).

The proconsul Statius Quadratus (it cannot be doubted) is the L. Statius Quadratus who was ordinary consul in 142.[3]

---

[3] PIR S 640; W. Hüttl, Antoninus Pius 2 (Prague, 1933), 52–55; G. Alföldy, Konsulat und Senatorenstand unter den Antoninen (Bonn,

In the nineteenth century, the excellent epigrapher William Waddington dated Quadratus' proconsulate of Asia to the proconsular year 154–155,[4] and his date was widely accepted for many decades,[5] though several scholars preferred to date both Quadratus' proconsulate and Polycarp's martyrdom one year later.[6] However, since 156 was a leap year, the second day of the month Xanthicus corresponded to 24 February in the Roman calendar.[7] Moreover, only former consuls of some years standing were permitted to draw lots for one of the two senior proconsulates, and epigraphical discoveries and prosopographical investigations since Waddington have established that in the Antonine period no proconsul of either Africa or Asia went out to his province after an interval of less than thirteen or more than sixteen years after he held the consular fasces in Rome.[8] Hence it

---

1977), 214–215; B. E. Thomasson, Laterculi Praesidum 1 (Gothenburg, 1984), 227–230; PIR² S 883.

[4] W. H. Waddington, Mémoires de l'Académie des Inscriptions et Belles Lettres 26.1 (Paris, 1867) 232–241, 268; Fastes des provinces asiatiques de l'empire romain depouis leur origine jusqu'au règne de Dioclétien 1 (Paris, 1872), 219–221, evaluated at length in the light of earlier discussions, by J. B. Lightfoot, Apostolic Fathers 2. S. Ignatius. S. Polycarp 1.1² (London, 1889), 646–677.

[5] See recently C. E. Hill, From the Lost Teaching of Polycarp (Tübingen, 2006), 73: 'I accept what is probably now the consensus date of 155 or 156 for Polycarp's martyrdom.'

[6] E. g, C. H. Turner, Studia Biblica et Ecclesiastica 2 (1890), 105–129; T. D. Barnes, JTS, N. S. 19 (1968), 513–514.

[7] E. Schwartz, Abh. Göttingen, Phil.-hist. Kl., N. F. 8.6 (1905) 125–130.

[8] R. Syme, ZPE 51 (1983), 271–290 = Roman Papers 4 (Oxford, 1988), 325–346. As a sole exception Syme admitted P. Mummius Sisenna, ordinary consul in 133, who was generally held to have been proconsul of Asia in 150–151 on the strength of an inscription from Thera (IG 12.3.325 = Sylloge³ 852), two years after T. Flavius

would have been anomalous for a consul of 142, as Quadratus was, to proceed to the province of Asia as proconsul before the middle months of 155. Quadratus, therefore, can hardly have been proconsul of Asia in 154–155. Accordingly, first Géza Alföldy, then Ronald Syme invoked prosopographical criteria to fix his probable proconsular year as 156–157.[9]

The chronological notice appended to the *Martyrdom of Polycarp* also dates the bishop's death to the year when Philippus was high-priest, that is, to the year in which Philippus was high-priest of the provincial council of Asia. Modern discussions of the value and accuracy of this statement have laboured under two serious misapprehensions which have long obscured a simple truth. First, erroneous assumptions were made about the date of the fifty-sixth Olympic games at Tralles, at which C. Julius Philippus was high-priest and agonothete for the second time (Inschriften von Tralleis und Nysa 127–130: in 126 and 131 the numeral is missing and has sometimes wrongly been supplemented as '53' or '57').[10] Although Louis Robert established many

---

Tertullus, one of the suffect consuls of the same year (CIL 6.858, cf. p. 3007; 16.76), who was proconsul in 148–149 (AE 1981.845), and he explained the anomaly by the hypothesis that Sisenna was governor of Syria when his time for the sortition came up (ZPE 51 [1983], 277–278). But K. Dietz, Chiron 23 (1993), 295–311, has shown that the proconsul attested at Thera is P. Mummius Sisenna Rutilianus, son of the consul of 133, consul suffect in 146 and probably proconsul of Asia in 160–161 (cf. ILS 1101).

[9] Alföldy, Konsulat und Senatorenstand (n. 3), 214–215; Syme, ZPE 51 (1983), 280–282.

[10] PIR² J 460, which appeared in 1967, appealed to Edhem bey, BCH 28 (1904), 80. But on the point at issue, Edhem bey had simply appealed to the communication from W. M. Ramsay printed by J. R. S. Sterrett, Papers of the American School of Classical Studies at Athens 1

years ago that the Olympic games of Tralles were founded at the time of Pompey's reorganisation of Asia Minor after the defeat of Mithridates in the later 60s B. C., he then went astray by accepting Lightfoot's erroneous date of 155 for the martyrdom of Polycarp and deducing that 'c'est en qualité d'*archiereus* municipal qu'il (sc. Philippus) apparaît sur les inscriptions de Tralles'[11] – a corollary mistakenly repeated long ago by the present writer.[12]

Second, the identity of Asiarchs and high-priests of the province of Asia seems to be guaranteed by a fragment of the third century jurist Modestinus, who stated that

ἔθνους ἱερ<αρχία> (*or* ἱερ<ωσύνη>) οἷον Ἀσιαρχία Βιθυναρχία Καππαδο-καρχία παρέχει ἀλειτουργησίαν ἀπὸ ἐπιτροπῶν, τοῦτ᾽ ἐστὶν ἕως ἂν ἄρχῃ

The high-priesthood of a province such as Asiarchate, Bithynarchate, Cappadocarchate confers exemption from the liturgy of being a guardian, but only during the tenure of the office. (*Digest* 27.1.6.14 = Modestinus, frag. 60 Lenel)

However, against the apparent identity of the two titles stand two facts. First, the lists of known high-priest of Asia and Asiarchs published by David Magie in 1950, Margarete

(1885), 102–104, where Ramsay rejected Sterrett's earlier view that the era of the Trallian Olympiads was 37 B. C. (Ath. Mitt. 8 [1883], 324). Ramsay's hypothesis, which Lightfoot, Apostolic Fathers 2.1.1² (1889), 628–635, 667, not only embraced with enthusiasm, but claimed to have reached independently (632 n. 2), was that Hadrian founded the games when he visited Tralles in 129, but that the Trallians numbered the first celebration as the fifty-first in order (as Ramsay put it) to lend the games 'a spurious antiquity by the fiction that they were already fifty penteterides old.'

[11] L. Robert, Rev. phil. 56 (1930), 33–35 = Opera Minora Selecta 2 (Amsterdam, 1969), 1133–1135; Études anatoliennes. Recherches sur les inscriptions grecques d'Asia Mineure (Paris, 1937), 423–428.

[12] JTS, N. S. 18 (1967), 433–437; 19 (1968), 512.

Rossner in 1974 and Maria Domitilla Campanile in 1994
contain more names than can comfortably be accommodated in the relevant time-span of less than 250 years: Magie
listed more than 70 high-priests and 120 Asiarchs, Rossner
well over 200 in the two categories together, while Campanile's numbered list of certain high-priests and Asiarchs
has 192 names, and Stephen Friesen, who excluded persons
recorded only by a unique item of evidence, assembled a
list of twelve men attested more than once as both Asiarch
and high-priest, fifteen attested more than once only as
high-priest and forty four attested more than once as only
Asiarch.[13] Second, an inscription of Tarsus honours a man
as ἀνυπέρβλητον κιλικάρχην ἀπὸ ἀρχιερωσύνης (SEG 27.947:
'Cilicarch after being high-priest').[14] The most probable
hypothesis, therefore, is surely that the two titles have different meanings: whereas the high-priesthood of Asia was an
office with an annual tenure, 'Asiarch' was a title of rank or
distinction conferred more widely on leading citizens of the
province of Asia.[15] Now C. Julius Philippus, who had been

---

[13] D. Magie, Roman Rule in Asia Minor 2 (Princeton, 1950),
1601–1603, 1604–1607; M. Rossner, Studi Clasice 16 (1974), 101–
142; M. D. Campanile, I sacerdoti del Koinon d'Asia (I sec a. C. – III
sec. d. C. Contributo allo studio della romanizzazione delle élites pro-
vinciali nell'Oriente Greco (Pisa, 1994), 29–157; S. J. Friesen, ZPE 126
(1999), 288–290. The earliest high-priest of Asia listed by Campanile is
M. Antonius Lepidus of Thyatira in 2/1 B. C. (W. H. Buckler & D. M.
Robinson, Sardis 7.1 [Leiden, 1932], 19, no. 8 lines 99–100), while
the latest datable with any precision is an Asiarch from the reign of
Caracalla (Inschriften von Ephesos 740, cf. 300).

[14] Published by L. Robert, BCH 101 (1977), 88, with Fig 16, and
reprinted in his Documents d'Asie Mineure (Paris, 1987), 46.

[15] For the long controversy over whether both titles refer to the
high-priesthood of Asia, see esp. Magie, Roman Rule (n. 13), 1298–
1301; J. Deininger, Die Provinziallandtage der römischen Kaiserzeit

honoured as an Asiarch at Olympia on the occasion of the 232$^{nd}$ Olympic Games in 149 (Inschriften von Olympia 455 = OGIS 498), is attested as high-priest of Asia when he presided over the fifty-sixth Trallian Olympic games (Inschriften von Tralleis und Nysa 127–130, cf. 126, 131). If these games were first celebrated in 64–63 B.C. (the precise year is not directly attested and Robert preferred 63–62 B.C.), then the fifty-sixth games were celebrated in 156–157 – and the author of the chronological appendix to the *Martyrdom* was correct when he stated that Philippus was high-priest of Asia in the proconsulate of Statius Quadratus. The convergence of the two independent calculations indicates that Polycarp was martyred on 23 February 157.[16]

## The Day of the Martyrdom

The letter of the church of Smyrna states that Polycarp was arrested on 'a great sabbath': ὄνῳ καθίσαντες αὐτὸν ἤγαγον εἰς τὴν πόλιν ὄντος σαββάτου μεγάλου (8.1), and the later notice

von Augustus bis zum Ende des dritten Jahrhunderts (Munich, 1974), 41–50; P. Herz, Tyche 7 (1992), 93–115; M. Wörrle, Chiron 22 (1992), 368–370; Campanile, Sacerdoti (n. 13), 18–22; M. Carter, GRBS 44 (2004), 41–68; for the strongest statements of the case for and the case against identity, Friesen, ZPE 126 (1999), 275–290; Steine und Wege, ed. P. Scherrer, H. Taeuber & H. Thür (Vienna, 1999), 303–307; P. Weiss, Widerstand – Anpassung – Integration, ed. N. Ehrhardt & L.M. Günther (Stuttgart, 2002), 241–254.

[16] Arguments for a date in the reign of Marcus Aurelius rely upon preferring Eusebius to the original *Martyrdom of Polycarp*: see the survey of modern opinions and arguments in favour of 167 advanced by P. Brind'Amour, AB 98 (1980), 456–462, accepted by P. Devos, AB 107 (1988), 212–213. The case advanced for a date of 177 by H. Grégoire & P. Orgels, AB 69 (1951), 1–38, is a travesty of scholarship.

appended to the letter gives the day and month of Polycarp's martyrdom according to both the calendar of the province of Asia[17] and the Julian calendar: it was the second day of the Asian month Xanthikos, and the seventh day before the kalends of March, that is, 23 February, and the day was a 'great sabbath' (21). Now the Roman and the Asian calendars diverged over how they accommodated the extra day needed in leap years. In a leap year the Julian calendar added an extra sixth day before the kalends of March, so that *ante diem septimum kalendas Martias* always corresponded to our 23 February. The Asian calendar inserted the extra day at the start of the month Xanthikos, the first four days (corresponding to 21–24 February) being Ξανθικοῦ Σεβαστή, Ξανθικοῦ Σεβαστὴ δευτέρα, Ξανθικοῦ πρώτη, Ξανθικοῦ δευτέρα so that in a leap year the Asian equivalent of *ante diem septimum kalendas Martias* was Ξανθικοῦ πρώτη, not Ξανθικοῦ δευτέρα.[18] Hence 23 February 156 is excluded, on technical chronological grounds, as a possible date for the martyrdom of Polycarp.[19] But in February 157, when Statius Quadratus was proconsul of Asia and Philippus of Tralles high-priest of the province, the 23rd of the month fell on a Tuesday, not a Saturday.[20] In 155, however, 23 February did

---

[17] Not the local calendar of Smyrna, in which the sixth month was called Hierosebaston: L. Robert, REA 38 (1936), 23–28 = Opera Minora 2 (n. 11), 786–791.

[18] A. E. Samuel, Greek and Roman Chronology (Munich, 1972), 181–182; Brind'Amour, AB 98 (1980), 459.

[19] Despite C. H. Turner, Studia Biblica et Ecclesiastica 2 (1890), 105–129; E. Schwartz, Abh. Göttingen, Phil.-hist. Kl., N. F. 8.6 (1905) 125–138, T. D. Barnes, JTS, N. S. 19 (1968), 513–514.

[20] Calculated from the tables in E. J. Bickerman, The Chronology of the Ancient World[2] (Ithaca & London, 1980), 60; Oxford Companion to the Year, ed. B. Blackburn & L. Holford-Strevens (Oxford, 1999), 832.

fall on a Saturday, and it was from this fact that Lightfoot argued that Polycarp's death occurred on 23 February 155.[21] Although Lightfoot's date held sway for many decades, it is too early for both the proconsulate of Quadratus and the provincial high-priesthood of Philippus.

What then of the correlation of 23 February with a 'great sabbath' on which Lightfoot relied? And what is meant by 'great sabbath'? Lightfoot stated the problem clearly long ago.[22] However, although the problem has often been discussed since Lightfoot, no generally agreed solution to it has emerged,[23] and some scholars have, perhaps unconsciously,

---

[21] Lightfoot, Apostolic Fathers 2.1² (n. 10), 677–722.

[22] Lightfoot, Apostolic Fathers 2.1² (n. 10), 709–715, noted that the day between Good Friday and Easter was first called 'the great sabbath' in the late fourth century and that 23 February was too early for a 'great sabbath' to be the sabbath preceding the Jewish Passover, but went astray by suggesting that the Jewish and pagan festivals were (1) the Feast of Purim, which (he argued on the basis of his dating of the martyrdom of Polycarp) fell on 23 February in both 155 and 250 and (2) a meeting of the provincial council of Asia connected with imperial cult.

[23] See P. Devos, AB 108 (1990), 293–206; L. Robert, Le martyre de Pionios prêtre de Smyrne, revised and completed by G. W. Bowersock & C. P. Jones (Washington, 1994), 50; G. W. Bowersock, Martyrdom and Rome (Cambridge, 1995), 82–84. Bowersock's discussion is variously defective: not only does he repeat from the Oxford Dictionary of Byzantium 2 (Oxford, 1991), 1205–1206, the false claim that Athanasius, *Festal Letter* 2 attests the celebration of Lent in Egypt in 330, when that letter was in fact written for Easter 352, but he ignores what appears to be the well-established fact that a forty-day fast before Easter was in origin a western custom, which was only introduced into the East in the fourth century, perhaps on the initiative of Constantine himself at the Council of Nicaea in 325: see L. Duchesne, Origines du culte chrétien⁵ (Paris, 1920), 255–256; T. D. Barnes, JTS, N. S. 41 (1990), 261–262; Athanasius (1993), 185, 186, 190–191. Hence, whatever, the words 'great sabbath' mean in the *Martyrdom of Polycarp*,

supplied a definite article and turned the indefinite 'great sabbath' into 'the great sabbath.'[24] As it happens, the correlation of 23 February and a 'great sabbath' is attested in only one other text. The *Passion of Pionius* states that the martyr was arrested and taken for preliminary questioning together with several other Christians of Smyrna on the second day of the sixth month, which was the anniversary of the death of Polycarp and also a great sabbath:

μηνὸς ἕκτου δευτέρᾳ ἐνισταμένου σαββάτου μεγάλου,[25] ἐν τῇ γενεθλίῳ ἡμέρᾳ τοῦ μακαρίου μάρτυρος Πολυκάρπου (2.1).

Moreover, this day, 23 February 250, was a holiday for both Jews and gentiles:

ἐγεμίσθη πᾶσα ἡ ἀγορὰ καὶ αἱ ὑπερῷαι στοαὶ Ἑλλήνων τε καὶ Ἰουδαίων καὶ γυναικῶν· ἐσχόλαζον γὰρ διὰ τὸ εἶναι μέγα σάββατον

the agora and the upper porticoes were crowded with Greeks, Jews and women; for they were not at work because it was a great sabbath (3.6).

That appears to imply that the distinguishing characteristic, or at least one of the distinguishing characteristics, of a great

---

they can have nothing to do with Lent, since Lent was completely unknown in second century Asia Minor.

[24] Thus Robert, Bowersock & Jones, Le martyre de Pionios (n. 23), cite P. Devos, AB 108 (1990), 293–306, for the fact that Epiphanius calls Christ himself 'the Great Sabbath' (Panarion 8.6.8 [1.192.2–22 Holl], 30.32.7 [1.378.14–15], 66.85.9 [3.128.15–17]; De fide 24.2 [3.525.5–7]) and then ask: 'Est-il possible que le grand sabbat dans ces martyres indique la saison du carême?'

[25] The recent edition by A. Hilhorst, Atti (1987), 154, prints the emendation suggested by Lightfoot, Apostolic Fathers 2.1.1[2] (n. 10), 719: μηνὸς ἕκτου δευτέρᾳ ἱσταμένου, σαββάτῳ μεγάλῳ. The transmitted text is retained by Robert, Bowersock & Jones, Le martyre de Pionios (n. 23), who translate it as 'le 2 du sixième mois, au commencement du grand sabbat' (21, 33, cf. 50).

Sabbath in Smyrna in the middle of the third century was the coincidence of the Jewish Sabbath with a pagan holiday, which on 23 February was the festival of the Terminalia,[26] and 23 February was indeed a Saturday in the year 250. It may be suggested, therefore, with due hesitation and caution, that the two occurrences of the phrase 'a great sabbath' in the *Martyrdom of Polycarp* were interpolated after 250 in light of the fact that in 250 the anniversary of the death of Polycarp on which Pionius was arrested did indeed coincide with 'a great sabbath.'

Whether or not this removal of the contradictions in the evidence is acceptable, 23 February is too early for its designation as 'a great sabbath' to have any reference to either the Jewish Passover or the Christian Easter, even though similar phraseology was applied to both. In the gospel of John, the Jewish leaders ask Pontius Pilatus to kill Jesus and the two brigands crucified with him quickly and to take down their bodies from the cross in order to avoid polluting the sabbath because 'that sabbath day was a high day' (John 19.31: ἦν γὰρ μεγάλη ἡ ἡμέρα ἐκείνου τοῦ σαββάτου). Centuries later the Byzantine writer Michael Glycas explained that the evangelist 'would not have called it "great" if that sabbath had not coincided with the first day of the Feast of Unleavened Bread which is called holy in the Law:' (*Annales* 406.5–8 Bonn), while John Chrysostom supplied the definite article when he used the phrase in connection with the Crucifixion: ἐν τῷ σαββάτῳ τῷ μεγάλῳ πάλιν, ὅτι παρεδόθη ἡμῶν ὁ Κύριος, ὅτι ἐσταυρώθη, ὅτι ἀπέθανε τὸ κατὰ σάρκα, ὅτι ἐτάφη (*In prin-*

---

[26] W. Rordorf, Pietas: Festschrift für Bernhard Kötting. JAC, Ergänzungsband 8 (Münster, 1980), 245–249, followed by A. Hilhorst, Atti (1987), 454.

*cipium Actorum* [PG 51.104]).[27] The salient fact is thus that the phrase a 'great sabbath' (without the definite article) appears to occur nowhere in any ancient Greek text apart from the *Martyrdom of Polycarp* and the *Passion of Pionius* and in both these texts it refers to exactly the same day of the same month, that is, 23 February.

---

[27] The phrase 'dawn of the great sabbatical <day>' occurs in Eudocia, *De martyrio sancti Cypriani* 1.252–253: ἀλλ᾽ ὅτε δὴ ῥοδόπηχυς ἐπήλυθεν ἀργέτιςἨὼς σαββατικῆς μεγάλης).

# 5

# The *Acts of Maximilianus*

Four manuscripts of the eleventh to thirteenth centuries (two in England, one in Ireland and one in Switzerland) preserve what appears to be the documentary record of the trial of one Maximilianus who was executed for his refusal to be inducted into the Roman army at Theveste on 12 March 295 (BHL 5813). The text is of exceptional historical and cultural interest. For Maximilianus was executed not as a Christian, but because he refused to serve in the Roman army. Maximilianus believed that military service was incompatible with Christianity and under questioning he declared: 'My military service is with my Lord; I cannot serve in the army of this world' (2.8: *non possum saeculo militare*). The proconsul's verdict is equally explicit about the charge: 'Because Maximilianus has with a rebellious mind refused the military oath, it is resolved that he executed with the sword' (3.1). The *Acts of Maximilianus* are therefore central to any discussion of early Christian attitudes to war.[1] Specifically, although the terms are strictly speaking anachronistic since they were not invented until many centuries later, the *Acts* unambiguously present Maximilianus as a conscientious objector and a pacifist.[2]

---

[1] J. Helgeland, ANRW 2.23.1 (Berlin, 1979), 777–780

[2] E.g., A. Harnack, Militia Christi. Die christliche Religion und der Soldatenstand in den ersten drei Jahrhunderten (Tübingen, 1905), 84–85; Delehaye, Mélanges (1966), 375–383; P. Siniscalco, Massimil-

Although the majority of modern collections of early and authentic *acta martyrum* include the *Acts of Maximilianus* (K-K-R XIX = Lazzati, pp. 139–140 = Musurillo XVII), the first critical edition was not produced until 1987, when A. A. R. Bastiaensen broke with the conventional procedure of reprinting Ruinart's text with occasional emendations.[3] Hence historians of the Later Roman Empire with virtual unanimity have until very recently adduced the *Acts* as completely reliable and contemporary evidence for the recruitment procedures of the Roman army in the reign of Diocletian.[4] In 1998, however, a penetrating analysis of two laws of the 370s by Constantin Zuckerman brought to light the uncomfortable fact that the *Acts* not only juxtapose two different methods of obtaining new recruits for the Roman army, but that these two methods are incompatible with each other and in fact succeeded each other in time.[5]

---

iano: un obiettore di coscienza del tardo impero. Studi sulla "Passio S. Maximiliani" (Turin, 1974); P. Brock, JEH 45 (1994), 195–209.

[3] A. A. R. Bastiaensen, Atti (1987), 233–245. Siniscalco, Massimiliano (n. 2), 159–165, had merely reprinted Ruinart's text with some discussion of textual problems.

[4] E. g., W. Seston, Dioclétien et la tétrarchie 1 (Paris, 1946), 289, 301 n. 2, 311, 326 n. 2; Jones, LRE (1964), 616–617; Y. le Bohec, The Imperial Roman Army (London, 1994), 70, who deduces that 'on 12 March 295 the promagistrate in Carthage journeyed to Tebessa in order to recruit troops'; B. Campbell, The Roman Army 31 BC–AD 337. A Sourcebook (London, 1994), 12 n. 5, 237 n. 384. An exception was E. Sander, RE, Supp. 10 (1965), 680, who dismissed the *Acta Maximiliani* as a thirteenth century forgery. Recently, Y. le Bohec, L'armée romain au Bas-Empire (Paris, 2006), 57, notes that 'l'authenticité vient d'être sévèrement contestée,' but asserts that the *Acts* give a realistic description of recruitment procedures under Diocletian.

[5] C. Zuckerman, RÉByz 56 (1998), 97–121, cf. already R. Grosse, Römische Militärgeschichte von Gallienus bis zum Beginn der byzantinischen Themenverfassung (Berlin, 1920), 212–214, who made no

Pompeianus, who is described as an *advocatus* (presumably therefore an *advocatus fisci* acting on behalf of the imperial administration), begins the proceedings with the following statement:

*Fabius Victor temonarius est constitutus cum Valeriano Quintiano praeposito Caesariensi, cum bono tirone Maximiliano filio Victoris: quoniam probabilis est, rogo ut incumetur.*

Fabius Victor the temonarius is present with Valerianus Quintianus the head of the Caesariani[6] with the excellent recruit Maximilianus, the son of Victor: since he meets the requirements,[7] I ask that he be inducted. (1.1)

Other evidence indicates that for most of the fourth century the sons of veterans were legally required to enlist in the Roman army: this obligation is clearly stated in a law of Constantine (*CTh* 7.22.1 [313$^S$: 319 ms.]), Sulpicius Severus reports that Martin became a soldier in 352 because imperial legislation ordered that 'the sons of veterans be enrolled in military service' (*Life of Martin* 2.5) and the *Acts*

---

reference anywhere to the *Acts of Maximilianus*, perhaps deliberately. Zuckerman's scepticism is endorsed by J.-M. Carrié, L'armée romain de Dioclétien à Valentinien. Actes du Congrès de Lyon (12–14 septembre 2002), ed. Y. Le Bohec & C. Wolff (Lyon, 2004), 385–386, though he rejects his major premiss.

[6] The transmitted text cannot be correct: no *praepositus Caesariensis* is attested elsewhere, and the adjective must mean either 'of Caesarea' or 'of (Mauretania) Caesariensis,' neither of which makes sense. M. Durry, Mélanges de philologie, de littérature et d'histoire anciennes offerts à Alfred Ernout (Paris, 1940), 129–133, argued that the man must be a *praepositus* in charge of recruitment. I propose therefore to emend *Caesariensi* to *Caesarianis*: Caesariani appear as an organised body in several inscriptions c. 300 and at no other date: S. J. Corcoran, AT 14 (2007), 224–249.

[7] For the meaning of *probabilis*, Durry, Mélanges Ernout (n. 6), 131.

*of Maximilianus* imply that the requirement and already existed under Diocletian. In 370 Valens changed the law to make the furnishing of recruits or payment of a suitable sum in gold an annual obligation shared by all taxpayers organised into consortia (*CTh* 7.13.3), while a law of 375 reveals that the individuals who were responsible for making sure that each group fulfilled its obligation were called *temonarii* (*CTh* 7.13.7) – a term which had no place in the earlier system of recruitment. It follows that, if the *Acts of Maximilianus* really are the contemporary record of a trial held in 295, then the word *temonarius* must have been added by an editor who revised the text after 370.[8] Admittedly, as several scholars have noted,[9] the text does not state explicitly that Fabius Victor was a veteran, but the status of Maximilianus' father was presumably made clear when Maximilianus was first presented for induction into the army. For the *Acts* record only the trial and execution of Maximilianus by the proconsul: they presuppose that he has already refused induction into the army on an earlier occasion to which Pompeianus' opening statement refers.[10] Hence, if the *Acts of Maximilianus* contain an authentic record of a trial that occurred in 295, a later hand has revised the original text a century later.

Another anachronism also appears to be undeniable. The *Acts* narrate the fate of Maximilianus' body as follows:

*et Pompeiana matrona corpus eius de iudice meruit et impositum in dor-mitorio suo perduxit ad Carthaginem et sub monticulo iuxta Cyprianum martyrem secus palatium condidit. et ita post tertium decimum diem eadem matrona discessit, et illic posita est.*

---

[8] Zuckerman, REByz 56 (1998), 136–139.
[9] M. Durry, Mélanges Ernout (n. 6), 130; Siniscalco, Massimiliano (n. 2), 11 n. 27.
[10] Delehaye, Passions (1966), 79.

The matron Pompeiana obtained his body from the magistrate and, after placing it in her own burial-chamber,[11] took it to Carthage and buried it at the foot of the hill next to Cyprian the martyr near the governor's official residence. Thirteen days later the matron herself died and was laid to rest there. (3.4)

The custom of burial *ad sanctos* is well attested and was certainly frequent from the fourth century onwards.[12] But the earliest clear, indisputable and unambiguous example is dated between 309 and 338: at Altava in Mauretania Caesariensis three clerics of the same family were buried next to the *mensa* of the martyr Januarius.[13] The only earlier example of the phenomenon which has been claimed to be historical occurs in the *Acts of Maximilianus*,[14] whose account of the martyr's burial contains some obvious obscurities and implausibilities: for example, who was Pompeiana, who suddenly appears out of nowhere and abruptly dies after taking the martyr's body to Carthage, where she too was buried *iuxta Cyprianum martyrem*? And how did Pompeiana acquire the body when Maximilianus' father was present at his son's trial? Although the best modern treatment of burial *ad sanctos* accepts the two alleged burials next to Cyprian in 295 as 'the first explicit and dated example' of the phenomenon,[15]

---

[11] Musurillo, Acts (1972), 249, translates *dormitorium* as 'in her own chamber:' for the correct meaning, which corresponds to the Greek κοιμητήριον, see TLL 5.2036, s. v. dormitorius b.

[12] Delehaye, Culte (1933), 131–140. It appears in the fictitious *Acta Sebastiani* (App. 7).

[13] Y. Duval, Loca Sanctorum Africae. Le culte des martyrs en Afrique du IVe au VIIe siècle 1 (Rome, 1982), 412–417 no. 195; 2 (1982), 724, 739.

[14] V. Saxer, Morts Martyrs Reliques en Afrique chrétienne aux premiers siècles (Paris, 1980), 108.

[15] Y. Duval, Au près des saints corps et âme. L'inhumation "ad sanctos" dans la chrétienté d'Orient et d'Occident du IIIe au VIIe

it is more plausible to see the passage as a later addition designed to glorify Pompeiana rather than Maximilianus.[16]

It has recently been argued that the *Acta Maximiliani*, so far from being a late fourth or early fifth century reworking of a text from 295, are a wholesale forgery concocted no earlier than the eighth century.[17] The argument has three stages. First, apart from the *acta*, there is no clear evidence for either the existence or the cult of Maximilianus before c. 838, when Florus included him in his martyrology.[18] Second, there are similarities of phrasing between the *Acta Maximiliani* and the Latin translation of the Greek passion of Theagenes of Parium, which was composed no earlier than the 380s (BHG 2416; BHL 8106, 8107).[19] And third, Maximilianus was ordered to accept a lead seal as a sign

---

siècle (Paris, 1988), 52–55, cf. Chrétiens d'Afrique à l'aube de la paix constantinienne. Les premiers échos de la grande persécution (Paris, 2000), 399–400, 526 Fig. 3.

[16] Delehaye, Passions (1966), 81, cf. Mélanges (1966), 383.

[17] D. Woods, Hommages à Carl Deroux, ed. P. Defosse 5. Collection Latomus 279 (Brussels, 2003), 266–276. P. Brock, The Riddle of St. Maximilian of Tebessa (Toronto: privately printed, 2000), had answered Woods' earlier thesis, posted on an electronic website, that the *Acts* were composed between c. 384 and 439.

[18] Quentin, Martyrologes (1908), 345, 421, 481. The ancient calendar of the church of Carthage has lost all its entries for March (AASS, Nov. II.1 [lxxi]), and Maximilianus is absent from the *Martyrologium Hieronymianum*, but Baronius slipped him into the Roman Martyrology the guise of 'Mamilianus,' allegedly a martyr at Rome: see Comm. Mart. Rom. (1940), 94. The earliest martyrology to include Maximilianus is that of Florus, whose notice Ado reproduced in his martyrology (Quentin, Martyrologes [1908], 345, 421, 481).

[19] On the origins of the cult of Theagenes, see D. Woods, Greek Orthodox Theological Review 44 (1999), 371–417; for the three extant versions of the text, P. Franchi de' Cavalieri, Note agiografiche 4. ST 24 (1912), 179–185 (BHG 2416); AB 2 (1888), 206–210 (BHL 8106); AASS, Ian. I.133–135 (BHL 8107).

of his conscription and threatened to break it if it was put around his neck:

*Dion ad Maximilianus dixit: milita et accipe signaculum.*
*Respondit: non accipio signaculum; iam habeo signum Christi mei …*
*Dion ad officium dixit: signetur.*
*Cumque reluctaret respondit: non accipio signaculum saeculi; et si signa-*
*veris, rumpo illud quia nihil valet. ego Christianus sum: non licet mihi*
*plumbum collo portare post signum salutare domini mei Jesu Christi, filii*
*Dei vivi, quem tu ignoras …* (2.4–6).

Now, while there is no other evidence that new recruits received a lead seal as a mark of their induction into the Roman imperial army at any period, the practice of using lead seals around the neck during a census was common under Arab rule, being attested for both Mesopotamia and Egypt in the eighth century: therefore, so runs the inference, the author of the *Acts of Maximilianus* was familiar with the use of lead seals in enumeration for the *jizya*, the poll-tax levied on non-Muslims.[20]

The case, though attractive, is not conclusive. First, the coincidences of wording between the *Acts of Maximilianus* and other similar texts could be due to the fact that, like Maximilianus, Theagenes asserts that military service is incompatible with Christianity: the similarities of wording are not so extensive as to prove literary derivation in either direction. Moreover, the *Acts* get three important technical details correct. First, the consular date *Tusco et Anolino* is correct for 295, once the second name is recognised as a natural variant for Anullinus.[21] Second, the central army is correctly described in the vocabulary of the Diocletianic period and the names of the reigning emperors are stated

---

[20] Woods, Hommages à Carl Deroux (n. 17), 270–273.
[21] CLRE (1987), 124–125.

correctly, although the fourth has been corrupted in transmission:

*in sacro comitatu dominorum nostrorum Diocletian et Maximiani, Constantii et Maximi\<ani\>, milites Christiani sunt et militant.* (2.9)[22]

Third, the proconsul of Africa is named as Dion all through the text. Now, while the *Acts of Maximilianus* provide the sole evidence that a Dio(n) was proconsul of Africa under Diocletian, a proconsulate of Africa in 294–295, after Dio's consulate in 291 and shortly before he was appointed *praefectus urbi* on 11 February 296, corresponds to known career patterns of the period.[23] It seems a priori improbable that a later writer of fiction centuries later could achieve such prosopographical accuracy. But the evident anachronisms, which amount to much more than superficial retouching by a later editor, mean that the *Acts of Maximilianus* should no longer be accepted as a contemporary record from 295.

---

[22] D. Hoffmann, Das spätrömische Bewegungsheer und die Notitia Dignitatum. 2. Epigraphische Studien 7.2 (Düsseldorf, 1970), 106 n. 537; M. Speidel, Roman Army Studies 1 (Amsterdam, 1984), 397–399. On the hypothesis that Aurelius Gaius (AE 1981.777 = SEG 31.1116) left the Roman army in consequence of Galerius' purge, see Chapter III n. 19.

[23] New Empire (1982), 98, 115, 169.

# Eusebius' *Martyrs of Palestine*

For only one area of the Roman Empire does there exist any sort of systematic account of the enforcement and impact of the persecuting legislation of 303 and subsequent years.[1] Between Galerius' edict of toleration, issued in April 311, and Maximinus' resumption of persecution towards the end of the year, Eusebius of Caesarea composed a memoir of the Christians of his acquaintance who had suffered martyrdom in the Roman province of Palestina in the persecution that began in 303. The preface to the long recension of the *Martyrs of Palestine* makes the scope and intentions of this memoir clear. It was incumbent, Eusebius believed, that 'those who dwelled with the combatants' should bequeathe to posterity a written record of 'the conflicts which were illustrious' in each province. As for himself,

I pray that I may be able to speak of those with whom I was personally conversant, and that they may associate with me – those in whom the whole province of Palestine glories, because even in the midst of our land the Saviour of all men arose like a thirst-quenching spring. The contests then of those illustrious champions I shall relate for the general instruction and profit. (*Mart. Pal* [L] 1.8, trans. Lawlor and Oulton, with slight modifications)[2]

---

[1] Chapter III.

[2] H. J. Lawlor and J. E. L. Oulton, Eusebius: The Ecclesiastical History and the Martyrs of Palestine 1 (London, 1927), 327–400, provide parallel translations of both recensions.

Eusebius thus states explicitly that he has not set out to record all the martyrdoms that occurred in Palestine between 303 and 311, only the glorious deaths of those with whom he was personally acquainted. Nevertheless, when Gibbon concluded his account of Christianity before 324 by drawing attention to the 'melancholy truth' that Christians 'have inflicted far greater severities on each other than they had experienced from the zeal of infidels' and to the fact that the number of Protestants executed in the Spanish Netherlands under Emperor Charles V, which, on the authority of Grotius, he estimated at more than 100,000, 'far exceeded that of the primitive martyrs in the space of three centuries' in the whole of the Roman empire, he based his argument on the premiss that a total of only ninety-two Christians were martyred in the Roman province of Palestine between 303 and 311, because he believed that Eusebius gives a complete account of all the martyrs of Palestine in these eight years.[3] Gibbon's assumption about the *Martyrs of Palestine* has often been reiterated,[4] and, although it has been shown to be completely untenable as contradicting what Eusebius himself says about the scope of the work,[5] it is still sometimes repeated by incautious scholars.[6]

---

[3] E. Gibbon, The History of the Decline and Fall of the Roman Empire 1 (London, 1776), Chapter XVI (2.137–139 Bury = 1.578–581 Womersley).

[4] Most notably by G. E. M. de Ste Croix, HTR 47 (1954), 100 = Christian Persecution, Martyrdom, and Orthodoxy (Oxford, 2006), 64: 'Of all the provinces of the empire, it is only Palestine … for which we have a full list of all the martyrdoms of the Great Persecution.'

[5] Constantine (1981), 154.

[6] E. g., J. E. Taylor, Christians and the Holy Places. The Myth of Jewish-Christian Origins (Oxford, 1993), 59–61, who cites only William Cureton's translation of the Long Recension (London & Paris,

The *Martyrs of Palestine* has a symbiotic relationship with
Eusebius' *Ecclesiastical History*, since he composed the short
recension of the *Martyrs* as an integral part of one of the
several editions of his large historical work. Eusebius began
the long recension of the *Martyrs of Palestine* soon after he
learned of the edict of toleration which the dying Galerius
issued in late April 311 en route from either Serdica or Thessalonica to Romulianum, the place of his birth, where he
had constructed a palace for his future retirement (modern
Gamzigrad in Serbia).[7] This, the earlier of the two extant
recensions, was an independent composition in which Eusebius celebrated the heroic deaths of his friends who had died
as martyrs in Palestine in 'the entire time of the persecution
in the province of Palestine' (*Mart. Pal.* [L] 13.11). In the
short recension 'the entire time of the persecution in the
province of Palestine' has become 'eight entire years' of
persecution from spring 303 to spring 311 (*Mart. Pal.* [S]
13.11), which confirms that Eusebius composed the original
edition of the *Martyrs* in 311, whether or not he had already
drafted or completed a history of the Christian church from
its beginnings down to c. 280 in seven books.[8]

The original version of the *Martyrs of Palestine* (the long
recension) has survived as a complete text only in Syriac
translation with some lacunae (between 1.2 and 1.5b, between 4.15 and 5.1, between 11.29 and 13.1 and between

---

1861) and opines that 'it is time for a new English translation of this
important text' (59 n. 48, cf. 58 n. 45).
  [7] New Empire (1982), 64.
  [8] As argued in GRBS 21 (1980), 191–201; Constantine (1981),
129–148.

13.5 and 13.9)[9] and some additions by the translator.[10] Eusebius completed it before persecution resumed towards the end of 311: the earliest precisely datable martyrdoms from this second phase of the 'Great Persecution' are those of the bishop Peter in Alexandria on 25 November 311[11] and of the prominent scholar and theologian Lucian of Antioch in Nicomedia on 7 January 312.[12]

When persecution finally ceased in 313 after Licinius' defeat of Maximinus and Maximinus' subsequent suicide, Eusebius produced an edition of his *Ecclesiastical History* which comprised Books I–VII and IX of the *History* in more or less their present form together with a rewritten and abbreviated version of the *Martyrs of Palestine* standing where

---

[9] These lacunae are duly marked in Lawlor and Oulton's translation, but I do not accept their postulate of a lacuna in 13.11 (Eusebius 1 [n. 2], 400).

[10] Apart from small verbal changes, the only demonstrable addition is an expansion of the brief speech of Theodosia in *Mart. Pal.* [L] 7.2 (p. 359 Lawlor & Oulton), where Eusebius' original Greek survives (E. Schwartz, Eusebius Werke 2.2 [GCS 9.2, 1908], 922.24–26). For most of the long recension, however, the original Greek is not available for comparison with the Syriac. Hence there may well be other passages where the Syriac translator has added to Eusebius, even though they can only be detected by a priori reasoning. A prime candidate is the miracle of Romanus speaking powerfully and preaching after his tongue had been cut out, of which the short recension has no hint whatever (*Mart. Pal.* [L] 2.3).

[11] Although the early martyrology preserved in a Syriac manuscript of 411 has 24 November (F. Nau, PO 10 [1915], 24), the weight of the evidence of ancient calendars and martyrologies points to 25 November 311 as the correct day: J.-M. Sauget, Bibliotheca Sanctorum 10 (Rome, 1968), 767–768; T. Vivian, St. Peter of Alexandria, Bishop and Martyr (Philadelphia, 1988), 40–50.

[12] For proof that the emperor who tried Lucian was Maximinus (not Galerius) and that he was executed on 6 January 312 (not twelve months earlier), see ZAC 9 (2005), 350–353.

Book VIII of the *History* stands in modern editions. This short recension of the *Martyrs* is transmitted only in some manuscripts of the *Ecclesiastical History* which preserve it in a truncated form without any introduction and lacking the full quotation of Galerius' edict of 311 which stands in Book Eight of the *History* (8.17.3–10), but with a conclusion printed by Eduard Schwartz as an appendix to Book Eight of the *History* (8 App.).[13]

It is certain that Eusebius composed the long recension of the *Martyrs of Palestine*, the short recension of the *Martyrs of Palestine* and the present Book VIII of the *Ecclesiastical History* in that chronological order, whether the edition of the *History* in nine books that Eusebius produced in 313/314 was the first or second edition of that work.[14] For Book Eight of the *Ecclesiastical History* is a rewritten version of the short recension of the *Martyrs of Palestine*, which Eusebius has, without complete success, tried to turn into a general account of the 'Great Persecution' down to the death of Galerius.[15] During the process of revision Eusebius has omitted something important and introduced serious chronological distortions. (1) The eighth book of the *History* omits the edict of early 304 ordaining universal sacrifice recorded in both recensions of the *Martyrs of Palestine* (3.1). (2) The *Martyrs* correctly placed the abdication of Diocletian and Maximian and the investiture of Maximinus as Caesar on 1 May 305 shortly after the martyrdom of Agapius of Gaza on 24 Dystros in the second year of the

---

[13] Schwartz, Eusebius Werke 2.2 (n. 10), 796–797 ('Kirchengeschichte VIII Anhang'), cf. GRBS 21 (1980), 196–199, 201.

[14] As powerfully argued by R. W. Burgess, JTS 48 (1997), 474–501. Studies in Eusebian and Post-Eusebian Chronology (Stuttgart, 1999), 21–98.

[15] Constantine (1981), 149–150, 154–158.

persecution, i. e. 24 March 305 (*Mart. Pal.* 3.7–4.1), but did not explicitly record the third year of persecution until the narrative reached the year 306 (*Mart. Pal.* 4.8). Book VIII of the *History* places the abdication before the end of the second year of the persecution, that is, on the computation of the years of persecution that Eusebius is using, before instead of after Easter 305 (*HE* 8.13.10). (3) Book Eight of the *History* includes the martyrdoms of Peter of Alexandria on 25 November 311 and Lucian on 7 January 312 in a narrative which explicitly concludes with the 'palinode' of Galerius and his death immediately afterwards at the end of April 311 (*HE* 8.17, which concludes: 'Such is the character of the edict in the Latin tongue …; now it is time to consider carefully what happened subsequently').

It is not plausible to argue that these outright chronological errors and the pervasive vaguenes and confusion of Book VIII of the *Ecclesiastical History* are intentional because 'the genre Eusebius adopts requires such chaotic narratives, which caused occasional error.'[16] For Eusebius composed his *Ecclesiastical History* as a history aiming at veracity – in marked contrast to his original version of *Martyrs of Palestine*, which he wrote in 311 as a work of hagiography, a memorial to friends whom he had lost in the 'Great Persecution' and whose memory he felt an obligation to record for posterity (*Mart. Pal.* [L] pref. 1.8, quoted above).

---

[16] D. Mendels, The Media Revolution of Early Christianity. An Essay on Eusebius's Ecclesiastical History (Grand Rapids & Cambridge, 1999), 100.

7

## The *Acta Sebastiani*

Late Antique and early medieval Rome produced a copious harvest of hagiographical legends. Albert Dufourcq (1872–1952) devoted much of his long life to the hagiography of the city of Rome, but too often reached unconvincing conclusions.[1] Hippolyte Delehaye analysed a selection of the same material with his customary magisterial touch.[2] Although the present work concentrates on history rather than legend, it uses the admittedly fictitious *Acta Sebastiani* as evidence for the cult of the apostles Peter and Paul.[3] That procedure is justified because, even if the *Acta Sebastiani* (BHL 7543: AASS, Jan. II [1643], 265–278 = 629–642, whence PL 17 [1844], 1021–1058 = 17 [1879], 1113–1150) are a historical romance filled with miracles, conversions, long discourses and descriptions of torture, the text was probably composed

[1] Dufourcq composed five volumes of a vast Étude sur les Gesta Martyrum romains, all published in Paris: volume I (1900) was later given the subtitle 'Vue d'ensemble. Le mouvement légendaire ostrogothique', while the remaining volumes were all published with subtitles, as respectively II: Le mouvement légendaire lérinien (1907); III: Le mouvement légendaire grégorien (1907); IV: Le Néo-Manichéisme et la légende chrétienne (1910); V: Les légendes grecques et les légendes latines (1988). For critical reviews, see H. Delehaye, AB 19 (1900), 444–447; 27 (1908), 215–218; H. Quentin, Rev. bén. 24 (1907), 537–546; R. Lane Fox, JTS, N. S. 43 (1992), 243–244.

[2] H. Delehaye, Étude sur le légendier romain. Les saints de Novembre et de Décembre (SSH 23, 1936).

[3] Chapter I.

in the first half of the fifth century.[4] Its relevance to the cult of Peter and Paul *ad catacumbas* is obvious.[5]

In their present form, the *Acta Sebastiani* appear to be a conflation of two originally separate texts. The first and much longer part of the *acta* narrates the story of the arrest and imprisonment of the brothers Marcellianus and Marcus and of the subsequent conversion and baptism of the fictitious *praefectus urbi* 'Agrestius Chromatius' (38–48) and his son Tiburtius, who could be a genuine martyr (I–XVII / 3–63). In this story Sebastian has the subordinate role of preacher and miracle-worker and a priest by the name of 'Polycarp' appears, who catechises 'Chromatius' (31, 48). The second and briefer part (XVIII–XXIII / 64–90) begins with a formal introduction of Gaius, the bishop of Rome (64: *erat autem papa urbis nomine Gaius, vir magnae prudentiae magnaque virtutis*), then offers a brisk narrative, set in the year 287 (65: *Maximiano et Aquilino consulibus*), of the martyrdoms of many Roman Christians, including Tiburtius, Castulus, Zoe, the Quattuor Coronati, Marcellianus and Marcus, and finally Sebastian himself (64–88), and it concludes with the burial of Sebastian on the Via Appia (88–90).

The second part shows a good knowledge of Roman topography.[6] After Sebastian has been used as target practice and miraculously healed (85–86), he stands 'on the steps of the temple of Elagabalus' and hails the emperors as they

---

[4]   A. Amore, I martiri di Roma (Rome, 1975), 184–185; Bibliotheca Sanctorum 10 (Rome, 1978), 1286; P. Cannata, ib. 11 (1978), 777.

[5]   M. Armellini, Le catacombe romane (Rome, 1880), 389–392.

[6]   S. B. Platner and T. Ashby, A Topographical Dictionary of Ancient Rome (London, 1929), 248; F. Coarelli, LTUR 2 (Rome, 1995), 372; 3 (1996), 10–11; F. Chausson, La Vigna Barberini 1. Histoire d'une site: Étude des sources et de la topographie (Rome, 1997), 74.

approach (87: *stans super gradus Heliogabali,*[7] *venientibus imperatoribus dixit: iniquis subreptionibus animos imperii vestri templorum pontifices obsident*), whereupon Diocletian, after a brief verbal interchange, orders him to be taken to the 'hippodrome of the palace' and to be beaten violently until he expires (88: *tunc iussit eum in hippodromo palatii duci, et tam diu fustigari quamdiu spiritum exhalaret*). Sebastian's corpse is then thrown into the Cloaca Maxima, but he appears in a dream to the matron Lucina and instructs her to recover his body from 'the sewer which is next to the circus,' to take it *ad catacumbas* and bury it 'at the beginning of the crypt next to the relics of the apostles' (88: *hoc [sc. corpus meum] tu dum levaveris, perduces ad catacumbas et sepelies in initio cryptae iuxta vestigia apostolorum*). This Lucina duly does. She then keeps vigil over Sebastian's grave for thirty days, converts her house into a church as soon as persecution ends, and finally leaves all her property to the church for the repose of Christians (89–90).

The burial of a martyr by a pious matron is a commonplace of hagiographical fiction.[8] But the author of the *Acta Sebastiani* knew that during the reign of Diocletian the joint cult of the apostles Peter and Paul was celebrated at the third milestone of the Via Appia.[9] Despite stating the date as 287, he might also have been aware that both Diocletian and Maximian were in Rome together for several weeks (it was in fact during November and December 303 for their joint *vicennalia* and the Persian triumph).[10] But his statement that Sebastian hailed plural emperors can hardly derive from a

[7] On the Heliogabalium, F. Chausson, MEFRA 107 (1995), 740–743.
[8] Compare Pompeia in the *Acts of Maximilianus* (App. 5).
[9] Chapter I.
[10] New Empire (1982), 56, 59.

written source which recorded authentic details about the
death of Sebastian: although the martyrdom of Sebastian
is registered in our earliest list of Roman martyrs (Chr.
min. 1.71), there is no sign that any contemporary account
survived.[11] In this Sebastian resembles Agnes, whose martyrdom is registered in the same list, for Prudentius' poem on
her (*Peristephanon* 14) is also total fiction.[12]

---

[11] Delehaye, Légendes (1927), 105.

[12] App. 2 at n. 4.

## Stolen Bones

Monsignor Ludwig Kaas (1881–1952) was a deputy in the German Reichstag from 1920 to the spring of 1933, when he left Germany and settled in Rome for the rest of his life.[1] Elected chairman of the *Centrumspartei* (the Catholic Party in the Weimar Republic) in 1928, Kaas was in this capacity instrumental in persuading his party's deputies in the Reichstag to vote en bloc in favour of the *Ermächtigungs-gesetz* of 23 March 1933, which empowered Adolf Hitler to rule indefinitely by decree, as he did until his death in April 1945. Later in 1933 Kaas acted as the agent of Pope Pius XI in negotiating the Konkordat between the Vatican and the Nazi regime. In 1936 Pius XI appointed him Economicus and Secretary to the Holy Congregation of the fabric of St Peter's Basilica. Three years later Cardinal Pacelli, whose acquaintance Kaas had made while Pacelli was papal nuncio in Berlin in the 1920s, became Pope as Pius XII and on 28 June 1939 authorised archaeological excavations under the high altar of St. Peter's. These excavations were carried out during the years 1940–1949 by Enrico Josi (1885–1975), a professor at the Pontificio Istituto di Archeologia Cristiana, the architect Bruno Maria Apollonj Ghetti (1905–1984), and the Jesuits Engelbert Kirschbaum (1902–1970), profes-

---

[1]  Unfortunately the three large volumes by G. May, Ludwig Kaas. Der Priester, der Politiker und der Gelehrte aus der Schule von Ulrich Stutz (Amsterdam, 1981–1982), are rather brief on Kaas's time in Rome and almost totally silent on the Vatican excavations.

sor of Christian Archaeology at the Gregorian University in
Rome, and the epigrapher Antonio Ferrua (1901–2003).[2]
These four men worked under the administrative authority
of Kaas and produced an official account of their findings
in two luxurious volumes which remain the basic repository
of facts about what was discovered in the western section of
these excavations.[3]

These 'explorations under the *Confessio Petri* on the Vatican between 1940 and 1949' established that a shrine (or
*aedicula*) was constructed between c. 150 and c. 170 as an
integral part of the so-called Red Wall as a memorial to
Peter, that this shrine must be the 'trophy' of Peter to which
Gaius referred a generation later, and that, when a large
and magnificent basilica was built on the site in the second
quarter of the fourth century,[4] no expense or effort was

---

[2] The latter pair are alleged to have attached themselves to the
excavation 'senza alcuna nomina ufficiale' by M. Guarducci, Le chiavi
sulla pietra. Studi, ricordi e documenti inediti intorno alla tomba di
Pietro in Vaticano (Casale Monferrato, 1995), 15: 'i due Gesuiti si
aggregarono spontaneamente … ambedue finirono col rimanere, senza
alcuna nomina ufficiale.'

[3] B. M. Apollonj Ghetti, A. Ferrua, E. Josi and E. Kirschbaum,
Esplorazioni sotto la Confessione di San Pietro in Vaticano eseguite
negli anni 1940–1949 (Vatican City, 1951).

[4] For disproof of the traditional assumption that Constantine
initiated the construction of the 'Constantinian basilica', see C. Piétri,
'Roma Christiana.' Recherches sur l'Église de Rome, son organisation,
sa politique et son idéologie de Miltiade à Sixte III 224 (Rome, 1976),
51–69, 366–380; G. W. Bowersock, St. Peter's in the Vatican, ed. W.
Tronzo (Cambridge, 2005), 5–15. Piétri dated the start of construction shortly before 333, while Bowersock shows that the most that
Constantine can possibly have done was to supply funds after 324 for
commencing construction – which was an empire-wide policy according to Eusebius, *VC* 2.45–46. Bowersock advances three very strong
arguments against associating Constantine with St. Peter's. (1) M.
Guarducci, Rendiconti della Pontificia Accademia di Archeologia 39

spared, despite the sharp slope of the terrain, to ensure that its focal point was centred exactly above the second century memorial.[5] Unfortunately, the official publication conspicuously fails to provide a full record of what was found during the excavations of 1940–1949, even directly under the altar of Saint Peter's. This was made clear by Jocelyn Toynbee and John Ward Perkins, who in 1956 evaluated, partly reinterpreted and supplemented the excavators' published findings.[6] Toynbee and Ward Perkins showed themselves expert guides as they confronted a series of complicated questions with unfailing precision and alertness. Yet they

---

(1967), 135–144, published a rather worn coin mentioned by the official excavators, though not documented by them, which was found in Mausoleum T: the coin came from the mint of Arles and dates from 317 at the earliest, since it appears to be an example of *RIC* 7 (1966), 249: Arles 148. The cemetery beneath the Vatican was therefore still being used for pagan burials some years after 312. (2) Eusebius, writing apparently c. 325, refers to crowds of pilgrims thronging the shrine of Peter in Rome 'as if it were a great temple of God' (*Theophany* 4.7), which implies that he knew nothing about the construction of a great new basilica at that date. (3) The brick stamps found in the apse of Old Saint Peter's when it was demolished in the sixteenth century had the name of Constantine's son Constans, not that of Constantine himself: G. Grimaldi. Descrizione della basilica antica di S. Pietro in Vaticano. Codice Barberini Latino 2733, ed. R. Niggl (Vatican, 1972), 205, fol. 165[v], reproduced in Bowersock, St. Peter's (2005), 10 fig. 3.

[5] See Esplorazioni 1 (n. 3), 152, Fig. 106; E. Kirschbaum, Die Gräber der Apostelfürsten. St. Peter und St. Paul in Rom[3] (Frankfurt, 1974), 151, Abb. 37.

[6] J.C. Toynbee and J. Ward Perkins, The Shrine of St. Peter and the Vatican Excavations (London, 1956); for the pagan necropolis, see subsequently W. Eck, ZPE 65 (1986), 245–293; Tra epigrafia, prosopografia e archeologia. (Rome, 1996), 230, 232–237, 251–270; H. Mielsch & H. von Hesberg, Die heidnische Nekropole unter St. Peter in Rom 1: Die Mausoleen A–D (Rome, 1986); 2: Die Mausoleen E–I und Z–Psi (Rome, 1995).

were debarred from revealing all that they knew. In their preface, they imply that, before they were allowed access to the excavations, they were compelled to give an undertaking that their work 'should be based (as any such work must be) on the findings of the official *Report* on the excavations.'[7] That such an undertaking not to use knowledge acquired independently of the official report was exacted from Toynbee and Ward Perkins is significant, especially since it had emerged very soon after the publication of the official report that its authors had omitted the discovery of 'a graffito that is not included in the official *Report*, but is referred to elsewhere by the individual excavators.'[8]

Monsignor Kaas made a habit of visiting the site after the excavators had finished work for the day and removing objects surreptitiously, as Kirschbaum stated later in a most emphatic manner.[9] He also secretly removed a human

---

[7] When Toynbee and Ward Perkins stated that for the section of the excavations under and close to the *Confessio* of St. Peter's that 'the official Report … is a definitive work,' they were consciously using the language of diplomacy rather than candid scholarship, since they later lamented the absence of any detailed report on bones found during the excavations (Shrine [n. 6], xix–xx, cf. 154).

[8] App. 9, cf. Toynbee & Ward Perkins, Shrine (n. 6), 165, 180 n. 33. Both the conduct of the excavations and the reliability of the Esplorazioni have been subjected to searching scrutiny by H. G. Thümmel, Die Memorien für Petrus and Paulus in Rom. Die archäologischen Denkmäler und die literarische Tradition (Berlin & New York, 1999), 15–72.

[9] E. Kirschbaum, Archivum historiae pontificiae 3 (1965), 310. Kirschbaum confirmed the plausibility of Guarducci's account of finding the bones in the box with the following two astounding sentences: 'Ausserdem war es nicht das einzige Mal gewesen, dass Prälat Kaas ähnliche Eingriffe vornahm, die den Ausgräbern verheimlicht wurden. Da Kaas als Leiter der Dombauhütte auch ipso facto dem Ausgrabungsunternehmen vorstand, hatte er sich wohl die Meinung gebildet, ein

skeleton from the *loculus* which had been hollowed out in
the north side of the short buttressing wall usually known
as the Wall of the Graffiti and then effectively sealed in by
the construction of a load-bearing wall built flush with its
face. This *loculus* remained undisturbed from being sealed
in the fourth century until 1941, when Kaas and a Vatican
workman removed its contents without the knowledge of
the official excavators, who have consistently and explicitly
stated that they found it virtually empty. The truth about
the removal of the bones remained hidden from the world
until 1995, when Margherita Guarducci (1902–1999), who
contended with some belligerence that the bones were those
of St Peter in a series of books and articles stretching over
more than three decades,[10] published the transcripts of two
sworn declarations by *sanpietrini* who described how they
assisted Kaas.

---

Recht zu solchen Eingriffen zu haben, zumal diese sich allein auf eine
Entfernung von Gebeinen beschränkt zu haben scheinen.'

[10] Guarducci's publications on Peter are listed in La tomba di san
Pietro. Una straordinaria vicenda (Milan, 1989; reprinted 2000). Her
most important books and monographs on the early cult of Peter are I
graffiti sotto la Confessione di San Pietro in Vaticano (Vatican, 1958:
three volumes); Le reliquie di Pietro sotto la Confessione della Basilica
Vaticana (Vatican, 1965; reprinted 1995); Le reliquie di Pietro sotto la
Confessione della Basilica Vaticana: una messa a punto (Rome, 1967);
Pietro ritrovato (Verona, 1969; 2nd ed., Rome, 1970); Archeologia Clas-
sica 24 (1972), 117–126; Pietro in Vaticano (Rome, 1983); Le reliquie
di Pietro in Vaticano (Rome, 1995); Le chiavi sulla pietra (1995).
Guarducci has stated that she did not visit the excavations under Saint
Peter's until May 1952, that is, one month after Kaas died on 15 April
1952 and six months after the official report of the excavations had
been published: San Pietro e Sant'Ippolito: Storia di statue famose in
Vaticano (Rome, 1991), 7.

On 7 January 1965, Giovanni Segoni declared

(1) that he removed bones from the cavity in the foundation
    of the Red Wall in the presence of Monsignor Kaas,
    which were placed in a zinc box with a cross and put in
    the semicircular ambulatory in the Grotte Vaticane;

(2) that he also removed the contents of the *loculus* in the
    Wall of the Graffiti in the presence of Kaas, which were
    put in a wooden box, and that he placed the box in the
    same ambulatory;

(3) that these contents included a certain quantity of bones
    markedly white in colour;

(4) that the wooden box in which he put these bones was the
    same box as he showed Guarducci in September 1953.

In a supplementary deposition on 22 January 1965, Segoni
further stated

(5) that the white bones in the marble receptacle in the Wall
    of the Graffiti were removed by him in the presence of
    Monsignor Kaas alone after the normal closing hour of
    the Grotte;

(6) that 'as normally happened with removals of this sort,
    no person was present, with the exception of Monsignor
    Kaas and myself ('come abitualmente avveniva per i
    prelevamenti di questo genere, nessun'altra persona, ad
    eccezione di Mons. Kass e di me stesso, era presente').

The full text of a similar deposition made by another *san-
pietrino*, Oliviero Zinobile, on 4 February 1965 deserves to
be translated:

I remember working on the opening of the plaster of the wall of the
graffiti in order to enlarge the existing crack with the aim of obtaining
a better view of the inside of the marble receptacle discovered inside
the wall. I also have the precise recollection that, as soon as the gap
under the plaster was enlarged, bones were seen on which had fallen
some fragments of mortar which came from the external plastering

which I was engaged in breaking. I do not know who took these bones from the marble receptacle or when this happened.[11]

Kaas died on 15 April 1952, apparently having disclosed his 'discovery' to Pope Pius XII,[12] and the discovery of these bones was announced to the world thirteen years later by Guarducci, who had the ear of Pope Paul VI and persuaded him to declare officially that the bones are the mortal remains of the apostle Peter. On 27 June 1968 the bones were placed under the high altar of Saint Peter's, where they have remained except for the temporary removal of one of them to aid the recovery of Pope John Paul II after he had been shot in St Peter's Square.[13]

---

[11] The documents paraphrased and translated here were published by M. Guarducci, Chiavi (n. 10), 121–123. Two other relevant documents published for the first time in this revealing volume are (1) a long statement by Antonio Ferrua, dated 28 April 1968, which has the heading 'Oggetto: Ossa attribuite alla cassetta marmorea del muro dei graffiti' (65–76), and (2) a memoir submitted by Guarducci to Pope Paul VI on 14 May 1968 rebutting it point by point (79–120). The volume also contains a full bibliography of Guarducci's writings about Peter (145–149).

[12] W. H. C. Frend, The Archaeology of Early Christianity. A History (Minneapolis, 1996), 272, acutely noted that the Pope announced on Vatican radio on 24 December 1950 that 'the tomb of the Prince of the Apostles has been found' (Acta Apostolicae Sedis 43 [1951], 51–52) and he suggested a connection in the Pope's mind with his recent proclamation (on 1 November 1950) of the doctrine of the bodily Assumption of the Virgin into heaven as a required belief for Roman Catholics.

[13] In this context, I need to state that I have visited the *scavi Vaticani* twice, on each occasion on a tour with a Vatican guide who gave the official interpretation of what I saw. On my first visit in January 1965, the high point of the exposition was the ceiling mosaic of Christ as Helios (in Tomb M). On my second visit in October 1997, this mosaic was not even included in the tour, although I did sneak a look at it. The guide concentrated exclusively on setting out the evidence that the bones found in 1941 are the bones of Peter – though he refrained

The bones alleged to be those of the apostle Peter were found in 1941, but their discovery was not published until 1965. What happened to them in the intervening period? Discussion of what ought to be a scientific question has too often been *ad hominem*, so that the controversy has generated more heat than light. The reason is both simple and discreditable. A man high in the Vatican hierarchy stole the bones in 1941, and ingrained Catholic respect for ecclesiastical authority prevented both sides in the controversy from calling theft by its proper name. Now that the protagonists on each side (Guarducci and Ferrua), who were bitter personal enemies and who contradicted each other's conclusions for thirty years, are both dead, the truth can at last be stated openly and dispassionately.[14] In 1995 Guarducci published documents regarding the finding of the bones in 1941 and her discovery of the stolen bones in 1953 in a box in an ambulatory under St Peter's where Kaas had hidden

---

from uttering the name of Ludwig Kaas, who surreptitiously removed them, until I asked him whether the bones about which he had been discoursing so learnedly were the bones found by Kaas. Apart from these two brief tours, my knowledge of the archaeology of the site is based entirely on published work.

[14] Ferrua makes his contempt for Guarducci plain in his contribution to the volume Saecularia Petri et Pauli (Vatican, 1969), 131–148. He dismisses her proposed supplement and interpretation of the graffito (below, p. 408) as advanced 'con un largo corteggio di supposizioni gratuite ed inverosimili, che non torna a conto esaminare' (135), and he comments on her reading of the graffito in Tomb H, which she alone saw, that 'chi ha pratica di acclamazioni e graffiti paleocristiani, al sentir tali cose sorride e passa ad altro' (137). Contrast the fulsome praise of Guarducci's three volumes of Graffiti (n. 10) by A. Prandi, Pellerinaggi e culto dei Santi in Europa fina alla Iª Crociata. Atti del IV Convegno di Studi sulla spiritualità medievale (Todi, 1963), 283. On her side, Guarducci made no attempt to conceal her detestation of Ferrua: see esp. Chiavi (n. 10), 109–115.

them. The box allegedly also contained a piece of paper 'che constatava la provenienza,' but the photograph of it which Guarducci published shows only the words 'ossa, urna, graf[fiti],'[15] so that there is only Guarducci's unsubstantiated word for it that anything more was ever legible.

In 1956, Toynbee and Word Perkins alluded to Guarducci's discovery or so it seems: they observed that the *loculus* in the Wall of the Graffiti 'had already been rifled' when the excavators opened it.[16] Since Toynbee and Ward Perkins knew perfectly well that the *loculus* had remained completely inaccessible from the fourth century until the excavators exposed it in 1941, they cannot mean that the *loculus* had been looted or robbed in Late Antiquity or the Middle Ages. It is, therefore, hard to see what they can mean other than that the contents of the *loculus* had been removed without the knowledge of the excavators, who were constrained to remain silent about what they knew and to avoid any overt mention of the finding and the theft of the bones in the official publication of their excavations. A new and properly independent scientific examination of the bones that Kaas stole is clearly needed:[17] the bones

---

[15] Guarducci, Reliquie (1967, n. 10), 23 fig. 6: the caption states that 'il biglietto, da me rinvenuto integro, ha molto sofferto della esposizione all'aria.'

[16] Toynbee & Ward Perkins, Shrine (n. 6), 166–167, cf. 221–222 figs. 23, 24: see also Esplorazioni 1 (n. 3), 201 fig. 154; Guarducci, Pietro (n. 10), 99–100; Chiavi (n. 10), 24 fig. 2.

[17] Guarducci, Reliquie (1965, n. 10), included the following four contributions by scientists: (1) V. Correnti, 'Relazione dello studio compiuto su tre gruppi di resti scheletrici umani già rinvenuti sotto la Confessione della basilica vaticana' (83–160); (2) L. Cardini, 'Risultato dell'esame osteologico dei resti scheletrici di animali' (161–168); (3) C. Latruo and G.C. Negretti, 'Risultato dell'analisi petrografica dei campioni di terra' (169–181); (4) M.L. Stein and P. Maltesta, 'Risultato

presumably have a DNA fingerprint and it should now be possible to establish whether the skeleton belonged to a Jew or not. A critical survey of the archaeological evidence has already suggested that these bones belong to a gentile who was bishop of Rome long after Peter.[18]

---

dell'esame merceologico dei frammenti di tessuto' (182). These documents are substantially reproduced in Reliquie (n. 10), 85–133.

[18] Thümmel, Die Memorien für Petrus and Paulus (n. 8), 70: 'etwa die Reste eines der römischen Bischöfe … deren Gräber man nach dem Liber Pontificalis bei dem des Petrus lokalisierte.'

# Vatican Graffiti

## I

Monsignor Kaas was not the only person who secretly pur-
loined items from what purported to be scientific archaeological excavations under Saint Peter's. In January 1952
Antonio Ferrua published a drawing of what the *aedicula*
of c. 160 might originally have looked like, in which there
appeared adjacent to it on the Red Wall a graffito naming
Peter which had not been included in the official report of
the excavation published only two months earlier.[1] When
asked where the graffito was, Ferrua at first said that it could
still be found *in situ* on the wall: that was a conscious lie,
since he had removed the graffito from Saint Peter's and was
keeping it in his room next to the editorial offices of *Civiltà
Cattolica* in the Via Ripetta, where it apparently remained
until he was compelled to return it.[2] Where precisely did
Ferrua find the graffito? The colour of the fragment of wall
on which it is written establishes that it came from the Red

---

[1] A. Ferrua published the *disegno* in Il Messagero on 16 January
1952 and in Civiltà Cattolica 103.1 (January 1952), 25/26, cf. E.
Kirschbaum, Stimmen der Zeit 150 (1951–1952), 330; J. Carcopino,
Études d'histoire chrétienne. Le Christianisme secret du carré magique.
Les fouilles de Saint-Pierre et la tradition (Paris, 1953), 279–282.

[2] M. Guarducci, Le chiavi sulla pietra. Studi, ricordi e documenti
inediti intorno alla tomba di Pietro in Vaticano (Casale Monferrato,
1995), 109–115, esp. 110, 111–112.

Wall, and there is no positive reason to reject the implication
of the illustration which Ferrua published in January 1952
or his later explicit statement that he took it from inside the
*loculus*.[3] But the unsupported statement of a convicted liar
deserves to be treated with some scepticism.

It is more important to ask what the graffito says. Margherita Guarducci maintained for more than forty years
that the first line is to be supplemented as ΠΕΤΡ[ΟΣ], that
the second line, in which the three letters epsilon, nu, iota
can be read, is preserved complete, and that the two lines
together form a complete sentence which says 'Peter is here,
i.e., inside.'[4] Now Guarducci's supplement of the first line
is highly probable, and her date of c. 320 for the graffito
could in theory possibly be correct. But her restoration of
the second line is demonstrably erroneous. First, there is a
technical, epigraphical objection: Guarducci bends the first
line downwards for no reason other than to preclude extend-
ing line two beyond the three letters preserved.[5] Second,
Guarducci's reading is linguistically most improbable and
perhaps completely impossible.[6] For, while the word ἔνι

---

[3]  A. Ferrua, Saecularia Petri et Pauli (Vatican, 1969), 131: 'lo
raccolsi con le mie mani nella cassetta marmorea, già inserito da Costantino nel muro dei graffiti, il cosidetto muro *g* che fasciava sul lato
settentrionale l'edicola eretta sopra il sepolcro di s. Pietro.'

[4]  M. Guarducci, I graffiti sotto la Confessione di San Pietro in Vaticano 2 (Vatican, 1958), 385–407; Le reliquie di Pietro sotto la Confessione della Basilica Vaticana (Vatican, 1965; reprinted 1995), 46–48;
Pietro in Vaticano (Rome, 1983), 74–77 (with Tavola XXXVII); Epigrafia greca 4 (Rome, 1978), 552–556 no. 7 (with bibliography);
Chiavi (n. 2), 28–34.

[5]  Most clearly brought out by E. Dassmann, in his 'Nachtrag' to E.
Kirschbaum, Die Gräber der Apostelfürsten. St. Peter und St. Paul in
Rom³ (Frankfurt, 1974), 243–245, with Abb. 56.

[6]  As noted in JTS, N. S. 21 (1970), 165–169.

(a synonym of ἔνεστι, the third person present indicative
of ἔνειμι) does indeed often mean 'there is / are inside' in
Homer and classical Greek,[7] in colloquial Greek of the third
or fourth century A. D. Greek ἔνι is invariably used in one of
three ways: (1) meaning 'there is,' often with the negative as
οὐκ ἔνι = 'there is not / there does not exist,' (2) meaning 'it
is possible,' or (3) as the copula meaning 'is.'[8] To the best of
my knowledge, the verb ἔνι never in late Greek means 'there
is / are inside.' Moreover, there are two obvious and linguistically acceptable supplements after the iota in line two: either
eta or rho as abbreviations of ΙΗ[ΣΟΥ] or ΙΡ[ΗΝΗ], i. e.,
'Peter in Jesus' or 'Peter in peace.'[9]

---

[7] See, e. g., R. J. Cunliffe, A Lexicon of the Homeric Dialect (Glasgow, 1924), 131.

[8] For example, the early Byzantine hymn *On the Departed*, edited
by C. A. Trypanis, Fourteen Early Byzantine Cantica (Vienna, 1968),
51–64, uses ἔνι in all three senses: (1) 3.3: οὐκ ἔνι δοῦλος οὔτ᾿ ἐλεύθερος
κτλ.; 14.2: οὐ γὰρ ἔνι ... μετάνοια, οὐδὲ ἔνι ... ἄνεσις; (2) 9.3–5: ἆρα ἔνι
ἐκεῖ ἰδέσθαι κτλ.; (3) 19.3, 20.3: ποῦ / οὗτος ἔνι ὁ δεῖνα κτλ. All three
meanings are attested in two series of acclamations and denunciations
chanted by pro-Chalcedonian bishops in Jerusalem and Rome in July
and September 518 and preserved in the so-called Collectio Sabbaitica,
nos. 27, 32: τίς ἔνι Νεστόριος, ἐγὼ οὐκ οἶδα· ἀνάθεμα αὐτῶι ἀπὸ τῆς τριάδος.
τίς ἔνι Νεστόριος, ἐγὼ οὐκ οἶδα· ἀνάθεμα αὐτῶι μετ᾿ Εὐτυχέος ... ὁ μὴ λαλῶν
οὐκ ἔνι πιστός ... ὁ βασιλεὺς ὀρθόδοξος ἔνι· εἰς αἰῶνας τὸ βασίλειον τοῦτο ...
ὁ Ῥωμαικὸς δόλιος ἔνι· τὸν Ῥωμαικὸν ἔξω βάλε ... Ἰουστῖνος βασιλεύει, οὐκ
ἔνι φοβηθῆναι· ὀρθόδοξος ἔνι. τοῦ αὐγούστου πολλὰ τὰ ἔτη· εἰς αἰῶνας τὸ
βασίλειον τοῦτο· νέος ἐστὶ Κωνσταντῖνος· οὐκ ἔνι φοβηθῆναι ... ὁ βασιλεὺς
ἐκέλευσεν ὡς εἶπεν ἡ σύνοδος· Ἀποσχίστης οὐκ ἔνι. λάβε τὴν θεοτόκον· εἴσβα
καὶ καθάρισον τὸν οἶκον τὸν ἅγιον· ὁ μὴ λαλῶν οὐκ ἔνι πιστός ... μία πίστις
γέγονεν, οὐκ ἔνι ἀταξία. ὁ σταυρὸς ἐνίκησε καὶ οὐκ ἔνι ἀταξία· ἡ τριὰς ἐνίκησε
καὶ οὐκ ἔνι ἀταξία (ACO 3.74.27–28, 85.24, 86.12–13, 86.19–21,
86.27–29, 87.2–3).

[9] P. Fraser, JRS 52 (1962), 218, proposed to read ᾽Πέτρ[ος] ἐν Ἰ[η] or
less probably Ι[Χ],᾽ the latter meaning 'Peter in Jesus Christ,' without
questioning Guarducci's assumption that in Greek of this date ἔνι has

## II

The aptly named Wall of the Graffiti presents a great contrast. It was covered with graffiti and even on the small area
which the excavators exposed Guarducci was able to read or
decipher no fewer than fifty eight separate graffiti or groups
of graffiti, which she published in three imposing volumes.
Paradoxically, it is unnecessary to decide whether Guarducci
read these texts correctly – or even whether most of them
really are or were legible or visible only to a believing eye.
For two salient facts stand out. First, a pair of graffiti as
deciphered by Guarducci allude to Constantine's victory at
the Battle of the Milvian Bridge and must therefore be later
than 28 October 312 (2.7–8: *HO[C] VIN[CE]*, with a chi-
rho monogram adjacent to the lower right).[10] Second, there
is not one single clear invocation of or reference to Peter. Admittedly, Guarducci's index to her publication of the graffiti
contains long entries for 'Pietro' among the 'concetti espressi
sul muro *g*' and an entry 'vicinanza a Pietro' among the
various 'auguri e pensieri salutari' found and this entry lists
more than a dozen certain occurrences (2.11, 12–13, 23, 45;
15.5; 17.1; 18; 18.1; 25; 25.6; 30.3; 32; 47.2, 3; 48.3, 6)
and two dubious ones (7.4, 46.24).[11] But many of the graffiti
indexed in this way may not refer to Peter at all and none
actually states that his body was close by. Guarducci obtains
her frequent mentions of Peter on the Wall of the Graffiti

---

the same meaning and linguistic range as ἔνεστι. Similarly, J. M. C.
Toynbee, Dublin Review 233 (1959), 243: 'Professor Guarducci's
equation of ἔνι with ἔνεστι is most acceptable.'

[10]  Guarducci, Graffiti 2 (n. 4), 14–33, justifies her reading at some
length. She dated all the graffiti of the Wall of the Graffiti 'alla prima
età di Costantino' (Chiavi [n. 2], 24).

[11]  Guarducci, Graffiti 1 (n. 4), 463–464, 465.

by invariably construing not only the pair of letters *PE*, but
also the single letter *P* as abbreviations for Peter.[12] In one
case her supplement can be positively disproved. Guarducci
expands the abbreviation *APE* as 'a*(d) Pe(trum)*' (32: *Nibe,
a(d) Pe(trum) vive*).[13] But the parallel case of an epitaph
from the cemetery of Domitilla, where the centred letters
*APE* form the last line (ICUR, N.S. 3.6837b),[14] indicates
that these letters by themselves do not necessarily carry the
implication that the body of Peter was believed to be nearby.


### III


A graffito with the name of Peter attached to the drawing
of a man's head, which comes from the tomb of the Valerii
(Tomb H), was published by Guarducci in 1953, who
devoted a whole monograph to it. Besides certain symbols
and abbreviations in line 1, her text reads:

*Petrus, roga / pro sanc[ti]s / hom[ini]bus / Chrestianis [ad] / co[r]pus tuum
sep[ultis]*[15]

Peter, pray for the holy Christian folk buried by your body.

That seems clear enough: whoever wrote these words believed that Peter was buried close by where he wrote them.

---

[12] Guarducci, *Graffiti* 1 (n. 4), 385–478 ('il nome di Pietro').

[13] Guarducci, *Graffiti* (n. 4), 1.465–469; 2.221.

[14] Photograph in Guarducci, *Graffiti* 2 (n. 4), 467–468, fig. 243,
where Guarducci implausibly suggests that in this inscription the letters
*APE* may represent the personal name *Ap(p)e*.

[15] M. Guarducci, *Cristo e San Pietro in un documento precos-
tantiniano della necropoli vaticana* (1953), 18, Tavole 17–28, 44. For
Mausoleum H, the 'mausoleum of the Valerii,' in which the graffito
was found, see now H. Mielsch and H. von Hesberg, *Die heidnische
Nekropole unter St. Peter in Rom* 2 (Rome, 1995), 143–208.

But at what date? Although Guarducci dates the head and graffito shortly before 300, her date is assumed rather than proved.[16] Toynbee and Ward Perkins argued that the drawing and its accompanying text, which could well be virtually contemporaneous with the construction of the basilica after c. 320,[17] merely reflect 'the prayers and aspirations of Christian workmen' engaged on filling in the tombs of the pagan necropolis and building the foundations of the new basilica.[18]

## IV

In brief, Guarducci's erudition and years of toil failed to produce any clear mention of Peter on the Wall of the Graffiti. And the graffito from the Red Wall proves nothing more than that the place had a close association with Peter, but that was already known, and the graffito fails to clarify the nature of this association in any way at all. The graffito in Tomb H, in contrast, if correctly read by Guarducci, not only names Peter but also indicates that his mortal remains were believed to lie nearby at the time it was written – whenever that was. It is most unfortunate, therefore, that the letters of the graffito faded completely away shortly

---

[16] Guarducci, Cristo (n. 15), 70: 'il ritatto di S. Pietro e la rispettiva preghiera sarebbero anteriori al 300.'

[17] On the problem of dating, see esp. J. Ruysschaert, RHE 49 (1954), 8–18.

[18] J. M. C. Toynbee and J. Ward Perkins, The Shrine of St. Peter and the Vatican Excavations (London, 1956), 15.

after Guarducci read it, so that her readings have never been verified by a second pair of eyes.[19]

---

[19] Toynbee & Ward Perkins, Shrine (n. 18), 13–17, 22–23 n. 39. A succinct evaluation of Guarducci's claims is offered by W. H. C. Frend, The Archaeology of Early Christianity. A History (Minneapolis, 1996), 272–275.

# 1. Names of Persons and Authors

(also titles of anonymous texts discussed)

This index covers historical personages, saints both real and fictitious whatever their date, other invented characters and anonymous texts from the ancient and medieval worlds which are mentioned in the text and footnotes of the present book. Also included are modern figures including painters, composers and authors who are named or to whom allusion is made. Modern scholars of the ancient world, however, from Cardinal Baronius onwards have a separate index of their own. Hagiographical texts are indexed by the name(s) of the martyrs or saints who are their subject, but the texts discussed in Appendices 2 and 3 are excluded unless there is a substantive discussion of them there.

# 2. Places and Peoples

This geographical index includes the names of places, groups identified by their local origin and the names of barbarian tribes and nations.

# 3. Modern Scholars

This index does not register all occurrences of the names of modern scholars who are cited as authorities in footnotes, but only those passages in the text or footnotes where the achievements, opinions or arguments of named scholars are evaluated or discussed. It excludes the editors of individual texts listed in Appendix 2.